BY THE AUTO EDITORS OF CONSUMER GUIDE®

THE COMPLETE HISTORY OF
CHRYSLER
CORPORATION 1924~1985

RICHARD M. LANGWORTH
JAN P. NORBYE

BEEKMAN HOUSE
New York

Louis Weber, President
Publications International, Ltd.
3841 West Oakton Street
Skokie, Illinois 60076

Library of Congress Catalog Card Number: 85-60088

ISBN: 0-517-44813-0

This edition published by:
Beekman House
Distributed by Crown Publishers, Inc.
One Park Avenue
New York, New York 10016

Manufactured in the United States of America
10 9 8 7 6 5 4 3 2 1

Principal Authors
Richard M. Langworth
Jan P. Norbye

Photo Credits
Chrysler Historical Collection
Richard M. Langworth

Special thanks to Karla Rosenbush

Photography
Terry Boyce
David Gooley & Associates
Vince Manocchi
Douglas J. Mitchel
Richard D. Spiegelman
Nicky Wright

Special thanks to the following owners whose Chrysler
Corporation cars are featured in the color sections:
Dennis Bernardy, Larry Desenville, Warren Emerson,
Richard Graves, William K. Hamilton, Robert L.
Joynt, Frank Kleptz, Guy Morice, Forrest Padon,
Bill Trnka, Neil Vedder, John Weiser.

Jacket Design
Frank E. Peiler

Contents

Introduction

While Chrysler Corporation's many contributions to the march of automotive progress have long been recognized, the story of its cars—both good and bad—has seldom been told. Moreover, the reasons why the cars turned out the way they did and the role they played in this company's turbulent 60-year existence have not often been explained. With *The Complete History of Chrysler Corporation 1924-1985,* we hope to answer both these long-neglected needs.

This book is primarily the story of Chrysler Corporation automobiles, yet it's equally the story of the people and events that shaped them. No book could have more expert or exacting storytellers than the two who have contributed to this volume. Noted historian Jan P. Norbye chronicles the Chrysler saga up to World War II. It starts with a profile of the daring, determined Walter P. Chrysler and the companies he brought together to create the last automaker to be established in this country that still survives today. It's a fascinating tale involving many legendary figures in the annals of U.S. automotive history. Here, too, is background on Dodge and its rise as one of the industry's leading independents before becoming part of Chrysler Corporation in 1928. Beginning with the first Chrysler of 1924, we chart the company's key product and business decisions on a year-by-year basis. You'll learn about the company's early high

success, its near-fatal mistake with the advanced Airflow of the Depression years, and the remarkable recovery that enabled Chrysler to overhaul Ford Motor Company as the nation's number-two automaker in the late Thirties. Renowned postwar authority Richard M. Langworth continues the story with Chrysler's stillborn wartime styling studies and on to its decline and resurgence in the Fifties. After yet another key marketing mistake in the early Sixties, the firm recovered once more, and went on to build some of the most revered high-performance cars of that decade. Bringing the tale up to date are the developments that led Chrysler from the heights of prosperity to the brink of financial ruin by the end of the Seventies and the amazing turnaround wrought largely by Lee Iacocca in the early Eighties. Throughout this book you'll find photographs and information on show cars, trucks, and Chrysler Corporation's various overseas connections. But our main focus is on the intriguing evolution of Plymouth, Dodge, DeSoto, Chrysler, and Imperial cars. The authors and editors gratefully acknowledge the enthusiastic assistance of Karla Rosenbush, curator of the Chrysler Historical Collection, and Dodge and Chrysler-Plymouth Public Relations, without whom this book would not have been possible.

The Auto Editors of CONSUMER GUIDE® January 1985

Walter P. Chrysler:
An All-American Hero

The story of a daring, determined railroad mechanic, his passion for winning, and his meteoric rise in the wild and woolly, high-stakes auto world of the Twenties.

In 1908, a 33-year-old worker at the Union Pacific Railroad shops in Olwein, Iowa traveled to Chicago for the annual automobile show. There he went crazy over a $5000 Locomobile. It was the first real exposure to cars for Walter Percy Chrysler, but it would set him on a course that would completely change the face of the American auto industry in just a few short years.

Chrysler saw that Locomobile on his first day at the show, and then spent another three days drooling over it. He was determined to own that car, and he wasn't about to be stopped by a modest $350-a-month income or meager savings that amounted to only $700. Walter knew Ralph Van Vechten, second vice-president of the Continental Bank of Chicago, and brashly applied for a $4300 personal loan without collateral. Amazingly, Van Vechten agreed, provided Chrysler could get someone to co-sign the note. Walter must have expected exactly that, for he had a friend waiting at the bank, Bill Causey, who held a senior post at the Union Pacific. Three years later, Walter owned the Locomobile outright.

Immediately after concluding the deal, Chrysler arranged to have the car shipped back to Iowa, then rushed on ahead to remodel his barn into a garage. His interest in the Locomobile had nothing to do with driving, nor did he want to see what made it tick, as some historians claim. Instead, he bought the car for the sole purpose of studying how its individual pieces were made. At this point, his only concern was manufacturing—materials, methods, machining. Building a *better* car was not his goal—at least not yet—only knowing *how* cars were built. But this passion for making parts would soon blossom into a near obsession with building cars of high quality at less cost and in great numbers.

Machines had been a big part of Chrysler's life since childhood. His father, Henry Chrysler, was an engineer with the Kansas Pacific Railroad (later absorbed by Union Pacific) and was descended from Pennsylvania Dutch settlers who had emigrated from the Palatinate region between the Rhine and Saar Rivers (the original family name was "Greisler"). Walter grew up on the family farm near Ellis, Kansas, where he avidly read *The Scientific American* and learned about the mechanical workings of steam locomotives at an early age. He seemed all set to follow in his father's footsteps when fate steered him toward the automobile. Though he never admitted it, this was no fickle change of heart but a conscious, mature decision. Walter saw that railroading had ceased to be a growth industry by 1900, while the automobile's potential seemed unlimited. There was a wild, speculative side to the auto business in its earliest days. Fortunes could be made or lost in a flash, and that's precisely why he wanted to break into the field in the worst way.

Walter P. Chrysler is perhaps the best example of the all-American hero in industrial history. We're talking about the enormously successful tycoon who rises from a poor childhood and minimal schooling to head a giant enterprise only by dint of imagination, willpower, stamina, and hard work. Almost everything about him fits the image, from his humble beginnings to his simple, straightforward way of dealing with employees as though he were one of them, a touch he never lost; from a cocky air that made him stand out from other railroad workers in his youth to his polished performances later in life as a corporate poker player able to outfox some of the best banking brains in the world. Wrote Christy Borth: "Chrysler has been called a jack of all trades. What made him different was that he was also master of them."

Chrysler wasn't unusually tall, about 5'10", but he did have a prominent nose, an impertinent grin, and a clear, unfurrowed brow. He was fiercely competitive, and in his earliest years insisted on proving himself superior to those around him, a trait that didn't win him any friends in the roundhouse. Perhaps it's not surprising that he also had a short temper, but he learned to use it to his advantage. There was also a roughness about him that never wore off. Though he was not sparing with kind words, the part of his vocabulary people remembered best was the cursing he learned during his railroad years.

Young Walter may have been a diamond in the rough, but he was one with many facets. He loved music, and played tuba and trumpet in band concerts and the piano at home. It was at a music class that he met Della Forker, with whom he fell in love and wrote to constantly whenever jobs took him to distant depots. Engaged in 1896 when Walter was 21, they married five years later, a union that would last the rest of their lives.

It was almost inevitable that Walter would feel stiffled at Union Pacific, so he decided to abandon the maintenance and repair end of railroading for a more lucrative manufacturing job. It wasn't long before he landed the post of plant manager at American Locomotive Company's Allegheny facility in Pittsburgh. This factory had

Walter P. Chrysler and a pre-production 1924 Chrysler

Walter P. Chrysler

piled up disturbing deficits, which Chrysler traced to their individual sources. The operation soon began making money, and Chrysler's salary was raised to $8000 a year, a princely sum in those years and one that enabled him to buy another new car, a six-cylinder Stevens-Duryea. But he was still an outsider removed from corporate decision-making.

One day, Chrysler got a call from James J. Storrow, a Boston banker who sat on the American Locomotive board and was also president of General Motors. Storrow wanted to meet with Chrysler, who quickly decided he'd better go once he learned who the man was. Storrow said he liked the way Chrysler was running things in Pittsburgh, and Walter began thinking about asking for another raise. To his surprise, Storrow said, "I need a new works manager at Buick, and I would like you to take the job. If you are interested, you should contact Charlie Nash and arrange to see him as soon as convenient." It was an offer Walter couldn't refuse, especially since he had no idea how long it might be before he got another chance to work for a car company.

Chrysler promptly wrote to Nash, who was then president of Buick, and started making noises about leaving the Allegheny plant. In response, American Locomotive raised his salary to $12,000 a year. Then, Nash arrived unexpectedly in Pittsburgh, the melancholy-looking executive meeting the brash candidate for the first time. Though nothing was decided at that point, Nash did invite Chrysler to Flint to see Buick's facilities. Walter naturally accepted, and spent three days looking things over. Then they sat down to talk. According to C. B. Glasscock in *The Gasoline Age,* their conversation went something like this: "What do you think of it?" "Great!" "Would you like to be works superintendent?" "Yes, I would." "What's your salary in Pittsburgh?" "Twelve thousand a year." "Oh, we couldn't pay that. This is the *automobile* business, not the railroad business. If it does what we expect it to do, we can pay that much, but not now. I'm sorry. We'd like to have you." Then Chrysler asked, "How much *can* you pay?" "Six thousand," replied Nash. Said Chrysler, "I'll take it."

Walter viewed that $6000 cut as the price he had to pay to get into the auto industry, but he figured he could make it up in no time. Unfortunately, he didn't know about Nash's pinchpenny frugality. Though Chrysler boosted production from 45 to 560 cars a day during his early years at Buick, he never saw a dime more than his starting salary. Not that he didn't ask. One day he walked into Nash's office and with quiet determination said, "Charlie, I want $25,000 a year." All Nash could utter was "Walter!!!," a panicky scream for sanity. When he recovered his normal voice, Nash stalled, telling Walter that Storrow would have to approve the raise. Storrow was due in Flint for a meeting with Nash, and Chrysler shrewdly chose this occasion to present his case—in the bluntest possible way. "Don't get excited, Walter. You're going to get your $25,000," Storrow said. "Thank you," said Chrysler, who stopped before walking out the door, turned around, and stunned his two bosses by saying, "And next year I want $50,000!"

It was a performance characteristic of Walter P.

Chrysler. The higher the stakes, the more he enjoyed gambling—and winning. He had been sure of winning this particular showdown because he knew he was too valuable—the best works manager anywhere, a uniquely resourceful master of his profession. And he wanted his just reward.

At Storrow's instigation, Nash became president of General Motors on November 11, 1912. He also continued as president of Buick, which effectively blocked Chrysler from advancing any further in that division. By late 1915 it was clear that W. C. Durant would regain control of GM, and that led to an unlikely alliance in Flint: an informal partnership between Nash and Chrysler.

With the promise of Storrow's financial backing, Nash and Chrysler decided to buy control of Packard Motor Car Company in Detroit. It would have been a wonderful acquisition for both men. Though they were totally different in character and temperament, they had always been completely honest with each other, and had developed a peculiar sort of trust. And Storrow's integrity was unquestioned. But Packard shareholders had no interest in selling, and the deal fell through.

Meanwhile, Durant offered the president's job at Buick to Chrysler, who told him with typical candor, "If my plans work out, I'll be leaving here soon." Walter didn't know Durant as well as Nash did, but Nash knew that he could not and would not work for Durant again and resigned from GM. With Storrow's backing he took over the Thomas B. Jeffrey Company on July 1, 1916. Jeffrey had built the Rambler up to 1913, when the name was changed to honor the company founder. For 1917, its car became the Nash.

Chrysler was asked to join Storrow and Nash at the firm's Kenosha, Wisconsin headquarters. But Walter planned to go back to Durant, not with hat in hand over the attempt to buy Packard but with a demand for more money regardless of whether he got to be president of Buick. Before he could issue his ultimatum, Durant offered him a $500,000 annual salary plus a three-year contract. Thus, Chrysler became president of Buick and a GM vice-president. And because he agreed to take a $120,000 annual cash payment and the rest of his wages in stock certificates, he also became a major GM shareholder.

Chrysler spent three years as Buick's boss. He fought with Durant much of the time, and threatened to leave unless Durant kept his hands off Buick. But wily Willy continued to transfer division personnel to other assignments and to interfere with Buick's sales administration in open conflict with Chrysler's decisions. A nasty break was inevitable, and when his contract ran out, so did Walter. Friends came to feel him out about new business opportunities, but he told them all he was retired—except Ralph Van Vechten, who along with James C. Brady asked for his help to save Willys-Overland. It wasn't long before he began turning that firm around, earning a reputation as something of a "company doctor," a crackerjack executive able to nurse sick corporations back to health. In Chrysler's case, however, a one-man "intensive care unit" would have been a more accurate description.

Getting Started:
Maxwell and Chalmers
1904-1924

The two main branches of Chrysler Corporation's family tree have roots that go back to the auto industry's earliest days. It's a fascinating genealogy with a host of legendary figures.

The first Chrysler was actually a product of Maxwell Motor Corporation. Although the Maxwell was offered as a lower-priced companion to the Chrysler in 1924-25, the make had been around for quite a few years. In fact, it was one of the most venerated names in the business. Comedian Jack Benny helped keep it alive for many years by claiming he drove a Maxwell decades after the last one was built.

The Maxwell wasn't made or sponsored by a house of coffee but was named for Jonathan Dixon Maxwell. As a young mechanic in Kokomo, Indiana, Maxwell had helped Elwood G. Haynes build his first car in 1893, together with Elmer and Edgar Apperson of Jackrabbit fame. He later moved on to Olds Motor Works, then left in 1902 to start the Northern Automobile Company in Detroit.

It wasn't long before Maxwell had made a set of drawings for a low-cost runabout, and he left Northern's affairs to his backers and went to see Benjamin Briscoe, a big sheetmetal supplier to Olds who also owned a large stake in Buick. While Maxwell had come from a working-class family, Briscoe had grown up with money, his father having made a fortune by selling various inventions to Michigan railroads. Briscoe was sufficiently intrigued by Maxwell's design to sell his Buick shares and invest in a new car to be called—what else?—the Maxwell-Briscoe. Production began at Tarrytown, New York, in 1904 in a leased factory where John Brisben Walker had built the Mobile steam car for a couple of years. Soon they took over a former textile plant at Pawtucket, Rhode Island, and tooled up for parts manufacturing. Though it was only a low-priced two-cylinder model, the Maxwell-Briscoe was significant as the first U.S. car with all-metal bodywork. It was also one of the first to employ shaft drive to the rear axle.

The new automaker astonished the experts by turning out 540 cars in its first year of operation. Leading the

1904 production race were Oldsmobile (5000 cars), Rambler (2342), Cadillac (2318), and Ford (1695). Maxwell did even better the next year, turning out 2450 units and sailing into third place behind Cadillac (4182) and Rambler (3807). (Olds fell behind when Ransom E. Olds left the firm he founded to establish Reo. Ford produced only 1599 cars in 1905.) The firm expanded in 1907 by adding four-cylinder models and a new plant at New Castle, Indiana. It soon acquired a big Olds factory on East Jefferson Avenue in Detroit.

A round-faced man with a well-waxed moustache, Benjamin Briscoe looked a lot like latter-day comedian Avery Schreiber. But there was nothing comic about him: he was deadly serious, especially when it came to business. And like W. C. Durant, he wanted to be the biggest of America's automobile magnates. It was around 1906 that he started making plans to merge his company with Ford, Reo, and Buick. Durant, then head of Buick, was all for it, recognizing a possible opportunity for himself, and Ransom Olds was not unwilling. But Henry Ford, displaying

Maxwell's four-cylinder "Mascotte," new for 1912

Getting Started

the obstinacy that would become his trademark, insisted on cash for his assets, and that torpedoed the idea.

Briscoe and Durant were master schemers, and they kept on scheming, sometimes together but most often separately. In June 1908, a mere four months before the official birth of General Motors, they plotted to combine Buick and Maxwell-Briscoe, and Benjamin Briscoe even had a name for the new outfit: United States Motor Company. To obtain the needed startup capital, Briscoe approached financier J. P. Morgan, from whom he had borrowed $100,000 in 1903 to expand his sheetmetal plant. Because he had repaid that loan on time, he thought he could tap Morgan for money help at any time. But despite additional pleading by Durant, Morgan refused to cough up more than a third of the $1.5 million required to put U.S. Motor on a sound footing. This irked the two schemers, who were not used to sitting still with no way to get their hands on something as trivial as a million dollars. Briscoe apparently did sit still for a while, but Durant had a plan of his own: the merger between Buick, Oakland, and Oldsmobile that would produce General Motors. Ironically, it was Briscoe who first secured an option to buy Cadillac from the investors behind that company's founder, Henry M. Leland. As we know, Cadillac became part of GM in July 1909.

Though Durant's maneuvering had apparently left Maxwell-Briscoe out in the cold, it was still hot property and a weighty piece of collateral for raising investment capital. In 1909 it remained a solid third in industry production (9000 units), behind Buick (15,000) and Ford (10,000). Throughout the second half of that year, Durant still had ideas of bringing Maxwell-Briscoe into General Motors. But Briscoe became more and more difficult to deal with as his company continued to prosper, and Durant, perhaps out of spite, quickly snapped up a few little companies, notably Welch, Elmore, Ewing, and Cartercar.

Briscoe knew that J. P. Morgan's reluctance to back U.S. Motor fully should not be interpreted as a cold shoulder from New York's financial world. He got busy, and in February 1910 actually launched the new automaker. His list of backers read like the *Who's Who* of Wall Street: John Jacob Astor, Anthony N. Brady, J. S. Bache, Eugene Meyer Jr., and Harry Payne Whitney. Brady took more than a passing interest in the automobile business. Now he kept a watchful eye on Briscoe, who went on a buying spree as if to outdo Durant at his own game, landing Brush, Columbia, Courier, Alden-Sampson, and Stoddard-Dayton. Brady expected that Briscoe would be forced to sell to Durant sooner or later. But Durant lost control of GM to two rival groups of bankers before the end of 1910. Suddenly, U.S. Motor Company began looking like an industry power: it produced about 30,000 cars (including 16,000 Maxwells) in 1911 and had a payroll of 14,000. But by September 1912, Briscoe's little empire had collapsed, overextended and undercapitalized, a victim of inept management.

In the aftermath of U.S. Motor, J. D. Maxwell got out of the automobile business completely. Meantime, Briscoe made several minor, short-lived attempts to get back in, launching new makes like Argo and Earl that faded from view after about 1922. Investor Brady, convinced of the Maxwell company's earning potential, decided to build it up until its stock was worth something again, then sell. Thus, when U.S. Motor's assets were liquidated, Maxwell-Briscoe wasn't part of the package.

Brady now brought in Walter E. Flanders to run the company. A Vermonter with little formal education, Flanders was a well-muscled ruffian with a total absence of social graces and a way with a bottle that would have pleased W. C. Fields. But high professional competence plus leadership qualities that were the envy of any shop foreman would enable him to leave a decisive mark on the company. In *The Gasoline Age,* author C. B. Glasscock quotes William Chittenden, manager of the Book-Cadillac Hotel in Detroit, who described Flanders as "a roughneck of the roughnecks. But I always got along beautifully with him and admired many of his characteristics greatly. He was a powerful man physically and mentally, and without fear, physical or otherwise. Whatever he wanted, he wanted without delay, and usually got it."

Flanders had learned his manufacturing skills as a tool salesman, and became so well-known around Detroit that he was hired by Henry Ford in 1906 to be general manager for his Bellevue and Piquette Avenue plants. By reorganizing Ford's production methods he raised annual volume from less than 9000 units to nearly 15,000. In 1908, six months before the Model T appeared, he left to start a rival organization with two business partners, taking three key Ford people with him. Backed by a million dollars of venture capital, they took over the Wayne and Northern companies in Detroit and began making a new car called the EMF, named for Flanders, former Wayne president Byron F. Everitt, and one-time Cadillac sales manager William E. Metzger.

A pioneer auto salesman and a master of the trade, Metzger set up a distribution arrangement with Studebaker for EMF's entire output. Studebaker wasn't really a car manufacturer at the time but a wagon builder, with excess factory capacity and a vast dealer organization. Thus it was that 8132 EMF cars were pumped through the Studebaker pipeline from October 1908 through December 1909. The South Bend firm took over EMF completely in 1911, and the 22,555 cars it built that year were the first to bear the Studebaker name.

Everitt, Metzger, and Flanders now went after new ventures. For a time they offered cars carrying the Everitt and Flanders nameplates. Then Flanders went off to run Maxwell, with a five-year contract plus $2,750,000 in stock certificates and a million dollars cash. Taking over on New Year's Day 1913, he again began to reorganize operations. Bodies, castings, and axles would be produced in the former Courier plant in Dayton. Other components would be supplied by the New Castle, Indiana plant, with engine production and final assembly carried out in Detroit. The Tarrytown facility was sold to Chevrolet, which still operates it today. To develop new products, Flanders brought in his chief engineer from EMF, William Kelly, who had also designed the Wayne.

Maxwell's 1913 line comprised three offerings. At the bottom was a 22-horsepower roadster selling at $785. Built on a 93-inch wheelbase, it was powered by a

This Model 25 touring was part of "The Good Maxwell" line for 1922.

176.7-cubic-inch T-head four (bore and stroke: 3.75 × 4.00 inches). Next came a new 30-bhp model (a replacement for the 1912 Mascotte), available as a roadster for $1110 and as a touring car for $1145. It too was powered by a T-head four, but with the cylinders cast in pairs. The big 40-bhp Maxwell, a carryover from 1912, also used a T-head power unit but with four individually cast cylinders. It listed at $1625 as a roadster and $1675 as a touring. For 1914, the former Everitt car and the Flanders 6-50 acquired Maxwell nameplates. A new offering was the Kelly-designed Model 25 on a 102-inch wheelbase. Replacing the 22-bhp model, it sold for $695 in touring form, with electric lighting and starter available for an extra $55.

All these cars were recognized as good value, and they sold well. By 1915, Maxwell had worked its way back up to fifth place, just ahead of Buick and right behind Dodge, which in turn trailed Studebaker by less than 2000 units. Under Flanders's direction, Maxwell's factories were steadily modernized for greater efficiency. By 1916 the Jefferson Avenue plant was turning out 250 cars a day on a moving assembly line about 800 feet long that could carry 100 cars at a time.

For 1915, Maxwell dropped its 40-bhp Four and the 6-50 model to concentrate on a new low-priced Four built on a 103-inch wheelbase and powered by a more modern L-head engine of 186 cid. This car was to be the core of Maxwell production up to 1921, and the company built 69,000 of them in 1916 alone. Still, that wasn't enough to keep pace with the rise of Buick (now under the command of Walter P. Chrysler), Dodge, or Chevrolet. So, despite its success, Maxwell slipped to sixth on the industry production list.

By this time, Maxwell's plants were running at close to full capacity, so Flanders began looking around for additional factory space. His eye fell on the Chalmers Motor Car Company, which had a colossal 38-acre complex on Oakland Avenue in the Detroit suburb of Highland Park, with 21 buildings and capacity for 30,000 cars a year. Flanders arranged to lease the entire facility, and Maxwells began coming off the Highland Park lines in 1917, interspersed with Chalmers models. With this move, Flanders became president of Chalmers, while company founder Hugh Chalmers stepped into the background with the title of chairman.

Hugh Chalmers had joined the National Cash Register company at the age of 14, and rose from office boy to vice-president before he was 30—with a salary of $75,000! Christy Borth once referred to National Cash Register as John Henry Patterson's "organization of freewheeling eccentrics," and several of them gravitated to the auto industry, including Charles F. Kettering, later of Delco and GM fame, and Alvan Macaulay, who became president of Packard. Chalmers set the pattern for Errett Loban Cord, Paul G. Hoffman, and other automotive super-salesmen of the next generation. He started in the auto business by buying the Thomas half of the company that made the Thomas-Detroit car, which he promptly renamed Chalmers-Detroit in 1908. The Detroit part of the name was dropped at the end of 1910.

Our interest in the Chalmers car centers on the Model 6-30, introduced in 1916 and produced with minor changes up to 1924. It was the direct predecessor of the first Chrysler, which explains why that make was born as a medium-price contender.

Getting Started

The first six-cylinder Chalmers was ready in 1911 (a prototype served as a press car in that year's Glidden Tour). It was designed by George Willis Dunham, a serious-looking young man who had worked for Olds, Hudson, and Royal Tourist (he would later build the light six-cylinder Saxon with Harry Ford). When it appeared as a regular production model for 1912, the Chalmers Six rode a 130-inch wheelbase and was priced at $3250. Chalmers-Detroit did not manufacture its own engines but had them supplied to Dunham's designs and specifications by Continental, American and British Manufacturing Company, and the Westinghouse Machine Company. The six was basically the existing 36-bhp four with two extra cylinders and the same 4.25 × 5.25-inch bore and stroke for a displacement of 446.8 cubic inches. The block was brand-new, however, cast in two three-cylinder halves. An F-head layout with side exhaust valves and overhead inlet valves was employed, the crankshaft ran in three ball bearings, and the multi-disc clutch was of the oil-bath type.

Chalmers began phasing out its four-cylinder models with introduction of the Master Six for 1913 and a Light Six the following year. The latter's engine was a T-head design with the cylinders cast in a single block, displacement of 288.6 cubic inches (3.50 × 5.00), and a 30-50-bhp rating. At the same time, the Master Six unit was redesigned as a T-head, with revised cylinder dimensions (4.00 × 5.50) giving 414.7 cid.

After Dunham's departure in 1914, former Olds engineer Carl C. Hinkley took over at Chalmers, with responsibility for production as well as new-product design and development. His first creation was a new 6-40 model with a single-overhead-camshaft engine and a new chassis featuring transaxle and cantilever rear suspension. His last Chalmers (completed before he left to start his own engine company) was the 6-30, powered by a 224-cid (3.25 × 4.50) L-head with a one-piece block. Intended for higher crankshaft speeds, this engine ran on only three main bearings but would spin safely to 3400 rpm, though its peak output of 45 horsepower was developed at 2600 rpm. Other features included Hotchkiss drive and a gearbox mounted directly behind the engine. Built on a 115-inch wheelbase, the 6-30 weighed 2660 pounds. Prices started at $1400.

With this car and Hinkley's plant management, Chalmers had its best year ever in 1916, production climbing from 9800 to 16,000 units. For 1917, a 122-inch-wheelbase chassis was offered for the 6-30, but sales declined. Part of that was due to the conservatism of vice-president and assistant general manager Lee Counselman, who delayed Chalmers in adopting the closed four-door sedan body style that more and more buyers in the medium-price market were demanding.

There were two innovations for the 1918 version of the 6-30. One was the hot spot, basically a heat-riser that used exhaust heat to warm up the fresh fuel/air mixture so as to assure better combustion with the poor quality gasoline of the day. The second was the "ram's horn," intended to prevent fuel droplet formation. It consisted of a smoothly curved intake manifold with two "horns" that extended from the central carburetor flange, bent

One of the last Chalmers, the 5-passenger coach of 1923

Also from 1923, the Chalmer 7-passenger touring

downwards, then curved up near the ports. At the same time, the front of the engine was reworked with a timing chain instead of gears on camshaft and crankshaft.

Walter Flanders resigned from Maxwell at the end of 1918, bought a farm and made plans for growing tobacco. But the call of the automobile was too strong, and he soon became chairman of the new Rickenbacker Motor Car Company (his old friend Barney Everitt had paid $25,000 to wartime flying ace Eddie Rickenbacker for the use of his name). History says nothing about his accomplishments there, and Flanders met an untimely demise in a traffic accident in the summer of 1923.

Meantime, W. Ledyard Mitchell had taken over as Maxwell president. Though there was no doubt about his managerial abilities, the firm nevertheless started to decline. Part of this was due to quality problems, especially weak rear axles that could shed gears all over the road without warning. Numerous cases were reported and, as the word got out, people stopped buying. So even though 34,000 Maxwells and almost 10,000 Chalmers cars were assembled in 1920, the firm was going broke.

Inevitably, Maxwell fell into receivership, which prompted the resignation of engineer Kelly and his assistant, E. J. Miles. L. C. Freeman moved in as executive engineer. Bankers representing the bulk of the firm's creditors felt there was only one person who could save Maxwell Motor Company: Walter P. Chrysler. But at the time, Chrysler had his hands full trying to save Willys-Overland.

Though it may be difficult for today's generation to appreciate, Willys-Overland was once a very big fish in the automotive pond. For years it ranked second only to

Ford in production and sales, and the extent of its holdings was so vast that it was almost impossible for any one executive to keep track of everything. So it's appropriate here to take a brief look at the situation faced by Chrysler, soon to be renowned as a corporate "Mr. Fix-It."

Overland was born in 1903 when the Standard Wheel Company of Terre Haute, Indiana, hired Claude Cox, a young engineer fresh out of college, to design an automobile. The make became Willys-Overland in 1907 when John North Willys, an upstate New York automobile dealer, assumed Overland's $80,000 in accumulated debts. He moved operations to Toledo, Ohio, and took over the factory where Pope Manufacturing Company had built the Pope-Toledo. Willys-Overland expanded during 1909, producing about 4000 cars. Things were running smoothly by 1910, and the firm turned out about 10,000 cars that year compared with Ford's 32,053 and Buick's 30,525.

Then Willys fell into the same trap that had already snared W. C. Durant and Benjamin Briscoe: empire building. First he organized Kinsey Manufacturing Company to supply sheetmetal components, then relocated Warner Gear Company to Toledo in 1912 to supply Willys-Overland with gears and other machined parts. He acquired Gramm trucks at the same time, and later snapped up Tillotson carburetor, Morrow transmissions, and Electric Auto-Lite. By 1915 the conglomerate ranked second in industry production at 91,780 cars. Output climbed the next year to 142,000 units, which exceeded the aggregate production of General Motors. All these acquisitions were consolidated into the Willys Corporation, which also controlled Willys-Overland, and the expansion continued, with Wilson Foundry and Machine Company, Fisk Rubber Company, Federal Rubber Company, Curtiss Aeroplane Company, New Process Gear Company, USL Battery, Moline Plow Company, and Duesenberg Motors all quickly folded in.

But the bubble was about to burst. John Willys spent most of his time in Washington and New York, leaving mere lieutenants to run things back in Toledo. But lucrative World War I defense contracts were drying up and some of his clever acquisitions were becoming liabilities. Nevertheless, he raised capitalization to $50 million, and continued to overspend on expansion projects in the euphoria of the immediate postwar period. Then came a seven-month strike that crippled production in the Toledo, Elmira, and Elyria plants, and suddenly it seemed that the entire Willys Corporation was about to collapse.

Worried about getting their money back, Willys's bankers sent a committee knocking on Walter Chrysler's door. The group was headed by James C. Brady, a shrewd man with a sharp legal mind, and included one Ralph Van Vechten, the same man who had loaned Chrysler the money to buy his first car. The delegation offered Chrysler a million dollars a year, a two-year contract, and the title of Willys-Overland executive vice-president in exchange for turning the company around. He accepted, and in January 1920 he moved from Flint to New York City, site of corporate headquarters. Significantly, his understanding with the bankers included a provision that Willys-Overland would produce a brand-new car carrying the Chrysler name—if Walter opted to stay on indefinitely.

Chrysler waded into Willys-Overland with a very sharp edge on his cost-cutting axe. He wielded it ruthlessly, laying off unnecessary staff and workers, selling equipment, and even going so far as to slash John Willys's salary by half. By the end of his second year Chrysler had pared the company's debt to about $18 million. But the Chrysler car would have to wait, because Walter was about to tackle the Maxwell mess.

Something good actually came from this delay, though "good" is really an understatement. It was an engineering team that Chrysler discovered at the Elizabeth, New Jersey plant where brothers Fred and August Duesenberg had built aircraft engines during the war and where Willys wanted to make cars. It was not just a bunch of guys with pencils and slide rules but a close-knit technical triumvirate that has no parallel in automotive history. Perversely presenting themselves in reverse alphabetical order, they were Fred M. Zeder, Owen Skelton, and Carl Breer. At the time, they were consulting engineers on Willys-Overland's new-car projects and were presumably hired by chief engineer Ed Belden, who had arrived from the body department at Packard in 1917 with the task of bringing order to Willys's chaotic group of makes and models.

Zeder, Skelton, and Breer were preparing a concept for a new medium-priced six-cylinder car, which we'll call the ZSB for want of any official code name. But the Cleveland bank that John N. Willys was counting on to finance this program backed out because of the high estimated costs of retooling the Elizabeth plant. Willys had nothing further up his sleeve. Belden and his assistant Harry Woolson had thought of slotting the engine from the ZSB car into the Willys-Overland, but it wouldn't fit due to the peculiar front suspension design and its quarter-elliptic springs. However, the ZSB car would not die on the drawing board, for business events soon created new opportunities.

After falling into receivership in late 1921, the Willys Corporation was liquidated. Many of its divisions survived, however, including Willys-Overland, which was soon operating profitably once more. It built 94,000 cars in 1922, up from about 48,000 cars the previous year. By 1923 it was making big money again, with car sales that year totalling 120,000 units. Nevertheless, the Elizabeth plant had to be auctioned off to provide capital for the various operating units. Zeder, Skelton, and Breer moved into a small factory building, appropriately located on Mechanic Street in Newark, and incorporated as a partnership of consulting engineers. It wasn't long before they were working on a second Willys-Overland project under contract to Walter P. Chrysler.

Chrysler had intended to buy the Elizabeth plant for $5 million, which would enable him to start building automobiles under his own name. But he was outbid by none other than W. C. Durant, who was willing to pay $525,000 more. In the process, Durant acquired not only the factory but all design and engineering drawings for the ZSB car. Miraculously, he managed to raise the necessary

15

Getting Started

money to tool up for production, and rushed it to market as the Flint.

Durant tried to secure the services of Zeder, Skelton, and Breer on a full-time basis. But though they agreed to develop another engine for him, they decided that they would be better off with Chrysler. They had good reason to think so, because Chrysler had signed on as chairman of Maxwell in the spring of 1921. John N. Willys had no objection to this "time-sharing" arrangement so long as Walter lived up to his contract with the Willys bankers. It's also likely he thought he could take advantage of Chrysler's presence at Maxwell. Interlocking directorates were nothing new even in those days, and Willys, an experienced corporate juggler, was quite familiar with other, more informal ways of finding out what was going on at rival companies.

Chrysler once credited James C. Brady, Willys's top banker, with giving him some of the best advice he ever got. Noting the big differences between the Willys and Maxwell situations, Brady said Chrysler should take a fat cash salary at Willys, because the firm had enormous assets, even though it was ailing. That was definitely not the case at Maxwell. If Chrysler wanted to play it smart, said Brady, he should opt for a low annual salary (say $100,000 or so) and take the rest in Maxwell stock, bonds, and commercial paper with an eye to one day gaining personal control of the company. That idea appealed to Walter. Trouble was, the Maxwell-Chalmers bankers were hoping to sell to Studebaker. As it turned out, Chrysler

was saved by a misunderstanding. Studebaker president A. R. Erskine had offered $26 million for Maxwell in the belief that Zeder and Chrysler would be included. When they refused to go along, the deal fell through.

Chrysler was able to leave Willys-Overland some time before his two-year tour of duty actually expired. Company bankers had arranged for a $16.5-million bond issue to retire the remaining debt, then put the firm in receivership, from which it would emerge leaner and in a better position to face the Roaring Twenties. Walter promptly moved back to Detroit, where his plan for saving Maxwell quickly took shape. That inevitably included new products, and in 1922, Zeder, Skelton, and Breer moved to Michigan to work exclusively for him.

The Chrysler car was now very much on Walter's mind, but there were still a few obstacles to hurdle before it could become a reality. Foremost was a stockpile of 26,000 Maxwells that nobody apparently wanted. Chrysler ordered every car into the plant for axle reinforcements, then sold each of them at a profit, a tiny one but still a profit. The big thing was to rid himself of worry about depreciation, deterioration, capital being tied up without bearing interest, and other inventory costs.

Following Maxwell Motor Company's liquidation, a new organization called Maxwell Motor Corporation had been formed in early 1921 and incorporated in West Virginia, with Walter P. Chrysler as chairman. That was the year of "The Good Maxwell," an advertising slogan intended to convince the public that a change had indeed

Priced at $1495, the 1923 Chalmers 7-passenger touring rode a 122-inch wheelbase. Few were sold.

Chalmers disappeared after 1923 in favor of Chrysler. Shown is that year's 5-passenger sport sedan.

been made to a product that had hardly changed at all since 1914. The most significant feature of the revised model was undoubtedly a new axle said to be "strong, quiet, and long-lived." Prices were $885 for the touring car or roadster, $985 for the club coupe, $1235 for the four-passenger coupe, and $1335 for the sedan.

For 1922 there was a "New Series" Maxwell, with an engine worked over by Harry T. Woolson, whom Chrysler had lured from Willys-Overland on Zeder's recommendation. Woolson had started out in shipbuilding, then worked five years as chief engineer for the Gas Engine & Power Company. He joined Packard as a truck designer in 1915, then went to Studebaker, where Zeder discovered him working as a research engineer in 1916. Basically, his improvements involved adding counterweights to the Maxwell crankshaft and substituting aluminum pistons for cast-iron ones. He also reworked the chassis until it was almost completely new.

With the worst of its problems addressed, Maxwell made a stunning recovery, recording a net profit of $2,678,000 in 1923. Most of this was Chrysler's doing, but some of the credit must go to banker William R. Wilson, who was installed as interim president of Maxwell Motor Corporation in 1922. A statistician and a vice-president of the Irving National Bank, Wilson knew business and the auto industry, having worked for both Studebaker and Dodge before going into banking.

The Maxwell-Chalmers association had never completely satisfied either company, and now that both were in the same bankruptcy court and under the same receiv-

ers, they began an internecine battle over bookkeeping practices. Chalmers filed a $6 million suit against Maxwell, which countersued for $3.5 million. The case was settled on December 7, 1922, when Maxwell purchased Chalmers Motor Car Company for just under $2 million, thus completing the long-deferred merger. Hugh Chalmers retired that year. He died 10 years later at the age of only 59.

The Chalmers car had made no great strides since 1916. Restyled models prepared under the direction of L. C. Freeman were introduced for 1922, but they were powered by the same 224-cid L-head six and had the same ladder-type frame and Hotchkiss drive. Wheelbase was stretched to 117 inches, however, and prices came down about $200 so that the roadster sold for only $1295, the sedan for $2245. Four-wheel hydraulic brakes appeared for 1923, a careful ZSB adaptation of the system patented by Malcolm Loughead in 1919 and first used on a production car by the Duesenberg brothers in 1921. There were no other changes worth mentioning, but Walter P. Chrysler ordered another cut in prices, which now ranged from $1185 for the roadster to $1585 for the 5-passenger coach.

Chalmers disappeared after 1923, joining Columbia, Brush, Midland, Regal, Speedwell, Standard, Abbott-Detroit, Pope-Hartford, Stoddard-Dayton, Dixie Flyer, and hundreds more in America's vast graveyard of makes. The car that could have become the 1924 Chalmers carried the Chrysler badge instead. Walter was about to realize his dream.

Dependable by Design:
Dodge Before Chrysler
1914-1928

The first Dodge Brothers car, a Four touring from 1914. Retail price was $785 f.o.b. Detroit.

The Dodge Company that Walter Chrysler would buy in 1928 was not the same one the Dodge brothers had started in 1914. Nor was it the same one that existed at the time of their deaths in 1920. The 1928 Dodge was fully up-to-date, and the industrial force behind it was among the strongest in America. Not that the Dodge brothers didn't have adequate facilities when they started car production in 1914. Their factory on Bismarck Street and Mount Elliott Avenue in Hamtramck was one of the most efficient and best-equipped in Detroit. In fact, it had supplied most of Ford's mechanical components since 1903 (Ford plants were limited mainly to assembly up to 1914).

Though they were the sons of a poor mechanic, John F. and Horace E. Dodge would rise to the very top of the social ladder. They were born in Miles, Michigan, some 15 miles north of South Bend, Indiana, John in 1864, Horace four years later. When they were old enough to work, they had to help their father at his workshop in Port Huron, experience that taught them the rudiments of a trade. They soon left the family to make their fortune in Detroit. Wherever they went, they went together. After a period

While Walter P. Chrysler was winning fame and fortune, two enterprising brothers were building an automotive empire. Here's how they did it—and what happened after fate intervened.

working as machinists in the printing-press business, they got into the bicycle trade with an advanced ball-bearing design. It wasn't long before they sold the concern at a good profit to Canadian interests, which kept them on the payroll.

When the brothers had amassed some $7500 between them, they returned to Detroit and set up a machine shop on Beaubien Street. They were hard workers and they did good work for their clients, so their business thrived. In 1901 they were able to move into larger quarters located at Hastings Street and Monroe Avenue, where they made 3000 transmissions for Oldsmobile the following year. Then came the Ford contract, which put them on the way to the millionaires' club.

As Ford prospered, so did the Dodge brothers, who began buying land for new facilities. But increasingly they recognized that it wasn't such a good idea to have one customer account for practically all of their business. In the spring of 1913 they decided to cancel the Ford contract and start building a car of their own. The formal break came in August of that year, and the Dodge Brothers company was incorporated about a year later (July 17, 1914) with a capital stock of $5 million.

As president of the new firm, John Dodge was the dynamic businessman and fearless entrepreneur. Horace, serving as vice-president, was more the technician and scientist, forever planning new processes, methods, and machinery. They still stuck close together, hanging out at the Pontchartrain Bar, an informal gathering place for thirsty auto moguls (or would-be moguls), and often keeping late hours at the Detroit Athletic Club. They were known as boisterous, two-fisted drinking companions who would stop at nothing to win an argument, and Detroit's gossip mills ground out hundreds of stories about their night life.

The first automobile to bear the brothers' name was completed on November 14, 1914, and carried an announced price of $785. Lead times were much shorter in those days, which is why the Dodge car appeared so soon after the company's formation. Production began with a force of 482 workers, and the firm completed nearly 2000 cars before the end of the year. The design was mainly the work of Ralph A. Vail, who had worked for Franklin and the Olds Motor Works before joining the Dodges in 1901. Ransom E. Olds had sent Vail to keep an eye on output of the Dodge plant, then supplying engines, transmis-

Dodge Center-Door Sedan arrived in late 1915.

A 1916 Dodge touring for General John J. Pershing

sions and axles to Oldsmobile. When its factory (next to Detroit's Belle Isle bridge) burned down, Olds moved to Lansing, but Vail decided to stay with the brothers. Others who had a hand in the first Dodge car were Fred Whitman, Ray deVlieg, George W. Kiernan, and master mechanic Charles B. deVlieg. Experimental work was directed by Henry L. Innes.

Built on a 110-inch wheelbase, the first Dodge was 156 inches long, stood 81 inches high, and weighed 2200 pounds. To suit the differing spans of unpaved rural roads in various parts of the country, the car was offered with a choice of front and rear axle widths, so track was

Dependable by Design

either 56 or 60 inches. The frame consisted of channel-section steel side members and three cross-members. The front axle was carried on semi-elliptic leaf springs, the rear on three-quarter elliptics. Steering was by worm-and-wheel gear. The external-contracting service brakes had internal-expanding emergency brakes on the rear wheels, acting on the same 12-inch drums. Bodywork was supplied by Budd, with sheet-steel panels either bolted or nailed to a wooden framework.

Like the Ford Model T, the new Dodge was powered by a four-cylinder engine with a one-piece block, detachable head, side valves in L-head formation, and a three-bearing crankshaft. The crankshaft and connecting rods were made of drop-forged vanadium steel, and gray iron was used for the pistons. The Dodges wanted a larger and more powerful engine than Ford's, however, so they chose a bore and stroke of 3.875×4.50 inches, which gave 212.3 cubic inches and 35 horsepower at 2000 rpm on a 4.0:1 compression ratio. (The 20-bhp Model T four displaced 176.7 cubic inches with 3.75×4.00-inch bore and stroke.) With this size and output, the first Dodge had adequate performance, though top speed was only about 55 mph. The plugs were fired by a high-tension magneto, and a combined electric starter-generator was standard. The brothers frowned on Henry's two-speed pedal-shifted transmission, and opted instead for a three-speed sliding-gear unit. Its shift pattern was unusual in being an upside-down H, reflecting John Dodge's desire that top gear be positioned up and away from the driver. Another unusual touch was a countershaft that disconnected in direct-drive third to reduce noise and friction.

The Dodge Brothers car was not in direct competition with Henry's Tin Lizzy but instead entered a field that included Maxwell, Willys-Overland, and the Studebaker Four. John Dodge wasn't at all worried about being undersold: "Just think of all those Ford owners who will someday want an automobile," he once quipped. And the new make was quickly recognized as a "real" automobile.

Changes for 1915 were minor. Linoleum-covered running boards were added, and a vacuum fuel feed replaced gravity feed. Advertisements proudly stated that "The front door is not a dummy but swings wide open," a poke at the Model T. Only two models were offered, a four-door touring and a two-passenger roadster, both carrying the same $785 price, unchanged from 1914. A closed sedan with a tall body and a single, central curbside door appeared at the end of the year, tagged at $1185 f.o.b. Detroit (Dodge's first four-door sedan wouldn't arrive until February 1919). A Dodge climbed the Twin Peaks of San Francisco higher than any other car in 1915. Also that year, a Dodge was the first car to roll onto the floor of the Grand Canyon and then climb out under its own power.

John Dodge had driven a Packard before the brothers built their own automobile. Because he appreciated the make's high quality, he began to wonder whether he could lure one of Packard's top engineers to his fledgling firm. His ultimate choice was Russell Huff, who had joined Packard shortly after its move from Ohio to Detroit. He became chief engineer at Dodge in 1916. George Goddard was brought in as assistant, and Vail was named vice-

Dodge pioneered the four-door hardtop in 1916-23.

It also introduced the first four-door sedan, in 1919.

president of engineering (Henry Innes had left to join Chevrolet the year before and Fred Whitman departed about the same time). The company also got its own body engineer through Huff, a man named Baskerville who had also moved with Packard to Detroit.

For 1916, wheelbase was extended to 114 inches and straight-bevel gears were abandoned in favor of spiral-bevel drive for the rear axle. The next major engineering changes weren't made until 1918. The engine got a heavier crankshaft that year, after which it would continue basically unchanged through 1923, and a new multi-disc clutch replaced the earlier leather-faced cone unit. New frames and lower bodies were designed and developed on a continuing basis after 1918 and announced at roughly 12-month intervals, thus making Dodge an early exponent of the annual model change.

The Dodge Brothers company went from strength to strength. Production climbed from 45,000 cars the first year to 71,000 in 1916. It topped the 100,000 mark in 1917, by which time the work force had ballooned to 18,000. Profits in 1919 stood at $24 million on sales of 121,000.

Then, both brothers died suddenly. Horace caught pneumonia in early 1920 while the brothers were in New York for the annual auto show. John nursed him back to health, but the effort wore down his own resistance so badly that he too came down with pneumonia and died a few days later. Horace lost his spirit after this and took no further interest in the business, retiring to his summer home in Florida where he passed away quietly that autumn. To Malcolm Bingay, who was editor of The Detroit *Free Press* for many years and knew them both, the Dodge brothers were "two of the most misrepresented men of the wild years" in Detroit. "Legend has them as two wild wastrels," he wrote. "They were not. No two men ever worked harder or more soberly toward their objectives.... Though both men enjoyed drinking in their off hours, they had a moral code as sincere as any churchman's, and they lived rigidly by that code. Sometimes their fiery tempers got the better of them, for they were born fighters. If they had not been, they would never have accomplished what they did."

One of the brothers' last accomplishments had been to initiate an expansion project that would double production capacity at Hamtramck, from 300 to 600 cars a day. This work was completed in 1920, when Dodge car output totalled 145,389 units. However, because of the heavy investment involved, the firm's net profits fell to $18.6 million that year. The plant's oldest buildings dated from 1910, when the brothers set them up for Model T engine production in what was then an outlying area of Detroit.

The eight years between the brothers' death and their firm's acquisition by Chrysler is a little known but very important era in Dodge history. John Dodge's will specified that his estate should be divided equally among Mathilda Rausch Dodge, his second wife, and her children. Horace Dodge left his entire estate to his wife, Anna Thomson Dodge, but on her death it would be divided equally between their two children. Both widows consulted Howard E. Bloomer, who had been the brothers' legal advisor since their earliest days. On his recommendation they decided not to sell their stock and resisted several offers to buy the firm outright, including one from steel magnate Charles M. Schwab. In addition to the Dodge company, which at the time had an estimated net worth of around $60 million, the estates included personal fortunes the brothers had been more or less forced to accept. These dated from a time when Ford Motor Company was strapped for cash and the brothers agreed to buy 100 shares of that company's stock. In 1919, Henry Ford wanted to buy them back as part of his plan to gain complete control of the firm, by which time those shares were worth a cool $27 million. The brothers had also realized nearly $10 million in dividends during their 16 years as Ford shareholders.

Dodge's success continued unabated despite the brothers' deaths, with sales of 139,000 cars in 1920, but ownership of the firm wouldn't be resolved until 1923. That fall, attorney Bloomer set up trusteeships that divided all company stock equally between the two estates. Directors who had held voting stock now became the new management. The question of running the company had been settled much earlier with the election of Frederick J. Haynes as president and general manager on January 11, 1921. Haynes had been with the Dodge brothers in their bicycle days. When they moved to Detroit, he went to study engineering at Cornell University. Later he became a factory manager for H. H. Frank-

lin in Syracuse. He rejoined John and Horace in 1912, and worked with them on car production plans. At first he was involved mainly on the manufacturing side. He became increasingly involved with managerial tasks, however, and by 1920 had developed a unique familiarity with every aspect of the brothers' business. He was thus the perfect choice to head day-to-day operations after their deaths. Bloomer had himself elected chairman of the board, only to relinquish the office in the spring of 1924, after which the title was abolished.

The economic recession ushered in with 1921 almost drove Fred Haynes to despair. Just as he was breaking in Hamtramck's expanded facilities, car sales fell to 92,476 units and profits dwindled to less than $3 million for the year. He decided to gamble on the growing market for closed cars, and won: by the fall of 1922, these models had climbed from 13 to 35 percent of Dodge's total annual production. He also banked heavily on the commercial market by offering standard chassis with van and truck bodies made by the Graham Brothers company in Evansville, Indiana. This business flourished, which enabled the Grahams to set up a new plant on Conant Avenue in Detroit in 1922, followed by another on Lynch Road two years later. Both these gambits helped Dodge to a handsome recovery. Total vehicle sales improved to 164,037 in 1922. The total rose again the next year, to 179,505.

The 1921 Dodge was a medium-price, no-frills work-

1914 Dodge Brothers touring

From 1922, a custom Dodge town brougham by Babcock

Dependable by Design

1924 Dodge Brothers five-window coupe. Price was $1035.

1927 Dodge Brothers Standard touring

1925 Dodge Brothers Standard "Type A" four-door sedan

1927 Dodge Brothers "Fast Four" DeLuxe four-door sedan

horse, plain-looking, simple and stark, and tremendously rugged. It offered quality and dependability for moderate outlay, a no-nonsense formula that nevertheless generated ample demand. It was also the same basic car the company had introduced in 1916, which in turn was simply an improved version of the original 1914 design. The only noteworthy alterations for 1921 were 32 × 4-inch tires, standard-equipment heaters, and available hand-operated windshield wipers. Dodge car production amounted to 132,000 units for the calendar year.

For 1922, the touring car was reduced from $985 to $880. Business coupe and business sedan body styles were added in the summer, priced at $980 and $1195, respectively. The following year the Dodge four acquired a new longer-duration camshaft, but power output stubbornly refused to climb. Wheelbase was again stretched, this time to 116 inches, the frame was lowered, and a new semi-floating rear axle was adopted. Also for 1923, rear leaf springs were lengthened from 45 to 55 inches, and 36¼-inch front springs were fitted. Semi-elliptic springs replaced the old rear quarter-elliptics on 1924 models.

In the spring of 1923, Haynes committed Dodge to a new $5 million expansion plan that would boost car volume to 1000 units daily, built by 20,000 workers. After turning out 180,000 cars that year, the company set a new sales record in 1924, with 225,104 vehicles and a net profit just shy of $20 million. By that time, Dodge was beginning to move with contemporary design trends. In 1922, Russell Huff had hired chassis engineer George B. Allen, who had started with Hudson and had also been with

Chalmers and Liberty. Allen would later be a Dodge experimental engineer, taking a hand in the development of most every innovation being considered for production. Meanwhile, Dodge hoodlines had been raised repeatedly under Baskerville's aegis, and the company got into "styling" for the first time with some 1924 variations called Special. Priced $50 to $100 above the standard offerings, they featured chrome-plated radiator shells, deluxe interiors, extra instrumentation, and various decorative refinements. Such product changes were made in an evolutionary fashion and without compromising the make's by-now substantial reputation for dependability.

It was in 1924 that the Dodge heirs decided to sell, and Howard Bloomer discreetly began to invite offers as administrator for the estates. In an unusual mood of acquisitiveness, General Motors president Alfred P. Sloan instructed the banking firm of J. P. Morgan & Co. to offer either $124,650,000 in cash or $59 million cash plus $90 million in non-interest-bearing installment notes that would mature in equal series over nine years. What Sloan had in mind is anyone's guess, because with Buick, Oakland and Oldsmobile already in the fold, the last thing GM needed was another medium-price line. In any case, the purchase would have meant a realignment of GM's entire product range, which would likely have changed the market position of all its makes, including Dodge. Perhaps it's just as well then that Sloan's bid wasn't accepted.

For about six months beginning in late 1924, Dodge

was actually run by Joseph B., Robert C. and Ray A. Graham, who would go on to establish Graham-Paige Motors. In mid-1925 the Wall Street investment firm of Dillon, Read & Co. paid $146 million to the two Dodge widows. The Graham brothers then sold their company holdings, and their truck company became a Dodge division. These moves allowed the Grahams to buy up Paige-Detroit and its factory on Warren Avenue in Dearborn, which set the stage for the Graham-Paige in 1927.

But why should bankers want to own a car company? Usually financiers invest in an industry only if they think there are big profits to be made, but things weren't so simple in this case. Clarence Dillon actually had ideas of becoming a motor tycoon, and he was not without qualifications. Born in Texas, he went to school in the east, graduating from Harvard in 1905. After holding managerial posts in iron, steel, and coal, he joined William A. Read & Co. in New York. After three years, in 1916, he was named its president. The firm became Dillon, Read & Co. in 1921, when it refinanced the Goodyear Tire & Rubber Co. Clearly, Dillon had a predilection for transportation. For example, his company handled all the bond issues for the Canadian National Railways, and he was personally involved with financing for Shell Union Oil Co. B. C. Forbes described him as "the most-discussed and least-known-about investment banker in the United States. He shrinks from self-glorification. He is extremely mild and gentle of manner; nothing boisterous or domineering about him."

It soon became apparent that Dillon, by now 42, had visions of a merger between Dodge, Packard, Hudson, and the Briggs body company, feeling that such a group could rival General Motors, which was smaller than Ford Motor Company at the time. Packard was running with regular profits of about $15 million annually in the mid-Twenties, while Hudson's profits fell from $21 million in 1925 to $5.4 million the following year. Packard was building 550 cars a week compared to 9400 for Hudson (including Essex) and 4800 for Dodge. The last had $13,746,656 in net earnings on sales of 167,686 cars in 1925, which rose to $21,591,919 and 219,446 cars the next year. Dodge was obviously in a very strong market position, and Dillon got nowhere with either Alvan Macauley at Packard or Roy D. Chapin at Hudson.

Fred Haynes stayed on at Dodge under the Dillon regime, supervised by newly appointed chairman Edward G. Wilmer (whom Dillon had installed as president of Goodyear four years earlier). However, Haynes had his differences with Dillon and left Dodge within a year of the takeover. (He then linked up with William C. Durant, and ultimately returned to Franklin in 1930.) Wilmer succeeded him as Dodge president in 1926.

Before the sale, Haynes and Vail had reorganized the engineering department. Dissatisfied with Huff's conservatism that let Dodge lag behind the times, they made Roy Cole chief engineer for new-product design, leaving Huff as chief engineer with responsibilities mainly in the area of reliability and quality control. In 1926, however, Huff became Director of Engineering and Clarence Carson took over his previous duties. Huff left in the fall of 1926 and went to work for John N. Willys on a new car to be called Falcon-Knight. He continued as a consulting engineer at Willys-Overland until his death in 1930.

Dodge scored two Detroit firsts with its 1925 models: vacuum-operated windshield wipers and sprayed-on lacquer for the exterior finish. Other new features included cowl vents and a one-piece windshield to replace the previous horizontally split type. The engine was still basically the same as before, but acquired silchrome exhaust valves and oil-control rings on the pistons. The following year a five-bearing crankshaft appeared and coil-and-battery ignition replaced the magneto.

There were a host of changes for 1927. These were largely the work of R. E. Cole, who had previously worked at Oldsmobile, Chalmers, Liberty, Saxon, and Continental Motors. He joined Dodge in 1924 at the age of 37, and formed a fast friendship with Vail. He also worked fast, producing not one but two new models. First came a 40-bhp four-cylinder car built on a 108-inch wheelbase and featuring four-point engine mounting, a single-plate clutch instead of the old multi-disc unit, standard-shift transmission, and four-wheel hydraulic brakes. Frames and bodies were lower, and Dodge contracted the Fisher coachworks to supply certain body styles. With its smaller wheels and fatter tires, Dodge now had a fashionably stylish automobile.

And there was more: the first six-cylinder Dodge, marking the firm's entry into a higher price bracket. Called the Senior Six, it rode a 116-inch wheelbase, the same as that of the larger carryover Four. It was joined in November by the Victory Six, built on a 112-inch chassis. Dodge completed about 15,000 six-cylinder cars in 1927, all powered by a 224-cubic-inch L-head engine with 3.25 × 4.50-inch bore and stroke. On its 5.3:1 compression, the six put out a rated 60 horsepower at 2800 rpm.

Despite all its new and improved models, Dodge lost sales to Oakland's new six-cylinder Pontiac in 1927, along with Hudson, Nash, and Durant. Deliveries for the year, dropped to only 124,000 units, and profits dried up. Accordingly, the four-cylinder line was discontinued in January 1928 and replaced by a new Standard Six on a 110-inch wheelbase. The Senior Six wheelbase was stretched to 120 inches, and its engine was bored out to 3.375 inches for 241.5 cid and 78 bhp at 3000 rpm. A new short-stroke 208-cid six powered the Standard and Victory models, with 3.75-inch bore, 3.875-inch stroke, and 58 bhp at 3000 rpm.

But by the second half of 1928, Dodge would be absorbed into Walter P. Chrysler's new corporation, marking the end of an era. As Vail and Cole faced the formidable engineering trio of Fred M. Zeder, Owen Skelton, and Carl Breer, they quickly realized their days at Dodge were over. They left to work briefly for W. C. Durant, then moved on together to Studebaker.

In its last year as an independent, Dodge built a total of 178,000 cars, all sixes: 82,000 Standards, 81,000 Victory models, and 15,000 Seniors. However, the dealer network was unable to move more than 150,000 of these, so the Chrysler takeover seemed timely. In fact, Dodge desperately needed some fresh design thinking. As part of the new Chrysler Corporation, that's exactly what it would get.

The first prototype Chrysler and its builders in 1923. Production models used chrome radiator shells.

1924

The public first set eyes on a car named Chrysler in January 1924. The place was the lobby of the Hotel Commodore on 42nd Street in New York City. Walter P. Chrysler had planned to display his car—with all appropriate pomp—at the annual New York Automobile Show, which opened at the Grand Central Palace on January 5. That, he figured, would enable him to attract dealers and investors as well as potential customers. But show managers denied him space on the grounds that the car wasn't actually in production. "If you don't build it, you can't sell it," they told him. "And the cars you see here are here to be sold."

It's not certain who had the idea first, Chrysler or Joseph E. Fields, but one of them noticed that the hotel where most of the exhibitors would be staying during show week—and where a lot of auto business would be conducted—was just four blocks away. If Chrysler could get his car in there, it would likely be noticed by more of the people who mattered than it would have been at the show. How the arrangements were made has never been put on paper, but it is known that Fields had a big smile on his face when he came back from seeing the hotel manager, saying to Chrysler: "Boss, we own the lobby."

Joe Fields was one of those wonderful salesmen who (along with Richard H. Grant of Chevrolet fame and Hugh Chalmers) had cut their teeth at National Cash Register. He got into the automobile business with Chalmers and later worked for Hupmobile, which had one of the slickest, most effective sales organizations in the country, if not the biggest. He had also helped Chrysler unload his stocks of Maxwell and Chalmers cars in 1922.

For a solid week the Commodore lobby was jammed with visitors, including a number of important investors and bankers. Chrysler was lying in wait for them, along with his financial advisor, B.E. "Hutch" Hutchinson (when your birth certificate reads Bertram Edwin, people call you "Hutch"). Walter desperately needed $5 million to get his car into production, and touted its merits to anyone even remotely connected with Wall Street. Some said no right away, while others gave a definite maybe. Then there was one who first said yes, then no. Ultimately, it was "Hutch" who cajoled R. Edward Tinker of Chase Securities into underwriting a $5 million issue of Maxwell Motor Corporation debenture bonds. Already a reality to those who had a hand in its creation, the new car would soon be a reality so impossible to ignore that not even the New York show organizing committee would be able to keep it out of the 1925 event.

The Chrysler shown at the Commodore was a touring car that would go on sale a few months later at $1335, just $40 more than the popular Buick Model 24-45. The idea of going after that market, if indeed a strategy had ever been formulated, came from Walter's experience at Chalmers, and it made sense. Though crowded, it was a big segment: Buick alone sold over 150,000 cars a year in 1923-24. Of course, Chrysler, in the form of Maxwell-Chalmers, was starting from far behind, with combined 1923 registrations of 49,546 units, most of which (42,788) were Maxwells. By contrast, Dodge, still an independent, sold more than twice as many cars (114,076). Besides Buick, this positioning also put the Chrysler in direct competition with Auburn's Six, the R-series Hupmobile, Nash's Advanced Six, Reo's G-series, the Studebaker Special Six, and the Velie.

Officially designated B-series, the initial Chrysler lineup consisted of six body styles. Besides the aforementioned touring it offered a roadster ($1525), phaeton ($1395), four-door sedan ($1625), two-door brougham ($1795), and the five-passenger four-door Imperial sedan, available in standard ($1895) and more elaborate Crown Imperial ($2195) variations. The Imperial name would later become synonymous with Chrysler Corporation's most luxurious cars, but it was originally used to denote a body type rather than equipment or model rank.

Some observers believe that engineers Zeder, Skelton, and Breer set out to create a "baby Lincoln" in the first Chrysler, though the same has been said about Edsel Ford and his 1928 Model A. Actually, what Walter P. Chrysler essentially told them was to come up with a car having a 110-inch wheelbase, a dry weight of 2400 pounds, and a top speed of 60 mph. The production model exceeded the target dimensions by small margins, but it also exceeded the performance goal by 10 mph.

Zeder, Skelton, and Breer started on the Chrysler project before leaving New Jersey, and completed it in their new Highland Park quarters. Chrysler's confidence in this trio was so solid that their finished design was approved on June 4th, 1923, *before* a single prototype had been built. Assistant chief engineer Howard E. Maynard now began to coordinate the massive efforts needed to get production rolling. Then 45 years old, he had worked for U.S. Motor Co. in Detroit and Lion Motor Car Co. of Adrian, Michigan, before joining Maxwell as chief production engineer in 1913. Former Maxwell-Chalmers executive engineer L. C. Freeman was displeased by the way Zeder, Skelton, and Breer were managing to concentrate all engineering authority in their own hands, so he left in March 1924 to sign up with Hupp Motor Car Co.

The first running Chrysler prototype was ready on July 31, 1923, less than 60 days after the design had been approved. Walter P. went for a demonstration ride with his engineers up Kercheval Avenue in Detroit in the dead of night. In those days, pre-production cars were tested on public roads. GM was then working on its first proving grounds at Milford, Michigan, but Ford had no similar facilities, nor did Maxwell. The Chrysler test program amounted to five weeks and 25,000 miles of running around the Allegheny mountains from Virginia to Pennsylvania.

Prime responsibility for producing the new car fell on George W. Mason, who had worked with Studebaker's sales force in 1913 and with Dodge in 1914-15. Hired by Chrysler in 1921, he became general manager for the Detroit plants the following year, but left in 1926 to become president of Copeland Products, Inc. He ended up with Nash-Kelvinator in 1936, where he would eventually become president, a position he would retain until his death in the mid-Fifties. Another newcomer to Chrysler's manufacturing team in 1922 was Charles E. Davy, a Michigander who had started as a machine shop foreman with Ford in 1913 and later worked for Denby Motor Truck, Universal Products, and Paige-Detroit. Davy would spend the rest of his career with Chrysler, ultimately rising to director of engineering operations before his retirement in 1955, but for the initial 1924 model he was mainly concerned with production methods and means. Tooling was duly installed in some of the buildings that made up the former Chalmers complex.

As the first cars were being shipped out, Walter P. Chrysler explained the new model's design concept to Maxwell-Chalmers dealers (according to author Chris Sinsabaugh in the book *Who, Me?*): "I am building the Chrysler because I have been convinced for years that the

Mr. Chrysler and his 1924 B-series roadster

1924 Dodge Brothers Standard touring

The first production Chrysler was this 1924 B-series touring.

1924 Chrysler B-series 5-passenger brougham cost $1795.

public has a definite idea of a real quality light car—one not extravagantly large and heavy for one or two people but adequately roomy for five, economical to own and operate." Then he went into technical detail: "[I chose] a perfectly balanced six-cylinder motor with a top speed of over 70 miles an hour—not because [people] want to drive at that rate, but to ensure quick getaway, flashing pickup, power to conquer any hill, and for the steady pull at low speeds. A small-bore powerplant, first for fine performance, and second for gasoline and oil economy.

Simplicity and accessibility throughout. Lots of room. I mean wide doors, deep comfortable seats, ample leg room. Real comfort: long, soft springs, extra-size tires, deep overstuffed cushions. Driving convenience and ease that will let a woman drive for long distances and through heavy traffic. Light weight so that a single passenger doesn't feel he's paying to haul a private Pullman, yet without squeaks or rattles or flimsiness. Wheelbase built to fit into an ordinary parking space and to ensure quick and easy hauling, but designed to ride well on rutted

Owen Skelton, Fred Zeder, and Carl Breer in 1933

Zeder, Skelton, and Breer: The Three Musketeers

Almost from the day they met, Fred M. Zeder, Owen Skelton, and Carl Breer guided Walter P. Chrysler in all matters technical. Chrysler was astounded by the natural way these three engineers worked together, communicating almost as if by a sixth sense to produce sound and often brilliant solutions to a variety of thorny problems. For this reason, he frequently referred to them as "The Three Musketeers," after the famous Alexandre Dumas novel.

Zeder was the team's "front man," the leader. He was the only one of the three who truly appreciated their collective worth and the only one able to negotiate lucrative contracts successfully on their behalf. By nature an entrepreneur and planner, he was always on the lookout

for new business opportunities. This and his uncanny ability to coordinate his partners' efforts toward a single goal constituted much of the team's strength, and it's interesting that none of the three had enjoyed particularly brilliant careers before they joined forces.

As an engineer, Zeder took no chances and always put a big safety margin into his work. His innovations were not eye-catching features but less visible and more enduring contributions, like the first Chrysler's hydraulic brakes, which were regarded as pretty far-out in the mid-Twenties. Yet despite his emphasis on long-lasting quality over fad ideas and peak performance, he was wild about new technology. In fact, he was attending an inventors fair in Florida

when he died in 1951.

Frederick Morrell Zeder was born in Bay City, Michigan, in 1886, making him nine years younger than Walter Chrysler. Growing up on a farm in Saginaw Valley, he worked during his school years as a mechanic for the Michigan Central Railroad. He then went on to the University of Michigan, and served a student apprenticeship with Allis-Chalmers before graduating in 1909. His work at the firm turned into a two-year stretch as an erecting engineer, and it was during this time that he met one of his future partners, Carl Breer. Next, he signed on a head of the E-M-F (Everitt-Metzger-Flanders) engine laboratory in Detroit, where he designed a new four-cylinder power unit. At the time, E-M-F was mainly a subcontractor to Studebaker, and this connection led Zeder to an appointment as a consulting engineer for the South Bend automaker in 1913. The following year he was named Studebaker's chief engineer by engineering director James G. Heaslet, at the princely salary of $15,000 a year.

It was at Studebaker that Zeder joined up with Breer and Skelton, and in 1918 the trio resigned to organize their own engineering laboratories. It wasn't long before they left Detroit to become consultants to Walter Chrysler at Willys-Overland's plant in Elizabeth, New Jersey, where they were assigned to draw up a new model Chrysler was planning to build there. As previously mentioned (see Maxwell-Chalmers), that car didn't appear as a Willys but instead became the Flint under the aegis of William C. Durant. As the direct precursor of the first Chrysler, the Flint was also powered by an L-head inline six, had coil ignition, and used a water pump for coolant circulation. However, it packed more displacement, 268.4 cubic inches (3.375 × 5.00-inch bore and stroke) versus the Chrysler's 201.5 cid, and was built on a 8.25-inch longer wheelbase (120.0).

Fred Zeder was a big man, not excep-

roads or a cobblestone street. Quality materials and workmanship to give long life and constantly good service instead of a job built to fit a price. Beauty that speaks for itself and good taste that is self-evident. Complete modern equipment built into the car, not hung on it merely as an afterthought."

At the outset, Herbert V. Henderson was the closest thing to a stylist Chrysler had. He was not an automobile man but an industrial designer with experience mainly in interior architecture. Zeder—and probably Chrysler himself—viewed "styling" not as overall vehicle design but as something that involved ornamentation—the look of hubcaps, radiator shells, instrument panels, lamp housings and the like. Not surprisingly, then, the major task for Henderson's staff of eight was to select interior color schemes and appointments, Henderson reported to chief body engineer Oliver H. Clark.

A former Studebaker engineer, Clark actually designed the body for the first Chrysler. Asked many years later about his styling theme for it, he could only say, "The

---

tionally tall or heavy but definitely corpulent. A jowly face gave no clue that it belonged to one of the nation's finest automotive engineers, and indeed he looked more like the stereotypical midwestern blue-collar worker. He had a cleft chin that would have been more prominent but for his massive neck, and an indeterminate nose that was set off by kind brown eyes under bushy brows. His hair was dark, but it began graying and thinning in his forties.

Author Malcolm Bingay described Zeder as "a very devout churchman, though you would never suspect it around the Chrysler engineering laboratories when something goes wrong. Fred goes to church every morning. He believes that God is 'The Great Engineer.' He [even] spent months up at Rochester, Minnesota, studying human anatomy with Drs. Charles and Will Mayo—[just] to get engineering ideas."

If Zeder looked the part of a factory worker, Owen Skelton looked the part of a movie actor. His appearance was smart—almost too smart for his own good—and he always dressed correctly even though he had no eye for fashion. Had he been an actor, he would not have made a convincing hero. Smooth hair parted elegantly on one side, and blue eyes set far apart but a trifle small and perhaps too almond in shape, combined with a tall, slender figure to give him a slightly suspicious air. He had a fine, manly nose and lips that seemed to smile even in repose. Though he worked slowly (certainly more so than Zeder) no engineer was more meticulous or exacting: on a Skelton drawing there was never an error.

Born in Edgerton, Ohio, and educated at Ohio State University, Skelton found his first auto industry job at Pope-Toledo, where he remained for two years. From the age of 23 to 30, a vital stage in an engineer's life, he worked at Packard, where he was known as "a good man on axles and transmissions." In 1913 he went into partnership with a friend named Goodman to build the short-lived Benham car in Detroit, then went on to the engineering staff at Studebaker, where he met Zeder and Breer and also brought Hotchkiss drive to the firm's cars in about 1917.

As a member of the "ZSB" triumvirate and during his many years at Chrysler Engineering later in life, Skelton would contribute substantially to the automobile's technical advancement. As early as 1928, for example, he evolved a mounting arrangement for a rear-engine car, consisting of a transverse leaf spring centered on the crankshaft axis. He also gets credit for development of four-wheel hydraulic brakes, all-steel body construction, and the fluid coupling. "Floating Power," for years a Chrysler Corporation selling point, was another Skelton innovation (with Ken Lee), and would become almost universal. The term refers to rubber mounts for the engine so that its roll axis coincides with its center of gravity for less motion under torque and thus smoother power delivery. Skelton was a co-founder of the Chrysler Institute of Engineering in 1933, and was given a seat on the Corporation's board of directors in 1937 after being named executive engineer. Though he retired in 1951, he served as a company consultant for another three years. He then moved to Palm Beach, Florida, where he lived until his death in 1969.

Carl Breer may have been first on the alphabet in name, but he was always the last "Musketeer" introduced. As noted, he met Fred Zeder in 1909 when they worked side by side as student apprentices at Allis-Chalmers. Breer made a big impression there by solving some rather intricate condenser problems. When Zeder took over as chief engineer at Studebaker in 1914, he remembered this and invited Breer to join him in South Bend.

Carl was a car nut from childhood. Born in Los Angeles in 1883, he attended Throop Polytechnic Institute in Pasadena. It was in his student days that he designed and built his own steam car, and it's safe to say that had he grown up in a later era, he probably would have been a hot rodder—and a general menace from Long Beach to Salt Lake City. His auto industry experience came early, but involved only obscure makes like Tourist and Duro. This convinced him that he needed more schooling, so he entered Stanford University and obtained a mechanical engineering degree in 1909. Following his apprenticeship at Allis-Chalmers, he went to work for the Moreland Truck Company, then organized the Acme Electrical Auto Works in 1914. At this point his career seemed to have gone slightly awry, but in 1915 he married Barbara Zeder, Fred's sister. About a year later, he was working under his brother-in-law at Studebaker.

There's no doubt that Breer was the most intellectual "Musketeer," He was the sort of quiet thinker who usually comes up with original and clever solutions, not necessarily new inventions but inspired applications of existing ones. Though engine development was his forte, he was interested in rethinking and remaking every aspect of a car's design, and avidly studied everything from front-wheel drive to aerodynamics. Though he was something of an "egghead," he didn't look like one. His open, trustworthy face was the kind you expect in a doctor, and his big blue eyes gave you a frank answer every time, though with age his lips curved more and more into a disappointed arc. Breer was the smallest of the "Musketeers" physically and the first to need glasses for work. As a young man he was quite handsome. Though not athletic, he kept himself fit even as he approached retirement. He was fastidious about attire and always impeccably groomed.

Breer officially retired in 1949, but retained his seat on the Chrysler board through 1953. In view of the order in which the "Musketeers" presented themselves, it's fitting that Breer should live the longest. He died at the end of 1970 at the ripe old age of 87.

shape just sort of happened." Indeed, the car didn't really look that different next to its rivals, but Clark claimed his design had been worked out "scientifically," based on the notion that all curves are actually sections of a sphere. Panel widths were thus graduated, with the smallest sections at the top of the body and the largest at the bottom. Even the gas tank and spring hangers were shaped to be pleasing to the eye. Bodies were supplied by Fisher, an arrangement Chrysler was happy to continue, as Hugh Chalmers had helped Fred and Charlie Fisher set up their coachworks and in return had enjoyed preferential treatment.

The new Chrysler inline six was miles ahead of the 1923 Chalmers unit. It was designed and built with little regard to cost and no compromises were made that might affect reliability, because this engine would help establish the new make's reputation. It was also an advanced design, far above the typical Detroit engine of this era for efficiency, silence, smoothness, and flexibility. It had a one-piece nickel-chrome-alloyed iron block and a detachable cast-iron head. Valves were disposed in an L-head arrangement, and the combustion chambers were laid out for high turbulence according to Ricardo principles so that compression could be uncommonly high without detonation problems. Zeder chose connecting rods made of forged steel and a chain drive for the camshaft. The crankshaft was a massive steel forging having integral counterweights and seven fully machined main bearings without shims. The crankcase was machined internally to

ensure adequate clearance for the counterweights. Tolerances were kept to a minimum throughout, calling for precision of a much higher order than was then normal in auto engine manufacturing. Besides these features, Chrysler pointed with pride to the full-pressure lubrication system, an oil filter with quick-replaceable element, an air cleaner that also functioned as a silencer, Ball & Ball updraft carburetor, and Remy coil-and-battery ignition. A water pump assured coolant circulation from the head to the cellular radiator, and the fuel feed from the rear-mounted tank was assured by an intermediate vacuum tank. The complete engine weighed about 660 pounds.

But was the Chrysler six a mechanical marvel? Not really. It wasn't exotic like the overhead-cam V-8 C. Harold Wills was building up in Marysville, Michigan. It didn't have an aluminum block, already common in aircraft and racing-car engines. And its configuration was hardly unique: Buick had introduced a valve-in-head six in 1914, and Nash followed in 1917. Nevertheless, this powerplant would have a great deal to do with the Chrysler's high initial success. One explanation for choosing an L-head straight six was the need to hold down tooling costs and to make the best use of the Chalmers plant's existing machinery. There were also highly valid technical reasons for this choice. An inline six is inherently balanced, while a V-8 is not. Overhead valves, even with overhead camshaft actuation, tend to be noisy, while side valves are very quiet as well as being easy to adjust

A custom town car with unknown bodywork on the B-series Chrysler chassis from 1924-25. Note unusual headlamps.

and grind. An aluminum block saves weight, but costs three or four times more to cast, not to mention the expense of the separate cylinder liners it requires. Then too, a lot went into the Chrysler engine that isn't readily apparent from its paper specifications. All "hot" parts got proper cooling, all sliding parts got better than average lubrication, and valves, gears, rods, and everything else were dimensioned to avoid damage and breakage. When Fred Zeder designed an engine, he didn't overlook a thing.

But it was the Lockheed four-wheel hydraulic brakes and not the engine that started people talking about the 1924 Chrysler, even though Chalmers had already offered this feature on some of its cars. The Chrysler system employed externally contracting bands for the brake drums, plus a mechanically operated emergency brake acting on the propshaft. The drums and brake bands were similar to those of the four-wheel system adopted by Rickenbacker in mid-1923 and standardized by Buick for 1924. But while those were purely mechanical arrangements, with rods and wires connecting foot pedal and drums, Chrysler's hydraulic lines afforded balanced brake force distribution, something that was impossible to achieve even with the best mechanical setups.

Brakes aside, there was nothing extraordinary about the first Chrysler's chassis engineering. Skelton stuck pretty close to Packard practice and Zeder did not want to stray far from what he had done at Studebaker, so the result was parallel leaf springs suspending conventional solid axles front and rear. The frame was made as wide as possible so the springs could be attached closer to the wheel hubs, thus affording greater resistance to side sway. The front frame members came close together, providing a strong base for engine mounting while simultaneously freeing space for the front wheels to turn at sharper angles. At the rear, the frame was kicked up above the axle to permit a low passenger compartment floor, and the chassis was indeed low and modern for 1924. The wood-spoked wheels carried 30×5.77 tires, Lovejoy hydraulic shock absorbers were fitted all round, and the relatively long, flat springs effectively brought everything closer to the ground. The semi-floating rear axle was equipped with a spiral-bevel final drive geared at 4.30:1. Hotchkiss drive via an open propeller shaft was specified, with the main drive taken from a three-speed gearbox (with central shift lever) through a dry multi-disc clutch. Worm-and-sector steering was adopted to give accurate wheel positioning with low effort. The tubular front axle was unusual in being made of chrome-molybdenum steel. Chrysler claimed it was 34 percent more rigid than an I-beam axle of the same weight: "It has over five times the resistance to horizontal strains in a fore and aft direction. Its resistance to torsion, or twisting, is 138 percent greater." The 1924 Chrysler measured just over 160 inches long overall and weighed about 2750 pounds ready for the road, depending on body style.

Despite the new car's size and weight, one observer noted that "you can drive it 60-70 miles an hour without the usual clutching of the steering wheel, without side sway and road weaving that ordinarily make speed a fear-

1924 Chrysler B-series 4-passenger roadster

1924 Chrysler B-series Imperial 5-passenger sedan

ful thing." And speed was definitely a Chrysler attraction. This was demonstrated all over the country, but particularly on the Pacific coast. On July 16, 1924, Ralph de Palma drove a Chrysler in the Mount Wilson hillclimb near Los Angeles. Over a road with 144 curves and a fast rise of 4635 feet in a mere 9½ miles, he set the fastest time of the day and was declared overall winner. He also ran two minutes faster than any previous stock car, which was also fast enough to beat the previous racing-car record by over a minute. The following September he put another Chrysler on the track at Fresno, and drove a distance of 1000 miles in 1007 minutes, an astounding accomplishment for the day.

Maxwell was still around in 1924, and entered the selling season with several important improvements. The engine now had a higher block with redesigned water jacketing to assure freer circulation around all exhaust ports and valve seats. The formerly siamesed exhaust ports on cylinders 2 and 3 were now fully separated, valve diameter was increased, and piston skirts were lengthened.

These changes put Maxwell on the upswing, but the low-price field was still dominated by Ford, which held a commanding 55-percent share of the market. By contrast, GM accounted for no more than 17 percent, and Dodge did well to secure a 6-percent share. The Chrysler-managed companies ended the year with a modest gain in registrations, about as much as could be expected: 2003 units for Chalmers, 44,006 Maxwells, and 19,960 of the new Chryslers, for a grand total of 65,969. Dodge registered 158,000 cars for the calendar year.

1925

Walter P. Chrysler had made all the right moves since his first contacts with Maxwell in 1921. At the end of 1924 he was contemplating the biggest move of his career. What went on in his mind at that point was probably akin to the tormented excitement General Dwight D. Eisenhower would experience in the last weeks before D-Day, because Chrysler was getting ready to take the same kind of no-return gamble. It was the sort of long shot that would have scared even habitual high-stakes players in the sport of kings.

Basically, his dilemma revolved around what to do next. On one hand, he could play it safe: stay on as chief executive of Maxwell-Chalmers, watch his earnings grow with each increasingly favorable balance sheet, and plan for a comfortable retirement. Thousands of middle-echelon auto executives dreamed of little more, and Chrysler only had to keep from rocking the Maxwell-Chalmers boat to assure his future. On the other hand, he could stake everything he owned on turning the firm into the Chrysler Corporation he longed for, an alternative that was not only bold but also wildly reckless. Hadn't Maxwell been sinking only a short time before with Chalmers little more than ballast? How could anyone hope to make this derelict into something even remotely like a force in the industry? Making the attempt might be thrilling as long as no serious setbacks occurred, but Chrysler had seen a lot of them, though always in other organizations. Was he immune to miscalculation, poor judgment, or just plain bad luck? No one can pretend to be so fortunate.

Now the salient point in this dilemma is not the alternatives but the man who would choose between them. And being who he was, Chrysler was simply incapable of taking the easy way out. For him, the question wasn't *if* he should set up Chrysler Corporation but *when*. And, again because of his personality, he was incapable of waiting when he saw a way to do something *now*.

Maxwell's 2-seat roadster from 1925. Price was $885.

He also had an advantage in the unfailing support of "Hutch" Hutchinson, the engineer-turned-financial expert who would lead him through the maze of money matters. Remember how he had helped secure $5 million to get Chrysler production underway? Well, Maxwell made a net profit of $4,115,540 in 1924, so that loan was paid off on time. But getting control of the firm was something else. The underwriting group of bankers had managed to capitalize Maxwell Motor Corporation at $40 million. How could Chrysler hope to buy that big a bundle —even if the bankers were willing to sell? True, Chrysler had earned a pile of money during his Buick and Willys days, but it wasn't a $40-million pile. Of course, he didn't want to be the sole personal owner but the majority stockholder, which amounts to the same thing. Ultimately, he sold his General Motors holdings, raised $15 million from Jim Brady's banking group and, together with friend Harry Bronner, purchased Maxwell's total assets. Amazingly, he did it without having to mortgage the Pasadena, California vacation palace he had bought from John N. Willys in 1921 at a reported price of $200,000.

Chrysler Corporation was officially born on June 6, 1925, and took over the whole of Maxwell's property and business. The designated officers were Chrysler as president and chairman, Hutchinson as vice-president and treasurer, Joe Fields as vice-president in charge of sales, W. Ledyard Mitchell as vice-president and secretary, and Fred M. Zeder as vice-president in charge of engineering. Within a month or so, Chrysler Canada was organized to handle north-of-the-border sales, but with an eye to production possibilities in that country.

While all this was going on, the Chrysler lineup was expanded for 1925. Prices now ranged from $1395 to $2195, and the previous six body styles were joined by the four-passenger Royal Coupe. Oliver Clark later claimed that Chrysler originated the annual model change and not General Motors, which usually gets the credit for it—or the blame, depending on your viewpoint—but appearance was nevertheless the same. There were engineering improvements, however. The most notable was a new friction-driven vibration damper mounted on the front of the crankshaft, similar in concept to the patented Lanchester vibration damper that Packard had introduced on its Twin Six in 1920. Now Zeder adopted it to give Chrysler's inline six the smoothness of a twelve. At the same time, he revised engine mounting to reduce vibration transmitted to frame and body structure, supporting the front of the power unit with a floating platform spring. For the same reason, a number of enclosed rubber pads and bushings were employed at the rear, centered around the flywheel, to eliminate metal-to-metal contact.

Though neither of these refinements did anything for performance, Chrysler continued to demonstrate its prowess in open competition. Ralph de Palma drove to victory in the 1000-mile stock car speed trials at Culver City speedway in California at an average of 73.6 mph. And a Chrysler appeared in the 24-hour race at Le Mans for the first time. Piloted by Henry Stoffel and Lucien Desvaux, it ran flawlessly from start to finish, only to be disqualified for having fallen two laps behind the minimum distance allowed for its displacement class.

1925 Chrysler Series B-70 5-passenger four-door sedan. As shown here, it had a base price of $1825.

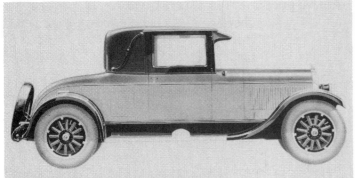

1925 Chrysler Series B-70 4-passenger coupe: $1895.

1925 Chrysler Series B-70 5-passenger phaeton: $1495.

Highland Park workers pose with the first four-cylinder Chrysler "58" in late 1925. Model arrived for 1926.

The Maxwell continued in production up to the end of the calendar year, after which the marque would disappear forever. It was not a high priority with Chrysler or his engineers, who felt that the name was simply no longer needed. Mechanical specifications were unchanged for this final year—including thermosyphon cooling, contracting mechanical brakes on the rear wheels only, and handbrake acting on the propshaft—and appearance alterations were confined to more deeply skirted fenders, wider and deeper radiator, and lower running boards. Prices stood at $885 for the roadster, $895 for the touring, $1025 for the club coupe, $1095 for the club sedan (a new name for the two-door five-passenger style previously offered), and $1345 for the four-door sedan. The bare chassis retailed at $735.

Though less than 2000 dealers sold Maxwells in 1923, the new Chrysler Corporation counted 3800 outlets in strategic locations from coast-to-coast at the end of 1925. Registrations for the year were 68,793 Chryslers and 36,236 Maxwells for a total of 105,029. For comparison, Dodge delivered 167,686 cars and Buick sales climbed to over 170,000 units. But though it was small, Chrysler Corporation was already quite profitable, raking in net earnings of better than $17 million for the year, more than either Nash or Studebaker. Against all odds, Walter P. Chrysler's gamble had paid off handsomely.

1926

By the end of 1925 it was clear to many financial analysts and auto industry observers that Walter P. Chrysler was in the process of pulling off another spectacular corporate coup. But America's newest motor mogul wasn't about to back off, and wasted no time in proceeding with the next phase of his master plan. That involved expanding his firm's manufacturing base as a prelude to a broader product line. That in turn meant a renewed commitment to heavy capital expenditures for new facilities and equipment, plus a liberal budget for new-product development.

Ideally, profits should have been sufficient to pay for both programs, but even at its 1925 income level the company would have to spread its spending over several years. Walter Chrysler wasn't interested in that. He wanted everything done in parallel and in a third the time his competitors would have taken. While it has never been clear how "Hutch" Hutchinson managed to get financial types to back his boss's plans, Chrysler Corporation did borrow heavily in its early years. Today, of course, we know the reasons why, and history would prove Walter P. Chrysler correct in tolerating a high level of indebtedness at that time. The plant modernization begun during 1925 returned early dividends, and by the start of 1926 the company was turning out 1250 cars a day. If the sales organization could sell 300,000 cars a year, at least the plants now had the capacity to produce them.

1926 Chrysler Imperial Series E-80 7-passenger sedan

Activity on the product front centered on greater variety. At the heart of the new three-tier 1926 Chrysler lineup was the G-70, essentially a warmed-over version of the previous year's B-70. A ⅛-inch bore increase raised displacement of the inline six from 201.5 to 218.6 cubic inches, which yielded a bit more torque but no more rated power. For the first time, the Imperial name was divorced from the standard short-wheelbase "70" line, which consisted of eight separate offerings, still carrying very competitive prices.

phaeton	$1395
coach	$1445
roadster	$1625
sedan	$1695
Royal coupe	$1795
brougham	$1865
Royal sedan	$1995
Crown Sedan	$2095
chassis	$1195

Though the Maxwell name disappeared this year, the car itself did not, continuing essentially unchanged under the Chrysler "58" label. It wasn't a bad car, but it wasn't a "real" Chrysler, and for this reason it may not have been wise to use that name for it. Joe Fields welcomed the change, since Chrysler carried a lot more prestige than Maxwell and that was bound to help sales. But apparently there wasn't much thought given to the possible liabilities, particularly dilution of Chrysler's first-class reputation. That could have had dire consequences. Once a car loses its good name, it's pretty difficult to recover and often means its makers are on their way out of business. Fortunately for Chrysler, there were numerous cars of questionable quality, mediocre engineering, and general lack of refinement competing against the "58" at the $1000 level, where customers tended to be more forgiving of design and performance flaws than those in the higher price classes.

The "58" line consisted of the same four body styles offered as the last Maxwells, but prices were reduced. The coupe was now $995, the coach (nee club sedan) listed at $1045, and the four-door sedan came down a whopping $250 to $1095. The touring remained unchanged at $895.

1926 Chrysler Series G-70 4-passenger roadster: $1625.

1926 Chrysler Series G-70 four-door sedan. Price: $1695.

Whatever risks may have been involved in extending the Chrysler name downmarket were offset in Walter P. Chrysler's view by a simultaneous move upmarket with a separate new Imperial series. This was not just a top-of-the-line Chrysler but a completely different design selling for about twice as much as a "70." Designated Series E-80, it had a longer and heftier new frame, a bigger engine, and a choice of three different wheelbases. The five-model lineup comprised a $2885 four-passenger roadster and a $3195 four-seat coupe mounted on a

120-inch chassis, a $3395 five-passenger sedan and a $3595 seven-passenger version on a 127-inch platform, and the top-line $3695 limousine sedan, a 4260-pound luxury car with room for seven. All were powered by what was essentially an enlarged version of the Chrysler six, though it did benefit from some material changes, such as pistons made of Lynite aluminum alloy. The 288.7-cid unit was developed by J. B. Macauley, who was then chief of dynamometer testing. To cope with their extra weight, Imperials were geared at 4.60:1, which gave tremendous

1926 Chrysler Series G-70 4-passenger roadster

1926 Chrysler Series G-70 4-passenger roadster

1926 Chrysler Imperial Series E-80 5-passenger phaeton

1926 Chrysler Imperial Series E-80 4-seat roadster

1926 Chrysler Imperial Series E-80 7-passenger sedan

top-gear pulling power, and their standard three-speed transmission had chrome-steel gears and a roller-bearing countershaft.

As Chrysler's first foray into Cadillac territory (Lincoln, Locomobile and Pierce-Arrow were costlier still), the Imperial "80" was also a rival for some Packard, Peerless, Franklin, and Kissel models. This was a well-calculated move. Every Imperial sold represented plus business for the firm, and each carried a bigger profit margin than a Chrysler "70." Also, the company's presence in the luxury segment could only enhance its public image.

Just as the "70" was named for its 70-mph top speed capability, the Imperial "80" could exceed 80 mph. And its over-the-road performance was quite outstanding. Auto dealer and accessory inventor Floyd Clymer drove a

stock Imperial from Denver to Kansas City in June 1926 in 13 hours and 56 minutes at an average speed of 51.8 mph, thus setting a record for production cars for distances of 500 miles or more. The feat was all the more remarkable for being achieved not on a smooth oval track but on 702 miles of open road, less than 200 miles of which was paved. Also this year, an Imperial roadster was selected as pace car for the Indianapolis 500, which not only gave the new line extra public exposure but also emphasized its sporty qualities.

Although 1926 sales did not measure up to Walter's expectations, they were no less than what realistic observers would have predicted. With registrations of 129,565 for the calendar year, Chrysler catapulted into sixth place in the industry, and the corporation realized a $17.4 million net profit. Yet Chrysler still had a long way to go: Buick sold 232,570 cars in the same period and Dodge retailed 219,466.

Walter Chrysler was eager to begin selling cars in Europe as a hedge against fluctuations in the North American market. Because of the customs and tariffs then in force, however, it was more expedient to set up local assembly operations in those countries that permitted it, rather than export fully built vehicles. His first assault on the market came in Belgium, where S.A. Chrysler was formed in 1926 with a plant at Antwerp. A year later, Chrysler Motors Ltd. began doing business in London.

A threat to Chrysler's domestic operations appeared this year when General Motors acquired the Fisher Brothers coachworks. While the move did not bring an immediate end to Chrysler's body supply, it did signal the eventual demise of Fisher as a contractor to non-GM

K.T. Keller

His full name was Kaufman Thuma Keller, but he was almost never called that. "Do not address him as Kaufman even if you are a fellow 33rd-degree mason. He doesn't like that name," advised author Malcolm Bingay.

K. T. Keller circa 1935

"Of course, K. Thuma Keller would hardly be an improvement among that hard-hitting group of colleagues. So to intimates and the great wide world he is known as K. T.—or 'Katy.'"

Keller's name is memorable for another reason that has nothing to do with its being an unusual one: it was the first to go up on the doors of Chrysler Corporation's president and board chairman offices that did not coincide with the company name. Keller replaced Walter Chrysler as president in 1935, a job he held through 1950 when he became chairman, filling a vacancy that had been created by Walter Chrysler's death a decade earlier. Neither appointment was a surprise. In fact, Keller had been groomed for years as Walter Chrysler's hand-picked successor.

Keller was 10 years younger than his boss, having come into the world in 1885 in a small Pennsylvania-Dutch community near Lancaster. After serving an apprenticeship with Westinghouse in his youth, he moved on to Metal Products Company in Detroit, where he inspected

axles that the firm supplied to Hudson and Chalmers. He then held a variety of jobs, including general foreman at Metzger Motor Car Company, heavy repairman and chassis tester for Hudson, and chief inspector at Maxwell. In 1911 he joined the office staff at General Motors' Manhattan headquarters, where he worked mainly on Cadillac matters. It was in this post that he met Walter Chrysler about a year later. Keller tired of waiting for a promotion at GM, so he left to join Cole Motor Car Company. In 1917, Chrysler invited him to Flint to take on the job of master mechanic at Buick, and the two men had daily contact over the next two years. When Chrysler left to patch up Willys-Overland, he told Keller to continue his career at GM, adding slyly: "When I have a better job for you, I'll call you."

That call wouldn't come for a long time, but Keller followed Chrysler's advice. In 1920, Chevrolet's manufacturing manager, Fred Hohensee, decided to throw in his lot with W. C. Durant, who was ready for new ventures only months

makes. Fortunately, Chrysler was beginning to build its own bodies by this time, having acquired the old Kercheval plant in Detroit about a year before. Now the firm began switching more of its remaining body business to the Hayes and Briggs concerns.

1927

1927 Chrysler Series 50 touring. It sold for $750 new.

Chrysler Corporation's relentless drive up the sales charts both gained and lost some steam in 1927. Only a sudden reversal on the sales front could blunt the company's progress and, in a way, that's what happened. Nevertheless, the firm's entire production apparatus was now humming along smoothly under K. T. Keller (see sidebar), who joined the corporation as vice-president in charge of manufacturing toward the end of 1926. This year, his plants regularly turned out an average of 4000 cars a week.

And what they turned out was an expanded line of cars in four series. The four-cylinder "50" (officially I-50) returned with only minor styling changes, continuing as a remnant of the old Maxwell. The familiar "70" was now called the "Finer 70" (factory designation G-70). The Series E-80 Imperial carried on at the top of the line, offering a variety of models on the same three wheelbases. The newcomer for the year was the H-60, which stemmed from a natural cross-pollination between the four- and six-cylinder lines.

The "60" was intended to offer the performance and

The 1927 Chrysler Series 50 four-door sedan cost $830.

smoothness of a six at a price not much higher than that of a typical four-cylinder car, and it was an expedient, though clever, piece of production engineering. While the old Maxwell platform was too short to accept an inline six, Chrysler engineers discovered that its frame could be

---

after losing control of General Motors for a second time. Keller was named to succeed Hohensee, and served at Chevrolet for four years before company president Alfred P. Sloan named him vice-president and general manager of GM Canada, Ltd. Finally, Chrysler telephoned one day in 1926 to tell Keller he needed him. K. T. promptly resigned from GM and joined the newly formed Chrysler Corporation late that year as its vice-president in charge of manufacturing.

Although Keller's accomplishments at Chrysler are described in later chapters, a word is in order here about his sense of aesthetics. Along with almost every other manufacturing person at Chrysler, he was opposed to the radically streamlined Airflow that was introduced for 1934. It was simply too outlandish for Keller, though some of his dislike probably involved construction that differed from what he was used to. His utterly conservative taste was blamed in later years for keeping many interesting projects from being completed. It was cer-

tainly reflected in the boxy, upright styling of Chrysler Corporation's first all-new postwar models, introduced for 1949.

Despite this, it's doubtful K. T. ever allowed personal preferences to cloud his judgement. If he turned down an idea, he always had a valid reason, usually cost. Yet he was no miser when he could see the benefit of spending extra money. In fact, he was quite liberal about improving Chrysler's physical facilities, provided the money directly enhanced productivity or product quality.

The Keller years at Chrysler produced stodgy-looking cars, but the man was not without artistic appreciation. He filled his home with beautiful objects, and ultimately assembled one of the finest collections of Chinese art in the entire country. He also served on the Detroit Art Institute's board of trustees until 1942, so he obviously knew something about relative aesthetic values. Yet he never saw the automobile as a possible object of art. Though he doubtless appreciated the pure decoration

that figures heavily in Chinese art, he had no use for decoration on a car. Remember that he was first and foremost a "machinery man," and to him, the beauty of any machine derived from its function. This philosophy naturally spilled over into the way he looked at cars, which, after all, are machines designed for a specific purpose. The more useful and practical the design, the better it would look to Keller.

We don't remember Keller as an advocate of the "form follows function" principle that has invariably inspired truly great automotive design. Chrysler certainly didn't produce styling "classics" under his regime, perhaps because he failed to recognize that a given function can be served well by different forms, some more attractive than others. When there was a choice, he almost always opted for the most serious and sober.

It has been said of Chrysler Corporation's early-Fifties cars that "they wouldn't knock your eyes out, but they wouldn't knock your hat off, either." For Keller, there was no finer testimonial.

1927 Chrysler Series 50 club coupe. Price was $750.

1927 Chrysler Series 60 5-passenger touring: $1075.

1927 Chrysler Series 60 4-passenger roadster

1927 Chrysler Series 70 sport phaeton. Price: $1495.

lengthened at low cost and the front axle relocated three inches further forward without difficulty. Accordingly, a smaller version of the Chrysler L-head six was prepared for the "60." Though "downsized" in both bore and stroke compared to the "70" unit, it incorporated some of the improvements made the previous year for the Imperial version, such as Lynite pistons. The gearbox came from the "70" and the rear axle (geared at 4.90:1) was borrowed from the "50." Naturally, anything less than Lockheed four-wheel hydraulic brakes wouldn't do for a Chrysler, so they were specified, along with Ross cam-and-lever steering. The usual array of body styles was fielded, with prices ranging from a $1075 four-door touring to a $1330 five-passenger landau sedan. A two-passenger coupe offered early in the year was phased out in favor of a four-passenger model with rumble seat.

Elsewhere in the 1927 line, the "70" came in for a number of improvements that don't show up readily on paper. Though appearance wasn't radically altered, bodies were considerably modernized inside and out. There were no changes to the power unit, but engine mounts were fine-tuned for further reductions in mechanical vibration. As in the "60" series, there were special landau versions of the two-door brougham sedan, marked by a rubberized fabric roof covering adorned with dummy landau irons and set off by smaller rear side windows. The "Finer 70" also gained a rumble-seat coupe this year, offered in Royal and "cabriolet" forms, and there was a new, fully enclosed four-passenger coupe with an extended roofline done in "Victoria" style. Black-painted fenders and headlamp buckets were standard on all models, which ranged in price from $1395 for the standard touring/phaeton up to $1795 for the five-passenger Crown sedan. Bolstering the touring car's sales appeal were snazzier Sport and Custom Sport variants. The former featured leather upholstery and glass wind wings, while the latter used wire wheels in place of the wood-spoke "artillery" types and added a standard left sidemount spare and accessory trunk.

The Imperial line saw a similar expansion of body styles and trim variations for 1927, though basic engineering was little changed. The only mechanical alterations of note were a reduction in tire size (to 6.75 × 30) and a corresponding numerical drop in the final drive ratio to 4.10:1 to reduce engine noise in the 40-60-mph range. New model permutations included a sport version of the touring, a fully enclosed five-passenger coupe, a standard version of the five-passenger sedan and, late in the season, a two-seat business coupe. The price spread was about $1000, with the standard phaeton/touring at $2545 and the seven-passenger long-wheelbase limousine at $3595. For those who demanded the ultimate, a five-passenger Imperial town car was offered for the first time, though only to special order, priced at a towering $5495. Features included an open chauffeur's compartment (with folding top and side curtains), leather roof covering, dummy landau irons, dual sidemount spares, and opulent trim.

Competition in the low-price field was stiffer than ever this year, but that didn't worry Walter Chrysler. Although no one knew it at the time, the relative lack of

1927 Chrysler Imperial Series 80 club coupe

change in the "50" signalled the arrival of a new four-cylinder car that would not carry the Chrysler badge. As we know, it arrived in 1928 as the Plymouth.

Looking back, it's safe to say that Walter's new car arrived none too soon. Oakland had made a big splash with the 1926 introduction of its new Pontiac Six, which proved so popular that it would completely supplant its parent make by 1931. Hudson had upgraded its low-price Essex from four to six cylinders in 1924, though this engine was not very durable, due in part to the 5.4:1 rear axle gearing that meant needlessly high rpm and correspondingly short engine life. Nevertheless, a cheap Six did wonders for Hudson sales. Studebaker had launched its equally inept six-cylinder Erskine in 1927, which wouldn't stay around long, and Willys had replaced its Overland Four with the six-cylinder Whippet the year before.

All these "bargain" sixes found a ready market, due in no small measure to the demise of the Model T. Chevrolet probably benefitted most from Ford's belated model change. Indeed, Chevy was among the first to field a low-price six, and the trend it helped start virtually killed demand for upper-class four-cylinder models. Among the last to yield was Dodge, which didn't drop its Four until 1927, and Hupmobile, which followed suit the next year.

With all this, it's no surprise that Chrysler found selling the four-cylinder "50" increasingly difficult, and this explains why overall 1927 sales were not as high as the boss expected. Chrysler did overhaul Dodge in calendar year registrations—154,234 versus 123,918—but Dodge was no longer so much a direct competitor with its move to an all-six lineup. A more telling comparison comes from Buick, steady as ever, with 232,428 registrations this year.

1927 Chrysler Series 70 4-passenger coupe

1927 Chrysler Series 60 touring

On a proportional basis, Chrysler's annual growth rate slowed in 1927, down from 57 percent the previous year to a mere 19 percent. Was Walter's balloon losing air? Was this the end of the Chrysler challenge? Not at all, as the events of 1928 would prove. In fact, Walter P. Chrysler was about to top all his earlier accomplishments.

And the success of Chrysler Corporation during its first two-and-a-half years had been nothing short of meteoric. From an initial launching point somewhere in the industry's top 20 it had rocketed to fifth place in annual sales. Only Chevrolet (648,000), Ford (393,000), Buick (232,000), and Hudson (225,000) were ahead by 1927. Along the way, Chrysler had passed minor leaguers like Jewett and Durant Motors and heavy hitters like Hupmobile, Studebaker, and Willys-Overland. Most recently it had bested Dodge, a name that would very soon occupy an important place in Chrysler history.

1928

The last full year of prosperity before The Great Crash witnessed Chrysler Corporation's historic emergence as a multi-make producer, a new power to rival the "Big Two," Ford and General Motors. It was a busy 12 months in Highland Park. Toward the end of the year the Dodge Brothers company became a separate Chrysler division following exploratory talks between Clarence Dillon, who headed the investment banking group that owned Dodge, and Walter Chrysler. The move only expanded a sales base that had already been enlarged by the introduction of two new nameplates, Plymouth and DeSoto, which arrived at midyear, shortly before the Dodge deal was formally concluded.

For all this, the company's outlook was decidedly mixed when the 1928 Chrysler models were presented in January. The firm was still profitable, of course, but its rate of growth was slowing and there were weaknesses in its production setup and dealer organization. Some said it couldn't hope to realize further sales gains without doubling its number of retail outlets; others said Chrysler couldn't build more cars economically until it had its own forge and foundry shops. And there was the naggingly urgent question of what to do about a body supplier, as the contract with Fisher, the firm's principal source, would run out at the end of the year.

There was nothing spectacularly different about the 1928 Chryslers, just the anticipated annual upgrading with the emphasis, as usual, on engineering. Though the basic four-tier lineup stayed the same, model designations were shuffled. The four-cylinder "50" became the 1928 Series "52," and the six-cylinder "60" and "70" became "62" and "72," respectively. The Imperial was still an "80," but with an L instead of an E prefix. The "72" arrived with new convertible coupe and sedan body styles designed by chief body engineer Oliver Clark and built by Locke. Fisher continued to supply several other "72" body types, while most bodywork for the two low-

end series had by now been shifted to Briggs.

It's interesting to note that Chrysler Corporation's "styling department" in the late Twenties consisted of only five designers, who were responsible for all interiors and exteriors. The team consisted of Henry T. King, Herb Weissinger, Bill Lindberg, Thomas L. Martin, and director Herbert Henderson. All worked closely with Ralph Roberts and his staff at Briggs Manufacturing Company, a relationship that would prove important to Chrysler in the years ahead.

Author Malcolm Bingay provided this concise history of how the Briggs company came to be in *Detroit is My Home Town:* "W. O. Briggs had been a switchman on the Michigan Central and had advanced to yard foreman of the C. H. Little Cement Company. Then he crossed the path of Barney Everitt, who represented the 'E' in the E-M-F company. Everitt had a small business at the time, a buggy and wagon, and—later—a body-painting shop. He wanted to get rid of his shop. This he turned over to Briggs, then known for only two things: his enthusiasm for baseball and his handsome profile. From this start grew the great body-making industry known as the Briggs Manufacturing Company."

On the mechanical front for 1928, the "72" boasted more displacement than the previous "Finer 70," with the same basic block carrying a reinforced bottom end with a longer-throw crankshaft (cylinder head and valvetrain were unchanged). Final drive ratios were stepped up across the board for improved top-gear performance, the "52" now at 5.11:1, the "62" at 4.60:1, and a

1928 Chrysler Series 52 5-passenger phaeton sold at $750.

1928 Chrysler Series 52 5-passenger sedan. Price was $795.

4.30:1 gearset for the "72" and Imperial.

The top-line Chrysler also gained displacement this year, but via a bore increase (stroke was unaltered). This beefier power unit rested at the front of an entirely new chassis with a long 136-inch wheelbase, common to all models, and channel-section side girders seven inches deep. Springs were switched from plain to chrome-vanadium steel and were wrapped in plastic covers. Front spring length went up to 47.5 inches, rear length to 58 inches. The semi-floating rear axle had spiral bevel gears with ratios of 4.63 or 4.27:1. The front axle was now an I-beam affair, with Elliott yokes and made of chrome-molybdenum alloy, as Skelton now apparently veered away from the tubular axle that had been such a big deal back in 1924. Driver-oriented refinements included a light switch mounted on the steering column, a feature found throughout the Chrysler line this year, and adjustable steering wheel. Semi-custom bodies available only to special order were offered for the first time on the Imperial chassis, with a variety of styles—sedans, coupes, and open models—supplied by LeBaron, Derham, Locke, Murphy, and Waterhouse. Today these cars are certified Classics by both the Classic Car Club of America (CCCA) and the Antique Automobile Club of America (AACA).

If Chrysler model numbers were still intended to indicate top speed potential, they were certainly conservative. A typical "72" could easily do 80 mph, and an Imperial could top 90 mph despite its massive size and weight. That Chrysler offered more than mere straight-

1928 Chrysler Series 72 close-coupled four-door sedan

line speed was proved conclusively this year in European road racing, where handling, braking, and general reliability counted as much or more than brute power. A team of four "72" roadsters drew a lot of attention at LeMans in June—and the attention turned to astonishment when these perfectly civilized cars finished third and fourth overall. French drivers Henry Stoffel and Andre Rossignol shared the fastest car, ending up with a 24-hour average of 64.56 mph. The fourth-place car was shared by two brothers named Ghica. The other two Chryslers didn't finish: the Gofreddo Zehender/Jerome

1928 Chrysler Series 52 4-passenger coupe

1928 Chrysler Series 62 four-door sedan. Price: $1245.

1928 Chrysler Series 62 4-passenger roadster: $1175.

The $875 Chrysler Series 52 DeLuxe four-door sedan from 1928

1928 Chrysler Series 72 4-passenger coupe. Price: $1595.

1928 Chrysler Series 72 4-passenger coupe sold at $1545.

1928 Chrysler Series 72 Standard 4-passenger roadster

1928 Chrysler Imperial convertible coupe by LeBaron

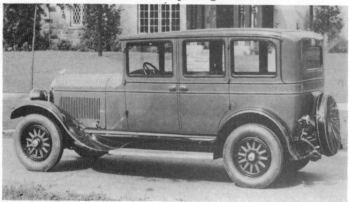

1928 Chrysler Series 72 four-door sedan

1928 Chrysler Imperial 5-passenger town sedan

Ledur car went out on the fifth lap due to an accident, and a similar fate eliminated the Louis Chiron/P. deVere machine after 63 laps. A few weeks later, an Imperial ran at the 24-hour endurance contest at Spa-Francorchamps in Belgium, and took second overall in the hands of deVere and Marcel Mongin behind an Alfa Romeo. Two of the team "72" roadsters captured third and sixth in the same event.

The four-cylinder Chrysler came to an end in May, when "52" production was halted and the assembly lines modestly retooled for the new Plymouth. There was less here than met the eye, however, as the new car was essentially a "52" with minor styling changes, standard four-wheel hydraulic brakes, and a winged goddess for the radiator cap. Use of the good ship Mayflower as a Plymouth symbol was still a few years off, though a representation of Plymouth Rock did appear on the radiator.

Though both Plymouth and DeSoto appeared in mid-1928, they are officially considered 1929 models and are thus more fully discussed under that heading. However, it's pertinent to relate a brief story about Chrysler's new low-priced car. The first Plymouth was built on June 11, 1928. The third one completed was personally driven off the line by Walter Chrysler, who immediately headed west and pulled up in front of the Ford Motor Company offices in Dearborn about a half-hour later. He proudly invited Henry Ford and his son Edsel to inspect and drive the car, and the three spent most of that afternoon together. After the demonstration drive, Henry earnestly confided: "Walter, you'll go broke trying to break into the low-priced market." Characteristically, Chrysler made no secret of his intended prices: the roadster would sell at $670, the four-door sedan for $725, both factory f.o.b. As a parting shot, Walter gave the Plymouth to the Fords and took a taxi back to Highland Park.

Time magazine commented that "Chrysler had gone into the low-priced field with the throttle wide open." And indeed, sales manager A. Vanderzee shipped 58,000 Plymouths during the remaining six-and-a-half months of 1928, which earned the new make a one-percent toehold in the market.

Meanwhile, events were moving forward that would bring the Dodge Brothers company into the Chrysler Corporation family. Actually, the idea had been discussed before, in 1926, by Walter Chrysler and Dodge administrator Clarence Dillon. The two men knew each other well, and had talked enough about a possible merger to know exactly where the other stood. When his imaginative plan for a merger with Packard, Hudson, and Briggs had fizzled, Dillon had started looking for a buyer. There weren't many candidates. Both Henry Ford and GM's Alfred P. Sloan had the means but had no need for Dodge. W. C. Durant would have been thrilled to get the company but couldn't pay. That left Walter P. Chrysler as the only chief of a major producer who had plausible reasons for acquiring Dodge. An important consideration for the bankers was Chrysler Corporation's position as a solid credit risk, with earning potential that was viewed as so high that it could get almost any amount of financing it cared to ask for.

The personal motivations behind the sale are significant. Dillon had gradually come to see the basic truth of the tenet that says bankers should stick to banking and let business types run businesses. He had also begun to feel that the money he had tied up in Dodge could be used more productively elsewhere. Not that Dodge was failing: it was a profitable company with a good product and a healthy industrial base. But Dillon knew he had to act before Walter Chrysler either lost interest or got sidetracked with other investments. Chrysler's primary motivation was acquiring a ready-made sales organization, though Dodge had several other attractions. Chrysler Corporation still lacked its own iron foundry, which meant it had to rely on outside suppliers for engine blocks and cylinder heads. It also lacked a drop forge, and was forced to pay whatever prices vendors set for crankshafts, connecting rods, steering knuckles, and various other parts. Dodge had a big foundry and a modern forge shop, and Walter wanted them. He also wanted the Dodge name and the goodwill and reputation that went with it. Far from entertaining any thoughts of killing the make, he wanted to make it more successful than ever.

Chrysler's interest in Dodge made Dillon think he could get a high price and thus satisfy his banker colleagues as to return on investment. But Chrysler knew that he was the only buyer for all practical purposes, and that put him in a very strong bargaining position. By the spring of 1928, both men knew the sale was just a matter of agreeing about price, but the formal negotiations involved a lot

1928 Dodge Victory Six four-door sedan. Price: $1095.

Dodge Victory Six sport sedan appeared in early 1928.

1928-29 Plymouth Model Q 2-seat roadster. Price: $670.

of theater, mostly for public image sake. Chrysler felt he had to feign lack of interest, while Dillon ricocheted back and forth from aggressiveness to indifference, teasing Chrysler with a barrage of telephone calls one week and none the next.

In May 1928, Chrysler told Dillon to make a written proposal: "Mind, your lowest price! Then I'll tell you yes or no." When Dillon began talking numbers, Chrysler added one of his own: the sale would have to be approved by 90 percent of Dodge stockholders. That way, he would avoid having to deal with a possibly disgruntled group at Chrysler Corporation's general meetings. When Dillon said he was ready, Chrysler hired a suite of rooms at The Ritz Hotel in New York, and moved in with "Hutch"

1928-29 Plymouth Model Q 5-passenger touring: $695.

1929-30 Plymouth Model U 2-passenger coupe cost $655-$670.

1929-30 Plymouth Model U two-door sedan sold for $675.

Hutchinson and corporation lawyer Albert Rathbone. When the delegation from Dillon, Read & Co. arrived, Walter declared, "We'll stay here till we come to an agreement, stay until one of us says yes or no." They were still there five days later, but they had finally pinned down the price.

Chrysler's terms did not involve a cash payment. What the bankers eventually agreed to was an exchange of stock: one share of Chrysler common for each share of Dodge preferred, one share of Chrysler common for every five shares of Dodge class A stock, and one share of Chrysler common for every 10 shares of Dodge class B stock. This new issue of Chrysler stock was evaluated at $170 million. In addition, Chrysler Corporation would assume all outstanding liabilities of Dodge Brothers, Inc., including $57,276,000 worth of debenture bonds.

It was near the end of May, and Dillon would have been the happiest man in the world had it not been for Chrysler's insistence on 90-percent approval by Dodge stockholders. Worse, Chrysler gave him a two-month deadline to get it, for "if we give you longer, the time for creating new car models will be on us and passed before the new management can get a chance to function." It wasn't until July 31st that Dillon had signatures representing the required 60,000 shares, and the sale was closed that day. "Hutch" Hutchinson phoned K. T. Keller with the news. The very next day, Dillon was back in Highland Park to assure Chrysler that the Dodge organization was in great shape and could run itself for a while, "three months, if you want to." A hired straight-man couldn't have given Chrysler a better line. "Hell, Clarence," he replied, "Our boys moved in last night." And indeed, a huge new billboard now stood atop the Hamtramck plant. It read: Chrysler Corporation, Dodge Division.

Chrysler's acquisition of Dodge Brothers, Inc. created an industrial giant ranking next to General Motors and Ford Motor Company in production and sales, with total assets of $450-$500 million. In later years, Walter remarked that "without Dodge, there would not have been Plymouth," a reference to the expanded physical facilities that made possible the subsequent growth in Plymouth volume. Besides the Hamtramck plant, real estate acquired with the purchase included the Dodge truck factory and forge, plus smaller shops at Conant Road and Harper Avenue in Detroit. Chrysler did not get a body plant as part of the buyout, but Dodge was the Budd Company's biggest customer, which thus provided a link to a new supplier to take over from Fisher.

In an official ceremony marking the formation of Dodge Division, Walter P. Chrysler said: "I am particularly pleased to bring under one general management two organizations so similar in their ideals of service to customers and high quality of product. I wish to pay tribute to the thousands of splendid dealers here and abroad representing Chrysler and Dodge products. Dodge dealers can look to the new management to continue the policies which brought the Dodge product to favorable acceptance of the American public, and I foresee in this move increased opportunities for all those associated with Dodge." As for personnel, Chrysler generally had his pick of the Dodge roster except for two top-ranking engineers, Ralph Vail and Roy Cole, who resigned. To reassure everybody, K. T. Keller appointed Fred Lamborn as operations manager of Dodge Main. Lamborn had joined the Dodge brothers in 1911 at the age of 22, becoming chief mechanic by 1919 and serving as the firm's production manager since 1924.

The Chrysler takeover brought no immediate change to Dodge design or specifications, and production of the three-tier, all-six-cylinder 1928 lineup continued uninterrupted. However, the sale did introduce a good deal of confusion into Chrysler's corporate engine stable. There were now no fewer than six separate six-cylinder designs, including the two existing Dodge units and a new 175-cubic-inch job reserved for the new DeSoto (see 1929). Simplification was clearly in order, and Chrysler would see to it in short order.

In new-car registrations, Chrysler Corporation made a

great leap forward in 1928. To the Chrysler marque's 142,024 units were added 149,004 for Dodge, plus 29,490 for the new Plymouth and 14,538 for DeSoto, all calendar year totals. The bottom line was over a third of a million Chrysler Corporation cars, precisely 335,056. Several rivals also advanced this year, including Hudson (226,900), Willys (231,000), and Pontiac (184,000). Buick didn't fare as well (196,000). GM's total calendar year sales came to 1.3 million units, while Ford registered only 488,000 cars, due partly to production delays with its new Model A. The balance of power in Detroit was beginning an historic shift.

While working out the technicalities of the Dodge sale, Chrysler's legal staff was also filing papers for two new companies as Chrysler Corporation divisions: Plymouth Motor Corporation and DeSoto Motor Corporation. After the Dodge deal was completed, Fargo Motor Corporation was set up to handle fleet sales for all car divisions. The year also saw the finishing touches put on the company's new engineering building in Highland Park and, in October, the start of construction for a separate Plymouth assembly operation on a 40-acre site at Lynch Road and Mount Elliott Street. The latter was begun at the behest of K. T. Keller in response to Joe Fields' glowing sales forecasts, and was completed in record time, coming on stream the following spring.

1929

Companion makes were big in 1929, especially the lower-priced variety. Oakland had introduced the six-cylinder Pontiac in 1926, and its success had inspired Buick to bring out Marquette and Oldsmobile to offer the Viking this year. The "junior edition" trend cut across all price levels and involved a number of makes: Cadillac had LaSalle, Studebaker its Erskine, Marmon the Roosevelt, Hudson its Essex, Reo the Wolverine, and Willys a Whippet. At Chrysler Corporation there were not one but three "companions": Plymouth, DeSoto, and Dodge. Actually, Chrysler was not so much fielding companion makes as setting up a family of cars, tiered by price class (though allowing some overlap) and thus imitating the "hierarchy" approach to marketing instituted by Alfred P. Sloan at General Motors. Since 1922, Sloan had moved Buick upmarket, while shifting Oldsmobile to the price bracket between Oakland and Buick.

From its inception, the Chrysler had been aimed squarely at Buick and, also as previously noted, the Chrysler Imperial was intended as a direct challenger to Cadillac. Plymouth arrived in mid-1928 as Chrysler's rival to Chevrolet in the low-price field, and acquisition of Dodge gave Chrysler a range of cars more or less equivalent to Oldsmobile's. That would leave Oakland/Pontiac, a job that was assigned to Chrysler's other 1929 model year newcomer, DeSoto. At first it missed that target, being more a competitor for Dodge than the GM makes, but the reasons are easily explained. DeSoto was actually planned long before Walter Chrysler was sure he would be

1929 Chrysler Series 65 4-passenger roadster: $1065.

1929 Chrysler Series 75 Royal sedan sold at $1535.

The $1040 Chrysler Series 65 business coupe from 1929

able to acquire Dodge. In case that deal fell through, DeSoto was to be his medium-price weapon, aimed right at Dodge but selling at lower prices. It would also naturally take on class rivals at GM and elsewhere. While Chrysler could have perhaps stopped the DeSoto project once Dodge was safely under his banner, he chose to let it go ahead and work out any in-fighting between the two makes later. As Chrysler's reply to the light, low-priced sixes from Oakland, Hudson, and Studebaker, DeSoto was priced below corresponding Dodge models in its early years, a reversal of their positions on the ladder in the future.

The effect of constantly upgrading makes doesn't seem to have been clearly understood by industry leaders in the late Twenties. The top of the price pyramid set a natural limit on how far this could go, so Cadillac, for instance, could not raise prices too much without losing volume. The result was a surplus of medium-price cars

1929 Chrysler Series 75 phaeton on the assembly line

Chrysler's Series 75 4-passenger coupe from mid-1929

1929 Chrysler Series 75 tonneau phaeton. Price: $1835.

1929 Chrysler Series 75 tonneau phaeton with top down

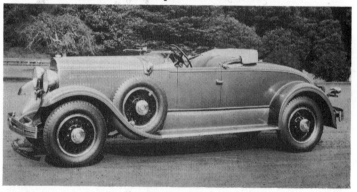

1929 Imperial roadster with Chrysler-built bodywork

and cut-throat competition in the $800-$1250 bracket. The battle for buyers would prove catastrophic for some companies, and Chrysler was as eager as any of them to enter the lists, unprepared for the consequences. Only Ford Motor Company steered clear, due to Henry's blindness rather than his foresight.

Nevertheless, the Detroit *Free Press* reported as early as May 6, 1928 that "probably no development of the past five years has created so profound a stir in the automobile industry as the current announcement that the DeSoto Six, which is to be presented to the public in the next three months, is to be built by Chrysler." That was enough to send 500 dealers clamoring for a franchise. As announced in January 1929, DeSoto prices started at

$845. Production had begun the previous July, and it should be noted that no Dodge facilities were involved for either components or assembly. By the end of 1928, over 34,000 DeSotos had been shipped to the 1500 dealers that had signed up, and registrations totalled nearly 15,000.

Joe Fields served as first president of the newly formed DeSoto Motor Corporation (see 1928), with C. W. Matheson as vice-president in charge of sales and "Hutch" Hutchinson as vice-president and treasurer. Walter P. Chrysler was listed as chairman. James C. Zeder was named chief engineer for both DeSoto and Plymouth in 1928. A younger brother of Fred Zeder, he was educated at the University of Michigan and the University of Dayton. Fred had invited him to work at

Maxwell in 1922, but Jim accepted a job offer from Handley-Knight and also worked for a while at the Timken bearing company before joining Chrysler Corporation.

The DeSoto engine, of course, was part of the growing family of sixes derived from Zeder's original Chrysler unit, and was built with much of the same tooling. The DeSoto version was designed by L. Irving Woolson, a 25-year-old Cornell graduate who had spent the summer of 1924 on the Maxwell assembly lines to help finance his schooling. (He was then transferred to the Chrysler laboratories, and subsequently went into chassis engineering for Dodge trucks.) This powerplant had no more displacement than the four-cylinder Plymouth engine, newly enlarged to 175.4 cubic inches for the Series U, the formal 1929 replacement for the initial Series Q, production of which was halted in February. However, the DeSoto unit offered 10 more horsepower and, being a six, had that silky smoothness associated with the breed —and notoriously lacking in the ex-Maxwell four.

The shared wheelbase length suggests the Plymouth and DeSoto chassis were similar. In fact, they were nearly identical. Styling was another matter. Both Series Q and Series U Plymouths were much like a scaled-down Chrysler "65" in appearance. Aside from the shorter wheelbase, they differed mainly in being four inches shorter overall and weighing about 450 pounds less. They also ran on 20-inch-diameter wheels and tires, while the senior make had gone to 18-inchers in the interest of achieving a lower, more rakish stance. DeSoto's exterior was more closely related to that of the Chrysler "75," and predictably contained no original styling elements. A small exception was the radiator emblem, which bore the family coat-of-arms of the car's namesake, 16th century Spanish explorer Hernando deSoto, discoverer of the Mississippi River.

With hindsight, the lack of design distinction between Plymouth, DeSoto, and Chrysler in the late Twenties may seem curious given the well-known relationship between styling and sales. But Chrysler Corporation's top officials didn't seem at all concerned, which perhaps isn't surprising for a company founded and run mainly by engineers. Their apparent disregard for fashion would have dire consequences five years hence. A more immediate explanation for the dull styling similarity lay in Oliver Clark's body engineering department and its eight-man "Art & Colour" staff, which now had design responsibility for not only Plymouth and DeSoto but Dodge as well.

Chrysler's newly acquired make revised its model offerings twice during the 1929 selling season. Beginning in July 1928, the Victory Six was dropped from the Dodge line and the Standard and Senior Sixes returned with smoother styling but no major mechanical modifications. Closed bodies were now 2-4 inches longer and an inch or two higher. New colors and accessories helped brighten appearance even more, and there were special sport versions of several open and closed body styles, distinguished by a standard sidemount spare tire. Bowing at the first of the new year was what was called "The New Dodge Brothers Six," officially the Series DA and essen-

1929 Chrysler Imperial 5-passenger sedan. Price: $2975.

Mid-1929 DeSoto Series K Cupe de Lujo (Coupe de Luxe)

1929 DeSoto Series K Roadster Espanol: $845.

1929 DeSoto Series K Sedan de Lujo. It sold at $995.

tially a rebodied continuation of the previous Standard Six. Though it looked somewhat like this year's lower-end Chrysler, the design had been virtually completed by the time of the Chrysler takeover. The Senior Six carried on through early July 1929, when it was similarly overhauled to become the new Series DB Six, a 1930 model.

1929 Dodge Series DA DeLuxe 4-passenger coupe

1929 Dodge Series DA 5-seat phaeton. Price: $1025.

1929 Dodge Series DA 4-passenger victoria, $1025.

A Dodge truck with wagon-like wood bodywork from 1929

The $945 Dodge Series DA business coupe, 1929

1929 Dodge Series DA two-door sedan

With transformation of the four-cylinder "52" into the new Plymouth, the Chrysler line was down to three series for 1929. Model designations changed once more, the "62" becoming "65" and the "72" now labelled "75." The Imperial continued with its previous L-80 tag. Styling was enhanced with a new "slim-profile" radiator and longer, more sweeping fenders, plus more attractively trimmed interiors and redesigned instrument panels. Ad writers crowed that "as for beauty, Chrysler now brings to the automobile an entirely new art." The 1929s were unquestionably better-looking, but Chrysler was hardly an industry styling leader this year.

On the other hand, it most definitely remained an engineering leader. For example, it was still alone in offering four-wheel hydraulic brakes, though many other makes were by now at least fitting a mechanical brake at each wheel. Invisible to most showroom-goers were the 1929 Chryslers' revised brakes, boasting larger drums with internal-expanding shoes instead of the old external contracting bands, the first modern automobile brake design and a change that made weatherproofing much easier. Simplified brake adjustment was also featured. Long springs mounted as close to the wheels as possible had always assured Chrysler passengers a smooth ride. This year it was improved with standard Lovejoy hydraulic shock absorbers. Fenders and other sheetmetal parts were "rust-proofed" on all models, and the "75" acquired thermostatically controlled radiator shutters color matched to body paint. If Chrysler lagged in any area it might have been in transmissions, largely due to Cadillac's 1928 introduction of "silent" synchromesh, which afforded "clashless" shifting with less effort.

Chrysler had nothing like it, and would later be forced to pay GM for the manufacturing rights to it.

The demise of the four-cylinder Chrysler also brought a realignment of chassis and engine sizes for 1929. Wheelbase on the bottom-line "65" was restored to the original 1924 length of 112.75 inches, and the L-head six was bored out ⅛-inch, boosting displacement by a modest 5.4 cubic inches. As on the 1928 Series 62, there were standard and "high-compression" engines known as Silver Dome and Redhead, respectively. Final drive ratio was standardized at 4.60:1. Chrysler's middle-size six continued unchanged in the same two states of tune, but the "75" it powered was stretched in wheelbase over its "72" predecessor, and final drive gearing was reset at 4.30:1. In July the "65" was supplanted by a mechanical twin called "66," technically a 1930 model (and described in that chapter). The first of these cars had the customary vacuum-tank fuel delivery system, but at the end of the year a mechanical fuel pump made by General Motors' AC Division was adopted, another example of engineering rivalry between Chrysler and GM.

The problem of describing the end result of the 1929 models' many changes must have puzzled even the most imaginative and poetic of Chrysler's ad writers. But someone was evidently up to the task, as witness this florid phrase: "Chrysler again transcends all standards and ideals of power, of riding ease, of roomy luxury, of smooth operation, of quality and of value."

We haven't forgotten the Imperial, which was set even further apart from the lesser Chryslers this year. There were no powertrain changes apart from adoption of 7.00 × 18 wheels and tires, which gave the luxury liners a more modern look in concert with a lower frame and more integrated styling. The best-looking models wore semi-custom bodywork, still supplied principally by Locke and LeBaron and comprising a variety of types, mainly the sportier roadsters and convertible coupes and sedans.

Walter P. Chrysler had passed the 50-year-mark in 1925, and was working as hard and bravely as ever. He was now splitting his time fairly evenly between his firm's Detroit-area production centers and its New York office. This year saw construction begin on the handsome Chrysler Building at Lexington Avenue and 42nd Street in New York. Completed in 1934, it was never intended as the corporation's headquarters, which would never budge from Michigan, but was instead simply a real-estate investment that Chrysler took on "to give my children something to do," as he said. If there was a note of regret in that remark it may have been because none of his four children—two boys and two girls—cared about cars or wanted to work for Chrysler Corporation. Maybe they were wise to stay out of it. Working for your dad can be a problem, particularly when dad is the absolute ruler of a big business, and there's no doubt that Walter P. Chrysler was a despot, if a benevolent one. (Perhaps Edsel Ford might have lived longer had his chosen career not made him so completely subservient to his father.)

On top of being vice-president for the entire corporation, K. T. Keller this year became president and general manager of Dodge Division, actually Dodge Brothers Corporation. Walter Chrysler realized that with his grow-

ing collection of facilities he needed more manufacturing experts like Keller. He found one in David A. Wallace, another Buick alumnus, who held 70 patents for various machines and processes. Born on a ranch near Castleton, Kansas, he had been a railroad machinist apprentice, served as a Buick service representative in Texas, and worked as a tool designer for Hart-Parr Tractors. About 1920 he joined John Deere in Waterloo, Iowa, where he advanced rapidly to become supervisor and works manager. Keller invited him to Detroit in 1929 and made him chief mechanic for Chrysler Corporation. Wallace would go on to the presidency of Chrysler Division in 1937. Today, he is perhaps best remembered as the originator of the wood-bodied Town & Country, which premiered for 1941.

Chrysler sales continued to hum along in 1929, but were nowhere near the firm's production capacity. By the eve of The Great Crash, total U.S. car sales had gone up from 3.1 to 3.9 million units, an increase of 25 percent, but Chrysler's registrations moved up only 3 percent. The figures show that the public was ready to embrace

1929 Plymouth Model Q four-door sedan: $725.

A 1929 Plymouth four-door sedan "body drop"

Plymouth, but some 22 percent of faithful Dodge buyers deserted that make, and the Chrysler marque lost a lot of ground to Hudson, Oldsmobile, and Cadillac's LaSalle. In fact, the Chrysler brand took a bath, sales plunging a full 40.5 percent from its 1928 level, which was nearly 8 percent down on record 1927. Registration figures for the year were as follows:

Chrysler	84,520
Plymouth	84,969
DeSoto	59,614
Dodge	115,774
Total	344,877

The situation was bad enough to make Walter P. Chrysler feel like a small fish in a big pond. Meantime, Ford recovered as the new Model A helped it top 1.3 million sales. GM trailed by about 40,000 units.

1930

Following Chrysler Corporation's disappointing sales results in 1929, the company founder and especially "Hutch" Hutchinson were more than a little concerned about the stock market crash that had occurred in October. Its effects were not yet much in evidence when the company showed off its 1930 models the following January. But ever since his days at GM, an unerring instinct had helped Walter P. Chrysler maintain what was often mistaken for so much good luck. Now that instinct told him that the car business was going to be a lot tougher, at least for the foreseeable future. With grim determination, he plunged into sweeping organizational and personnel changes that would assure Chrysler Corporation's long-term survival while improving its near-term prospects in a market that was bound to shrink. Price cutting was seen as essential in view of growing national unemployment and dwindling personal income, which would put pressure on the entire industry to hold the line on production costs. Like most other companies, Chrysler carefully reviewed its marketing policies and began repositioning whole car lines in light of the new economic realities.

The corporation's incoherent engine lineup presented a wonderful opportunity for rationalization, though it had not been possible to do anything about that for 1929. However, some streamlining was accomplished by the start of 1930 production. Both Dodge sixes were discontinued, leaving five in the corporate stable. Though there was some gross overlap at the small end of the displacement scale, this was a reasonably spaced quintet: a 190 cubic-inch unit for Dodge and DeSoto; the 219 cubic-inch six dating from 1927 and a brand-new 196-cid unit, both for Chrysler; the long-stroke Chrysler six, now bored out to 269 cid; and the Imperial 310, which continued unchanged. But now complicating the picture was a brace of straight eights, a 207.7-cid engine for Dodge and a 221-cid unit for DeSoto, both manufactured at Dodge

The $845 Chrysler Series Six four-door sedan from 1930

1930 Chrysler Series Six 4-seat roadster. Price: $835.

1930 Chrysler Series 66 roadster

Main. And Plymouth's four-cylinder job was still around, enlarged this year to 196 cid by adding a half-inch to its stroke.

With hindsight, it's obvious that Chrysler could have saved money by not fielding the new eights. Why, then, did they appear at a time when economic hardship should have been driving more and more people toward a good little four-cylinder car? The reasons had to do with marketing and manufacturing. Packard had started the swing to straight eights in 1923. By 1927, Auburn, Elcar, Gardner, Hupmobile, Jordan, Kissel, Marmon, Paige, Stutz, and several others had chimed in. Nash followed in 1929, Hudson and Studebaker in 1930, and Willys-Overland in '31. Buick ultimately switched completely from sixes to eights. Chrysler could not afford to ignore the trend, and by 1927 it looked like the firm would need

1930 Chrysler Series 66 phaeton. Only 26 were built.

1930 Chrysler Series 70 4-seat roadster

1930 Chrysler Series 77 convertible coupe

1930 Chrysler Series 77 roadster with optional two-toning

The $1495 Chrysler Series 77 Royal coupe, 1930

1930 Chrysler Series 70 4-seat roadster

an eight pretty quick. That's when Walter Chrysler asked Fred Zeder to lay one out.

At first, the eight-cylinder project had no definite timetable. Then, around Thanksgiving Day 1927, Chrysler decided he wanted the engine in his 1929 models. Zeder completed design work by April 1928, and testing and development started about midyear. It was likely K. T. Keller who held back on tooling orders until it was clear that no further large-scale design changes would be needed. That was prudent, but it killed any chances of an eight-cylinder Chrysler for 1929.

If Chrysler's first straight eight was conceived out of marketing considerations, it was born out of manufacturing necessity. The decision to discontinue the Dodge sixes meant that the plant that had built them would stand idle until it could be retooled. By the end of October

1929, machining lines for the new engine were in place and eight-cylinder blocks, heads, camshafts, and crankshaft blanks were piled up in vacant spots all over Hamtramck. It was too late for second thoughts, so the eight appeared for 1930.

As to why the new powerplant did not appear in a Chrysler, we have to go back to high-level discussions that took place during the winter of 1927-28. The original idea, of course, was an eight-cylinder Chrysler, for the DeSoto had yet to appear and Dodge was still an independent competitor. But the marketing people worried about price, for the new model would surely have to sell for less than a comparable Imperial, which still had only a six. Then there was the size dilemma: the eight then under development was too small for Imperial, but making it big enough would then make it too big for Chrysler, with the result that engine tooling would be underutilized, given the top-line series' low production volume. While it was possible to build two versions, the cost would be prohibitive unless they could share main components. And even with eight cylinders, it would be difficult for one basic block to accommodate the anticipated displacement range of 220-440 cubic inches. There was also the risk that the large unit would prove fragile, while the small one would certainly be too heavy relative to output.

So at the end of 1929, Chrysler was hoping that its new eight would put a fresh wind in Dodge's sagging sails and flagging sales. Meanwhile, Joe Fields's staff had worked out a last-minute plan for a new low-priced Chrysler to drum up new business for the marque, even if it meant a loss of prestige. Plymouth, however, would get the biggest selling push, because it was the volume line that had to tackle Ford's Model A as well as the six-cylinder Chevrolet. It might steal some business from W. C. Durant's falling Star and perhaps cut into Essex sales, but its main mission was to carve big hunks out of Ford's and Chevy's markets.

Accordingly, Plymouth prices were cut shortly after the May 1930 debut of the new 30-U series. Up to that point, the 1929 Series U cars had been sold as 1930 models, but were bodily and mechanically unchanged. Confusingly, the price reductions came after the new line had been on the market less than three months, and were accompanied by an expanded range of body styles and a 1931 model year designation. Everything was sorted out by July, and there were now two new price leaders, a $535

business roadster and a $565 business coupe. Previously, the least expensive Plymouth had been the $590 two-passenger coupe. The rumble-seat coupe dropped from an initial $695 to $625. There were similar cuts on most other models. Two exceptions were the DeLuxe four-door sedan and Plymouth's first convertible coupe, priced at $695 and $745, respectively, through the entire 1930-31 model run.

Billed as the "New Finer Plymouth," the 30-U boasted the larger four previously mentioned, with an extra 21 cubic inches but only three more horsepower than the former unit. Apart from this, there were several other refinements, courtesy of Jim Zeder. Wheel diameter contracted to 19 inches for a lower stance and a look of greater stability, and hydraulic shock absorbers, a mechanical fuel pump, and an electric fuel gauge were fitted as standard. Plymouth remained the only member of what had yet to become the "low-price three" with all-steel construction on closed body types.

Walter P. did not drive out to Dearborn to leave a Plymouth with Henry Ford this year. It's doubtful Henry lost any sleep over that, or the 30-U. However, 1930 did bring a problem that may have kept him up a few nights, the resignation of sales chief Frederick L. Rockelman, who had shepherded the Ford dealer body through the difficult transition from Model T to Model A and put Ford back on top in sales. Not surprisingly, perhaps, Rockelman was lured away to Chrysler, becoming president of Plymouth Division.

Initially, Plymouths had been sold only through

1930-31 DeSoto CF Eight convertible coupe

Chrysler dealers. In March of this year, shortly before the 30-U arrived, the company announced that its low-priced cars would henceforth be retailed through all Dodge and DeSoto outlets as well, which immediately brought the Plymouth dealer network up to 7000 strong. This would prove an excellent strategy for "hard times," because it effectively insulated the more expensive makes from the Depression by giving dealers a more readily saleable product.

Also in early 1930, the company made two key personnel changes. W. Ledyard Mitchell was named chairman of Chrysler Export Corporation, and Dave Wallace was assigned to be general manufacturing manager for Chrysler Division.

Like the good support players they were, engineers Zeder, Skelton, and Breer studiously continued to avoid stealing Walter Chrysler's limelight. However, in a rare press mention this year, *Fortune* magazine gave the following character studies: "Mr. Breer devotes most of his energies to experiments with motors. Mr. Skelton at present devotes himself to bodies and chassis and is directly responsible for the spring and axle designs. Mr. Zeder is the head of the entire engineering organization...[and] can make a scholarly analysis of events to date and a learned prognostication for the future of design."

We have seen how the first Chrysler was designed without compromise. It had to be a winner regardless of cost. Five years later, after a lot of winning, cost had become a dominant issue for Chrysler Corporation. What Walter wanted now was a new low-cost six to serve as the basis for a whole family of engines, a design so flawless and modern that it would remain competitive for 20 years or more without major modification. What his engineers came up with would continue in production for nearly 40 years—not bad considering its design specifications were originally determined by cost.

The initial version of this new low-cost L-head six had only 195.6 cubic inches and 62 horsepower. Cylinder dimensions were close to those of the 1926 Chrysler six, with an identical 3.125-inch bore and a half-inch shorter stroke, 4.25 inches. The main architectural difference was the use of four main bearings instead of seven. This saved some in crankshaft tooling costs, made for a cheaper block-and-crankcase casting, and reduced the number of small parts (bearing caps, shells, and bolts). It also reduced friction by nearly half. Bearing loads were actually lightened at the risk of putting higher stress on the crankshaft. The timing chain was abandoned for simple timing gears, silent running and lack of roughness being viewed as far less important than keeping production costs as low as possible. In all other respects—cooling, lubrication, breathing, firing, and so on—the "little six" resembled the original design.

The new engine arrived in February 1930 to power a bargain-basement Chrysler known simply as the Six, and made it possible for the firm to price this line very low without losing money. Officially designated the CJ series, the group comprised six body styles spanning a $100 band, from the $795 two-passenger business coupe to the $895 convertible coupe. Though the Six had a 109-inch

1930 Dodge Series DD four-door sedan: $865

1930 Dodge DD sedan with optional dealer-installed bed

The $935 Dodge Series DD convertible coupe, 1930

1930 Dodge Series DC Eight 4-seat roadster: $1095

wheelbase like Plymouth, it was built on a completely different platform, with a new lower frame and "steelweld" body construction produced in cooperation with the Budd Company. This basic structure was also used for the six-cylinder DeSoto. Like other Chryslers, the Six was available in standard-compression Silver Dome and higher-compression Redhead forms. A very short 4.70:1 final drive was fitted across the board, which limited top speed to no more than 65 mph. However, the Six had excellent top-gear flexibility and acceleration worthy of a Chrysler.

The Chrysler "66," introduced at midyear 1929, continued without change through May 1930, still available in six body styles priced from $995 to $1095. It was succeeded by the "70," which began coming off the lines at the end of November 1929. Power was supplied by the enlarged long-stroke Chrysler six in both Silver Dome and Redhead tune, and wheelbase was stretched by 3.7 inches over that of the "66." The previous year's "75" was upgraded to become the "77." It shared the "70" engine fitted with Stromberg's new downdraft carburetor, which Chrysler was first in the industry to adopt as original equipment (the "66" used a Carter updraft instrument). Both "70" and "77" engines boasted mechanical fuel pumps, and the cars were factory-wired for installation of a radio. Also featured was a new "multi-range" four-speed gearbox, really the standard three-speed transmission with an overdrive tacked on. Front and rear axles were mounted on "paraflex" springs, so-called as a promise of improved ride comfort, and bodies were advertised as "architonic," presumably to indicate that people could indeed sit in the seats as well as get in and out of the car. The "77" was available in nine body types listing at $1625 to $1825. The "70" offered seven choices one step down the price ladder, spanning a $1295-$1545 range.

The prestige Imperial returned for 1930 with no mechanical changes, as Chrysler was waiting to see what would happen to the luxury market in the wake of the stock market crash. As before there were factory and semi-custom body styles, and all open models save the standard roadster were supplied by Locke. Among the latter was the beautiful, four-seat dual-cowl phaeton first seen in 1929, with auxiliary rear windscreen and standard sidemounts. It was tagged at a lofty $3995, making it the costliest Imperial. Standard offerings ranged from $2995 for the rumble-seat roadster to $3595 for the massive seven-passenger limousine.

Dodge Division's initial 1930 models were 1929 carryovers with minor modifications. The Senior Six acquired the factory designation DB and a standard four-speed transmission, but was otherwise unchanged, retaining its familiar 120-inch-wheelbase chassis and a 241.5-cid six with 78 horsepower. Dodge's junior line, the Series DA Six, was also a rerun except for addition of a price-leader two-door standard sedan at $925. Prices on other models stayed the same.

The "real" 1930 model year began at Dodge on January 1 with the introduction of two new lines, the Series DD "New Six" and the make's first eight-cylinder cars, designated Series DC Eight. The DD shared its chassis and bodywork with the DeSoto CK Six and used the same 109-inch wheelbase, also shared with Plymouth. The DD borrowed the DeSoto engine too. This was not related to Chrysler's new "little six" but was an older, seven-main-bearing design originally developed for DeSoto and later enlarged. The Series DC arrived on the same 114-inch wheelbase as DeSoto's corresponding CF-series Eight, and had an identical overall length of 177 inches. Again, power was supplied by the equivalent DeSoto engine, but with a 0.125-inch longer stroke giving 13 more cubic inches and 5 extra horsepower. Reflecting Chrysler's efforts at rationalizing its engine lineup, the same block, heads, pistons, and valvetrains were used in each version. The basic design was typical Zeder, with a turbulent L-head layout, but neither version used the Chrysler's downdraft carburetor. However, both employed a chain-driven camshaft and a counterbalanced crankshaft running in five main bearings. To handle its slightly greater power, the Dodge eight drove through a slightly larger clutch than the DeSoto CF unit, and pulled a 4.60:1 final drive compared to the DeSoto's 4.90:1.

A timely round of price reductions accompanied both new Dodge series. The DD "New Six" offered fewer body styles than the previous DA, but was about $100 cheaper model for model. Differences between the DB Senior Six and the new DC Eight were even more dramatic: the rumble-seat coupe, for example, came down by nearly $500.

1930 Dodge Series DD Six four-door sedan

The "New Finer Plymouth" Model 30-U Sport Roadster, 1930

1930-31 Plymouth Model 30-U convertible coupe, $695

The straight-eight Dodge and DeSoto were not designed with performance in mind and Chrysler had no thought of racing either, but the company did set up an interesting performance test this year for advertising purposes. A DeSoto Eight was taken to Ligonier, Pennsylvania, some of Chrysler's favorite road-test country, where it was pitted against several rival eight-cylinder models, all priced around $2000. As long as the hills were steep enough the DeSoto would pull away, aided by its short final drive, but on level ground it proved undergeared and could not keep up.

Even so, Chrysler had a real talking point in the DeSoto CF. Billed as "the world's lowest-priced straight eight," it offered a seven-model lineup that comfortably underbid corresponding Hudson and Hupmobile offerings. The line leader was the $965 business coupe; at other end of the scale stood a $1075 rumble-seat convertible coupe.

DeSoto finished 1930 building more Eights than Sixes— 20,075 versus 12,200—but we shouldn't overlook the latter because they were the foundation of the make's spectacular early success. In fact, DeSoto had made history in the summer of 1929 with completion of its 100,000th car just 14 months after production began, an industry record. The milestone car was a Series K four-door sedan, part of the 1929 line that continued into 1930 unchanged. Its successor appeared at the end of April as the Series CK, advertised as the "Finer Six." Apart from the mechanical changes already mentioned, it differed from the K only in having a wider radiator and slightly lower list prices. Incidentally, both DeSoto series benefitted by sharing Dodge bodywork, with Budd "steelweld" construction for closed body styles. Previous DeSotos had carried Hayes bodies built around a wood framework.

On the sales front, all Chrysler Corporation makes fared poorly in 1930. Walter Chrysler himself was pessimistic about the year anyway—he never feared facing reality—but it's likely that even his sales department's lowest projections were higher than actual registrations. Figures for the calendar year are as follows:

Chrysler	60,908
Plymouth	64,301
DeSoto	35,266
Dodge	64,105
Total	224,580

Looking at production numbers, however, it's clear that company planners did a remarkably good job of anticipating the market. Of course, the firm had the ability to trim production if demand dried up in any segment, but Chrysler was unusual in ending the year without a large surplus of unsold cars. Dodge, for instance, built 4000 more units than it sold but, considering the size of its dealer organization, that did not pose a serious inventory problem. Margins were smaller for the company's other makes, and DeSoto actually delivered more cars than it built in 1930, starting the year with a modest backlog from 1929.

It could have been worse. Chrysler Corporation's unit sales shrank by 34.9 percent, very close to the overall industry average of 33.3 percent that represented a decline from 3.9 million to 2.6 million units. Other companies did fare worse: Hudson plummeted 63 percent and Willys-Overland took a 67-percent dive. GM's total slipped below the 1-million mark for the first time since 1926, while Ford managed more than a million, thanks to its tremendous strength at the low end of the market.

1931

Chrysler Corporation's 1931 model plans were largely determined by the sales performance of its 1929 offerings. The reason was that production of each year's upcoming models always began well in advance of the calendar year, although the concept of a "model year" beginning in the fall had yet to be adopted throughout the industry in the early Thirties. In this case, only the first few months of 1930 could be taken into account, because Chrysler's '31s had to be more or less locked up by the middle of that year. Industrial commitments such as plant construction and remodeling and contracts with outside suppliers were less urgent, as most wouldn't take effect until 1932-33. But personnel could be shuffled at any time, just as minds could be changed at a moment's notice and projects redirected or put on hold even in their final stages.

Personnel changes at Chrysler continued as the national economy plunged deeper into the Depression. B. E. Hutchinson now relinquished all his other duties to concentrate solely on the corporation's day-to-day and long-term financial health. Though he was nominally chairman of both Plymouth and DeSoto Divisions, this involved no extra work on his part and mainly served to push his income higher. The presidents of these two divisions were the real managers. At the time Fred Rockelman moved over from Ford to take over at Plymouth (see 1930), Byron C. Foy became his counterpart at DeSoto. Foy's credentials were almost in a class with Rockelman's. Born in Dallas, he had worked as a Ford salesman fresh out of college, then became vice-president of Reo's branch operation in California at the age of 28. In 1924 he married Walter Chrysler's daughter Thelma, and became a partner in a Detroit-area Chrysler dealership at the same time. Elsewhere, Joe Fields continued as president of Chrysler Sales Corporation, and this year was given additional responsibilities as president of Chrysler Division. Over at Dodge, K. T. Keller promoted Fred Lamborn to the post of general plant manager.

Despite all the cutbacks now being made in investment, production, and payroll, the engineering department continued business as usual. Zeder, Skelton, and Breer kept their staff intact, and even added to it. C. Harold Wills, who had masterminded Ford's Model T and later produced the Wills Sainte Claire, signed on to work in metallurgical research. And Robert N. Janeway, after spending a year or so as an engineering consultant to Chrysler Laboratories, joined the firm in 1931 as a research engineer assigned to the staff of R. K. Lee. Janeway was a combustion specialist who held a patent on a special combustion chamber design.

As 1930 opened, both K. T. Keller and Walter P. Chrysler believed that straight-eight engines would eventually dominate the medium-price field where the Chrysler marque had been pitched, now supported by DeSoto and Dodge. Their belief led to some costly conclusions. To free production capacity for more eight-cylinder engines,

Keller slashed the number of sixes to just three: a 205 cubic-inch unit for DeSoto, a 211-cid Dodge powerplant, and a new 218-cid design for Chrysler. There were now no fewer than five eights. The small 207.7-cid DeSoto unit was dropped in favor of the 221, while a new 240-cid engine was readied for Dodge and Chrysler. The latter would also offer 261- and 282-cid engines plus a 385 reserved for Imperial, all of them new.

Curiously, these engines were not related to the previous year's Dodge and DeSoto eights. The Imperial unit was actually based on the existing big six, with an extra cylinder grafted onto each end. It used the same 5.00-inch stroke and a bore brought back to the original E-80 six's 3.50 inches. A new nine-bearing crankshaft was developed, with larger-diameter main bearings and greater crankpin overlap. It drove a side camshaft via silent chain, with the camshaft geared to a slanted shaft

1931 Chrysler CD Eight Royal coupe (Second Series)

1931 Chrysler CD Eight 4-passenger coupe (First Series)

1931 Chrysler CD Eight Standard 5-passenger sedan

that drove oil pump and distributor, as on the six. The 261 and 282 eights were scaled-down versions of this design, though they had specific block castings, only five main bearings, and shared no major components.

On the six-cylinder side, the largest engine represented the wave of the future. This was the new 218-cid unit, a scaled-up derivative of the low-cost, four-bearing 195.6-cid engine of 1930. Initially offered in the 1931 "New Six" CM-series Chrysler, it had direct counterparts in the engines that powered the 1931-33 DeSoto SA, SC, and SD series and the 1931-32 Dodge DH and DL series, as well as Chrysler's DI and CO series of 1932-33. The two smaller sixes were simply enlargements of the existing Dodge/DeSoto six, the biggest change for '31 involving a new crankshaft for the Dodge version. And let's not forget the Plymouth four, which had grown to 196 cid for the 30-U series, the same size as the Chrysler "65" six.

The upshot of all this was nine different engines spread across total 1931 production of less than 230,000 cars. That hardly made sense from the standpoint of production economics. At the time, Ford was producing nearly three-quarters of a million Model A engines a year, all exactly the same, and Chevrolet made nearly as many sixes, again a single design. The break-even point for a company like Chrysler was somewhere between 100,000 and 250,000 units per engine family, depending on whether it was produced in Chrysler or Dodge facilities.

Technically, the 1931 Chrysler lineup consisted of seven separate series, but it really wasn't as complicated as that. Per usual practice, the "early" 1931s were actually 1930 carryovers, comprising the CJ-series Six, the "66," and "70," all unchanged from their previous specifications. The genuine '31s—and our focus here—started coming off the lines in December 1930, and they were

1931 Chrysler CD Eight sports roadster (First Series)

1931 Chrysler DeLuxe Eight dual-cowl phaeton by Locke

1931 Chrysler CG Imperial roadster by LeBaron

1930-31 DeSoto CF Eight phaeton (export model)

1931 DeSoto SA Six 4-passenger roadster: $795.

1931 DeSoto SA Six roadster with six-wheel equipment

1931 Dodge Series DG Eight 4-seat roadster: $1095

1930-31 DeSoto CF Eight DeLuxe 5-passenger sedan

1931 DeSoto CF Eight business coupe (Second Series)

1931 Dodge Series DH Six touring/phaeton

stunning. At the bottom of the new order was the CM-series "New Six," built on a 116-inch wheelbase and powered by the 78-bhp, 218-cid engine already discussed. Next up was the CD-series "New Eight" on a generous 124-inch-wheelbase chassis and packing the 82-bhp 240-cid powerplant. Topping the line was the elegant CG-series Imperial, with the big 385 engine and a massive 145-inch wheelbase. Just to confuse matters, there were also "early" and "late" versions of the CD. The latter, appearing in April, was essentially the same car carrying the 261-cid engine and designated DeLuxe Eight. Another round of price reductions was instituted through all this shuffling—even the carryovers were cheaper than they'd been as 1930 models. Among the true '31s, the six-cylinder line started at $865 for the business coupe, while the New Eight roadster and Royal Standard coupe were each offered at an attractive $1495.

But besides low price, Chrysler could now count on styling to help sell its cars for the first time. The '31s really looked new, and they were elegant and tasteful as well. The styling spoke for itself, but advertising was silent on the subject, curious after all its earlier and less justified hyperbole.

The new look was largely the work of Herb Weissinger, a member of Herb Henderson's small "Art & Color" staff. Taken with the lines of Alan Leamy's beautiful Cord L-29, Weissinger doodled variations on the same theme, particularly the front end. Henry T. King and other colleagues encouraged him, and soon Oliver Clark saw nothing in the Chrysler studio but Cord-inspired fronts wherever he looked. Eventually he came out in favor of two slightly differing proposals; one ended up on the Chrysler, the other on the Imperial.

Thanks to Weissinger, this was the first time in company history that the styling department was involved with a design from the beginning. Before, a complete chassis would be prepared without consulting the designers, whose main task was to put in seats, decorate the interior, and wrap up the whole thing. This time, the chassis was devised to meet the demands of body design, and it emerged with a lower ride height and smaller, fatter wheels and tires. As a result, even the plainest Chrysler Six looked far more expensive than it was, and the custom-bodied Imperials looked like a million bucks. All Eights wore Cord-like vee'd radiator shells, tilted back ever so slightly but with tremendous visual impact. Fender lines were allowed to flow in a way that was natural and pleasing. Overall proportions were perfectly balanced, particularly on the Imperials, their extended chassis allowing the proverbial mile-long hoods that made them truly majestic and imposing machines. And the '31s seemed even wider and lower than they actually were. Suddenly, Chrysler was the style leader among the industry giants. Harley Earl had brought "styling" to Detroit with his lovely 1927 LaSalle, which had made a reputation for itself and its designer mainly on looks, but its popularity was already on the wane. Now, all the people in Highland Park could wonder was how much their spectacular new styling would help Chrysler sales.

While styling was becoming an important sales factor, it was from the top of most buyers' priority list in the early Thirties. Good looks are why we remember the Cord and Auburn of these years, but both were still victims of the Depression. Styling wasn't enough to keep Packard from losing three-quarters of its business in four years, and it did nothing to stave off the deaths of Marmon, Kissel, Stutz, and others. However, everyone at Chrysler felt sure that no car had a chance of selling unless it was fashionably up to date and not too far out. And if looks had anything to do with sales success, then the '31 Chrysler looked like a winner.

Other than the engine and wheelbase changes already mentioned, the '31 Chryslers did not differ much technically from their 1930 counterparts. One notable exception was the arrival of freewheeling as an extra-cost option. This device saved fuel by allowing the engine to "coast" at idle speed whenever power was not needed, and made for easier shifting whenever the accelerator was released. It also made more work for the brakes. For safety, a manual override button was fitted so the driver could lock out the system.

Chrysler continued to make competition news in 1931. A pair of Imperials, a roadster and a sedan, went to the sands of Daytona Beach, where drivers Billy Arnold and Harry Hartz wrote 12 new Class B stock car marks in the American Automobile Association (AAA) record book. The roadster reached 90.4 mph in the flying mile. The sedan was just 0.1 mph slower in the same trial.

Plymouth also made the record books this year when Louie Miller drove a new PA model coast-to-coast and back again—a distance of 6237 miles—in 132 hours and 9 minutes. It was a sensational "media event" for the PA, the first completely new Plymouth since the nameplate's debut. The end product of a development program tagged at approximately $2.5 million, it arrived at midyear to replace the carryover 30-U series. It was better in every way. A revised camshaft, larger valves, higher compression, and a bigger carburetor all combined to boost output of the 196-cid four by 8 horsepower. But the big news was "Floating Power," an intelligent solution to a difficult problem: namely, how to minimize the rocking and vibration inherent in a four. Owen Skelton had been analyzing it for years.

Torque reaction tends to make any engine rock from side to side, a trait most noticeable on sudden application or lifting off of the accelerator. The reaction is stronger the fewer the number of cylinders. The axis of the motion depends on the location of the engine mounts. Skelton decided to place the mounts so that the engine's natural rocking axis would intersect with its center of gravity, thus forestalling any amplification of the motion that would occur on a "top-heavy" engine. He devised a two-point mounting system, with a high front mount at the water pump housing and a low rear mount below the aft gearbox flange. The idea was not to prevent the rocking but to keep its associated vibration out of the frame and body structure. As it appeared in production, "Floating Power" employed mounts anchored in rubber bushings, which provided ample flexibility, and a torque-stabilizing quarter-elliptic leaf spring was mounted next to the flywheel to keep the engine in proper alignment with the rest of the drivetrain.

Though it was a relatively minor advance, "Floating Power" seemed simply astonishing in a low-price car. Plymouth advertising made the most of it by claiming that the PA offered "the smoothness of an eight and the economy of a four." Touted as the industry's most significant engineering advance in a decade, it would be a Plymouth hallmark for the next 20 years.

The Plymouth PA is officially considered a 1932 model, but we're including it here because of its public introduction in July 1931 and the fact that it was not advertised with a model year. Its advanced debut date was matched by advanced styling, at least compared to that of prior Plymouths. Despite retaining the familiar 109-inch wheelbase, the PA was altogether prettier, lower and sleeker overall, and thus right in step with this year's Chryslers. The snazziest of the nine available body styles were the open cars, especially when equipped with accessory sidemounts and wire wheels. PA prices were roughly comparable with those of corresponding 30-U models, the business roadster remaining the least expensive entry at $535.

The Plymouth PA borrowed much of its body structure from the new DeSoto SA-series Six, which in turn was related to this year's Chrysler CM. The successor to the previous CK "Finer Six" (carried over for the first por-

1931 Dodge Series DG Eight 5-passenger four-door sedan

1931 Dodge DH Six suburban commercial, body by Cantrell

1931-32 Plymouth PA taxi. Only 112 were built in all.

1931-32 Plymouth PA two-door sedan. Price was $575.

The $565 Plymouth PA coupe from 1931-32

1931-32 PA 7-passenger sedan (prototype)

The 1931-32 Plymouth PA convertible coupe sold for $645.

Prototype Plymouth PA convertible sedan, not produced

tion of the '31 model year), the DeSoto SA boasted a new double-drop frame, a longer hood, and smoother overall contours. However, the 109-inch wheelbase was unchanged, and DeSoto was still very much "a Plymouth with more cylinders." Remember that the make had been created as Chrysler Corporation's lower middle-price product well before the Dodge takeover, and was intended to take advantage of the "economies of scale" by sharing Plymouth's basic chassis and bodies. Evidence of this basic relationship would be maintained in at least a portion of the DeSoto line well into the Fifties. Interestingly, the kinship was strengthened with advent of the SA series, as DeSoto production was transferred from Highland Park to the new Plymouth facility on Lynch Road. Aside from its larger engine, the new six-cylinder line differed little from its CK predecessor. A revised 4.33:1 final drive

ratio yielded a 75-mph top speed, and optional freewheeling was available beginning at midyear, priced at $20.

Even fewer changes marked this year's DeSoto Eight, the "second series" CF that would continue through most of calendar 1932. Appearance alterations were confined to different radiator trim and a reworked hood and headlamp tie-bar. The increase in engine size to 221 cid brought a heavier crankshaft, and final drive gearing was revised downward numerically, to 4.60:1, for lazier open-road running. Prices were unchanged.

Down in Hamtramck, the company's third main production center turned out a four-series Dodge lineup that was, again, part old and part new. The existing DD "New Six" and DC Eight lines were carried forward from 1930 without change, except for a $100 across-the-board price cut. Arriving around the first of the year were two new

1932

model lines, a Six and an Eight designated DH and DG, respectively. Each was essentially an upgraded replacement for its predecessor, the Six moving up to the DC Eight's 114-inch wheelbase and the new DG riding a 118.5-inch span. Dodge did not quite match its sister divisions in the beauty department this year, but ride height on all eight-cylinder models was reduced slightly, which helped their looks. The division held to its previous pricing, with the four-model DH Six series overlapping the DD line in the neighborhood of $800-$950.

Chrysler Corporation more than maintained market share in this deep Depression year; in fact, its slice of the pie grew from 8.25 percent to fractionally under 12 percent. However, this growth was attributable solely to Plymouth, the firm's other nameplates falling below their previous year's results. The registration figures tell part of the story:

Chrysler	52,650
Plymouth	94,289
DeSoto	28,430
Dodge	53,090
Total	228,459

Overall company sales were up about 4000 cars over 1930, though unit prices were generally lower and profit margins correspondingly slimmer. Nevertheless, Chrysler did not lose money in 1931 despite the decline in total industry volume to 1.9 million units. Though General Motors lost only 10 percent of its previous volume, Ford Motor Company's sales fell by half and Willys-Overland sold only 51,000 cars for the calendar year despite announced cumulative production of 2,425,000 units. The picture was certainly grim throughout most of the industry. Durant Motors, Inc. went under this year, and Studebaker, Nash, and Hudson were facing a similar fate.

Chrysler analysts saw Plymouth's success in this difficult 12 months as the result of several factors: a basically sound product selling at fair prices and backed by a proper parts and service organization, plus dealer advertising bolstered by strong national promotion and two features exclusive in the low-price field, hydraulic brakes and "Floating Power." Don't underestimate that last one. PA series production didn't begin until June, yet over 105,000 of these cars were built before the end of the calendar year. Nearly half were four-door sedans, with the two-door sedan and business coupe following in popularity. This success is even more remarkable considering Plymouth's price handicap next to Ford. The Model A two-door coach listed at $490, while the equivalent Plymouth sold for $575. A Plymouth roadster listed at $535 and the four-door sedan at $645, both more than $100 higher than their Model A rivals. Undeterred by this disadvantage, Plymouth president Fred Rockelman decided to upgrade his products for 1932 while instituting a more aggressive price structure.

Over at DeSoto, division president Byron Foy looked at the market, the national economy, and his work force and plant capacity. He made some quick decisions. The most far-reaching one was to dump his eight-cylinder line after 1931. For the next two decades, DeSoto would rely exclusively on sixes.

It didn't look like a bright year coming in, and 1932 looked even grimmer going out. From all we know of his viewpoint, Walter Chrysler remained in a moderately pessimistic mood and prepared accordingly.

The corporate engine lineup was pared down to the minimum number possible to reduce production costs in the most sensitive and obvious area. The Plymouth four was slated for extinction, but it was still the only engine the make had this year. The six-cylinder stable shrank by one and the eights dwindled by three for a total of three each, distributed among Chrysler (including Imperial), Dodge, and DeSoto. Just as important as the paring is the fact that the remaining sixes and two of the remaining eights used the same 3.25-inch bore, which meant that all five powerplants could be machined on the same lines and share pistons, rings, wrist pins, etc. Evidently, Chrysler found it more expedient to manufacture a variety of crankshafts for a range of strokes than vary bore sizes. And the stroke dimensions spanned quite a narrow range: 4.25 to 4.50 inches. The DeSoto 211, Dodge 218, and Chrysler 224 shared the same six-cylinder block and heads, and the Dodge 282 and Chrysler 299 straight eights had the advantage of similar commonality. The 205-cubic-inch six and the 221-, 241-, and 261-cid eights were dropped. Two of the firm's 1932 engines shared

1932 Chrysler Series CI Six business coupe: $865.

Chrysler's 1932 Series CI Six convertible sedan

1932 Chrysler CD DeLuxe Eight coupe (with Barney Oldfield)

The $885 Chrysler Series CI Six roadster for 1932

nothing with the rest: Plymouth's mass-produced 196-cid four and the big Imperial straight eight, the latter built in very small quantities. Neither engine could be easily brought into line with the others unless the cars they powered were drastically changed so as not to be left underpowered or overly thirsty.

Chrysler Corporation product changes this year were not staggering in their importance, but they made a lot of sense and were generally accomplished at modest cost. The most comprehensive—and expensive—was the switch to double-drop, bridge-type frames with X-bracing on all car lines. This design effectively lowered the passenger compartment floor, which in turn allowed stylists to lower rooflines a little. But the main reason for it was the simultaneous extension of "Floating Power"

from Plymouth to all the company's nameplates, which necessitated the X-bracing.

The first Plymouth introduced with a specific model year arrived in April. Designated PB, it featured a three-inch longer wheelbase and a more rakish appearance, the latter aided by adoption of 18-inch-diameter wheels and tires. An exterior recognition point was the absence of the familiar tie-bar between the headlamps. Mechanical changes were few, but a new downdraft carburetor boosted output of the little four by 9 horsepower. Prices were not revised much. The business roadster was still the line leader at $495. The most expensive offering was the new five-passenger convertible sedan at $785. Also new to the Plymouth line this year was a seven-seat sedan built on a long 121-inch chassis. Advertising now asked

1932 Chrysler Series CP Eight 5-passenger sedan: $1475.

1932 Chrysler Series CI Six 5-passenger sedan: $895

1932 Chrysler Series CP Eight 4-passenger coupe: $1435.

1932 Chrysler CL Imperial convertible sedan by LeBaron

1932 DeSoto Series SC Six Standard four-door sedan

1932 DeSoto Series SC Six Custom convertible coupe

buyers to "Look at All Three," to compare Plymouth with Ford and Chevrolet. Many apparently did just that: Plymouth was one of the few makes to gain sales during the early Thirties, and would continue on a solid upward trend through most of the decade.

DeSoto entered the new year with just a single six-cylinder series, the straight-eight line having reached the end of the road at the end of 1931. Designated the Series SC "New Six," it used the Plymouth PB chassis. However, DeSoto stood apart from Plymouth and Dodge for the first time, thanks to a horizontal-bar radiator likely inspired by that of the famed Miller racing cars. DeSoto shared a first this year with Graham's new Blue Streak models by offering General Tire's "jumbo" 15-inch tires. This would be the last year for DeSoto as a step above Plymouth and a step below Dodge on the corporate ladder. For 1933, the make was deliberately moved closer to Chrysler in technical makeup, trim and equipment levels and, of course, price.

Though the new six-cylinder Plymouth being readied for 1933 was on a par with the existing Dodge Six, there was no thought of downgrading Dodge to accommodate DeSoto's move upmarket. In fact, quite the opposite happened. Announced on New Year's Day 1932 were the biggest Dodges ever seen. Flagship of the fleet was the new DK-series Eight, built on a 3.5-inch longer wheelbase than the DG Eight and boasting 90 horsepower. Its six-cylinder counterpart was the DL series, with a scant 0.3-inch added between wheel centers compared to the DH Six. These were arguably the best-looking cars in Dodge history too, with windshields and radiators tilted back at a modest angle and longer, more smoothly curved Chrysler-like fenders. However, the DK Eight's impressive size would be a bone of contention in discussions about reorganizing Chrysler Corporation's make structure. Some high-ranking executives saw the big, elegant Dodge as a rival for the Chrysler; it certainly looked like a competitor for an upgraded DeSoto. K. T. Keller had been solidly behind the DK, partly because he thought it would make money and partly because he thought it would add luster to the Dodge image. In the end, it did neither: only 6187 were built for the model year, which wasn't enough volume to polish up anything. The DL Six fared far better at 21,042 units.

The DK and DL series were piled on top of a confusing

1932 Dodge lineup that was otherwise made up of 1930-31 models. The DD "New Six" and DC Eight cars sold this year were simply leftovers, while the DG Eight and DH Six were little-changed continuations of the previous season's offerings. There was a curiosity, though, in that each of the latter lines gained a five-passenger phaeton body style; production was just 43 and 164, respectively. A DG business coupe was also fielded, but saw just 119 copies. The brand-new DK and DL lines offered similar body style choices: business and standard coupes, convertible coupe and sedan, and four-door sedan. Prices were set a notch lower than the previous year's, the DL Six ranging from $795 to around $1000, the DK Eight spanning an $1115-$1395 bracket. A new I-beam front axle replaced the former tubular design on all models, and

1932 DeSoto Series SC Six Custom convertible sedan

1932 Dodge Series DK Eight four-door sedan: $1145

1932 Dodge DK Eight (left) and DL Six four-door sedans

1931-32 Dodge DG Eight 4-passenger roadster

1932 Dodge DK Eight convertible sedan: $1395.

a kick shackle with a rubber buffer against the frame was added on the left front spring to counteract shimmy. Also, Oilite discs were inserted between the front and rear spring leaves to control interleaf friction.

This year's Chrysler lineup was also riddled with carry-overs, at least until January 1 when the "genuine" '32s appeared. There were no obvious external changes except for a split windshield on the CI6, also known as the "Second Series" Six and basically a continuation of the previous CM series. A really sharp eye might detect the one-inch longer wheelbase on this year's successor to the CD Deluxe Eight, designated CP. Both CI and CP ran larger engines than their predecessors, but cost much the same. The Imperial line was now split in two, a standard CH series on a 135-inch wheelbase and a "custom" CL series on a long 146-inch platform. Powertrains were the same for both.

Chrysler Corporation still lacked a synchromesh transmission, but it flirted with a number of ideas to ease the gear-shifting task. One was a vacuum-operated automatic clutch. First offered as an option on the 1931 Plymouth PA, it was extended to all the corporation's car lines for '32. Basically, it worked by a connection between the clutch throwout lever and a vacuum cylinder operated by manifold pressure. On closed throttle the clutch would automatically disengage, so that all the driver had to do was lift off the accelerator, wait a second, and then move

the gearlever without touching the clutch pedal. The device could be locked out by a dashboard pushbutton. Freewheeling was still around, and many buyers ordered it. It was a cam-and-lever device activated by a button on the gearshift, and cars so equipped came with bigger brakes to handle the extra wear imposed by the freewheeling and its consequent lack of engine braking.

Although Plymouth production was running along smoothly at 1000 units a day built by 5500 workers, Walter P. Chrysler decided to double capacity before introducing the six-cylinder line for 1933. "That will cost 10 million dollars," said K. T. Keller, who was never far wrong in such matters. The records show that $9 million was allocated to new tooling for the Plymouth plant in 1932, and there must have been bits and pieces charged to other budgets that added up to a million dollars. In June of this year, DeSoto production was again shifted, this time to the Chrysler plant on Jefferson Avenue. Also during 1932, Chrysler Motors of California was formed to operate a new plant in Los Angeles that could be set up for assembly of any of the company's makes. Among this year's personnel changes was the appointment of W. Ledyard Mitchell as chairman of Chrysler Canada, Ltd., and the death of assistant chief engineer Howard E. Maynard at the age of only 53. Harold Hicks, who had designed the Model A engine for Ford, joined Chrysler's research team, and A. B. "Buzz" Grisinger came to the

1932 Dodge DK Eight 4-passenger coupe. Price: $1115

1932 Plymouth PB sedan for taxicab use

The $895 Dodge DL Six convertible coupe from 1932

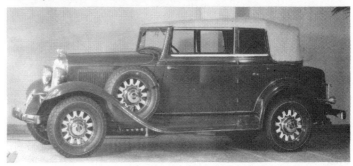

1932 Plymouth PB convertible sedan. Base price: $785.

Highland Park design staff from the Boeing School of Aeronautics.

U.S. auto sales all but dried up in 1932, less than 1.1 million new cars finding owners, a 42.5-percent drop in only one year. General Motors took it on the nose, falling below the half-million mark. Ford sales were cut in half for the second straight year, its total of 262,000 cars only a bit more than what Hudson had sold in 1929. Chrysler fought against the trend and did itself proud by holding the decline to a mere 16.2 percent. The breakdown on 1932 registrations is as follows:

Chrysler	26,016
Plymouth	111,926
DeSoto	25,311
Dodge	28,111
Total	191,364

For the year, Chrysler lost a little more than $10 million, small potatoes compared with Ford's frightening $71 million loss. Inexplicably, GM lost only $4.5 million.

Now in a gloomy mood and, uncharacteristically, at a loss for a purposeful course of action, Walter P. Chrysler was ready to shut the company's research laboratories and dismiss their employees. Then he heard about staff progress on an aerodynamic test car. Harold Hicks brought results showing that body changes had enabled its top speed to be upped from 83 to 98 miles an hour with

the same engine but different gearing. At that, Walter remarked, "Well, if that's what research can do, then we must always have research." The laboratories would keep their full budget and staffing throughout the Depression.

1933

At the start of 1933, a high-ranking GM official reportedly declared: "Chrysler Corporation will stand or fall with the Plymouth." The remark was undoubtedly prompted by the mixed buyer reaction to the first six-cylinder Plymouth, unveiled the previous October. It was a completely different car—and before the model year was out there would be two more Plymouths completely different from that one. It was an odd and unfortunate situation for the year in which the national economy hit bottom. In a way, it signalled the start of Chrysler Corporation troubles to come.

Walter Chrysler had long maintained that a four-cylinder engine was the only logical choice for a low-price car. But the advent of Ford's low-cost flathead V-8 for 1932, added to the continuing popularity of the six-cylinder Chevrolet, made it clear that Plymouth would have to change to stay competitive. And change it did.

1933 Chrysler CO Six convertible sedan: $945

1933 Chrysler Series CO Six 5-passenger sedan

Chrysler's 1933 CO Six 4-seat coupe cost $775 basic.

1933 Chrysler CT Royal Eight convertible coupe

1933 Chrysler Series CT Royal Eight 4-passenger coupe

The 1933 Plymouth, designated PC, arrived on a 107-inch wheelbase, two inches shorter than that of the previous PA and five inches less than that of the 1932 PB. And that was the rub, because despite its sassy, modern lines —with skirted fenders and a slightly raked, chrome-plated radiator shell—the PC not only looked much smaller than the previous four-cylinder cars, it *was*—too small, some said, even for a low-price make.

While the PC was a completely new Plymouth, it was not a completely new car. Its 189.8-cid L-head six was really the old 1930 DeSoto unit, which in turn dated from the 1928 Chrysler "62." The chassis was a cut-down version of the previous year's frame, with new "Floating Power" motor mounts to support the physically longer engine. Front springs were beefed up to take the six's greater weight, but the front axle was the same as before and the rear axle and transmission were both taken from the DeSoto parts shelves. With so few new components, the PC cost Chrysler next to nothing in mechanical tooling, which allowed the firm to put more money where it showed, mainly body styling, and to keep prices attractively low. Indeed, the price tag on the least expensive offering still read only $495, though it was now attached to a business coupe as Plymouth dropped the old-fashioned phaeton and rumble-seat roadster this year. However, you could still get a convertible coupe, the priciest of the pack, for just $70 more, and the popular four-door sedan cost a reasonable $545.

On paper, at least, the Plymouth PC looked like a winner. It was not only Chrysler Corporation's first low-price six-cylinder car but the only one of the low-price three with "Floating Power." It may have been shorter between wheel centers than the PB, but it was only an inch or so shorter *overall.* Moreover, Walter Chrysler, K. T. Keller, Fred Rockelman, and a host of others had all given it their blessing.

Nevertheless, production had barely begun when engineers Zeder, Skelton, and Breer were called in and told to get a revised model ready—*fast.* What worried the boss was that Plymouth had scored an 18.7-percent sales gain in 1932, a year that had been a disaster for most everyone else in Detroit. If Plymouth had managed that with its old styling, then the reason must surely be that it had something else going for it. And as the PC's disappointing sales returns suggested, that something was a longer wheelbase. Despite its "new" six and more streamlined appearance, the Plymouth PC looked like less car, not more.

As the crash fix-it program got under way in January 1933, two camps within the executive corridors wrestled with the question of what the fix should be. One camp wanted all Plymouth models on a longer wheelbase; the other maintained that the short chassis was long enough. With his customary daring, which seemed to increase in direct proportion with the gravity of a problem, Walter Chrysler opted for both. The result was a 108-inch-wheelbase line designated PCXX, marketed as the Standard Six, and a 112-inch-wheelbase group, the PD DeLuxe. The latter was actually a badge-engineered version of the 1931-32 DH-series Dodge, which explains why it appeared with record speed. Prototypes were shown at

Walter Chrysler's personal 1933 Imperial CL sedan

the New York Automobile Show in late January, and finished cars hit dealer showrooms the following March. But the tactic worked, and Plymouth sales moved upward again beginning in the spring. By the end of September, they were double those of 1932.

But there was something even more radical afoot. K. T. Keller had been an ardent supporter of the Plymouth PC,

and he was still thinking about how small a practical American car could be. His thinking led to an interesting project. Carl Breer had called Walter Chrysler's attention to *Horizons,* a book filled with drawings of futuristic aircraft, ships, and automobiles. It was written and illustrated by industrial designer Norman Bel Geddes, who was signed on as a company consultant in September. Bel

1933 Chrysler CT Royal Eight 5-passenger sedan (prototype)

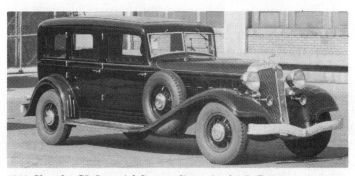

1933 Chrysler CL Imperial Custom limousine by LeBaron

1933 Chrysler CL Imperial Custom phaeton by LeBaron

Clay modelers sculpt the 1933 DeSoto SD front end

1933 DeSoto Series SD Custom 5-passenger sedan

1933 DeSoto Series SD Custom 4-passenger coupe: $750

1933 DeSoto Series SD business coupe

Geddes was charged with three tasks: suggest styling improvements for the streamlined Chrysler and DeSoto Airflow, scheduled for 1934; develop a 100-inch-wheelbase version of the Airflow, possibly for the Plymouth badge; and draw up a proposal for a compact even smaller than the PC. The purpose of these studies was not to devise a competitor for the likes of the little Willys 77 but to reduce freight expenses. Calculations showed that twice as many 100-inch-wheelbase compacts would fit in a railroad boxcar compared to typical standard-size automobiles, which meant lower unit shipping costs.

Breer was accordingly instructed to design such a car. What he came up with was a 1700-pound vehicle on the required wheelbase and powered by a small 130-cid V-8. If that weren't unusual enough, the design envisioned unit body/chassis construction, an early attempt at applying aircraft-style build techniques to an automobile, engineered by Joseph Ledwinka of the Budd Company. Even if no production cost savings were realized, the reduction in freight would be enough, according to estimates, to shave $100 off the cheapest '33 Plymouth PC.

But the compact-car project was abruptly cancelled

DeSoto Foursome prototype for 1933 Chicago Auto Show

1933 DeSoto Series SD Custom convertible sedan: $975.

because engineering resources were needed for more immediate and important tasks, namely finalizing the production '34s. Beyond that were plans for a new generation of Chevrolet-size Plymouths, a task that fell to Newton F. Hadley, who had been named the division's chief engineer the previous year. Hadley had been at Willys-Overland since 1913, where he linked up with Zeder, Skelton, and Breer about eight years later. Later, Fred Zeder brought him to Maxwell as an experimental engineer.

Efforts at streamlining Chrysler Corporation's mixed bag of engines were showing results by now. With the end of the Plymouth four, a tight group of sixes met nearly 90 percent of the company's powerplant needs on the basis of sales. The old 211-cubic-inch six was dumped this year in favor of the 190-cid Plymouth unit (which wasn't really new, as we've seen) and a 201-cid engine that went into the 1933 Dodge DP-series Six. The DeSoto 218 and Chrysler 224 continued unchanged, sharing a common bore but using different strokes. The Dodge 201 shared stroke with the DeSoto engine and bore with the 190, and would replace the latter as Plymouth power for nine consecutive years beginning with 1934. A quartet of straight eights comprised 274-cid Chrysler, 282-cid Dodge, and 299- and 385-cid units for the Imperial CQ and CL, respectively. Cylinder dimensions on the largest were unique in this group, while the other three engines employed a 3.25-inch bore.

The 1933 DO Series would be the last eight-cylinder Dodge until the modern "Red Ram" V-8 arrived for 1953. Built on the 122-inch wheelbase customary for the Dodge Eight, the DO line consisted of five body styles at prices around $1100-$1200 for all but the five-seat convertible sedan, which retailed at $1395. Production was low, a reflection of "hard times." The aforementioned top-line offering saw just 39 copies.

Nevertheless, Dodge sales recovered in 1933, and the reason was the new DP-series Six. Like the companion Eight, it was totally new from road to roof, marked by an attractively curved new radiator canted rakishly to the rear and topped by the make's new ram mascot, introduced the previous year. Body lines were more fashionably rounded than before, hoods were longer, and a switch to steel-spoke wheels added a modern touch. The new line arrived on a 111.25-inch wheelbase, but when the longer Plymouth PD and PCXX appeared, Dodge hastily stretched the DP to 115 inches between wheel centers to maintain its place in the corporate size and prestige pecking order. However, the extra chassis length brought no increase in prices, which ran from the $595 business coupe to the $695 rumble-seat convertible coupe.

DeSoto fared less well than Dodge, which may have contributed to the situation by stretching its DP-series wheelbase so that it was actually a bit longer than that of its sister make. With straight eights no longer in the picture, this year's DeSoto line consisted of just a single series, designated SD, essentially a continuation of the 1932 Series SC "New Six." Split windshields were more in evidence on the '33s, but the main design distinction was at the front, where a more severely raked, rounded radiator was now cradled by "air-flow" one-piece front

1933 Dodge DO Eight 5-passenger sedan. Price: $1145.

Dodge's DP Six convertible coupe sold at $695 for '33.

fenders, joined at the centerline under the radiator. As before, the rumble-seat coupe and the two- and four-door sedans were available in Standard and Custom versions, the latter carrying higher prices but more equipment and better trim. However, the differences were rendered more or less academic beginning in June, when the division added many of the Custom's features—wipers, dual horns, taillamps, and such—to the Standard models and cut prices throughout the line by $60 in an effort to spark sales. But they didn't spark, and DeSoto finished the year well down on its 1932 performance. Speaking of per-

1933 Plymouth PC Six 2-seat coupe. List price: $495.

1933 Plymouth PC Six four-door sedan, priced at $545

1933 Plymouth PCXX Six two-door sedan: $465.

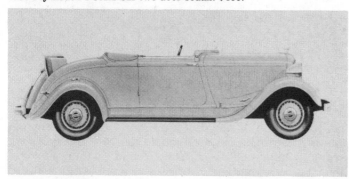

The 1933 Plymouth PD DeLuxe Six convertible coupe

1933 Plymouth PC Six convertible coupe sold at $565.

formance, this is another area where the Dodge Six may have hurt DeSoto, which weighed 500 pounds more on the average for a correspondingly poorer power-to-weight ratio and slower off-the-line acceleration.

All Chrysler Corporation makes adopted the model year concept for 1933, which made for a much less confusing succession of models, with no carryovers or half-year introductions to worry about—aside from the hastily revamped Plymouth, that is. As at Dodge, there were extensive changes in this year's Chrysler. At the bottom of the line was the Six, officially designated Series CO and built on a one-inch longer wheelbase than its CI predecessor. The standard eight-cylinder models were now named Royal, officially Series CT, and rode a five-inch shorter chassis than the previous year's CP series. The two-tier Imperial group continued from 1932, with Custom models still designated CL and retaining their 146-inch wheelbase. However, the standard Imperial, now designated CQ, also got a wheelbase chop, a full nine inches. All Chryslers retained the previous year's Cord-inspired radiator, but now stylishly leaned to the rear, and this plus fuller front fenders made the cars as regal-looking as ever despite their shorter chassis. Split windshields were now used on virtually all body types, and vertical rectangular doors replaced louvers on the hood sides. Mechanical improvements included "silent-running" transmissions with helical-cut gears, an industry first, plus a starter switch activated by the accelerator pedal, an automatic choke for the downdraft carburetor, and an automatic heat-riser valve on the manifold. The broad price spectrum ran from the six-cylinder business coupe at $745 to the magnificent Custom Imperial phaeton at $3395.

Though the Chrysler marque still carried a lot of prestige, it was Plymouth that kept Chrysler Corporation afloat in 1933. Actually, the company was positively buoyant, recording twice as many sales as it had the year before. By contrast, GM deliveries were up by about 20 percent and Ford's by one-third in a year that saw the industry as a whole make only a partial recovery, to 1.5 million cars. Chrysler's U.S. registrations for 1933 were as follows:

Chrysler	28,677
Plymouth	249,667
DeSoto	21,260
Dodge	86,062
Total	385,666

There was another achievement in 1933, less spectacular perhaps, but no less important, especially for the long-term future. This was the formation of the Chrysler Institute of Engineering, organized by James C. Zeder, who became chief engineer of Chrysler Laboratories this year, a post he would hold through 1946. In its early days the company had depended largely on talent brought in from other organizations, often rival automakers. With the founding of the Institute, the firm would now have a facility for training its own technical staff, executives, and designers. Said K. T. Keller: "The men who are worth most are usually the ones we develop—and that takes time. If you cannot develop an organization, you are apt to remain without one. You cannot go out and pick one off trees. You can get capable, intelligent, industrious men, but before you can develop a smoothly working organization, you have to study the men and fit them into your business." It was a clear recognition of the familiar principle that a well-managed organization is a whole greater than the sum of its parts.

1934

Renewed national prosperity seemed to be just around the corner in 1934, and Chrysler Corporation was preparing to celebrate its 10th anniversary. The firm had enjoyed spectacular success during its first decade, largely because of the superior engineering of its products. So it was no surprise that the radical new Chrysler and DeSoto Airflow that appeared this year were largely the products of engineers. What *was* surprising was that the normally canny Walter Chrysler approved this advanced concept without much apparent regard for whether the public would accept it. And that would prove to be Chrysler's—both the man's and the company's—first serious mistake.

The Airflow was unquestionably a mistake of major proportions, a failure so complete that it would cast a pall over Chrysler Corporation design for the next 20 years. In introducing the Airflow, Walter Chrysler declared: "I sincerely believe it will bring about a whole new trend in personal transportation." And, judging by the similar but far more successful Lincoln-Zephyr, he was right. But if the Airflow is remembered today as a marketing flop—for years its name was the best-known synonym for same, at least before the Edsel—then it is also remembered for the valuable lesson it taught the industry: no matter how well engineered, ugly cars don't sell. It was a costly lesson for Chrysler, which wouldn't fully recover from this folly for almost 10 years. And tellingly, the company would have to relearn the Airflow lesson in the postwar period, not once but twice.

Nevertheless, the pioneering Airflow must rank as one of the most significant individual designs in U.S. auto-

Pre-production prototype for the 1934 Chrysler CU Airflow

motive history. Though it was indeed ugly, at least to contemporary eyes, it did introduce streamlined styling and, with it, the basic shape of the automobile as we know it today. And in body construction, engine placement, ride quality, and several other areas, it marked a complete break with existing design conventions, which were simply evolutions of "horse-and-buggy" practices.

As the story goes, the Airflow concept originated in 1927, when engineer Carl Breer went out one day for a drive in the country. Returning home by way of a road that approached Selfridge airfield, he spotted what he first thought was a flock of geese, only to find it was a squadron of Army Air Corps fighter planes practicing maneuvers. This led him to an idea that would have been familiar to Leonardo da Vinci. Like the Renaissance artist/engineer, Breer was struck by the way nature so

1934 Chrysler CU Airflow four-door sedan. Price: $1345.

The Chrysler Airflow body line in Highland Park, 1934

1934 Chrysler CV Airflow Imperial four-door sedan: $1625.

1934 Chrysler CU Airflow four-door sedan (prototype)

DeSoto's first Airflow, the 1934 Series SE coupe.

1934 DeSoto Series SE Airflow four-door sedan

1934 Chrysler CW Airflow Custom Imperial sedan limousine

often suggested solutions for man's mechnical problems. Even if an automobile didn't have to fly, perhaps it could be made to move on the ground more efficiently if its design borrowed something from the shape of birds—or aircraft.

Breer discussed this notion with none other than pioneer aviator Orville Wright, and also began making up scale models of very different-looking cars to be tested in the wind tunnel at Dayton. Their basic shape almost suggested itself: a teardrop, modified to allow for a hood and windshield. Breer also talked with William Earnshaw, a research engineer at Dayton, and gave him a car for making measurements of air-pressure lift and distribution. Breer soon found money for construction of a wind tunnel at Chrysler's main headquarters complex in Highland

Park. "In those days, when we needed something, we just went ahead and built it," he told *Automotive News* in 1964. "Walter Chrysler never questioned us about what we were doing. We pioneered by not wasting time."

Even so, the Airflow took the better part of six years to develop. Many more scale models were built and tested along the way. Some of them didn't look much like cars, but were necessary trial-and-error experiments for discovering the "rules" of aerodynamics. There were also at least 10 full-size semi-streamliners evaluated in the wind tunnel. According to author Maurice D. Hendry, the aerodynamic model for the production Airflow was devised by Dr. Alexander Klemin, head of the Guggenheim Foundation for Aeronautics.

Breer soon engaged fellow "Musketeers" Zeder and

Skelton to help him develop a running prototype for a car employing aircraft-type design principles. Completed in December 1932, it was dubbed "Trifon Special," mostly for secrecy's sake (and after one of the engineering lab's employees). Power was supplied by a standard Chrysler six, mounted 20 inches further forward of its conventional position and equipped with a crankshaft-driven fan. The experimental's front-end styling prefigured that of the eventual Airflow: a short, curved nose with faired-in headlamps, "alligator" (rear-hinged) hood, and one-piece windshield. However, the prototype was a semi-fastback four-door sedan with integral trunk, not the full fastback style ultimately chosen.

Although a front-mounted engine was more or less assumed throughout most of the Airflow's gestation, Breer also drew up plans for a rear-engine version, though it likely never got off his drawing board. He abandoned the layout not so much because of its different weight distribution and the unusual handling characteristics associated with that but rather because it would wreak havoc with existing production procedures.

Initially, Breer had envisioned a passenger compartment with seating for three abreast in front and two in the rear, in order to get the desired teardrop body shape. But there were insurmountable problems. With more than two in front, elbow room was deemed insufficient for best driver control, and the marketing people would never accept a back seat for less than three. A central driving position was tried but rejected.

Shortly after the Trifon Special was completed, Walter Chrysler took his first demonstration ride in it and came away impressed. Breer had been struggling with weight distribution in order to reduce ride-motion frequency and to synchronize front and rear suspensions to reduce pitching. The forward engine, with its center of gravity above the front axle, definitely helped the ride. It also allowed the back seat to be moved forward a corresponding distance so that the entire passenger compartment was cradled comfortably within the wheelbase. The results were weight distribution reversed from the typical 45/55 percent front/rear, plus considerable interior space within rather compact external dimensions. There was more than enough head, shoulder, hip, and leg room to suit even the burly boss, and the ride was smoother than anything else on the road, especially for rear seat passengers.

For these reasons, not to mention the forward-thinking design that likely appealed to his ego, Walter Chrysler gave his wholehearted support to the Airflow project. By early 1933, production engineering was moving ahead at full steam and fresh funds had been allocated for tooling, final design details, and other expenses. The first production prototype quickly took shape in a sealed-off area of the Highland Park engineering building. Initial road tests were not conducted in or around Detroit but at a place called Strubles Farm, located on the Au Sable River about 200 miles to the north. The element of surprise would be important in launching the new car, especially such an advanced one, and Chrysler obviously didn't want rivals finding out what it was up to.

Originally, the Airflow was to have appeared only with

Jumping off a cliff in a 1934 Airflow publicity stunt.

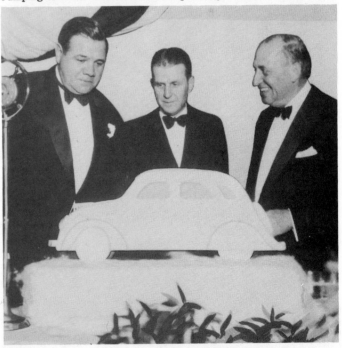

Babe Ruth (left), DeSoto Division manager Byron Foy, and Walter Chrysler (right) with a DeSoto Airflow cake in 1934.

A brace of 1934 DeSoto Airflows at a crossroads in LA

the DeSoto badge, but that changed when the boss decided there ought to be a Chrysler version to mark the 10th anniversary of his namesake marque. Thus, the new model debuted under both nameplates, encompassing five different wheelbases and as many engines. Smaller versions were also being prepared for Dodge and Plymouth in anticipation that the public would flock to the futuristic Airflow concept. It didn't.

This strategy created a near disaster for DeSoto, which relied exclusively on the Airflow for 1934, while Chrysler

protected itself by hanging onto conventional styling for its six-cylinder models. Designated Series SE, the DeSoto Airflow was built on a 115.5-inch wheelbase and offered a choice of four body styles—two-door coupe and brougham sedan, six-window four-door sedan, and four-window four-door town sedan. All were powered by a 241.5-cubic-inch L-head six rated at an even 100 bhp. There were four Chrysler Airflow groups: the 123-inch-wheelbase Series CU Eight, 128-inch-wheelbase Series CV and 137.5-inch-wheelbase Series CX Imperial Eights,

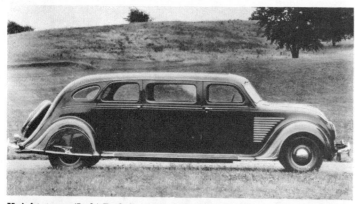

Knightstown (Ind.) Body's 156-inch-wheelbase 1934 DeSoto Airflow for funeral director Frank Stanley

Taxi!! Hailing a DeSoto Airflow sedan in 1934.

1934 DeSoto SE Airflow town sedan listed at $995.

The sleek tail of the 1934 DeSoto Airflow SE coupe

and the top-line 146-inch-wheelbase Series CW Imperial Custom Eight. Engines ranged from 299 to 385 cubic inches, horsepower from 122 to 150. There were no open Airflow body types.

Beginning in March 1934, both the DeSoto and the Chryslers gained an automatic overdrive for their standard three-speed transmission. Geared to give a 30 percent reduction in engine rpm at a given road speed, it was a simple planetary gearset mounted on the transmission's output shaft and engaged via a centrifugal clutch, which locked the satellite cage to the shaft at speeds above 40 mph depending on throttle position. Automatic downshifts were made at or below 25 mph. Invented by William B. Barnes, it was supplied by Warner Gear and, together with the streamlined styling, made the Airflows quite economical. One test car averaged 21.4 mpg on a run from New York to San Francisco.

The Airflows also had fine performance. The DeSoto set many speed records under American Automobile Association (AAA) auspices: 86.2 mph for the flying mile, a 76.2-mph average for 500 miles, and a 74.7-mph average for 2000 miles. On the Bonneville Salt Flats in Utah this year an Imperial coupe ran the flying mile at 95.7 mph, averaged 90.04 mph over 500 miles, and did 84.43 mph for 24 hours.

The Airflow was not an old-fashioned chassis in modern dress but a thoroughly re-engineered "car of the future." Its "interlocking" body structure was not true unit construction but rather a more tightly integrated body/frame arrangement, with the body panels extended below the frame and attached to its cage-like superstructure. The result was less weight and much greater torsional strength compared with conventional cars. In one of the well-known publicity stunts for which it had a fondness in these years, Chrysler proved the point by purposely sending an Airflow off a 110-foot cliff in Pennsylvania. The car landed wheels down and drove away under its own power. In concept, the Airflow's structure was not Breer's alone but also reflected input from engineers at Budd and Chrysler's chief body engineer, Oliver Clark. Budd ended up supplying most Airflow sheetmetal aft of the cowl, while the entire front end was built up as a sub-assembly at the Dodge plant in Hamtramck.

While this year's Plymouth boasted a newly designed independent front suspension, the Airflows were a throwback in having a tubular front axle, the same type found on the very first Chryslers. Nevertheless, one DeSoto advertisement claimed that you could read a newspaper in the Airflow "at 80 miles an hour over a rough dirt road." Besides the improved weight distribution, long leaf springs enhanced ride comfort. On the Chrysler CU, for example, the front springs were 44.125 inches stem to stern, while the rear ones were 52.5 inches. No fewer than 10 leaves were used at the front, eight at the rear. Another comfort bonus were seats mounted high off the floor on tubular chrome frames and measuring an impressive 50 inches wide. Upholstery was typically Bedford cord cloth with leather trim, and the unusual seat mounting allowed full air circulation within the passenger compartment to prevent the distressing clamminess expected in hot weather.

Actor Dick Powell tries a 1934 DeSoto Airflow sedan.

For all the Airflow's sterling virtues, most buyers just couldn't ignore its strange new shape, and it quickly became obvious that Chrysler's "car of the future" didn't have much of a future at all. Aggravating this basic problem was the cars' initial scarcity in the showrooms. Because of the considerable retooling necessary to convert to Airflow production, Chrysler had to delay the new models' public debut until January 1934. The Custom Imperials didn't go on sale until June. Lack of cars blunted whatever public interest may have existed initially, and it also led to rumors that the Airflow was flawed, a lemon. Negative press reaction hardly helped. Said industrial designer Henry Dreyfuss, the Airflow was "a case of going too far too fast." Frederick Lewis Allen, editor of *Harper's* magazine, described it as being "so bulbous, so obesely curved as to defy the natural preference of the eye for horizontal lines." In a year that saw most companies boost production by up to 60 percent, Chrysler's volume rose only 20 percent. The division would continue to lag behind its competitors for several years. DeSoto actually moved more Airflows than Chrysler (a bit over 4500 more), but it had no companion lines to fall back on and thus ended the year in a considerably weakened position. By contrast, the squared-rigged Series CA and CB Sixes accounted for more than half of Chrysler Division sales. The corporate sales breakdown for the year is as follows:

Chrysler	28,052
Plymouth	302,557
DeSoto	11,447
Dodge	90,139
Total	432,195

Obviously, Plymouth had again brought the bacon home to Highland Park. If it hadn't, company sales would have totalled only about 130,000 units, about twice Buick's volume. And of that, about three-fourths would have been accounted for by Dodge, which, like Plymouth, was not saddled with the Airflow. So before we leave this year, it's important to take a look at developments at Chrysler's junior divisions.

Plymouth's amazing success in 1932-33 was a valuable lesson to those who knew how to interpret it. Charles W. Nash thought he could cash in on the same market with a

1934 Dodge DR DeLuxe Six convertible coupe: $765.

1934 Dodge DS DeLuxe Six Special convertible sedan

1934 Dodge DS Special convertible sedan cost $875.

sion president this year and Dan S. Eddins was promoted to succeed him ("Hutch" Hutchinson remained chairman). Eddins, who hailed from Waco, Texas, began his career in the locomotive repair shops of the International & Great Northern Railroad at Mart, Texas. After 3½ years, he found a job with the Dallas branch of Studebaker, then became a partner in a Maxwell dealership in Denver. In 1918 he joined the sales force of fast-rising Chevrolet. When A.B.C. Hardy, the tough old president of Oldsmobile, needed help, Eddins was transferred to Lansing as general sales manager. In a few years he was Olds president and general manager. Eddins was happy there, but in 1932 he was brought into the GM corporate office by Richard H. Grant to develop marketing plans and sales projections for all the firm's car divisions. Eddins began to get bored, started looking around, and soon made contact with Chrysler. He resigned from GM to become vice-president and general manager of Plymouth in April 1934. Eight months later he was division president.

Shortly before this, on August 10th, the one-millionth Plymouth came off the Lynch Road assembly line. It was a symbol of the make's growing popularity, and its sales would continue strong for the rest of the year.

The 1934 Plymouth was distinguished by several new features. One was obvious at a glance: a radiator mascot with the image of the good ship Mayflower, a reminder of the Plymouth Rock connection, instead of a winged goddess. Under the hood was a larger six-cylinder engine, the 201-cid unit seen in the previous season's Dodge DP series, with an aluminum cylinder head newly available at extra cost.

Once again, Plymouth ended the year with more models than it started with. The first to arrive were the 108-inch-wheelbase Series PF Standard and the 114-inch-wheelbase PE Deluxe. Showroom visitors who bent down to look at the front axles on these cars were surprised to find that there weren't any. Still alone in its class with hydraulic brakes, Plymouth now brought independent front suspension to the low-price field. However, it was not alone in this, as Chevrolet introduced the "Knee-Action" system on some of its 1934 models, based on the patented Andre Dubonnet design. In April a price-leader Standard series, designated PG, appeared on the shorter chassis with a non-independent I-beam front suspension. Then in June, Plymouth announced a fancier version of the PF designated PFXX, offering the same body styles plus a new town sedan. With standard hydraulic brakes and independent front end, the PFXX was priced at just $5 above comparable Fords and, predictably, proved a big hit.

Plymouth's new ifs looked like it was copied from Cadillac's. Cadillac's chassis group, under Maurice Olley, had been working for four years on a coil-spring design with upper and lower A-arms. Chrysler Corporation hadn't been working on anything similar, largely because its fabled engineering triumvirate had other preoccupations. Although Chrysler offered freewheeling, vacuum clutch, and helical-cut gears, Fred Zeder was bothered by the lack of a synchromesh transmission. He was already beginning to think about an automatic transmission, and

cheaper LaFayette, and Roy D. Chapin tried to do the same by transforming his Essex into the Terraplane. But neither lived up to their creators' hopes, because both were based on a 1927 marketing concept, not the new realities of 1934. General Motors had rushed to kill its Viking and Marquette, and nearly did away with the LaSalle. There would be no more low-priced companion makes from GM, and a new policy evolved by which each division was given full freedom to dip into the next-lower price bracket. Thus was born the Buick Special, for example. At Ford, engineers were busy with a smaller V-8. A six would have been more logical, but Henry had an inexplicable aversion to sixes that likely stemmed from the lack of success of his first such car, the 1905-06 Model K.

Having put Plymouth firmly in the same league with Ford and Chevrolet, Fred Rockelman bowed out as divi-

The Plymouth PE DeLuxe convertible coupe for 1934

1934 Plymouth PE DeLuxe two-door sedan sold at $610.

1934 Plymouth PG Standard business coupe: $485.

1934 Plymouth PE DeLuxe town sedan: $695.

that became his main research interest for a time. Owen Skelton was mainly concerned with engine development in 1930-33, investigating high-compression cylinder heads and hemispherical combustion chambers. Carl Breer was up to his ears in the Airflow.

It was almost too late to change anything for the 1934 Plymouth chassis when Chrysler's engineers got wind of GM's "Knee Action." Chrysler was not engaged in industrial espionage; it found out simply because of casual contacts between friends and neighbors who happened to be working for rival companies. But once the word was out,

1934 Plymouth PE DeLuxe four-door sedan. Price: $660.

Chrysler knew it had to reply immediately. Though there is no proof that GM's actual suspension drawings were smuggled to Chrysler, the Highland Park engineers likely worked from freehand sketches on the backs of used envelopes.

Chrysler's chief chassis engineer was still Harry T. Woolson, who had been around since 1921 at the Maxwell company. It was his assistant, A. G. Herreshoff, who became manager of the independent front suspension project. Born into America's best-known family of yacht builders, Herreshoff graduated from the Massachusetts Institute of Technology, then gave up a career in naval engineering to work as a draftsman with the Edwards Motor Car company beginning in 1911. After spending six years with Mack Truck and shorter periods with Bethlehem Truck and the Fifth Avenue Coach Company in New York, he spent four years as an engine development engineer at Rushmore Laboratories. He moved to Chrysler in 1928, when Fred Zeder put him in charge of engineering for Dodge and Fargo trucks. From 1930 to 1933 he was responsible for coordinating production between the company's various makes and reducing the number of parts unique to each. In 1934 he became the firm's executive engineer for design development.

Chrysler's new independent front suspension was not reserved for Plymouth but also found its way into this year's Chrysler Six and the entire 1934 Dodge line. Because it was a rush job, it saw little testing. Road testing had just come under the aegis of Paul C. Ackermann, who had been with Maxwell in 1922-24, then left for a time, returning to Chrysler Corporation this year. He continued as road-test director up to 1938, when he acquired additional responsibilities as supervising engineer for car testing, engine development, and the general labs. Ackermann returned too late to be involved with the new ifs, so it was Swedish-born experimental engineer Tore Franzen who saw the idea through its hurried testing phase. Despite the rush, the ifs suffered no serious service problems in customer use, so Herreshoff and Franzen had obviously done their homework. This makes it all the more curious, then, that Chrysler reverted to non-independent front suspension for Plymouth, Dodge, and the low-end Chryslers beginning with the 1935 models.

Herreshoff's work on streamlining the corporate engine roster continued to pay dividends, and the list was shortened from eight to six basic units this year. The 190- and 224-cid sixes disappeared along with the 274- and 282-cid straight eights. The crankshaft from the Chrysler 224 was combined with a bigger-bore block to create a 241.5-cid six used for the DeSoto Airflow and the conventionally styled Chrysler CA and CB. A new 323.5-cid eight was created for the CV/CX Imperial Airflow by boring out the 299.

Dodge and Plymouth styling moved cautiously toward streamlining for 1934—nothing as radical as the Airflow, but definitely smoother and more modern. Skirted fenders and "potato" window shapes were more in evidence, and the Dodges were particularly handsome with their longer chassis and a restyled, Cadillac-like radiator. The all-six-cylinder lineup comprised the DR-series Deluxe and DRXX New Standard models on a 117-inch wheelbase and the prestige DS Special on a 121-inch span. Prices ranged from $645 for the New Standard business coupe to $875 for the Special convertible sedan.

Completely overshadowed by the Airflows were this year's six-cylinder Chryslers that, as noted, literally saved the division's hide. There were now two series instead of one, the entry-level CA on a 117-inch wheelbase and the 121-inch-wheelbase Custom Six Series CB. The latter was roughly equivalent to the Dodge DS, and offered the same two body styles, a close-coupled sedan and convertible sedan. As a matter of fact, the six-cylinder Chryslers shared the Dodge chassis, including steering and suspension, and bore similar evidence of streamlining within a more traditional styling approach than the Airflow's.

An oft-ignored fact about 1934 is that Chrysler Corporation actually made money for the year despite the Airflow's underwhelming sales performance. It was, to be sure, a mixed year for the industry as a whole. Though total car sales rose to about 1.9 million units, a number of makes were in trouble. Studebaker and Willys-Overland were both in receivership, and moved just 41,560 and 6600 cars, respectively. Hudson could manage no more than 60,000 (including Terraplane) and Nash failed to exceed 25,000 even with its low-cost six-cylinder LaFayette. Two revered makes, Stutz and Marmon, went out of business, and stalwart Franklin was on its last legs.

But Walter P. Chrysler's corporation was making money again. Now he could count on meeting his payroll and the interest on his debts. More importantly, he could plan ahead for future expansion.

1935

At the end of 1934, Walter P. Chrysler looked ahead to a year of expansion. He also looked ahead to changing in his own role within the company he had founded, for he was approaching 60 and wanted to let his lieutenants take over tactical command. So, he turned the presidency of Chrysler Corporation over to K. T. Keller in 1935, which brought a certain realignment among the other directors. Included were B. E. "Hutch" Hutchinson's appointment as chairman of the finance committee and Fred M. Zeder's being named board vice-chairman.

In the darkest days of 1934—in the early spring, when it first became clear that Airflow was going to be harder to sell to Americans than refrigerators to Eskimos—Walter Chrysler had decided that further cost cutting would be imperative. He called a meeting of his top-level executives and told them he wanted budget reductions of not less than 30 percent. Nobody argued, but then nobody wanted to cut their particular activity. Zeder said that instead of cutting it back, the engineering effort must be doubled to stimulate future demand. Keller said he had to have more money for new buildings, tools, and machinery. There were mutterings from the sales department about funds for new marketing studies, which would surely pay off in time. And so it went.

As Reginald M. Cleveland and S. T. Williamson tell the story in their book, *The Road is Yours:* "Chrysler listened patiently for a couple of hours, then turned to Hutchinson. 'Haven't we got a book which lists salaries and personnel?' 'Yes,' said Hutchinson, 'everybody from president to office boy is in it.' 'Let's see it,' said Chrysler. When the book arrived, he riffled its pages and held it up. 'Well,' he said, 'that's about one-third. Suppose we lay off everybody from here down?' 'Oh, Mr. Chrysler,' the chorus wailed, 'don't you think that's a hell of a way to cut expenses?' 'Sure!' he said. 'But you fellows haven't suggested anything else, and you will admit my way will work, won't you?' 'He gave us the night to think the thing over,' K. T. Keller related, 'and I will say that the next day an excellent job was done.'" A year later the corporation was debt-free, having weathered the depths of the Depression to pay off obligations totaling almost $60 million. Said *Fortune* magazine: "Rarely in any industry at any time does a late starter, entering competition at a time when the windward berths are all occupied and stretches of open water are scarce, drive so quickly into a commanding position."

But what sort of president now commanded this successful "late starter?" Having a production man at the helm had become something of a trend in the auto industry by this time, what with William S. Knudsen as president of General Motors and Charles E. Sorensen as Henry Ford's right hand. K. T. Keller did not try to be part of everything that went on. He kept close to the product, which held a particular attraction for him, but when he delegated authority to someone he usually left that person alone. Keller explained his attitude this way:

1935 Chrysler Airstream (left) and Airflow Imperial prototypes

1935 Chrysler C-1 Airflow 6-passenger coupe: $1245.

1935 Chrysler C-1 Airflow 6-passenger coupe

"There is nobody alive who can sit around and keep track of everything. That kind of superman does not live in this world. What we have to do is to break it down into the size package that a man of ability can handle. We think of our business as plants and departments and activities. It is important to think of it also as men who are running the plants for us and still other men who are helping them to do the job." Note Keller's awareness of human factors, the need for job satisfaction, opportunities for promotion, better pay, and so on. Though he was a man devoted to machinery, he was not a robot. He was well organized, and he always found time to reflect on all aspects of a question, on all consequences of an action.

Most of Chrysler Corporation's 1935 business moves had been arranged by Walter Chrysler. Acknowledging the growing importance of comfort among car buyers, he had laid the groundwork in 1934 for the purchase of Airtemp, Inc., an air-conditioning and heating equipment manufacturer. This year the corporation acquired the former Wills Sainte Claire factory in Marysville, Michigan, and also opened a new Plymouth/Dodge assembly plant in Evansville, Indiana.

While K. T. Keller might have preferred to drop the controversial Airflow, he knew that Walter Chrysler was strongly in favor of it, so he decided to try to salvage it, somehow. There was no question about its mechanical integrity or construction quality, just the styling—or rather the lack of it. Although no one has stepped forward to claim design credit for the Airflow, Carl Breer and Oliver Clark are said to have cooked it up between them, with perhaps some minor retouching here and there by the Budd people. Regardless, consultant Norman Bel

1935 Airflow and Airstream shared the same assembly lines.

1935 Chryslers and DeSotos await shipment in Highland Park.

Geddes was now asked to do what he could to fix it. Detroit's lead times are long, however, and it takes several years to alter a plan once it's in motion. Chrysler had banked heavily on the Airflow's success to inspire the design and sales of its cheaper makes. But with the car going nowhere and time short, a hasty regrouping was all the firm could manage for 1935.

Nevertheless, the Airflow got some badly needed sales support this year, and it came from two directions. First, both DeSoto and Chrysler versions were modestly face-lifted, with extended hoodlines, more conventional grilles, and more prominent hood side louvers, all courtesy of Bel Geddes and intended to minimize the snub-nose look of the '34s. The waterfall radiator was replaced on the Chryslers by a handsome vee'd prow that was strikingly close to the front-end treatment of the production Lincoln-Zephyr that was still a year away. The DeSoto grille was a more elliptical affair, with a rounded top and vertical bars bisected by four, slim, irregularly spaced crossbars. Wheelbases were unchanged and mechanical modifications were few on all Airflows. The DeSoto was designated Series SG. Chrysler's nomenclature read C-1, C-2 Imperial, and C-3 Custom Imperial (the 146.5-inch-wheelbase models were still called CW).

But the big news for 1935 was more conventional "Airstream" styling in two new companion lines for both Chrysler and DeSoto. These cars shared most body panels with this year's restyled Plymouth and Dodge. All were largely the work of famed designer Raymond H. Dietrich, who joined the Chrysler styling staff in 1934. In the Twenties, Dietrich had founded the renowned LeBaron Carrossiers of New York with Ralph Roberts and Tom Hibbard. The firm later merged with the Bridgeport Body Company, and both were taken over by Briggs Manufacturing Company in 1928. Dietrich did not stay with Briggs, choosing instead to set up his own styling studio in Detroit. In this venture he was sponsored by the Murray Corporation, another body builder, and was expected to work mainly on Ford and Lincoln projects. It wasn't long before he was working in Highland Park. The important thing about Dietrich's arrival at Chrysler is that he almost singlehandedly elevated the Art & Colour department to the same level of importance as Engineering.

The Airstream's speedy completion and quick production startup was a dramatic demonstration of Chrysler's ability to respond quickly to changing market conditions. More importantly, this car was the firm's reply to those

1935 Chrysler CZ Airstream Eight DeLuxe touring sedan

1935 Chrysler CZ Airstream Eight DeLuxe touring sedan

1935 DeSoto SG Airflow sedan at the Indianapolis 500

Prototype for the 1935 DeSoto SG Airflow four-door sedan

buyers who wanted a Chrysler or DeSoto but were put off by the Airflow. The Airstream design was nowhere nearly as radical, of course, but its basic theme included pontoon fenders, raked-back radiators, teardrop headlamp pods, and other streamlining "cues." Overall, there was a strong family resemblance with the Airflow, yet the Airstream wasn't as far out and was thus far more acceptable. Not surprisingly, it literally carried both divisions in the mid-Thirties.

Because the Airstream was intended to attract far more buyers than the Airflow, it arrived in a broad array of models, with no fewer than five different wheelbases and a choice of six- or eight-cylinder power. The DeSoto Airstream, Series SF, shared its 116-inch-wheelbase chassis and most suspension components with the 1935 Dodge DU series. There were base models and fancier DeLuxe offerings, including two- and four-door sedans with and without trunks. Power was provided by the 241.5-cid inline six fitted to the Chrysler equivalent, the Series C-6, which differed mainly in having a two-inch longer chassis. Exclusive to Chrysler was an eight-cylinder Airstream, the Series CZ, mounting the familiar 274-cid power unit. This lineup comprised standard and Deluxe models on a 121-inch wheelbase, plus a Deluxe

seven-passenger sedan riding a 133-inch platform. Airstream prices were quite a bit downstream of comparable Airflows. The DeSoto Airstream four-door sedan, for example, cost over $220 less than its Airflow counterpart, while the Chrysler CZ four-door came in $260 below the closest straight-eight Airflow C-1.

Though Dodge and Plymouth didn't play up the Airstream theme as much as their sister divisions, their 1935 cars bore much the same look, with definite GM overtones in each case. Dodge was adding a lot of sales gravy to Plymouth's meat and potatoes, but the make's commercial importance wasn't reflected in this year's lineup. There was now just the single Series DU, advertised as the "New Value Six," with a choice of six basic body styles plus two long sedans on a 128-inch wheelbase. The price spread was $645 to just under $1000. Dodge observed a milestone during 1935 with production of its 3-millionth passenger car.

After all the hoopla about independent front suspension the year before, both Plymouth and Dodge reverted to rigid front axles on semi-elliptic leaf springs for 1935. However, the springs were made of a new kind of steel that delivered a smooth ride comparable to that afforded by the ifs. This year's Plymouth lineup consisted of three

1935 DeSoto SF Airstream four-door sedan: $795

1935 DeSoto SF Airstream convertible coupe. Price: $835.

The $695 DeSoto SF Airstream business coupe for 1935

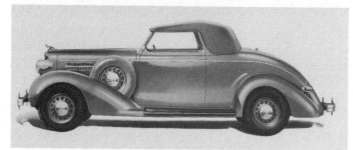

1935 Dodge DU New Value Six convertible coupe: $770.

1935 Dodge DU New Value Six four-door sedan. Price: $735.

Dodge reached a milestone with this 1935 DU touring sedan.

series, all carrying the PJ code designation and sharing a 113-inch wheelbase. Beginning in January, a less expensive Business coupe and two- and four-door sedans supplanted the coupe and two-door sedan initially offered in the Standard line. The volume seller was the DeLuxe, with a full range of body types priced from $575 to $765,

plus two long-wheelbase sedans listing at $895 each. The most expensive standard-chassis model was the Westchester Suburban wood-body station wagon. This was not strictly a factory offering but a conversion carried out by the U.S. Body & Forging Company of Tell City, Indiana.

Although Carl Breer felt he shouldn't be blamed for the Airflow's poor sales, he was nevertheless bothered by his close identification with the design. What he wanted now was to be identified with a winner, a new car that would make people forget about the Airflow—and everyone connected with it. Taking his cue from Keller's interest in the 100-inch-wheelbase project (see 1933), he began devoting a lot of attention to small-car engineering. He had seen the Willys 77, of course, and was familiar with the American Austin, which later evolved into the American Bantam. He also studied the layout and construction of several European cars that Chrysler had purchased for comparative evaluation. At the time, no one in Detroit could be certain that the Depression was over, and for Breer it was not unthinkable that the American public would turn to smaller cars in the event of a sudden economic downturn. It thus became his responsibility to make sure that if the market sagged, Chrysler would be ready with more intelligent small cars than its rivals.

Actually, both Ford and General Motors were designing and testing a variety of small cars around Detroit in the early Thirties, but these were destined for their European subsidiaries. GM had acquired England's Vauxhall in 1926 and added Opel of Germany in 1929. Ford fielded the small Y-model Junior in 1932 to supplement the Model A being produced at its British plant in Dagenham. But Breer's concepts went far beyond anything contemplated for near-term production by European mass-producers or Chrysler's American rivals. After securing a reasonable budget for small-car studies, he outlined his broad ideas to a trusted assistant, Ken Lee, who took charge of the project with a small group of designers and test engineers.

A central idea in Breer's small-car concept was an engine and drivetrain combined into a very compact unit. The main impetus for this was that it would save weight, but it would also permit maximum design freedom. Engineers working on advanced designs are supposed to be free of the constraints imposed by mass production considerations, but this time they really let their imaginations run wild, envisioning front-wheel drive and a five-cylinder radial engine. The engine's cylinder formation suggested the project name: Star Car.

The interest in front drive came not from the fwd Millers that won so many races at Indy and elsewhere, nor from production front-drivers like Ruxton or the Cord L-29, which had stirred up a general awareness of it. The attraction for Lee and Breer was the layout's packaging advantages for a smaller car, not to mention the superior traction it afforded. They did not like the rear-engine layout for the usually well-known reasons of weight distribution and atypical handling characteristics. Because the entire powertrain would be situated at the front of the chassis, the seating compartment could be solidly within the wheelbase, as on the Airflow.

In profile, the Star Car prototype bore a striking resem-

1935 Plymouth PJ DeLuxe four-door touring sedan: $685

1935 Plymouth PJ DeLuxe four-door touring sedan

blance to the contemporary Lancia Aprilia from Italy. Overall dimensions were similar, but the American, surprisingly enough, had the shorter wheelbase (100 versus 110 inches). For sheer ingenuity, the Star Car was almost the Lancia's equal. The reason Chrysler did not go ahead with it had nothing to do with its manufacturing practicality. Lancia *knew* the European market would eagerly embrace the Aprilia, while Chrysler knew just as well that American buyers would reject the Star Car.

As for the radial engine, it was not so much unheard of as just rare. Adams-Farwell had offered one in 1905, as did North-Lucas in 1923, both rear-mounted air-cooled units with the cylinder axes arrayed horizontally. The Star Car radial was water-cooled, and it was mounted at the front with a 30-degree tilt to the rear. That tilt served a dual purpose: it left adequate ground clearance for the bottom cylinders without raising the engine's center of gravity, and it permitted an equal tilt for the radiator, which yielded a lower hoodline. Clutch and flywheel were mounted on the back end of the crankshaft. The transmission shaft went straight through a hollow final-drive pinion to a three-speed gearbox, which had an output shaft integral with the worm-drive pinion shaft. This placed the differential in line with the wheel hubs and the gearbox inboard of the wheel axis, so as to counterbalance engine weight. This power package was not only

compact but also very light, about 440 pounds including gearbox and differential. Although the engine's bore and stroke have never been revealed, cylinder volume is known to have been about 67 cubic inches and maximum output about 36 bhp. An L-head design, like all Chrysler production engines of this era, the radial had a separate head and chain-driven camshaft for each cylinder. One of the camshafts drove an accessory shaft that turned an oil pump at the lower end (an oil tank was carried below the crankcase) and the distributor on top. The cooling fan was bolted to a flange on the nose of the crankshaft, with a separate V-belt drive to the generator, while the water pump was gear-driven from another camshaft. A single Carter carburetor fed the mixture from a manifold mounted atop the engine.

Carl Breer's small-car thinking naturally included unit body/chassis construction evolved from Airflow principles. For the Star Car he devised what we would now call a space-frame, made up of square-section steel tubes forming a cage or skeleton, to which the body panels were attached. The first prototype had a primitive cobbled-up body, almost military in its starkness and absence of curves. A second, more finished car wore a pretty Airflow-style body penned by Ted Pietsch, who was not on Henry King's staff but had been hired by Breer in 1934 to help develop futuristic body designs.

1935 Plymouth PJ DeLuxe Westchester Suburban wagon

1935 Plymouth PJ two-door sedan with 20-inch wheels

1935 Plymouth PJ two-door business sedan. Note rear door.

The Star Car's chassis components were created by Ed Shea, one of Chrysler's top suspension engineers, with help from Robert Janeway and A. G. Herreshoff. Frederick William Slack, who came to Chrysler this year after 22 years with Peerless, was put to work on prototype construction in Breer's department. A chassis engineer rather than an engine man, Slack was also a good project manager who could be counted on to produce results. The compact's independent front suspension was quite modern and based on well-founded principles. Long triangular lower control arms were employed, with pivot points below the inner universal joints so that the arms' swinging arcs conformed to that of the driveshafts. The upper kingpin bearings held brackets for the eyes of a transverse leaf spring, which crossed the chassis above the differential. This setup gave a high degree of roll stiffness, and no anti-roll bar was deemed necessary. Telescopic shock absorbers were mounted vertically on the lower arms, ahead of the outer universal joints and as close to the wheel hubs as practical. Rear geometry was non-independent. The hubs were linked by a straight tube located by trailing arms, and a transverse leaf spring was bolted to a structural crossmember at its center, an arrangement that also assured excellent roll stiffness.

All of the Big Three's small-car projects would ultimately be sidetracked by the economic recovery that began in the early Forties as the nation began gearing up for war. Preoccupied with military production, Chrysler broke up its Star Car prototypes sometime during World War II, and wouldn't get around to another compact for some 15 years. Both Ford and Chevrolet reactivated their small-car programs toward the end of the war, this time with a definite eye to U.S. sale. As it turned out, there was no need for either of these scaled-down but conventionally engineered designs in the booming seller's market of early-postwar America. However, the efforts did lead to models badly needed overseas. Ford's domestic "Light Car" evolved into the French-made Vedette, and Chevrolet's proposed Cadet became the basis for the late-Forties Holden produced by GM's Australian subsidiary.

The Star Car could have been a viable proposition. Each of the prototypes covered some 200,000 test miles with a clean bill of health, and the basic design was a modern one that could have lasted well into the Forties and maybe beyond. But, as in the postwar era, a recovering market rendered such a car unnecessary. Total industry sales for 1935 climbed to 2.7 million units, the first time in several years the tally had pushed past the 2-million mark. General Motors scored 1.05 million deliveries, Ford 829,000. Chrysler continued its advance largely on the strength of the Airstream's strong public acceptance, the Airflow accounting for only about 20 percent of Chrysler and DeSoto volume. The make-by-make breakdown for the year shows Dodge's strong comeback as well as Plymouth's still-growing popularity:

Chrysler	40,536
Plymouth	382,985
DeSoto	26,952
Dodge	178,770
Total	629,243

Chrysler Corporation recorded a good profit for 1935. It was now poised to overtake ailing Ford Motor Company as the industry's number-two producer.

1936

Every now and then, every automaker has a "non-year," a year with no product developments worth talking about. Engineering departments may not need such breathers, but the consumer often benefits in that workmanship tends to improve the longer a model is in production without significant change. Just ask any Volkswagen Beetle owner.

For Chrysler Corporation, 1936 was kind of a "non-year." Both Chrysler and DeSoto retained several Airflows in their lineups, but the conventionally styled and much more saleable Airstreams got all the emphasis and Ray Dietrich was emerging as the top man in the Art & Colour section. There were no new engines this year, so the corporate stable continued with three sixes and three eights. However, the company's switch from spiral-bevel to hypoid rear axles, which began with the 1935 models,

The Chrysler C-9 Airflow 6-passenger coupe for 1936

was completed this season. Plymouth had always had a class exclusive in its hydraulic brakes, which put pressure on Chevrolet and Ford to follow. The former finally did this year, but Ford wouldn't get around to it until 1939. Plymouth was still the only one of the low-price three with Floating Power, though, just as Chevrolet was the only one with a valve-in-head six and synchromesh transmission. Ford's exclusives were not as convincing from the sales standpoint: transverse-leaf-spring suspension front and rear and the flathead V-8.

This year's Chrysler line comprised five series (down one from 1935): C-7 Six and C-8 DeLuxe Eight Airstreams and C-9, C-10 Imperial, and C-11 Custom Imperial Airflows. Wheelbases were unchanged. A minor facelift for the Airstreams brought more barrel-like grille shapes, revamped headlamp pods, and reworked hood louvers. Airflows got a similar freshening, though it wasn't as immediately apparent. This would be the last year for the Imperial version of Chrysler's controversial "car of the future."

This would also be the last year for DeSoto's Airflow, now known as the Series S-2 Airflow III and offered in just two models, four-door sedan and five-seat coupe/sedan. Once again an attempt was made to improve appearance via detail trim changes, mostly at the front, but it was a halfhearted gesture. The bulk of DeSoto's 1936 volume came from the Airstream Series S-1, which offered an expanded lineup of DeLuxe and Custom models priced from $695 to $1095. All DeSoto Airstreams now rode the 118-inch Chrysler chassis, and a trio of long sedans on a 130-inch platform appeared under this badge for the first time. "Touring" sedans with integrated trunks were more widely available, and all models bore cosmetic retouching similar to that of their Chrysler counterparts. DeSoto advertising touted the Airstreams' "custom design," an indirect reference to Ray Dietrich's presence in the styling studio.

Dodge applied more extensive appearance alterations to its 1936 models, though in the wake of the Airflow debacle the changes were predictably evolutionary. Once again the division fielded but one series, designated D-2 and advertised as the "Beauty Winner," with the same body style offerings as before. Wheelbases, mechanicals, and prices were all roughly as for the '35s.

A cutaway Chrysler Airflow exhibited at 1936 auto show

1936 Chrysler C-9 Airflow four-door sedan: $1345.

The '36 Chrysler C-9 Airflow four-door from the rear

There was little need to tamper with the winning Plymouth formula, but the 1936s nevertheless claimed more than 40 improvements. Bodywork became more closely aligned with that of Dodge and the Airstream DeSoto, with rounded vertical radiators, bullet-shaped

1936 Chrysler C-10 Airflow Imperial four-door sedan

1936 Chrysler C-7 Airstream Six convertible coupe

1936 Chrysler C-8 Airstream DeLuxe Eight town car by LeBaron

1936 DeSoto S-2 Airflow III coupe. List price was $1095.

Only 8 of the 1936 Airstream town cars were built.

1936 DeSoto S-1 Airstream Custom touring sedan: $865.

1936 Chrysler C-7 Airstream Six convertible sedan

1936 DeSoto S-1 Airstream Custom convertible coupe

headlamp pods, and fully skirted fenders. The three long-wheelbase sedans returned from 1935 on a three-inch shorter chassis (125 inches) while other models retained the 113-inch size. Prices stayed the same, but Plymouth made a more obvious play for the commercial market by labelling its lower model group the "Business" series, officially P-1. The more popular DeLuxe line was coded P-2, and included the long-wheelbase trio. The year also brought a new ad slogan, "Plymouth Builds Great Cars." It proved highly effective, and would be retained well into the Forties.

This may have been a quiet year for Chrysler Corporation products, but the firm was the proverbial beehive of activity in other areas. After years of being shunted between Chrysler and Plymouth facilities, DeSoto finally got its own "home" plant this year. The announcement came in July from K. T. Keller, and Herman L. Weckler was put in charge of laying out the new factory and supervising its construction. Built at a cost of $5 million, it was ready for occupancy by September, situated on 42 acres

on Wyoming Avenue in Dearborn, just south of the Graham-Paige complex. Initial production capacity was 500 units a day with a workforce of 2500. Besides complete assembly of all DeSotos, this plant was kept very busy producing heaters for all Chrysler Corporation divisions and providing sheetmetal stampings for Plymouth, DeSoto, and Chrysler as well as Dodge trucks.

When the new DeSoto factory came on stream, Weckler became division general manager. He was an old friend of Keller's, the two having worked together at Buick for many years. Previously, Weckler had been with the American Locomotive Company, where he got to know Walter Chrysler, who brought him to Buick in 1912. He joined Chrysler Corporation as an assistant to the general manager in 1932, and would be named Chrysler Division general manager in 1940. Meantime, the task of planning the next DeSotos was given to Irving Woolson, newly named this year as the division's chief engineer. Formerly of Dodge Truck, he came to the Plymouth engineering department in 1934 and was named that division's top

DeSoto's 1936 S-1 Airstream DeLuxe business coupe

1936 Dodge D-2 Westchester Suburban commercial wagon

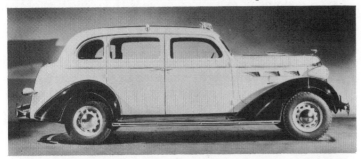

A prototype taxi on the long 1936 DeSoto S-1 chassis

The $620 Plymouth P-2 DeLuxe convertible coupe for 1936

1936 Dodge D-2 "Beauty Winner" 7-passenger sedan

1936 Plymouth P-1 Business 2-passenger coupe: $510.

engineer the following year. He would retain his job at DeSoto through 1943, when he turned to planning and supervising the DeSoto plant's war material production.

This year also saw several engineering appointments destined to have long-lasting effects. Robert N. Janeway was named director of the dynamic research department, and began a scientific study of why cars behave the way they do on the road. In the course of the following five years, he developed suspension systems with reduced friction and vibration, invented the constant-friction

Plymouth's 1936 P-1 Business coupe with utility box

1936 Plymouth P-2 DeLuxe 7-passenger sedan. Price: $895.

1937

Body drop for a 1936 Plymouth P-2 DeLuxe coupe

shock absorber, and took out a number of patents on ride and handling improvements. Also this year, K. T. Keller made Fred Lamborn vice president of manufacturing for Dodge and installed a 26-year-old engineer named George Huebner as assistant chief engineer at Plymouth. Huebner had started with Chrysler as an experimental engineer in 1931, assigned to the mechanical laboratories under Jim Zeder (who was married to Huebner's sister). He stayed with Plymouth for three years, then went back to the labs as assistant director of research. On the executive roster, P. C. Sauerbrey, another Keller appointee, became Plymouth Division general manager in 1936. Unfortunately, the division would lose him after less than four years, for he died in 1940.

Chrysler Corporation could well afford to undertake ambitious investments in 1936. The company showed a net profit for the year of $62,110,000 and paid out $2.3 million in year-end bonus money. The firm's glowing financial health reflected the gathering momentum of a recovery that was returning most of Detroit to solvency. Studebaker and Willys-Overland came out of receivership, Nash gained new strength by merging with appliance power Kelvinator, Hudson was back in the black, and Packard moved ahead on positive public response to its low-priced One-Twenty. Total industry sales for the year swelled to 3.4 million units, the highest volume since 1929. Chrysler Corporation set a record for annual production, topping a million vehicles for the first time to move decisively ahead of Ford Motor Company. The make-by-make registrations were as follows:

Chrysler	58,698
Plymouth	499,580
DeSoto	45,088
Dodge	248,518
Total	851,884

General Motors sales climbed to 1.5 million cars, but Ford could do no better than 764,000. Suddenly, Chrysler Corporation was a *big* Number Two.

Chrysler Corporation attacked 1937 from a position of strength. The Airflow was in its final year, and the firm had more than recovered from that miscalculation, aided by the general industry recovery and Plymouth's sparkling sales. This year, all the company's makes boasted new styling, though they were mechanically much the same as before. Meantime, Chrysler continued to pour profits back into its physical facilities while moving key personnel into strategic new posts. The year's main plant expansion came with acquisition of the Kokomo, Indiana factory that once belonged to the Haynes Automobile Company. It was earmarked as a transmission manufacturing operation for Dodge Division.

Walter Chrysler had always maintained that it was better for an automaker to manufacture key components rather than relying on outside suppliers, mainly because it avoided "middle men" with their needless markups. Yet it was Chrysler who, back in 1917, had tried to prove to William C. Durant that he could save $1500 by contracting with A. C. Smith of Milwaukee to manufacture Buick frames instead of spending $6 million on setting up a chassis factory. Was Chrysler now contradicting himself? Not at all. Any component supplier can be profitable given sufficient volume, which can come from several different customers. But a car company is, in a sense, its own best customer for most of whatever parts it chooses to make, since these are normally unique to its products and therefore unsaleable to most competitors. There have been numerous exceptions to this principle down through the years. In general, though, an automaker's decision on whether to make certain components hinges on whether anticipated volume is high enough to offset their production costs. And that varies with the component, its complexity and anticipated "service life," and the cost of raw materials, machinery, storage, and freight.

Chrysler had not been satisfied with the Briggs-engineered bodies of its 1935-36 models, so for 1937 it engineered new bodies for all its makes, though Briggs still built most of them. By this time, Chrysler also had some body stamping, welding, and finishing facilities of its own. Boasting one-piece roof construction, the '37 bodyshells would be retained with a minor facelift for 1938 and with a major one for 1939.

Ray Dietrich was still in charge of styling, and Chrysler Corporation's 1937 cars bore his imprint. This year he adopted a rounded-curve theme and used minor trim differences—grilles, hood vents, moldings, and other body hardware—to set the various makes apart from one another. He also supervised the final facelift for the ill-starred Airflow, which was now restricted to a single two-model series in the Chrysler line. Designated Series C-17, it was built on the 128-inch-wheelbase chassis of the previous Airflow Imperial Eight, and sported a gently raked and rounded front, both of which made this arguably the best-looking Airflow of all. And oddly enough, the basic design no longer looked so odd in its

1937 Chryslers were popular with Great Lakes Naval officers.

1937 Chrysler C-16 Royal Six coupe. List price was $860.

1937 Chrysler C-14 Imperial Eight convertible sedan

1937 Chrysler C-16 Royal Six 7-seat sedan. Just 138 were built.

$1100 bought this '37 Chrysler C-14 Imperial Eight sedan.

fourth year on the market. Time had finally caught up with the Airflow, and the styling elements that had seemed so radical in 1934 were now more or less established design orthodoxy in Detroit. Perhaps it hadn't been so "wrong" after all.

Corporate engine availability was simplified this year by restricting straight eights to Imperials and the lone Airflow series and discontinuing the 385-cubic-inch eight. Everything else on the model roster was powered by an L-head six. The workhorse 241.6-cid six was replaced by a short-stroke 228-cid version of same for the DeSoto and the low-end Chrysler.

Plymouth arrived on a one-inch shorter wheelbase (112 inches) for 1937, but the cars looked longer thanks to revised hood/body proportions courtesy of Dietrich. The

engine, still the old-faithful 201.3-cid six, was pushed six inches forward in the chassis, and a stabilizer bar appeared between the front wheels. The same array of body styles returned in two series, the P-3 Business and P-4 DeLuxe. The latter still included a seven-passenger sedan and limousine, but their wheelbase was an even longer 132 inches, up seven from their 1936 counterparts. There were no noteworthy mechanical changes for any '37 Plymouth. Prices averaged about $15 higher than in '36, perhaps reflecting the country's return to "good times"— at least compared to recent years. Along with other Chrysler Corporation makes, Plymouth stressed a "safety-styled" interior this year, featuring recessed control knobs and a rounded-off lower edge for the dash, plus a roll of "crash" padding on the front seatbacks and

1937 Chrysler C-15 Custom Imperial convertible coupe by Derham

The $880 DeSoto S-3 touring sedan for 1937

1937 Chrysler C-17 was the final Airflow. Sedan is shown.

1937 DeSoto S-3 convertible sedan (Indy 500 pace car)

1937 DeSoto S-3 convertible coupe: $975.

1937 Dodge D-5 touring sedan with optional two-toning

interior door handles curved inward so as to avoid snagging occupants' clothes. A blower fan and hidden defroster vents became standard (the latter devised by interior designer Fred Selje). Plymouth marked another milestone this year with production of its 2-millionth car.

Dodge carried on with a single six-cylinder series, coded D-5. As at Plymouth, the seven-seat sedan and limousine returned on a longer chassis, in this case 132 inches (up four), while standard models lost an inch. Everything else stayed the same except prices, which were somewhat higher. The line-leader business coupe went from $640 to $715, while the attractive but slow-selling convertible sedan rose from $995 to a hefty $1230. As elsewhere in the industry, "trunkback" styles had far outstripped "trunkless" sedans in popularity by this time.

Many of the above comments also apply to this year's

DeSoto line, now bereft of the unlamented Airflow. DeLuxe and Custom models disappeared, as did use of the Airstream name, replaced by a single series designated S-3. The standard wheelbase shrank by two inches to 116 and the brace of long-chassis sedans was stretched three inches between wheel centers to 133, thus aligning DeSoto precisely with the six-cylinder '37 Chryslers. Overall appearance can be fairly described as lumpy, but DeSoto avoided Chrysler's ungainly "high-nose" look thanks to hood side trim artfully blended into the barrel-shaped radiator. Though it moved up only one notch in the industry standings, DeSoto recorded more than double its 1936 production volume for the model year.

Chrysler likewise abandoned the Airstream name for 1937 and carried out a similar model consolidation at the bottom of its lineup. The junior offerings were now sold

1937 Dodge D-5 convertible coupe. List price was $910.

1937 Dodge D-5 with wood-wagon commercial bodywork

1937 Dodge D-5 lwb 7-passenger sedan: $1075.

Plymouth's 1937 P-4 DeLuxe four-door touring sedan

1937 Plymouth P-4 four-door touring sedan sold at $755.

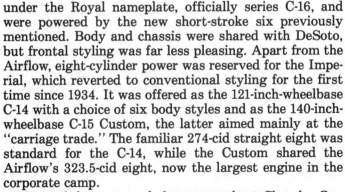

1937 Plymouth P-4 DeLuxe 7-passenger sedan: $995.

under the Royal nameplate, officially series C-16, and were powered by the new short-stroke six previously mentioned. Body and chassis were shared with DeSoto, but frontal styling was far less pleasing. Apart from the Airflow, eight-cylinder power was reserved for the Imperial, which reverted to conventional styling for the first time since 1934. It was offered as the 121-inch-wheelbase C-14 with a choice of six body styles and as the 140-inch-wheelbase C-15 Custom, the latter aimed mainly at the "carriage trade." The familiar 274-cid straight eight was standard for the C-14, while the Custom shared the Airflow's 323.5-cid eight, now the largest engine in the corporate camp.

Many of the personnel changes made at Chrysler Corporation during 1937 were logical promotions intended to keep certain senior executives from being overburdened.

Joe Fields, for example, had amassed so many titles and duties by this time that he felt he could no longer be effective as head of Chrysler Division. K. T. Keller accordingly let him concentrate on the head office and put Dave Wallace in charge in July. At DeSoto, Clarence E. Bleicher stepped in to replace president Herman Weckler, who left the division to assume a vice-presidency in the firm's industrial relations department. Starting at Maxwell in 1923, Bleicher had risen through the ranks to become a member of Keller's staff by 1930. Plymouth got a new general manufacturing manager in the person of E. S. Chapman, who would become division chief in 1940. He had joined Chrysler in 1928, when Keller made him staff master mechanic, the troubleshooter who was always sent out whenever a plant had a problem. Also this year, Texas-born Max Roensch, who had started in

1938

1937 Plymouth P-4 DeLuxe 2-passenger coupe. Price: $650.

Walter Chrysler in the millionth '36 car, a '37 Plymouth

the engine lab under J. B. Macauley in 1926, was named experimental engineer and head of the Highland Park engine laboratories. His work would never be seen by the public, but it enabled the firm to modernize its power units and prolong their production life.

On balance, Chrysler Corporation had a good, though not sensational, sales year in 1937. Though DeSoto leaped ahead and Chrysler advanced strongly, Dodge gained only fractionally and Plymouth sales actually dipped. Calendar year registrations are as follows:

Chrysler	91,622
Plymouth	462,268
DeSoto	74,424
Dodge	255,256
Total	883,570

In a market that stabilized at just under 3.5 million units, Chrysler stayed ahead of Ford, which retailed 791,176 cars. However, GM opened up its lead on Number Two by delivering some 1.4 million units.

On a model year basis, Chrysler Corporation's strength is more readily apparent. Plymouth was still a solid third behind Ford and Chevrolet, in that order, and number-four Dodge was comfortably ahead of Pontiac, Buick, and Oldsmobile. Chrysler, in ninth, trailed Packard by about 17,000 cars. DeSoto brought up the rear in 12th, but that was ahead of Nash, Willys, Hudson, and Graham, not to mention Lincoln and Cadillac/LaSalle. Highland Park had every reason to be optimistic about 1938.

At the beginning of 1938, no one in the auto industry could know that the year would bring a severe recession, which would cut auto sales nearly in half. Chrysler Corporation continued to prepare for sustained growth, however, as K. T. Keller and his crew could envision no other sort of future. A new Dodge truck plant built on Mound Road in Warren, Michigan, came on stream in October. At the same time, Keller appointed W. J. O'Neill as president and general manager of Dodge Division, while A. Van DerZee became a Chrysler Corporation vice-president. Robert Cadwallader replaced Ray Dietrich as top designer. Though he was outranked by Herb Weissinger, Cadwallader was known as the more creative artist, and enjoyed a free hand.

Overshadowing all other events of 1938 was the illness that struck Walter P. Chrysler on May 26th. From here on, he would no longer take any part in the management of the corporation he founded. Chrysler's wife died in the fall, and Walter spent the final two years of his life as an invalid. His death came on August 18, 1940. If his health had been failing, he had kept it to himself all along. If he was drained of energy and slowed down his pace, people thought it was due merely to a combination of age and prosperity. In 1937 he had told Boyden Sparkes, his biographer, that he was no longer to be regarded as one of those running Chrysler Corporation. What was he doing then? "Me? I'm just watching it," he said. His watch was cut cruelly short, but it was long enough to satisfy him that the company would stay on the course he had charted for as long as his hand-picked men were in command.

The company's 1938 cars were not strikingly different from their predecessors, but the year brought two significant technical improvements. One was Superfinish, which set a new standard for bearing surface smoothness. The second was a radical new option, Fluid Drive.

Superfinish was Chrysler's answer to a problem involved with shipping new cars over long distances. In storage or on a rail car, a car's static weight bore down on a few individual balls in its wheel bearings, and with time and motion pounded them into the races. As a result, the bearings would make clicking noises when the car was put into service. Dave Wallace realized that a "Brinelline" effect had occurred on the outer layer above the bare metal, and got the idea that the grinding "fuzz" on the race surface might be at fault. He asked his toolmaker to remove this material by hand from a few sets of new bearings, which were then installed on a few cars that were shipped to California. Factory representatives were on hand when the cars arrived. Each unit was unloaded and driven slowly down the road. None had any clicking noises. Encouraged by this evidence, Wallace met with his ball-bearing supplier and a machine-tool builder, which led to development of machines designed to produce much smoother bearing races. Chrysler called the process "Superfinish."

The first automatic Superfinish machine was built for the Timken Roller Bearing Company by a team from Ex-Cell-O headed by Hank Kreuger. By 1940, the process had been applied to all sorts of bearing surfaces in Chrysler components, from crankshaft main bearings to brake drums, distributor shafts to clutch pressure plates.

Fluid Drive was in no way a "me-too" reaction to Oldsmobile's semi-automatic transmission that had appeared in May 1937. Rather, it was the product of an independent, in-depth study and development program and was inspired by the same factors that led to GM's Hydra-Matic.

Hydraulic transmissions were not a new idea in the Thirties. Wilhelm von Pittler had experimented with a fluid coupling in Berlin in 1903. It was installed in the 1905 Hydromobil prototype in lieu of a friction clutch, in combination with a regular countershaft gearbox. Marine engineers picked up on the concept a lot more easily than the motor-vehicle crowd. It wasn't until 1926 that Harold Sinclair in England began to develop the Vulcan hydraulic coupling, which attracted the interest of Laurence H. Pomeroy, technical director of the Daimler Company. Some 1930 Daimler and Lanchester models featured a so-called "fluid flywheel," which was constructed so that it would not work correctly without a normal clutch between the coupling and the gearbox. For the first year or so, Daimler used a four-speed countershaft gearbox, but the arrangement wasn't fully satisfactory, so later cars were equipped with the Wilson planetary transmission.

General Motors started experimental work on fluid flywheels in 1932, a year after Fred Zeder had started a research project on automatic transmissions at Chrysler. The engineering brain behind Chrysler's Fluid Drive was Augustin "Gus" Syrovy, a Czechoslovakian who had emigrated to America in 1923. After brief stints at International Harvester and the Caterpillar Tractor Company, he came to Dodge and thus to Chrysler, where he launched his research into automatics in 1931. Familiar with both Hermann Fottinger's work and the Daimler fluid flywheel, he began testing low-cost adaptations of these designs, combining existing Chrysler components with a hydraulic coupling.

Fluid Drive employed a conventional manual gearbox and a pedal-operated plate clutch mounted behind the fluid coupling. The advantage of the coupling was that it provided smoother starts. Although gear selection still had to be done manually and demanded use of the clutch, Fluid Drive did obviate the need for most normal shifting. Top gear, for example, could be used to pull away from a standstill, though acceleration was necessarily quite leisurely. Another problem was that the coupling was, in a sense, too efficient—in other words, it did not really disengage, thus producing the "creep" now familiar in automatics. Chrysler minimized it by filling the coupling to only 80 percent of its fluid capacity.

Chrysler Corporation now had enough flexibility in its engine manufacturing operations that it could "juggle" individual power units in or out of production without much expense or downtime for retooling. Accordingly, this year saw a revival of the 241.5-cid six last seen for 1936, which brought the corporate engine count to four

1938 Chrysler C-18 Royal four-door touring sedan: $1010.

1938 Chrysler C-19 New York Special touring sedan

1938 Chrysler C-18 Royal convertible sedan. Price: $1425.

DeSoto's 1938 S-5 touring brougham two-door: $930

1938 Dodge D-8 convertible coupe. It cost $960 new.

1938 Dodge D-8 four-door touring sedan. Price: $910.

sixes and only two eights. Now called the "Gold Seal Six," the resurrected powerplant was installed in Chrysler's volume Royal series, now designated C-18 and built on three-inch longer wheelbases, 119 inches standard and 136 inches for the seven-seat sedan and limousine. The 274-cid straight eight was supplanted by a revived 299 for this year's Imperial series C-19, now built on a 125-inch wheelbase, up four inches over '37. A similar chassis stretch was applied to the 1938 series C-20 Custom Imperial, which retained its 323.5-cid eight.

Basic body styling on all 1938 Chryslers followed Ray Dietrich's well-established "Airstream" theme, but the awkward 1937 "face" was replaced by a more attractive design marked by a U-shaped, horizontal-bar radiator. Headlamps were relocated from the sides of the radiator shell to a lower position in the "catwalk" area between it

and the front fenders. A new hybrid offering for '38 was the New York Special, a five-passenger four-door sedan based on C-19 Imperial chassis and running gear but considered part of the Chrysler line. (A business coupe was planned but never actually built.) Identified by a slightly different, split grille, the Special carried a spiffy interior with full carpeting and upholstery tastefully color-keyed to exterior finish. Most people referred to this model simply as the "New Yorker." Chrysler would do the same for 1939, thus beginning a tradition that's with us yet.

DeSoto maintained its rank in the 1938 corporate hierarchy as a detrimmed, lower-priced edition of the Chrysler Royal, powered by a smaller six. This year's S-5 models paralleled the Royal in styling and dimensional alterations but continued with the 228-cid powerplant. Advertised as "America's Smartest Low-Priced Car," the

Ray Dietrich on Chrysler's Leaders: an Interview with Richard M. Langworth

The great coachbuilder Raymond H. Dietrich served as director of Chrysler Corporation's small styling department from 1932 through 1938. He left the company when Walter Chrysler did, for he was very much Chrysler's protege. His memories of company personalities were as vivid when I interviewed him in 1974 as they must have been in the 1930s.

"I first met Mr. Chrysler at the New York Automobile Salon in 1926 or 1927. He came up to me and said, 'I've gone through your exhibit. Will you come with me and tell me about your work?' That's how we met. WPC, to my way of thinking, was a gentleman all the way through, though a hard master. He knew what he was doing and how he was going to do it, but he had to fight with his engineers, as well as the public at times. Zeder and Skelton were always talking

about 'service' for cars—how much 'service' you'd get from this and that. Chrysler used to say, 'It reminds me of when I was a kid and my father would say, "take that cow down and get it serviced." They never let me in the barnyard but one day I peeked in, and now when I hear the word "service" I know somebody's getting just that.'

"There was dynamite in WP's step, his walk, his smile, and his piercing blue eyes. He never doubted what you would say to him, but he was always trying to get more out of you. The best times I remember were when he would spend mornings in the little design studio, discussing our clay models. It was always a matter of decoration: too much to put on, too little to take off. He would sit in my office and talk, with nobody around to second-guess him, and he'd talk about design, I think just to get

away from the pressures of the Engineering people. About half-past eleven he'd say 'How about having a frankfurter and a bottle of beer?', and we'd go out for lunch. He was that kind of man.

"I was head of design. That really meant I took all the working drafts and clays from Briggs back into Chrysler, and all was done under my supervision from the latter part of 1932 on. I didn't, however, have much to do with the Airflow. That was a purely mechanical design, an engineer's dream, simplifying all kinds of design rules. When they went to change something they had to change all of the construction, and I had to square that away. They couldn't sell those beetles, so I had to alter the front end on the later ones, give the trunk more accent to get away from the original flatness. They used 100-150 pounds of lead to change construction. It was still the beetle idea from the old Renaults. I never liked it and it had no practical value either, for it had never been wind-tunnel-tested.

"I never hit it off with the engineers, and I don't think Fred Zeder approved of my association with WPC, who often

1938 Plymouth P-6 DeLuxe convertible coupe: $850.

Plymouth's P-6 DeLuxe coupe for 1938, priced at $770

'38 DeSoto was a solid if stolid piece, good value but far from exciting.

The familiar "Dodge Brothers" insignia made its final appearance on this year's D-8 series, which offered the same body styles on wheelbases unchanged from 1937. A complete restyle added about a foot to overall length, but the cars looked little different anyway and carried no significant design changes. As at Chrysler and DeSoto, Dodge headlamps moved outboard to a lower position in the front fender "catwalk" area.

Plymouth retained high-mount headlamps and changed little in other areas for 1938—curious, considering the make was celebrating its 10th birthday (as was DeSoto). However, there were a few firsts. One was the addition of a station wagon as a regular catalog model, though this body style had been available on the Plymouth chassis to special order as early as 1934. Called Suburban, it was offered only in the upper-level DeLuxe series, designated P-6 this year, and except for the long-wheelbase seven-passenger sedan and limousine it was the most expensive offering in the line, priced at $880. Its body was all-wood from the cowl back (front-end sheetmetal was shared with other models) and required a lot of care to keep in sound condition. Glass windows all around could be ordered at extra cost to replace the normal side curtains, though front door glass was standard. There was no rear bumper at all, but the tailgate-mounted spare acted as sort of a substitute. Suburban bodywork was supplied by the U.S. Body & Forge Company of New York and Indiana.

A new Plymouth series for '38 was the Roadking, actually this year's P-5 Business line with a new name.

called me 'son.' In those days I liked a bottle of beer or a highball with my lunch, and one day, after lunch, Zeder called me into his office. He accused me of being drunk. The next day in front of Mr. Chrysler I walked up to him and saluted, and said, 'Sir, First Mate reporting sober.' 'He really gave it to you that time, didn't he Fred?' said Walter Chrysler.

"I remember that event because it was just before WPC died. He'd come up to Styling and asked if there was anything he should see. I told him I'd show him everything he *wasn't* supposed to see, and we went through tons of models under lock and key. He'd knock the locks off all the cases and look at them. It got to be about 11 and we adjourned for lunch. I said, 'You don't look well, Mr. Chrysler. Why don't you take it easy?' This was in 1938. Two weeks later I [resigned]. K. T. Keller was mad as hell, said they'd lost the best man they had, but he had no power to stop them. They were in and I was out.

"Walter Chrysler was a hard-working man, and like Edsel Ford a gentleman first. Like Edsel, he would be so helpful.

He'd lead you to an answer—not the one he wanted, but one that suited your problem. He was not a hard man to know. When he died, the automotive trade lost one of its greats. I was lucky to know him well, and I also got to know Mrs. Chrysler, his son-in-law Byron, his daughters and Walter Jr. I always felt that if the damn engineers would have left him alone he would have been able to enjoy himself a lot more. As it was, he'd always ask for something, and Engineering would say he couldn't have it.

"K. T. Keller, though I never worked directly with him, was much the same as Walter Chrysler. He understood. You couldn't pull the wool over his eyes. He was tough, but he had a sense of humor too.

"When I was at Dietrich, Inc. doing designs for Chryslers, he would come over and bring out a little pencil and act like he was going to write something on my drawings. 'Put that damn pencil away,' I'd say, 'Those are my drawings!' When I became associated with Chrysler and K. T. was president, he'd get the pencil out, but he wouldn't touch anything—and I'd just keep still. Finally

he'd say, 'What the hell is the matter with you? A couple years ago you'd have tore my head off if I tried to touch those drawings.' I said, 'K. T., these are *your* drawings now. You paid for 'em, and you can do anything you want with 'em!' And he laughed like the devil."

After leaving Chrysler, Dietrich became an independent consultant to the automotive industry. He helped Preston Tucker in the late Forties, and again when Tucker tried to make a comeback in the early Fifties. His postwar firm of Ray Dietrich, Inc. in Grand Rapids, Michigan, designed many bodies for prototype purposes, including Kaisers, Packards, Checkers, and Fords. He was a consultant in Ford Motor Company's Mark II Continental project. But no production postwar car was fully entitled to wear the Dietrich badge, though a few did; the Murray company owned the name and did what they pleased with it.

Dietrich retired in 1969, and moved with his wife to Albuquerque, New Mexico. He died there in March 1980 at the age of 86. Those of us privileged to have met the man will never forget him.

1938 Plymouth P-6 DeLuxe two-door touring sedan: $785.

1939 Chrysler C-22 Royal business coupe: $918.

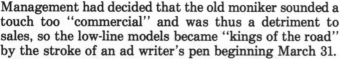

1938 Plymouth P-6 DeLuxe Westchester Suburban wagon

1939 Chrysler C-23 Imperial brougham. Price was $1165.

Management had decided that the old moniker sounded a touch too "commercial" and was thus a detriment to sales, so the low-line models became "kings of the road" by the stroke of an ad writer's pen beginning March 31.

Plymouth styling for 1938 was mostly a carryover of '37, with a slight redo for grille, headlamps, and hood ornament. Mechanical changes included a handbrake relocated from the middle of the floor to a position under the center of the dash, a revised clutch with reduced pedal release effort, and a new higher-geared steering system with roller-bearing kingpins for easier parking. Plymouth also marked one "last" for 1938: non-independent front suspension would be banished from here on.

The 1938 recession withered the total U.S. car market, which shrank back to 1934 size as deliveries again dropped below two million units. General Motors declined to 848,000 cars but managed to increase its market share by four points, while Ford dropped two percent on sales of 387,514 units, thus trailing Chrysler once again. Highland Park's penetration eased fractionally, but one out of every four new cars sold in the U.S. during 1938 bore the words "Made by Chrysler Corporation." Make-by-make calendar year registrations were as follows:

Chrysler	46,184
DeSoto	35,259
Dodge	104,881
Plymouth	286,241
Total	472,565

Besides Ford, the big losers this year were Hudson, Nash, Willys-Overland, Studebaker, and Graham-Paige.

Meanwhile, the first faint rumblings of war could be heard from Europe. The wide Atlantic Ocean seemed to insulate America from any conflict that might erupt there, and for the time being the nation looked forward to continuing with business as usual. And indeed, business began taking a turn for the better as America listened to pleas for material assistance—mostly arms—from its worried allies. In time, however, the country would discover that this was one war it could not avoid.

1939

Both Ford and General Motors poured a ton of money into new styling for 1939 and, as a result, this year's Ford and Chevrolet looked dramatically different. GM's total expenditures came close to $20 million, while Ford, having fewer makes to worry about, spent about half that much. However, Dearborn made a significant move this year with introduction of the Mercury, its new medium-price make. Elsewhere, Studebaker invested $3.5 million to tool up for a new six-cylinder line, its belated entry in the low-price market. Called Champion, it bore deftly designed bodywork created by the renowned Raymond Loewy. Largely because of this and its good performance, the Champion headed straight for the top of the sales charts and, in the process, hoisted Studebaker up to fourth place in the industry. Other 1939 developments included Hudson's new 112 series, a replacement for the Terraplane that provided a welcome sales boost, and dramatic new body designs from Nash, the work of George M. Walker.

Chrysler Corporation also had new styling for 1939, though it was far less extensive than most rival efforts. It amounted to a heavy facelift for each of the firm's four model lines, conceived by Ray Dietrich before his departure from Highland Park. Completed under the direction of Robert Cadwallader by a staff that included Buzz Grisinger, Herb Weissinger, Rhys Miller, and Ed Sheard, it was remarkably effective. Though based on 1937 bodyshells, Chrysler's '39s were not only different but also fresh, contemporary, and mostly tasteful.

The most striking features throughout the company's 1939 lineup were V-split windshields, headlamps nestled neatly in the front fenders, more pronounced Ford-like prows, and smoother, more elongated "pontoon" fenders. Several models were particularly attractive. Noteworthy was a trio of coupes with fleet, semi-production bodywork by Hayes. Offered as the DeSoto Custom Club Coupe, Chrysler New Yorker Victoria, and the Dodge Deluxe Town Coupe, it featured rakishly slanted B-pillars and a rounded rear roof with a novel split back window that tapered down to a curved decklid. Unfortunately, only about 1000 of these bodies were built, but the design was a forecast of things to come. Plymouth brought back the convertible sedan style for a one-year reprise, and it looked particularly handsome with this year's new lines. Plymouth also boasted an attention-getter in its vacuum-operated power top for the convertible coupe, an industry first. Plymouth's rumble-seat convertible was in its farewell year.

On the engine front, the company retained its four six-

1939 Chrysler C-24 Custom Imperial 7-passenger sedan

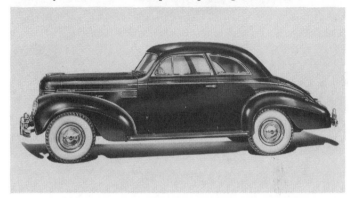

1939 Chrysler C-23 Imperial New Yorker victoria by Hayes

cylinder power units unchanged from 1938. The 299-cid straight eight disappeared again, leaving only one eight in production, the faithful 323.5-cid engine reserved for Chrysler New Yorkers and Imperials.

All 1939 Chrysler Corporation cars boasted two new features. A gearlever mounted on the steering column instead of the floor was standard on most models. So too

1939 Chrysler C-22 Royal (left) and C-23 New Yorker sedans

1939 DeSoto S-6 Custom coupe. Base price was $923.

1939 DeSoto S-6 Custom 7-passenger formal sedan

DeSoto's S-6 Custom four-door touring sedan for 1939

1939 DeSoto S-6 Custom club coupe by Hayes: $1145.

1939 Dodge D-11 "Luxury Liner" DeLuxe business coupe

1939 Dodge Westchester Suburban wagon did not see production.

1939 Dodge D-11 "Luxury Liner" DeLuxe town coupe by Hayes

A Dodge TC-series pickup from 1939. Price was about $375.

was the "Safety-Signal" speedometer, so called because it glowed green up to 30 mph, amber from 30 to 50 mph, and red at about 50 mph. Ralph Nader would have loved it. Plymouth and Dodge added two inches to their wheelbases, the latter going up to 117 across the board, the former to 114 inches except for the four-door convert-

ible (117) and long-chassis sedans (134).

Dodge returned to prosaic advertising titles for its 1939 model line. Officially designated D-11, it was promoted as the "Luxury Liner," a term that has since become more or less a part of the auto writer's lexicon. The division also reinstated a two-series lineup, the first since 1934,

1939 Plymouth P-8 DeLuxe convertible coupe: $895.

Plymouth's $685 P-7 Roadking utility sedan for 1939

1939 Plymouth P-8 DeLuxe Suburban wagon with side glass

1939 Plymouth P-8 DeLuxe convertible sedan. Price: $1150.

wheelbase reserved for the low-volume long sedans and limos. The Chrysler lineup itself became quite complex, with a new Windsor sub-series in the C-22 Royal family and a similar Saratoga line within the C-23 New Yorker/Imperial series. As before, the Custom Imperial, Chrysler Corporation's finest, rode its own 144-inch wheelbase.

For the first time in recent memory, nobody in the U.S. auto industry was a real "loser" in the 1939 selling season—though, of course, a number of makes had expired since the onset of the Depression. An expanding market allowed everyone to tally higher sales than in 1938, and total registrations climbed to 2.65 million. Of this, General Motors took a 44-percent chunk (off 1 percent from the previous year) and moved 1.16 million cars. Chrysler Corporation maintained its lead over Ford, continuing to run a solid second for the third consecutive year with a 24-percent share of the 1939 market compared to Dearborn's 21.5 percent. However, the new Mercury did extraordinarily well in its debut year, securing a 2.5-percent penetration all by itself and coming in ahead of DeSoto. The make-by-make breakdown for Chrysler's calendar-year registrations are as follows:

Chrysler	63,956
Plymouth	348,807
DeSoto	51,951
Dodge	176,585
Total	641,299

During 1939, Chrysler Corporation opened a new Canadian plant at Chatham, Ontario, as well as a new U.S. facility in San Leandro, California. Also this year, work began on a giant new engineering building at Highland Park. The additional production sites came none too soon: Adolf Hitler and his Nazis invaded Poland in September, thus beginning World War II.

1940

Following the long illness that had forced him to leave Chrysler Corporation two years earlier, Walter P. Chrysler died in 1940. With his passing, the board was moved to amend the corporation's bylaws, eliminating the office of chairman and confirming K. T. Keller as president. Herman Weckler was given a seat on the board to fill the vacancy left by the death of the company founder.

A war was now raging in Europe, and Chrysler Corporation was forced to close its Belgian assembly operations in Antwerp. The firm had delivered about 25,000 trucks to the U.S. Army in 1939. This year it filled additional truck orders from France and Great Britain. Chrysler also began construction of a new tank arsenal at Warren, Michigan. Completed in 1941, it would have the capacity for turning out five 25-ton tanks per eight-hour shift. In late 1940 tooling began for production of the M-3 28-ton medium tank and fuselage sections for the Martin B-26B bomber. Like other American industrial giants,

fielding three base Special models and a more complete DeLuxe range. Plymouth continued with a wide variety of body styles in P-7 Roadking and fancier P-8 DeLuxe trim. The DeSoto line was subdivided for 1939 into DeLuxe and Custom groups. Both shared the 119-inch-wheelbase Chrysler Royal chassis, with a 134-inch

1940 Chrysler C-26 New Yorker convertible coupe: $1375.

1940 Chrysler C-25 Windsor business coupe. Price: $935.

Chrysler was gearing up for war.

Meantime, the company debuted a 1940 passenger-car fleet bearing fairly extensive changes. Wheelbases were longer on every line, up 2.5 inches for Dodge and 3.5 inches for Plymouth, DeSoto, and Chrysler. Bob Cadwallader put the extra chassis length to good effect, and all makes bore fresh styling for the second year in a row, though still based largely on Ray Dietrich themes. The main elements of this year's look were lower, more horizontal grille styling; flatter, more squared-up fenders; less prominent running boards (they'd been shrinking in size for several years), optional on some models; lower

Fluid Drive

Fluid Drive was one of Chrysler's many splendored engineering feats, probably the most popular option (when it wasn't standard equipment) on Mopars of the Forties. It was usually sold along with Chrysler's hydraulic transmission of that time. The impetus for Fluid Drive was simple enough: eliminate shifting. The actual concept was a bit more complicated.

Fluid Drive discarded the conventional flywheel in favor of a fluid-coupling torque converter that performed all the same functions except providing a contact surface for the clutch plate (a separate clutch was mounted behind the coupling). All other flywheel services were provided: storing of energy, smoothing of power impulses, and carrying the ring gear that meshed with the starter pinion. The coupling was a cylindrical drum, filled to ⅞ths capacity with low-viscosity mineral oil. It contained a casing, or "driver," with radial vanes on its inner surface. This faced a driven "runner" having another set of vanes running freely inside a cover, which was welded to the opposing drum to make a solid unit. The oil allowed the casing to be sealed for life, since it provided essentially permanent lubrication. The coupling was bolted to the crankshaft as a flywheel would be,

and the fluid was retained by a leakproof seal around the rotating central shaft. The filler hole was designed to avoid overfilling.

When the engine was started, the fluid coupling revolved as a flywheel would, but the vanes attached to the driver casing also rotated, thus throwing the oil outward in whirlpool fashion. The oil circulated across a quarter-inch gap between the driver and runner and onto the vanes of the runner. The runner then turned through the action of the moving oil, though always a bit slower than the driver. This transfer provided a "cushioning" effect that accounted for the smooth flow of power for which Fluid Drive was known. There was no metal-to-metal contact. The cushioning effect prevented the engine from stalling when the car was stopped with a gear engaged, allowing the gearlever to remain in position without depressing the clutch pedal.

There were two Fluid Drive gearlever positions. "Low" controlled first and second gear and was used only for extra pulling power. "High" connected to third and fourth gears, and was used for all normal driving. "Low" was located where second would be on a conventional column shift; "High" was in its usual place. To start off, you normally shifted into High and stepped on the accelerator. At 14 mph you released the pedal slightly, waited for an audible *clunk,* and continued on in fourth or High. To stop, you braked as you

would with a modern automatic transmission. To start again, you just stepped on the accelerator. The system eliminated about 95 percent of all gear shifting.

Ted West provided one of the most entertaining driver's impressions of Fluid Drive in a 1968 issue of *Road & Track* magazine. West was certainly the first journalist to suggest that this semi-automatic transmission could be used like a manual four-speed: "To shift from high range of low gear to low range of high gear (second to third) it is necessary to de-clutch, change the shift lever position to high, reengage the clutch, press the accelerator to the floor to activate the electrical kick-down switch, and with luck you will continue forward. See how simple and relaxing? To reach high-range high, just let off the gas again ... you can run through the gears or simply leave it in high, à la Dynaflow (another legend of the Old West), let the torque converter do its stuff. This latter method results in very 'dignified' acceleration and is recommended only for people with several gasoline credit cards."

Fluid Drive must have been a boon to neophyte drivers in its day, but the factory had a strong warning about it: "The fluid used in the coupling must be of the correct chemical analysis and viscosity. This fluid is obtainable ONLY through the Chrysler Parts Corporation, and no other should be used under any circumstances." A small price to pay for so many virtues?

The $2445 Chrysler C-27 Crown Imperial limousine for 1940

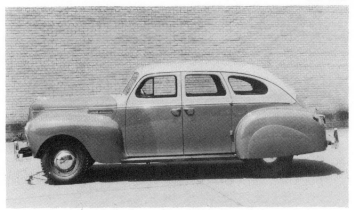

1940 Chrysler C-25 Windsor four-door sedan (prototype)

ride height; and simplified exterior ornamentation. The Chryslers arguably looked the best, announced by a simple grille composed of delicate horizontal bars and pointed in the center. Dodge had a fussier face, its grille resembling a diamond with the side points cut off. DeSoto showed a more heart-shaped front, while Plymouth stuck to horizontal bars either side of a 1939-style prow.

There were no significant engineering changes for 1940. Chrysler's innovative Fluid Drive transmission, which had been standard on the Crown Imperial and optional on the eight-cylinder Chryslers for 1939, was now extended to all makes as an extra-cost item. Sealed-beam headlamps were adopted across the board in keeping with industry practice, but Chrysler scored an important safety exclusive with the "Safety-Rim" wheel, featuring a raised circumferential bead that kept the tire from popping off the rim in the event of a blowout. Engines changed only in detail, but rated horsepower went up fractionally for Chrysler and DeSoto. Newly available for selected 1940 models was a Warner Gear overdrive unit with an improved shift mechanism. This involved a powerful solenoid instead of the old centrifugal clutch. The new unit was able to upshift into overdrive from 25 mph,

1940 Chrysler C-26 New Yorker two-door sedan, priced at $1230

1940 DeSoto S-7C Custom convertible coupe: $1095.

DeSoto's 1940 S-7S DeLuxe business coupe. It sold for $845.

The two-tone DeSoto Sportsman sedan from mid-1940

1940 Dodge D-14 DeLuxe sedan with optional two-toning

Plymouth's P-10 DeLuxe four-door sedan, $805 for 1940.

1940 Dodge D-14 DeLuxe business coupe. Price was $803.

A squadron of 1940 Plymouth police cars for New York City

and the solenoid went into a "freewheeling" mode when the overdrive was disengaged.

The 1940 Chrysler lineup was quite complicated, though it nominally comprised only two standard series plus the low-volume Crown Imperials on a special 145.5-inch wheelbase. The "junior" Series C-25 was made up of base Royal and fancier Windsor models, the latter distinguished by higher-grade trim and appropriately stiffer prices, plus eight-passenger sedans and limousines on a 139.5-inch-wheelbase chassis. Riding a 128.5-inch wheelbase, the "senior" Series C-26 included a solitary Saratoga four-door sedan, a New Yorker sub-series with a full-range of body styles, and the interesting new Traveler coupes and sedans, the latter mainly detrimmed, lower-priced alternatives to their New Yorker counterparts. For the first time, there were no standard-chassis Imperials. At midyear a special Highlander trim package was introduced as an option for Windsor and New Yorker coupes and convertibles. It consisted of brightly colored tartan-plaid cloth upholstery combined with trim made of "moleskin," a precursor of vinyl, plus small exterior nameplates.

DeSoto retained its existing two-tier lineup and basic body styles for 1940. As before, the cheaper offerings were called DeLuxe (Series S-7S), while the nicer ones bore the Custom label (Series S-7C) and were identified by a little extra chrome around windshield and side windows. The Custom line still included long-wheelbase sedans and limos, which now measured 139.5 inches be-

tween wheel centers, plus the division's sole convertible coupe.

Model choices also stayed the same at Dodge, except for the return of a seven-passenger sedan and limousine on the long DeSoto chassis. There were again two "Luxury Liner" series, the D-17 Special and the more comprehensive D-14 DeLuxe, the latter including the long-chassis variants.

The story was the same at Plymouth, which carried on with the base Roadking (P-9) and costlier DeLuxe (P-10) series in roughly the same body styles. Long-wheelbase derivatives were now built on a 137-inch chassis, and continued to be low-demand items.

Chrysler Corporation got into two-toning this year, offering special combinations for Chrysler, Dodge, and DeSoto. None of these were very well conceived. The Chrysler treatment was delineated by the normal high-set, full-length bodyside moldings, with the contrasting color on the greenhouse and cowl but not the hood. Dodge contrasted the central body with everything else, which made the car look like a circus wagon. DeSoto's was arguably the best, with the second hue used above the bodyside moldings all the way forward to the upper portion of the grille. This scheme was applied to a special four-door sedan called the Sportsman, introduced in March. However, even decked out with whitewall tires and the Custom series trim, this model looked like a taxicab without a roof light.

Model year 1940 saw some new activity in the low-price

1940 Plymouth P-9 Roadking two-door with 20-inch wheels

Plymouth's 1940 P-10 DeLuxe wagon. List price: $970.

1940 Plymouth P-10 DeLuxe convertible coupe: $950.

A 1940 Plymouth Panel Delivery on the P-9 Roadking chassis

field, with Nash's new unit-construction 600 and the compact Willys American. Even so, the major makes took the lion's share of sales. All by themselves, Chevrolet, Ford, and Plymouth accounted for nearly 54 percent of total 1940 sales. The market as a whole expanded again, this time to 3.4 million units, which enabled most every automaker to score sales gains. Chrysler's make-by-make registrations are as follows:

Chrysler	100,117
Plymouth	440,093
DeSoto	71,943
Dodge	197,252
Total	809,405

Chrysler Division recorded a first in exceeding the 100,000-unit figure. Plymouth, Dodge, and DeSoto also helped the corporation as a whole to widen its lead over Ford, which failed to reach 645,000 sales this season. However, General Motors outsold Chrysler by a margin of 2 to 1, retailing 1.6 million cars.

1941

Ever since the ill-fated Airflow experience, aerodynamics had not been a favorite subject in the engineering building at Highland Park nor in Chrysler Cor-

poration's executive offices. But the irrepressible Carl Breer had never lost his fascination for advanced bodywork—nor his missionary zeal. Finally, he managed to get James C. Zeder to listen. Zeder waded into a study of how improved aerodynamics could benefit automobiles, and in 1941 he presented a paper to the Society of Automotive Engineers entitled "Is It Practical to Streamline for Fuel Economy?" What interested him most was the "total design" approach to more economical cars. Unfortunately, his paper was long forgotten by the time Chrysler resumed civilian car production after World War II, but it likely figured in a styling feature that appeared on the 1942 DeSoto: hidden headlamps.

Nevertheless, Chrysler Corporation's approach to styling had become very conservative by the early Forties. K. T. Keller wanted it that way. Both he and engineer Owen Skelton were very cautious, no doubt because memories of the Airflow were still fresh. Yet it's curious that Keller never seemed to realize that exceptionally good styling can help a car's sales as much as exceptionally bad styling can hurt. Still, Chrysler had been stung once with an advanced design, and Keller wasn't about to repeat that mistake. He had his supporters, among them the aforementioned Jim Zeder and his brother Fred, who were likewise not design-oriented and also were far more concerned about the integrity of Chrysler engineering. Given this atmosphere it's no wonder the company earned a reputation for dumpy styling. It would take years before management felt secure enough to market

1941 Chrysler C-28S Royal business coupe. Price: $995.

Chrysler Town & Country wagon bowed as a 1941 C-28W Windsor.

1941 Chrysler C-30N New Yorker four-door sedan: $1389.

1941 Chrysler C-28W Windsor four-door sedan with rear skirts

1941 Chrysler C-30N New Yorker town sedan. Price: $1399.

more adventuresome concepts.

That's not to say that Chrysler styling stagnated completely in these years. In fact, two of the industry's first "dream cars" appeared under the Chrysler badge in 1940-41, both quite radical for the time. Surprisingly, the impetus for them was Keller, who ordered them up with a "generous" 90 days for design and construction.

The more predictive of these exercises was the Thunderbolt, a rakish convertible created by Alex Tremulis of Briggs. "Styling at Briggs was almost a 'good will' department," the designer once recalled, where the body company "could offer our clients a fresh viewpoint free from engineering restrictions..." The Thunderbolt was certainly fresh. Built on the 127.5-inch-wheelbase chassis of the 1941 Chrysler New Yorker/Saratoga, it carried a smooth, slab-sided "envelope" body made of aluminum and with nary a hint of separate fenders. The front had no grille, only a small rectangle for the license plate. Headlights were hidden behind "peek-a-boo" lids that lifted whenever the lamps were switched on. Contributing to the long, low look were wheels covered by skirts and anodized aluminum trim that almost completely encircled the lower body. The cockpit, finished mostly in leather, featured a single seat wide enough for three, plus electrically operated side windows and pushbutton exterior and interior door handles. Instruments were edge-lighted, another innovation. But the real topper was literally that: a one-piece metal roof that raised or lowered electrically. When stowed, it was completely hidden under the rear deck. In this, the Thunderbolt was a forecast of the production Ford Skyliner "retractable" hardtop of more than 15 years later.

Chrysler's other early-Forties show stealer was the Newport, a genuine dual-cowl phaeton in the grand tradition but styled along more modern lines. Created principally by Ralph Roberts of the LeBaron coachworks (which became a Briggs subsidiary in the late Thirties), it also featured hidden headlights and a road-hugging envelope body, but it had open front wheel wells (only the rears were skirted) and softer lines. Notable were the sculptured, flow-through front fenders that sloped gently downward, kicking up to form the rear fender line. The grille was made up of a small, high-set upper section and an oval lower portion, the latter set just behind a delicate twin-bar bumper. There were four doors, of course, and the twin cockpits were sumptuously trimmed in leather and fine carpeting. Doors were cut away at the sides and had no windows, as the Newport was intended primarily as a parade car for sunny days.

Six copies of both the Newport and the Thunderbolt were built, and they were the centerpieces of Chrysler's exhibit at various auto shows. Both designs were very favorably received, and the Newport was selected as pace car for the 1941 Indianapolis 500. Four Newports and at least two of the Thunderbolts survive today.

Ralph Roberts recalled that Keller himself was pleased with the results: "K.T. liked to have outside talent around to encourage Chrysler's own designers, though he actually used very little of what we designed *in toto*..." Significantly, these show cars helped inspire concepts for the 1943-45 Chrysler Corporation production models that

1940-41 Chrysler Newport show car. LeBaron built six in all.

Chrysler Thunderbolt show car of 1940-41, styled by Alex Tremulis

Thunderbolt featured envelope body, retractable hard top.

1941 Chrysler C-33 Crown Imperial four-door sedan

1941 DeSoto S-8C Custom four-door sedan. Price: $1085.

DeSoto's 1941 S-8C Custom two-door brougham: $1060.

1941 Dodge D-19 Custom four-door sedan. It cost $999 new.

D-19 Custom four-door sedan was the most popular '41 Dodge.

would have appeared had not World War II intervened.

America would be drawn into the widening war all too soon. As the U.S. auto industry unveiled its 1941 models, no one could know that this would be the last full year of production until 1946. Changes at Chrysler Corporation were fairly extensive for 1941. All makes bore revised styling, and all except Plymouth acquired two new body types, a revived three-window club coupe and a four-door "Town Sedan" with blind rear quarters. Chrysler in-

troduced the first of a classic line, the wood-bodied Town & Country wagon, and shortened wheelbases slightly on its volume models, the latter change also affecting DeSoto. Engineering efforts aimed at easier driving, which included a lower-cost alternative to Fluid Drive. It arrived this year as a semi-automatic transmission marketed as "Vacamatic" at Chrysler and "Simplimatic" at DeSoto.

This new transmission was similar to initial versions of

GM's Hydra-Matic, though it did not provide totally "clutchless" shifting. Basically, it consisted of a four-speed gearbox with a vacuum servo operated by lifting off the accelerator. The servo would "automatically" shift from first to second gear or from third to fourth, but moving between Low range (1-2) and High range (3-4) still required use of the clutch pedal and shift lever. The gearbox, designated M-3, was a heavy-duty three-speed unit cleverly converted to four forward ratios. How was it done? The key was mounting the forward (main) gear on the countershaft, with a cam-and-roller overrunning clutch providing about a 2.5:1 reduction. Power flow for first gear was normal, with gearing to the output shaft at the rear of the countershaft. For second, the countershaft was driven through a center pair of gears with a 1:1 ratio, using the same connection to the output shaft. For third, the countershaft was again driven via the forward reduction gear, but power flow was taken through the 1:1 pair to the output shaft. In other words, the power flow was reversed relative to second. Fourth gear was direct drive, with the countershaft spinning but not transmitting torque.

All normal driving with Chrysler's semi-automatic was done in High range, which was geared (approximately 1.7:1) to provide a fairly smart getaway, with slip diminishing with speed. Low range was intended only for situations like restarts with a full load on steep hills, towing a trailer in the mountains, or emergencies like getting out of soft sand or mud. The mechanical gearing for first was about 3:1, for second about 2.2:1. This transmission was a good try at greater driving convenience, but it still wasn't *fully* automatic, something Chrysler wouldn't be able to advertise until 1954.

Though unchanged in size, all Chrysler power units boasted a bit more horsepower for 1941, anywhere from 3-5 bhp depending on make and engine. Generally, these gains were achieved in the time-honored way: revised camshaft profiles, new intake manifolds, and slightly higher compression.

By far the most interesting newcomer to the 1941 Chrysler lineup was the Town & Country, the first station wagon ever to wear the badge. David A. Wallace, who had taken over as Chrysler Division president in 1940, had decided the make needed a station wagon. But he didn't like the clumsy, boxy creations then being ladled on various chassis by traditional bodybuilders, envisioning instead a tighter, more streamlined style that was closer to a sedan in appearance. Because most outside coachbuilders looked on the idea with bewilderment, Wallace turned to his own engineers, who gave him what he wanted.

And they succeeded brilliantly. In place of the typical rattling, awkward-looking wagon, the Town & Country arrived as a smooth, fastback-style four-door featuring double "clamshell" rear doors hinged at the sides. These opened to expose an enormous cargo bay, and didn't prang anybody's knees like a conventional tailgate. The interior held two or three large bench seats, thus affording six- or nine-passenger capacity.

T&C historian Don Narus has pointed out that Chrysler had to "learn" to build the new model, largely

1941 Dodge D-19 Custom two-door brougham (prototype)

The $862 Dodge D-19 DeLuxe business coupe from 1941

because Briggs, the firm's regular body supplier, had no experience with wood construction. Briggs was primarily a metal-working company, and it did produce the T&C's cowl and floorpan, front end, and steel roof. Everything else was Chrysler's. Wallace had picked another outside firm, Pekin Wood Products of Helena, Arkansas, to supply the new wagon's white ash body framing, and conjecture has it that Wallace, who just happened to be Pekin's president as well as Chrysler Division's, devised the T&C just to keep that company business. Town & Country inner body panels, those between the main ash members, were initially made of Honduran mahogany, though synthetic materials would be used in future years.

Wallace earmarked a section of Chrysler's Jefferson Avenue plant in Detroit for T&C assembly. Required jigs and fixtures were installed and a small force of craftsmen was trained to build the body, welding the steel roof to the steel cowl and mating wood to metal with angle irons and steel butt plates. With its unfamiliar construction, the T&C required more than the usual amount of hand labor, so perhaps it's not surprising that only 997 were completed for the 1941 model year. Of these, all but 200 were nine-passenger models.

Chrysler had considered offering its new wagon with straight-eight power, but the T&C was available only in the six-cylinder Windsor series (C-28W), which was now a line distinct from the entry-level Royal (C-28S). Both junior model groups rode a one-inch shorter wheelbase (121.5 inches) than their 1940 counterparts, though the

1941 Dodge WC-series pickup

1941 Plymouth P-12 Special DeLuxe 7-passenger sedan

139.5-inch chassis was retained for long-wheelbase sedans and limos in each line. Further up the scale was the eight-cylinder Series C-30K/C-30N, with New Yorker and Saratoga offerings on a 127.5-inch chassis, again an inch shorter than before. There was now a fuller range of Saratoga body styles, priced from $1245 to $1350, but the convertible remained exclusive to the New Yorker and Windsor lines. The previous Traveler twosome was dropped. Styling changes for all models were minor: a grille with fewer horizontal bars and taillamps with more ornate chrome housings. Brightening up interiors was an expanded selection of trim and upholstery packages. The Highlander returned with its striking combination of Scots plaid and leatherette. New on certain open models was Saran trim combined with woven plastic and leatherette. Also new was Navajo, a pattern inspired by American Indian art. Continuing at the top of the Chrysler heap was the Crown Imperial, which retained its 145.5-inch wheelbase for all models except a special town sedan, a mid-year addition to the line combining the New Yorker chassis with Imperial-style cabin appointments.

DeSoto was much better-looking for '41 thanks to a heavy sheetmetal revamp on the existing bodyshells. The biggest improvements were seen at the front, where a bolder grille with prominent vertical bars appeared, a motif that would be a DeSoto hallmark through 1955. As with Chrysler, wheelbase contracted by one inch on standard models. Seven-passenger sedans and limousines continued on their previous 139.5-inch chassis. The model

lineup still comprised DeLuxe (S-8S) and Custom (S-8C) offerings, with the new corporate town sedan style appearing in the upper-price series. Prices were higher across the board, initially by an average of about $58, with another $42.50 tacked on later in the season. DeSoto wooed buyers with more optional extras than ever, including Fluid Drive for the first time, the new "Simplimatic" semi-automatic transmission, and comfort/convenience goodies like pushbutton radio and an underseat heater.

Dodge also wore a new face for '41, and an effective makeover it was. A lower and wider horizontal-bar grille flanked a more prominent "beak," chrome trim was more artfully placed, and running boards were all but gone (again optional at the buyer's discretion). Series names for this year's D-19 lineup were juggled, with DeLuxe moving down a notch to replace the Special and a new Custom group slotted in above. Standard for the latter were "Airfoam" seat cushions, additional exterior bright trim, a passenger's door armrest, and twin electric windshield wipers. Standard wheelbase was unchanged, but long sedans were cut two inches between wheel centers. All models rode a redesigned box-section frame without the familiar X-member. Turn signals were now an extra-cost accessory, along with Fluid Drive.

Engineering changes at Plymouth were minor: oil-bath air cleaner, relocated battery (from under the passenger compartment floor to under the hood), and optional "Powermatic," the vacuum-assisted semi-automatic transmission. More noticeable in the showroom was the nicely updated styling, with a near heart-shaped horizontal-bar grille and "speedline" fenders with modest bright embellishments. As at Dodge, series names were changed, the DeLuxe (P-11) now denoting the lower-price models and Special DeLuxe (P-12) the pricier ones. Overall, Plymouth lagged behind Ford and Chevrolet in styling for '41, though this was undoubtedly one of the better-looking Plymouths. Prices averaged about $55 higher across the line.

Both Chrysler Corporation and General Motors set new production records in 1941, Chrysler moving more than 900,000 cars against GM's 1.77 million. Overall industry volume swelled to 3.7 million units, and Chrysler maintained a solid 24-percent market share against 19 percent for a declining Ford, which fell about 200,000 cars short of Highland Park's sales. Plymouth was still advancing, though not at the same explosive rate as 1934-36 or 1939-40, but Dodge and DeSoto had a fine season, and Chrysler Division made a spectacular gain, recording about one-third Plymouth's volume. Calendar 1941 make-by-make registrations are as follows:

Chrysler	143,025
Plymouth	452,187
DeSoto	91,004
Dodge	215,563
Total	901,779

In all, 1941 was one of the most successful years in Chrysler Corporation history. Unfortunately, world events were about to bring a swift end to these good times.

1942

Model year 1942 was only a few months old when the devastating Japanese attack on Pearl Harbor forced America out of troubled neutrality and onto the Allied side in World War II. Before that tragic event, Chrysler Corporation seemed all set for another great year, although, like other automakers and U.S. industry in general, it was already heavily involved with war production. That involvement became total within weeks of President Franklin Roosevelt's impassioned speech before Congress on December 8, 1941, seeking a formal declaration of war. That came promptly, and all civilian car production was suspended for the duration under government order. Dodge shut down on January 29, 1942, DeSoto closed the next day, and Chrysler and Plymouth followed on the 31st. When the end came, the corporation's 1942-model output stood at just over 152,000 units for Plymouth, about 68,500 at Dodge, approximately 25,000 at DeSoto, and nearly 35,000 for Chrysler (including just 448 Imperials).

Virtually all 1942 American cars are highly prized today for their historical significance as the last prewar models and for their lower original production and consequently greater scarcity now compared to, say, 1940-41

1942 Chrysler C-34W Windsor club coupe. Price: $1228.

cars. Considering that an increasing proportion of its resources had been shifting to war work since 1940, Chrysler Corporation's 1942 models bore a surprising number of changes. Chief among these was revised styling, which has special interest today because it would be retained in mildly modified form for the firm's first postwar cars that would continue all the way through the first part of calendar 1949.

Plymouth and Dodge were the most heavily restyled Chrysler Corporation makes for 1942, both virtually all-

1942 Chrysler C-36N New Yorker convertible coupe ("blackout")

1942 Chrysler C-36N New Yorker town sedan: $1520.

1942 Chrysler C-33 Crown Imperial limousine: $3065.

1942 Chrysler C-34W Windsor four-door sedan ("blackout")

1942 Chrysler C-34W Windsor club coupe ("blackout")

Dodge's 1942 D-22 Custom convertible coupe sold at $1245.

new. Highlights included door sheetmetal extended down to cover the running boards, lower front fenders, and more massive, horizontal-format fronts. Ride height was also noticeably lower. Plymouth bore a simple, divided bar grille, while Dodge's more ornate treatment spanned the car's full face and featured a prominent eggcrate central section. Rear fender skirts carrying bright trim were optional for both. Senior makes were more modestly revamped. Chrysler came in for a flatter, less sculptured nose, and its 1940-41 horizontal grille bars were now ex-

tended right around to the sides. Some models also bore matching horizontal "speed streaks" on the rear fenders. DeSoto picked up a very chromey and shallower grille with finer vertical teeth, as well as a show car-inspired innovation, hidden headlamps. Called "Airfoil," the lamps remained "out of sight except at night," and marked the return of this feature to American production for the first time since the lovely Cord 810/812 of 1936-37. Interestingly, however, it would not return on any of Chrysler Corporation's postwar continuations.

The last Chrysler built for the duration of WWII

All 1942 DeSotos featured "Airfoil" hidden headlamps.

1942 DeSoto S-10C Custom four-door sedan. Price: $1152.

1942 Dodge D-22 Custom 7-passenger sedan. Price: $1395.

1942 Dodge D-22 DeLuxe business coupe: $895.

1942 Plymouth P-14C Special DeLuxe wood-body wagon

1942 Plymouth P-14S DeLuxe two-door for Michigan state police

Paint replaced chrome on late 1942 Plymouths.

Bodyshells, wheelbases, and model offerings for 1942 were basically carried over from '41, though lineups were fine-tuned in some cases. Plymouth, for example, lost its low-volume long sedans this year, but again fielded DeLuxe (P-14S) and Special DeLuxe (P-14C) series, the latter now including the corporate blind-quarter town sedan style previously available at other divisions. Dodge likewise retained a two-tier group, DeLuxe and Custom, all designated D-22. Stretched-chassis sedans were still around at Dodge, but few were called for: a mere 210 in all. Ditto DeSoto, except that its long sedans could be had in base DeLuxe (S-10S) and upper-crust Custom (S-10C) trim. Chrysler rationalized its offerings around names that would be thoroughly familiar in the postwar era. At the bottom were the six-cylinder Royal (C-34S) and Windsor (C-34W), followed by a new separate eight-cylinder Saratoga line (C-36K), with the New Yorker (C-36N) and Crown Imperial (C-33) as before. The singular Town & Country wagon made its reprise in the Windsor series, and was one of the few 1942 models to score higher production than in '41. The total was exactly 999, of which 150 were six-passenger types.

Engineering revisions for '42 centered on larger engines with more rated horsepower. The smallest unit in the company stable, the 201-cubic-inch six, was phased out and Plymouth moved up to the 218-cid Dodge unit, still around after a decade and a direct descendant of the 1930 Chrysler CJ-series six. Dodge, in turn, was moved up to a longer-stroke 230-cid derivative of this powerplant, producing 105 bhp against the previous 91 (the '42 Plymouth 218 was rated a bit higher, 95 bhp). DeSoto's 228-cid six was bored out a miniscule 0.06-inch for 236.6 cid and 115 bhp (against 105 for '41), and Chrysler's six was similarly enlarged to near 215 cid for an extra 5-10 horsepower. As before, the company's lone straight eight was restricted to the senior Chrysler models, and was untouched at 323.5 cid and 140 horsepower.

Though abbreviated, the 1942 model year witnessed increasing shortages of certain raw materials, which the government earmarked exclusively for war production, not civilian goods. One of these was aluminum, and the shortage showed up at Highland Park in a return to cast-iron pistons for both the Chrysler and DeSoto sixes. As elsewhere in the industry, chrome and rubber also became progressively more difficult to come by, so many of the last '42s off the line either did without components made from these materials or used substitutes.

By the end of 1942, Chrysler had poured some $40 million into its Chicago facility for increased tank production as well as a huge aircraft-engine manufacturing operation. For the duration, Chrysler would turn out a variety of war material, including Bofors guns, engines and fuselage assemblies for the B-29 Superfortress bomber, and tank engines. More down-to-earth products came from the Canadian factories, which churned out vast quantities of Dodge three-ton trucks with the civilian-model cab and front sheetmetal. The Dodge truck factory in Detroit tooled up for a one-ton four-wheel-drive tactical truck. It saw duty as a staff car, reconnaissance vehicle, and ambulance, but was officially known by the snappy title of "Bucket Seat Weapon Carrier."

1943-45

Although America's entry into World War II meant the immediate end of civilian car production, it did not mean the complete end of civilian car design activities. Like most other automakers, Chrysler Corporation was well along with plans for its 1943-45 models when the Japanese attacked Pearl Harbor. Naturally, these had to be put on hold as design and engineering talent was directed to the crucial task of winning the war. Yet interestingly, designers did come back to these proposals when time permitted, developing further extensions of them, as well as more advanced concepts, in anticipation of an Allied victory and its promise of peacetime prosperity.

A similar situation existed at Ford Motor Company, and the photographs and drawings that survive from its wartime automotive projects make a fascinating comparison with Chrysler's. Both companies were literally working along the same lines, with a basic body shape that represented the logical evolution of mid-Thirties design thinking. Today we know it as the "upside-down bathtub." Significantly, neither company was engaged in corporate espionage, but were merely moving with the general trends of the era: curved, somewhat thick body lines, rounder and more integrated fenders, broader glass areas, skirted rear wheels, ornament-free hoods, wraparound bumpers, "all-of-a-piece" grilles. Some of these ideas would be reflected in each firm's postwar products, but crisper shapes didn't emerge at Chrysler until 1949 and Ford didn't fully abandon "bathtub" styling until 1952. It does seem that the wartime Chrysler designs would have had an edge on their Ford, Lincoln, and Mercury counterparts had not the war interrupted things. Chrysler's glass wrapped more, its window frames were thinner, its grilles better integrated, and the overall lines of its proposals were more smoothly flowing. Of course, the war *did* intervene, and the sales figures in later years reflect what happened. And don't forget that GM had something to do with it, too. In fact, GM's senior makes had brand-new styling for 1942 that was already ahead of most anything that Ford and Chrysler developed in the mid-Forties.

The funny thing about all these wartime machinations was neatly summed up by E. T. "Bob" Gregorie, who headed Ford's styling staff at the time: "It never dawned on any of us that, right after the war, anything on wheels would sell whether it was restyled or not. We just never sat down and thought about it enough to figure that out. So we went right ahead as though the first thing we'd have to do after the war was restyle...not realizing until the last minute that a suitable facelift would do as well. In fact, we had until about 1948-49 before we'd have to come up with anything really different."

Of course, in late 1941 no one in Detroit could predict how long the war would go on. Yet by mid-1943, it had been going on long enough to suggest that the civilian car population would be sufficiently depleted to ensure

This 1941 drawing for the '43 Dodge shows integral fenders.

A more radical Dodge idea was fender-mounted air scoops.

DeSoto might have retained hidden lights in '43, as this front-end buck shows.

A less "toothy" DeSoto front displayed concave grille bars.

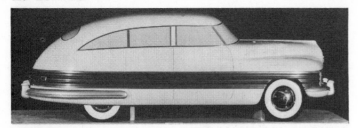

A Plymouth proposal from early 1940 shows how the postwar cars might have looked.

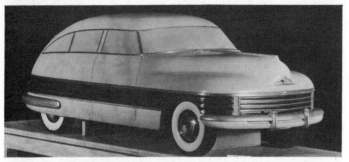

Stylists played with wraparound grillework and hidden headlights.

By mid-1942, Plymouth planning had progressed to this.

strong sales for three, four, maybe even five years once peace returned. Thus, it was hardly surprising that Chrysler, like every other U.S. producer, resumed production in late 1945 with a line of 1946 models that were little more than facelifted continuations of 1942 designs. In Chrysler's case, part of this was attributable to postwar material shortages and government controls. But clearly, as Bob Gregorie noted, there was no immediate need for anything new from any producer. Besides, it hardly made sense to scrap unamortized prewar tooling simply for the sake of newness. The only company to break ranks was Studebaker, which, in retrospect, probably should have saved its all-new 1947 design until 1949 or '50 despite gaining a temporary, though valuable, image boost by being "first by far with a postwar car."

One former Chrysler insider recalled, "The plan was for each company to wring the profits out of its old models and stave off the rapidly rising cost of retooling right up to the point where the law of diminishing returns began to operate. [This was] the psychological point at which the buyer was beginning to make up his mind about the car he would purchase when he had a free choice. Before that point was reached, something new had to be added. But when? For each company the problem was slightly different."

The problem for Chrysler was that its prewar styling, though much improved by 1941-42, was still dumpier and not as modern as GM's. It was arguably better than Ford's, but that company had a glamorous style leader in the Lincoln Continental, plus the only V-8 engine (dated though it was) in the low-priced field. One can only wonder how the timing of the war affected Chrysler's design planning, because the surviving record of its wartime styling efforts suggests that it very well might have closed the "styling gap" with GM somewhere in the mid-Forties. As it turned out, the Big Three leapfrogged a styling generation ahead with their first all-new postwar designs for 1949.

Work on Chrysler's 1943-45 models proceeded in the small styling unit that copied GM by calling itself the Art & Colour Section. Despite its traditional subservience to Engineering, it possessed ample talent. Robert Cadwallader was still in charge of exteriors, though he would leave Chrysler in 1946 to join newly formed Kaiser-Frazer, where he would briefly head the Kaiser design studio. Buzz Grisinger and Herb Weissinger were still around, though they would also leave to join K-F.

The direct inspiration for Chrysler's mid-Forties design thinking was the prewar Newport and Thunderbolt show cars (see 1941). The latter was created by Alex Tremulis, then a designer with Briggs Manufacturing Company, who had high praise for the Chrysler team. He remembered Weissinger as a skilled artist and a clay-model perfectionist, "a maestro in the execution of a line on a surface. He regarded a 1/64-inch deviation in a roofline as unthinkable, and would work hours on end seeking its correction. His chrome appliqués were done with the perfection of a Cellini; he was easily the best of us in this area. He had the qualifications of a brilliant body engineer, and could cross swords with the best of them in the defense of Styling. After 40 years in the business, I feel qualified to judge those whom I consider best. Herb Weissinger was truly one of the greatest."

Grisinger, said Tremulis, was "the greatest sculptural design modeler of all time. Tremendously talented, he did very little on paper—usually a quick sketch. That was all he needed to attack a full-size clay model singlehandedly. In his field he was in a class by himself. The body engineering draftsmen told me that they never had to surface-develop any irregularities in his models; they merely took templates off the clay and used his lines verbatim."

Chrysler's Art & Colour staff never exceeded several dozen, including clay modelers. During the war, it lost the services of many, including Grisinger (who was assigned to the Manhattan project, which developed the atomic bomb). Cadwallader and Weissinger remained long enough that they can be credited with many of the stillborn 1943-45 designs—as well as the mildly facelifted '42 models that became Chrysler's 1946-48 production cars.

The starting point for 1943-45 was the styling concept first seen in production for 1940, laid down by Ray Dietrich before his departure from Highland Park in 1938 and executed by Cadwallader. Though the wartime prototypes retained this basic "fat bathtub" shape, they differed from both late-prewar and early-postwar production styling in having integral instead of separate fenders and

Later that same year, a peaked grille and two-toning were tried.

Grille on this wartime Plymouth model is close to the '46.

Odd headlamp shape was used on this '41 proposal, probably a Chrysler.

Wraparound side trim and bumpers were favorite wartime styling themes.

This 1942 fastback sedan is somewhat Ford-like.

Ford and Chrysler worked with similar ideas, as on this 1942 model.

Complex grille marks this design as a Chrysler. Note upper "nostrils."

"Pregnant" wheel wells of this model probably wouldn't have been popular.

more unified grilles. Styling was uniform in that it didn't differ much from make to make. While Plymouths, Dodges, DeSotos, and Chryslers all bore identifying medallions or script and were scaled to appropriate dimensions, surviving photographs reveal that they were a closely related family.

The Forties were the years of "second-generation streamlining." Styling had progressed past the rounded fenders and teardrop body shapes of the initial mid-Thirties era. Now, the look was becoming more "organic": headlights were disappearing into fenders, freestanding bumpers were moving closer to the bodies, wheel wells were being covered by skirts. Chrysler's war-

time work followed these trends, with integral fenders (which did not appear in production form until 1955), wraparound bumpers and side moldings, and wrapped windshields and backlights. The glass industry's technology in those days didn't allow for much curvature, which is why the wraparound windows on these styling models would not be practical for another decade. Up front, designers tried to combine various components as a complicated, chromey grille. More expensive models were apparently slated for hidden headlights, as on the '42 DeSoto, while on others the headlamps were part of the basic grille shape. A few hood scoops were in evidence; most of the cars carried clean hoods, lacking even an ornament. (The clean-hood idea—to the horror of salesmen—was reflected in the 1947 K-F cars finalized by Grisinger, Weissinger, and Cadwallader.)

Chrysler continued its design experiments sporadically throughout the war years, and some influenced the corporation's '46 facelifts. The busy front end seen on one Imperial proposal, for example, worked its way into the 1946-48 Chrysler grille. The pointed horizontal-bar grille of one Plymouth was closely matched in postwar production. And DeSoto's trademark "teeth" really emerged from the design work of 1943-45. But there were some elements that would never be seen. Hidden headlights were written off after the war as unnecessary and expensive. Fender skirts, especially for the front wheels, were thought to be taking streamlining too far. Thin upper window frames (very much like those of the production 1949-51 Lincoln and 1952-57 Nash) were abandoned, too. They would have required expensive plated metal or extruded aluminum.

Though wartime studies were examined when Chrysler began planning its first all-new postwar cars, they actually contributed very little to that program. For one thing, they were obsolete by then. The industry was moving away from bulky, rounded styling—if not in current 1948-49 products, then at least for those to come in the early Fifties. And K. T. Keller, who was adamant about the need for adequate headroom, wanted boxy, upright cars rather than streamlined torpedos. That is exactly what he got.

Ironically, Keller's boxy '49s were far more efficient in use of space and raw materials than the 1943-45 prototypes, yet the wartime designs probably would have sold better. The public resisted the "boxes" in increasing numbers after about 1950, and Ford passed Chrysler in volume by 1952. Chrysler styling, which had been the industry's most practical in 1949-54, became flashy but handsome for 1955-56. The 1957 models ushered in the age of tailfins. After that, things would never be the same.

While compiling a proud record of service in the nation's war effort, Chrysler raked in huge profits from fat government contracts. It thus entered the postwar world in splendid financial shape, still under the no-nonsense leadership of Kaufman Thuma Keller. Once the hard-boiled protege of Walter Percy Chrysler, Keller had become the dominant corporate officer once the founder took ill in 1938. Like his mentor, he remained a man with definite likes—and dislikes. One postwar writer described him as "short, bull-shouldered, profane, his approach as direct and decisive as Dempsey's right to the ribs. He appears to run Chrysler exactly as he pleases, with results that generally please the stockholders." And he did run it—characteristically, from a modest office within the Highland Park factory and not from a grand cloister in downtown Detroit.

Yet for a time, it appeared that the Chrysler company had lost its soul when it lost its founder. Observed *Fortune* magazine in 1948: "That the roll call of Chrysler Corporation's more romantic achievements ceases when the active life of Walter P. Chrysler ceases is scarcely a fact to be set with as pure coincidence. It is equally true, however, that Chrysler Corporation hasn't ceased to be

successful, and it is never so rich, of course, as it is today." The latter half of that statement is purely ephemeral, however, for Chrysler's wealth varied directly with its ability to field exciting cars. And whenever the excitement ran out—or the bizarre set in—the wealth trickled away just a few years later. By the early Fifties, after a near decade of design stagnation, Chrysler was outproduced by Ford for the first time in years, as noted, and faced a severe sales shortfall. The company would bounce back in 1955, only to stagnate again late in the decade. This cycle would be repeated in the Sixties, and once more—with almost fatal results—in the Seventies.

But those turbulent times lay far ahead as Chrysler resumed peacetime operations in late 1945. It remained the conservative, engineering-oriented company it had always been, one that had enjoyed remarkable success and had managed to survive the Depression despite a near-disastrous marketing mistake. And Chrysler wasn't about to change its way of doing business. B. E. "Hutch" Hutchinson, vice-president for finance and now 61 years old, defined it this way: "It is to engineer good products, provide good facilities with which to make them, pay off your debts, and divide what is left with your stockholders, giving them as much as you can." That was about as straightforward as a business type ever gets. Hutch said nothing about industry "leadership" or "contributions." He didn't even look back to the firm's illustrious heritage. To *Fortune* magazine's William B. Harris, his tone had only "the cold, clear ring of the counting-house."

Ultimately, Chrysler would come to be dominated by accountants, in the Sixties, yet somehow it would always retain its aura as an "engineers' company." It certainly entered the postwar world that way, continuing to stress steady plant modernization and improvement just as Walter P. Chrysler always had. And even at the lowest points in its history, Chrysler would never sink to the level of, say, Studebaker, which gave away most of its earnings to its workers, executives, and stockholders to the ultimate detriment of its factory. Facilities were never figured high on Chrysler's balance sheets, but they were constantly improved. In fact, Chrysler Corporation had the lowest ratio of fixed assets to sales of any domestic auto builder. In 1941, for example, with production at capacity, Chrysler's figure was 12 cents to the dollar, against 36 cents for GM.

Because of this steady modernization program, Chrysler's facility depreciation expense was enormous. "Just what the eventual cost of replacing facilities now in use may be is obscure," Keller once said, noting "government indices show that industrial building construction costs have risen 83 percent since 1939. There have also been substantial increases in the prices of machinery and equipment. The level at which prices may stabilize is, to say the least, uncertain."

Of all Chrysler operations, those in or near Detroit comprised 70 percent of its facilities and employed close to 80 percent of its workforce. Most division assembly plants were in the Detroit area. Employment in 1950, for example, was 12,000 for Plymouth, 4000 for DeSoto, and

continued on page 129

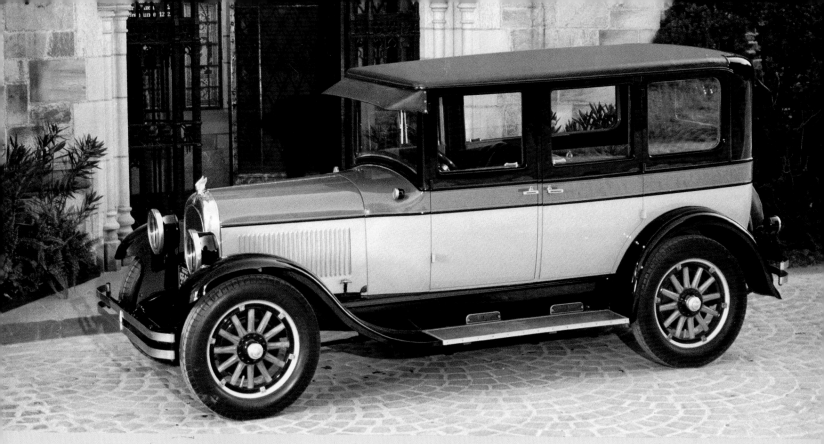

The six-cylinder "70" was the mainstay of the Chrysler line in the make's early years. Shown above is the 1926 Series G-70 four-door sedan. Left: Also from 1926, a four-cylinder Series 58 coupe with Fisher bodywork and an unusual left sidemount. Lower left: A handsomely restored example of the 1928 Chrysler Series 52 rumble-seat roadster. Original list price was $725. Below: One of the earliest Plymouths, a 1928-29 Model Q DeLuxe coupe. It cost $720 new.

Chrysler styling reached its peak in the Classic era with the 1931 models, inspired by the Cord L-29. *Above and right:* The magnificent 1933 Imperial Series CL five-passenger dual-cowl phaeton. *Lower right:* One of only 49 built, this 1932 Imperial CL convertible sedan boasted LeBaron bodywork and a smooth 385-cid straight eight. *Opposite page, clockwise from top left:* The 1932 Imperial Series CH five-passenger sedan; 1931 Chrysler CD "New Eight" convertible coupe; 1934 Custom Imperial Airflow Series CW seven-passenger sedan (with '35 grille conversion); 1934 Chrysler Series CU Airflow Eight brougham; 1936 DeSoto Series S-3 Airflow III brougham.

*S*hown top left is one of the last Airflows, a Chrysler Series C-17 sedan from 1937. Top right: 1938 Chrysler Royal business coupe. Above: From 1939, the DeSoto Series S-6 Custom four-door touring sedan. Right: Chrysler Corporation's only convertible sedan for 1939 was this Plymouth P-8 DeLuxe. Just 387 were built. Opposite page, top left: 1940 Chrysler New Yorker convertible coupe. Top right: 1940 Chrysler Royal coupe. Center: One of the six Newport show cars from 1940. Bottom: 1941 Chrysler New Yorker convertible coupe.

The first Chrysler Town & Country (right) appeared in the 1941 Windsor series as a six- or nine-seat wagon with unique "clamshell" rear doors. Production totaled 997 units. Center: The 1948 Chrysler Royal business coupe. Bottom: Also from 1948, the Chrysler Town & Country convertible. Opposite page, top left: 1948 Chrysler New Yorker convertible. Top right: The rare 1950 Chrysler Town & Country Newport hardtop. Only 700 were made. Center: The 1950 four-door sedan from Dodge's topline Coronet series. Bottom left: Plymouth's Suburban was one of the first all-steel postwar station wagons. Shown is the 1950 model. Bottom right: 1950 Chrysler Windsor four-door sedan.

Chrysler's 1951-52 Imperial Newport tops the facing page. Center left: The 1954 Chrysler New Yorker Deluxe convertible saw only 724 copies. Center right: Production of the 1953 Chrysler New Yorker Deluxe convertible was a mere 950. Bottom: The 1955 Chrysler C-300, first of "The Beautiful Brutes." This page, top left: Dodge's 1956 Royal hardtop coupe (prototype lacks rear fender script). Top right: The "Forward Look" came to Chrysler for 1956, as exemplified by this Plymouth Belvedere convertible. Center left: 1956 Chrysler New Yorker Newport hardtop coupe. Center right: Also from '56, the snazzy DeSoto Firedome Seville hardtop coupe. Left (clockwise from top): DeSoto Fireflite four-door sedan, Chrysler New Yorker hardtop sedan, the Imperial Southampton hardtop sedan, Dodge Custom Royal convertible, and Plymouth Belvedere hardtop sedan, all from 1956.

Chrysler Corporation became Detroit's styling leader for 1957-58 with cars like the ones shown here. Right: 1957 Chrysler New Yorker two-door hardtop. Center: 1957 Dodge Custom Royal Lancer two-door hardtop. Bottom: Plymouth's hot Fury two-door hardtop, also from 1957. Opposite page, top: The performance Chrysler for 1958 was the 300D, available as the two-door hardtop shown or as a convertible. Center left: The 1958 DeSoto Fireflite convertible, photographed with some flattering lens trickery. Center right: The 1958 Chrysler Windsor two-door hardtop. Bottom: Among the pricier Plymouths for 1958 were the Belvedere hardtop coupe (foreground) and convertible (right) and the Custom Suburban, this year's top-line wagon.

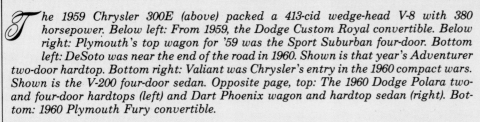

*T*he 1959 Chrysler 300E (above) packed a 413-cid wedge-head V-8 with 380 horsepower. Below left: From 1959, the Dodge Custom Royal convertible. Below right: Plymouth's top wagon for '59 was the Sport Suburban four-door. Bottom left: DeSoto was near the end of the road in 1960. Shown is that year's Adventurer two-door hardtop. Bottom right: Valiant was Chrysler's entry in the 1960 compact wars. Shown is the V-200 four-door sedan. Opposite page, top: The 1960 Dodge Polara two- and four-door hardtops (left) and Dart Phoenix wagon and hardtop sedan (right). Bottom: 1960 Plymouth Fury convertible.

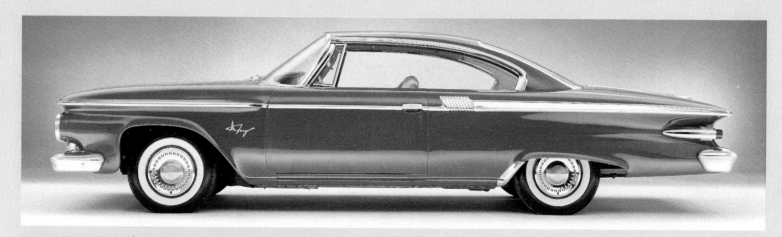

A quartet of two-door hardtops (opposite page) shows how fins began to disappear at Chrysler Corporation after 1960. From top: 1961 Plymouth Fury, 1961 DeSoto, 1962 Chrysler Newport, 1962 Plymouth Fury. This page, top: Dodge, along with Plymouth, radically downsized its big cars for 1962. Shown is that year's hot bucket-seat Polara 500 two-door hardtop. Above left: From 1962, the pert Dodge Dart 270 convertible. Above right: 1963 Chrysler New Yorker four-door hardtop. Left: Bucket-seat Sport Fury was Plymouth's equivalent to Dodge's Polara 500. Shown is the 1963 two-door hardtop.

*C*omplex grillework marked the mid-size 1963 Dodges, as on this Polara (shown above). Below left: The prestige Imperial Crown convertible for 1964. Left: Dodge revived a full-size model during 1962 under the Custom 880 label. Shown is the '63 four-door hardtop. Below: The sporty bucket-seat Dodge Dart GT two-door hardtop for 1964.

continued from page 112

34,000 for Dodge (whose Hamtramck plant built castings, stampings, motors and bodies for other divisions in addition to assembly of Dodge cars.) Dodge Truck accounted for another 5000 workers, and the Chrysler plant at Jefferson Avenue—which also produced engines—employed close to 10,000. Other Detroit-area plants included Lynch Road (axles and housings), Dodge Forge, Nine-Mile Press (stampings), Winfield (foundry), and Dearborn (bodies and motors). At Highland Park on Detroit's near-north side were the executive, styling, and engineering offices as well as Mopar spare parts and Fluid Drive production facilities.

Chrysler would begin diversifying after the war, setting up plants in Newark, Delaware; Trenton, Michigan; Indianapolis; and New Orleans. However, assembly plants outside Michigan were confined to the Dodge/Plymouth points in California and Indiana. Some transmissions and front-end parts were built in Kokomo and New Castle, Indiana, and some minor parts were supplied from Marysville, Michigan. Centralization would ultimately prove a problem, since Chrysler lacked the economies of scale enjoyed by GM and Ford, who had far more assembly plants scattered throughout the country. Yet Chrysler made more profit per car than its two major rivals, and this gave management little cause to worry that Plymouth was always outsold by Ford and Chevrolet. What mattered was the bottom line.

K. T. Keller once remarked with a smile, "How flattering to be considered one of the Big Three." In 1946, Chrysler was not only "considered" but *was* one of the Big Three. Actually it was still one of the Big Two. And as the vast extent of demand in a car-starved market became apparent, it seemed nothing could budge Chrysler from that hard-won position. But there was something and, as events would prove soon enough, it was the corporation itself.

1946

Chrysler Corporation had built a variety of defense equipment during World War II, and the output of its various divisions was astronomical. Included in the count were 120,000 anti-aircraft guns, half of all the Bofors and 40mm "pom-pom" naval weapons; over 18,000 nine-cylinder Wright-Cyclone aircraft engines; 20,000 land-mine detectors; 2000 radar units; 1500 searchlight reflectors; 5500 Sperry Gyrocompasses, built under license; 7800 "Sea Mules" or utility harbor tugs; and 29,000 marine engines. But the product for which Highland Park was most renowned was the tank, in particular the Sherman tank. Of the some 25,000 tanks produced by Chrysler, 18,000 were the impervious, indomitable Shermans, all built at the Detroit Tank Arsenal that K. T. Keller had constructed for their production. No one can question Chrysler's dedication to the war effort. Not only were its products durable, but its profits as a

1946-48 Chrysler C-38W Windsor convertible: $1861-$2414.

1946-48 Chrysler C-39N New Yorker club coupe

1946-48 Chrysler C-39K Saratoga four-door sedan

1946-48 Chrysler C-38S Royal two-door brougham sedan

percent of sales were below average for the wartime motor industry.

The government ban on auto production was lifted fairly late in 1945, and the company produced only a handful of 1946-model cars that year. A semblance of normal volume appeared in early 1946. No one was in the least surprised that, as at other producers, Chrysler's '46s

1946-48 Chrysler C-38W Windsor 8-passenger sedan

1947-48 Chrysler C-38W Windsor Traveler sedan

1946-48 Chrysler C-38/39 Town & Country convertible

Prototype 1946 Chrysler Town & Country hardtop coupe

were merely mildly facelifted extensions of its 1942s. And they would remain so for the next two model years.

With the company hauling out prewar dies, its various makes continued their traditional differences in wheelbases and engine specs, and this remained a very closely knit family stylistically. The 1946 Chrysler used multi-

bar, cross-hatched grillework reminiscent of a harmonica. DeSoto had established a vertical-bar grille motif before the war, and this was retained for '46. It also had an attractively sculpted woman as a hood mascot instead of Chrysler's twin wings. Dodge continued its '42 eggcrate grillework and usual ram hood mascot. Plymouth still relied on a horizontal-bar front and customary sailing ship mascot. Lucite plastic was something unusual at the time, and some DeSoto and Plymouth hood ornaments were made of it, wired to light up at night.

As was often the case in the prewar period, the Chryslers were easily the best-looking of the firm's 1946 cars because they rode longer wheelbases than the junior makes: 121½ inches for the six-cylinder Royals, Windsors, and Town & Country sedan; 127½ inches for the straight-eight Saratoga, New Yorker, and Town & Country; and 145½ inches for the Crown Imperial limousine. There was also a quartet of long-wheelbase Royals and Windsors (139½ inches) to serve the less posh commercial trade. As with the lesser makes, wheelbases and body styles followed a logical progression. The standard four- and two-door sedans (the latter known as brougham) were sold alongside a long-deck club coupe with a shorter greenhouse and roughly triangular side windows. A variation was a "turret-top" business coupe, with a huge deck and single bench seat placed ahead of a cargo platform inside the "turret." Long-wheelbase models were just stretched sedans, the chauffeur's compartment done in traditional leather and the rear section upholstered with cloth. Convertibles were built on a heavier frame to preserve rigidity, hence their greater weight and price. Availability was limited to two in the Chrysler lineup and one each for DeSoto, Dodge, and Plymouth.

Postwar materials shortages made whitewall tires scarce for a time, so Chrysler dealers substituted painted steel or white plastic "doughnuts" that were hung around the hubcaps to separate the plain black tire from the hub. These were sometimes standard, but as an option they rarely cost more than $15 per set and were quite popular.

Early-postwar Chrysler interiors were not known for breathtaking color, but convertibles were well-trimmed, with two-tone Bedford cord and leather. The brilliant prewar "Highlander plaid" upholstery was revived, using a tartan cloth in combination with red leather bolsters. The Chrysler instrument panel was one of the most ornate and opulent in the industry, heavily embellished with chrome and plastic, the latter still considered an exotic material. A full set of engine instruments conveyed vital information in a straightforward manner.

The mechanical makeup of Chrysler Corporation's early-postwar products was almost entirely carried over from prewar models. Chryslers had one of two engines depending on model: the "Spitfire Six" for the junior C-38s (250.6 cubic inches, 114 horsepower at 3600 rpm) and the "Spitfire Eight" (323.5 cid, 135 bhp at 3400 rpm) for the senior C-39s and C-40 Imperial. Driving impressions hardly differed, since the eight's incremental power advantage was nullified by the senior models' greater weight, and it takes a Chrysler expert to tell what is under the hood from behind the wheel. Both power units provided ample torque but leisurely, low-revving horsepower, and were quiet runners that took a long time to work up to cruising velocity.

As before, all Chrysler Corporation engines continued to feature Dave Wallace's "Superfinish" for '46. The company description of this patented process touted "mirror-bright" engine parts that "reduce break-in...reduce wear...preserve compression...hold gasoline and oil consumption to an efficient minimum...keep Chrysler engines young." All powerplants rode on sturdy ladder chassis of box-section steel. Watching his car being assembled at Jefferson Avenue, one customer asked if the frame that a crew had just picked off a pile was a good one. "Mister," came the reply, "if we got a bad frame, we wouldn't waste it on a guy like you. We'd send it to the Smithsonian Institution as a curiosity."

Fluid Drive remained Chrysler's most popular option of the day. It was optionally available on Dodges, DeSotos, and Chryslers in 1946, and was standard on Dodges and Chryslers after that. It was another of those Chrysler engineering feats that had intrigued *Fortune* magazine and many others in the years when Walter Chrysler was still around. Fluid Drive first appeared in 1938 and was standard on the 1939 Custom Imperials, but was not widely specified until after the war. In retrospect, it appears over-complicated, combining a conventional clutch with a torque converter and electric shifting circuits. Altogether, as one wag commented, Fluid Drive "afforded a full range of potential transmission trouble." But Americans were thinking of shiftless motoring, and the successful car manufacturer had to have it in one form or another.

The most memorable Chryslers of 1946-48 are the fabulous Town & Country convertibles and sedans. Beloved by such celebrities as Bob Hope, Barbara Stanwyck, Ray Milland, and Clark Gable, the T&C has gained an unmerited reputation as a sort of Duesenberg of the Forties, which it was not. While the Duesenberg was mechanically impeccable and an aesthetic triumph, the T&C was a stock Chrysler mechanically, and its styling was deplored as much as praised. What sold it was uniqueness. The application of wagon-style wood planking made the prewar bodies new and striking, especially in 1946.

The Town & Country name had been applied to special models in the past (it was seen in one of the 1934 Airflow brochures), but the most direct reference came from Paul Hafer of the Boyertown (Pennsylvania) Body Works, which occasionally supplied woody bodies to the industry. In 1939, Hafer made sketches of wood-bodied wagons intended for the Dodge chassis, one of which he called "Town & Country." Said Hafer in 1973: "The steel front end looked 'town' and the wood portion looked 'country,' so I thought it natural." The first production models to bear the name were the 1941-42 station wagons (see year entries).

Reaching for something unusual to attract customers, Chrysler Division originally planned a whole fleet of Town & Country models for '46, including a brougham, roadster, hardtop, sedan, and convertible. The first three were never released for production, though one brougham and seven hardtops were built experimentally (the latter

1946 Chrysler Town & Country eight-cylinder sedan

1946-47 Chrysler C-38W Windsor Highlander convertible

1946-48 Chrysler C-38S Royal business coupe

1946-48 DeSoto S-11C Custom two-door brougham sedan

1946-48 DeSoto S-11C Custom Suburban 8-passenger sedan

were actually the first postwar pillarless coupes). Ultimately, the division settled for a four-door sedan on the shorter six-cylinder C-38 platform as well as a convertible and four-door on the eight-cylinder C-39 chassis. (One short-wheelbase six-cylinder convertible was also built but never officially offered.)

Priced at $2743, the convertible was the first T&C announced, and grew to become the most famous and favored of all. The wood trim added grace and beauty to the familiar Chrysler lines, and the ragtop was the most luxuriously trimmed model in the range. Its white ash framing added structural rigidity to doors and decklid, was beautifully fitted with interlocking miters, and was varnished to perfection. Mahogany veneer plywood decorated the spaces within the framing. All body surfaces were covered by wood from the cowl back, with the exception of the rear fenders. Equipment included two-speed electric wipers, cut-pile carpeting and, initially, spotlights. There was a wide variety of interior trim, including leather and Bedford cord.

Upkeep was a problem. Shop manuals gave detailed instructions, informing the owner that any car so aristocratic deserved special care. Special, indeed! To maintain their glossy looks, T&Cs really had to be stripped and revarnished every year, with special attention given to corners and seams where water had entered the grain. Few owners followed the instructions, so most T&Cs began to look tatty after a while. Body panel replacement costs were very high. A Windsor front door cost $58.17, for example, against $304.78 for a Town & Country door.

Chrysler produced 8368 Town & Country convertibles through 1948. Company records also show 100 eight-cylinder sedans and 4049 six-cylinder sedans built for the same period. Though industry records show all three styles were available for 1946, Chrysler states that neither sedan went on sale until January 7, 1947 and that only 124 six-cylinder sedans were considered 1946 models. The eights didn't sell well and were dropped during 1947-48.

Town & Country sedan interiors were magnificently finished with rich grained wood paneling, and boasted color-keyed headliners, seats, and carpets. A novel Saran plastic of great durability alternated with Bedford cord as upholstery choices. Wood also decorated headliners and door panels. Some sedans came with a wooden luggage rack and roof runners, which were changed to chromium-plated metal in June 1947. The rack was an option for Royal and Windsor limousines at $115 and became standard on T&C sedans beginning July 16, 1947. But the chrome rack lacked the elegance of the wood one, which blended perfectly with the lower body's heavily varnished planking.

Below the 1946 Chryslers were the S-11 DeSotos, priced roughly $200-$250 less. These rode a 121½-inch wheelbase and were powered by a 236.6-cid flathead six that developed 109 bhp, incrementally smaller and less powerful than the Chrysler six. DeSoto also offered one long-wheelbase chassis (139½ inches) for a limousine and a Suburban sedan. DeSoto bodies thus matched those of the Chrysler Windsor exactly, the only differences being at the front end and in minor trim details. The DeSoto

1946-48 Plymouth P-15C Special DeLuxe four-door sedan

1946-48 Dodge D-24C Custom convertible. Just 9500 were built.

grille, a ponderous affair composed of large vertical bars, was die cast and thus cheaper to produce than the Chrysler eggcrate. This and somewhat less lavish interiors continued to separate the two makes. Nevertheless, these DeSotos were big, rugged cars, competing squarely in the middle of what was then the medium-priced field against GM's smaller Buicks and Oldsmobiles and Ford's Mercury. DeSoto had three improving years in 1946-48, moving from 67,000 units in model year 1946 to nearly 100,000 in 1948 and holding on to a consistent 12th place in industry sales, ahead of Mercury but well behind Buick and Olds. With the limited options available in those days, there was a strict price differentiation between DeSoto and its flanking linemates, Chrysler and Dodge. But as time passed and Dodges grew more luxurious, DeSoto would ultimately be crowded out.

As in 1941-42, DeSoto's 1946 lineup was divided into base DeLuxe and fancier Custom series. The former listed only coupes and sedans, with the latter containing the convertible and long-wheelbase sedans as well. A surprise postwar newcomer was the eight-passenger Suburban sedan introduced in November 1946. Designed to provide the ultimate in stylish hauling for hotels, airports, and well-heeled individuals, it featured a fold-down rear seat without trunk partition, thus providing a huge cargo hold. A metal-and-wood roof rack, beautifully finished wooden interior panels, and seats upholstered in Delon plastic completed the package. The whole contraption weighed nearly two tons and cost $2093, the most expensive postwar DeSoto by far. Between introduction and the end of the 1949 "First Series" models, DeSoto built 7500 Suburbans, which was no mean feat for a low-volume marque in those years. (Incidentally, DeSoto did contemplate a wood-trimmed Suburban. At least one proto-

1946-48 Plymouth P-15C Special DeLuxe wagon

Dodge's 1946-48 D-24S DeLuxe business coupe

type was built, but nothing came of the idea.)

Chrysler's slowest-starting division after the war was Dodge, which produced only 420 of its 1946 models by the end of 1945. But Dodge turned out cars rapidly between January and December of 1946, finishing the year fourth behind Chevy, Ford, and Plymouth and contributing mightily to Chrysler's success. The make's 1946 facelift was handled by Buzz Grisinger, John Chika, and Herb Weissinger. Allowed bolt-alterations only, they opted for a new grille with very wide horizontal and vertical bars that formed a rectangular pattern. Square parking lights were located at either side of the grille, with the Dodge nameplate displayed above. Mechanical revisions included changing the starter from a foot pedal to a button on the dash, front brakes equipped with twin wheel cylinders, and a modified transmission. An inline fuel filter and full-flow oil filter were made standard.

One component that was easy to change on any car, despite carryover bodies, was the dashboard, and Dodge's went through continuous alterations in the Forties. Prewar Dodge instrument panels were spartan and symmetrical; postwar dashboards were asymmetrical and gaudy. Dodge paid attention to practicality, however, by retaining needle gauges that clearly delivered their messages.

Fluid Drive, a 1946 option that became a Dodge standard the following year, was an important aid to sales in the early postwar era. None of the low-priced three had anything like it. Dodge therefore had the cheapest semiautomatic car on the market, only a couple of hundred dollars more than a Ford, Chevy, or Plymouth.

Like DeSoto, Dodge used one basic (119½-inch) wheelbase, with a longer (137½-inch) platform for its seven-passenger models. DeLuxe and Custom series returned from

1942, the latter still including the sole convertible. Prices began at $1229, and no model except the convertible ($1649) and long sedan ($1743) cost more than $1500.

Dodge's flathead six was only fractionally smaller than DeSoto's, with a smaller bore and longer stroke. One wonders why Chrysler bothered with two separate engines, since they were only 4 bhp apart in output and varied in displacement by only six cubic inches, but a Dodge was quicker than a comparable DeSoto because it was lighter. Indeed, the make's future reputation as the "hot" Mopar could be said to have started just after the war, although Dodge was by no means in the same class with the Ford V-8 in these years. Dodge would later introduce Chrysler Corporation's first, low-price V-8, which transformed the make's performance and its image.

The 1946 Plymouth was altered from its 1942 predecessor by elongated rear fenders, a simpler grille (a clean brace of horizontal bars), and bumpers that now wrapped around at all four corners. Like Dodge and DeSoto, the model lineup continued with two series, the price-leader DeLuxe and the more elaborate Special DeLuxe, though body choices were fewer than in 1942. Each series contained a pair of coupes and sedans; a woody wagon and convertible were exclusive to the Special Deluxe. You could buy a Plymouth for as little as $1100 in 1946, about $100 more than a Chevrolet. The most you could pay was about $1550 for the woody wagon. The convertible cost $1439. Also like DeSoto and Dodge, Plymouth continued with its prewar flathead six, the familiar 217.8-cid longstroker, still rated at 95 bhp. A sturdy if uninspired powerplant, it would continue in one form or another through 1959.

Plymouth's sales performance was impressive in the early postwar years. Although Chrysler records do not break out individual model year production for 1946-48, proportional calculations from the *Encyclopedia of American Cars 1930-1980* suggest that Plymouth came closer to Chevrolet and Ford than most historians realize—and it would never again come so close to Ford.

Model Year	1946	1947	1948	Total
Chevrolet	398,028	671,546	696,449	1,766,023
Ford	468,022	429,674	430,198	1,327,894
Plymouth	264,660	382,290	412,540	1,059,490

Plymouth built a million cars in 1946-48 to hold down a solid third place in industry sales, and combined Dodge/Plymouth output was almost equal that of first-place Chevrolet in each of these model years. It was on this combination—and combined Dodge-Plymouth dealerships—that Chrysler had built its position as the number-two producer after GM in the prewar era, a rank it would hold in the early postwar period.

Another holdover from 1942 was the three types of Mopar dealerships: Chrysler, DeSoto, and Dodge, each teamed with Plymouth. While the factory carefully avoided having too many outlets in a given territory, the fact that they all sold Plymouths made for a good deal of rivalry. It also made for good sales. Because of Dodge's greater volume, however, it was the Dodge-Plymouth franchises that enjoyed the highest total annual sales.

1947

Chrysler Corporation's 1947 lineup was largely a carryover from 1946. Although there were some changes, none of them were major. The marketing and manufacturing considerations that led to the use of prewar dies still applied, and the nation's demand for automobiles still exceeded the industry's ability to supply. Chrysler's corporate planning called for continuing the same basic models through model year 1948 as well.

The 1947 Chryslers looked almost the same as the '46s except for detail changes to fender trim, hubcaps, colors, carburetors, wheels, and instruments. Chrysler also phased in Goodyear low-pressure Super Cushion tires between August and November of 1947. Prices were about $100 higher this year. Fluid Drive was standard on the Crown Imperial, optional on other models.

Chrysler's main attraction for 1947 was the unique Traveler, a new offering in the Windsor line. It was perhaps inspired by DeSoto's more ambitious Suburban, but the two cars were not merely different versions of the same theme. The Traveler rode a standard 121½-inch wheelbase and had a roof rack and fixed rear seat. The DeSoto, on the other hand, had a 139½-inch wheelbase, triple seats that could be folded or switched, plus wooden planking in the trunk area and no partition between trunk and seats. If the Suburban was more versatile than the Traveler, it's probably because the Briggs Body Company had taken an interest in it. According to former DeSoto body engineer James Shank, interviewed in *Special-Interest Autos* magazine, Briggs created the trim work and styling, while DeSoto mounted body to frame and completed the detailing.

Though the Traveler was more like a conventional sedan, the Suburban was a genuine payload hauler, designed with an eye to maximum space utilization. It was, in fact, designed primarily for commercial use. Hence, its middle and front seats were completely interchangeable. Even with all three seats in use, there was room for eight suitcases and a golf bag in the trunk. The middle and third seat could be folded down, opening up the entire area behind the front seat for cargo. The Traveler was also carefully planned. There was an optional canvas cover for roof rack luggage, and even little step plates that hooked into the rear of the running boards to make it easier to reach the roof. Only 4182 Travelers were built for the 1947 and 1948 model years, making them among the rarer postwar Chrysler Corporation products.

DeSotos changed even less than Chryslers for 1947. In fact, there were no exterior alterations at all. The only way to differentiate between the two model years is by looking at serial numbers. The beginning number for 1946 was #5784001; for 1947, it was #5825784. The model year started in January.

Dodge made Fluid Drive standard for 1947, but aside from this important sales feature the cars themselves were little altered. The same models and body styles

1946-48 Chrysler C-40 Crown Imperial limousine

returned, but prices were about $110 higher across the board. One change, known mainly by very devoted students of the marque, was that the traditional ram hood ornament was more detailed for 1947-48.

Plymouth made no changes at all for 1947, except to assign a starting serial number in January. Prices were up about $50 model for model.

If Chrysler didn't find it necessary to alter its cars very much for 1947, certain others did. Chief among them was the Derham Bodyworks of Rosemont, Pennsylvania. One of the few coachbuilders still operating at the end of World War II, Derham devised several interesting conversions of Chrysler products. There were tandem-windshield phaetons (one built for the King of Saudi Arabia), a

1946-48 DeSoto S-11C Custom Suburban 8-passenger sedan

1946-47 DeSoto S-11C Custom two-door brougham sedan

1946-48 Dodge D-24C Custom club coupe: $1384-$1792.

1946-48 Plymouth P-15C Special DeLuxe four-door sedan

pair of Lincoln Continental-like two-door coupes on stretched wheelbases, a seven-passenger Pullman limo (built for cereal fortune heiress Marjorie Merriwether Post), and a fleet of formal sedans and limousines with blind rear quarters and leather- or canvas-covered padded tops. DeSotos were reworked by a few commercial body builders, notably Superior, which built hearses and flower cars, and the Sky-View Taxicab Company, creators of the "moonroof" DeSoto cabs once common in big cities. Superior also carried out commercial modifications on long-wheelbase Dodges, and the Canadian firm of John Little built a unique lwb Dodge ambulance. Perhaps the most memorable of all these early-postwar customs was a Chrysler coupe commissioned by the Zippo lighter com-

pany of Bradford, Pennsylvania, with the passenger compartment reworked to look like a huge Zippo lighter, lid raised and an enormous illuminated "flame" trailing out the top. None of these specials were very important to the Mopar sales picture.

1948

A postwar expansion program begun by K. T. Keller in mid-1945 added 4.5 million square feet to Chrysler Corporation plant facilities over the next three years. A new Dodge factory employing 1200 workers was opened in San Leandro, California, in 1948. Plymouth was already established in Los Angeles. But Chrysler remained largely a Detroit manufacturer, and it was the Michigan facilities that were most responsible for its success. Model year production rose dramatically: from 580,000 units in 1946 to 832,000 in 1947, then to 885,000 in 1948. Throughout these three years, the company relied on its prewar styles. Indeed, there was no reason to change. The postwar seller's market was in full bloom, the nation needing over 25 million new cars during that time.

Once again, Highland Park's cars were hardly altered for 1948. The Chryslers were introduced on January 2, with prices again higher, by $75 to $95. Chrysler's hydraulic transmission and Fluid Drive were combined as one option, and whitewall tires and stainless-steel wheel trim rings became available in April for the first time since the war. But there was still no fully automatic transmission. Chrysler Corporation gave *Fortune* magazine "the impression that it will string along with the Fluid Drive [though] everyone else in the business is scrambling to build something as good as Buick's Dynaflow.... Reasonable fuel consumption, plus good acceleration, is a Chrysler talking point; accommodation of interior design to the facts of human anatomy is another; mechanical integrity is still another. In short, Chrysler is selling transportation. K. T. Keller has said, 'Wide as our research interests range, you may be sure that more time and attention, and more money, is spent year in and year

1946-48 Plymouth P-15C Special DeLuxe convertible

1946-48 Plymouth P-15C Special DeLuxe wagon

1946-48 Chrysler C-38W Windsor Highlander convertible

1946-48 Plymouth P-15C Special DeLuxe convertible

1946-48 DeSoto S-11C Custom four-door sedan

1946-48 Plymouth P-15C Special DeLuxe four-door sedan

1946-48 Dodge D-24S DeLuxe four-door sedan

1946-48 Plymouth P-15C Special DeLuxe club coupe

out on these quiet means of individual satisfaction than upon creating revolutionary vehicles and power plants.'"

This certainly seemed to be the case on the lower-echelon Chrysler makes, which were likewise little changed for 1948. DeSoto marked the new model year by starting with a new serial number (#5885816). Dodge did the same (#31011766), and Plymouth followed suit.

By now the firm was well along on its first totally new postwar designs, but the long-awaited models wouldn't be ready for January 1949. Accordingly, the company continued selling its '48s into the first several months of '49. These cars thus became known as the 1949 "First Series," though hardly anyone (except maybe their owners) considered them true '49s.

The Chrysler Town & Country was mostly a carryover this year. Prices were up slightly. The convertible now stood at $3395, a truly stratospheric sum that was higher than for a Cadillac. Di-Noc decals had replaced the T&C's genuine mahogany veneer in late 1947. This year, the optional dummy whitewall "doughnuts" were dropped once true whitewalls became available. The 1948 T&C was available with the usual upholstery choices of leather or Bedford cord, but the cars could be somewhat customized because so much of them was built by hand. Though the six-cylinder sedan was still around, the convertible got most 1948 publicity. "Chrysler's work or play convertible," read one ad, was "magnificent in its utterly new styling, in the smooth, responsive power of Chrysler gyro Fluid Drive and improved hydraulically operated transmission...another triumph of Chrysler's imaginative engineering—first in the field with the developments that really matter!" You can't say Chrysler didn't try to get as much PR as possible out of its fabulous woody.

It would be hard to come up with another three years as proportionally successful for Chrysler as 1946-48. Starting literally from ground zero, the company had poured its huge resources into plant expansion and production, and by 1948 it was as solidly entrenched as the industry's second largest producer as it had been in the immediate prewar years. The troubles would come later. For now, Chrysler faced 1949 with its make-or-break redesigns against equally new models from GM, Ford, and the independents. That the road ahead would be rocky was unknown to K. T. Keller. He maintained that Chrysler products were primarily intended to be comfortable and well engineered, not industry design pacesetters. Keller would soon learn whether or not this was the right formula for future success.

1949

One thing about K. T. Keller: he always meant exactly what he said. When he announced to the postwar public that Chrysler would shun fads in favor of stolid practicality, everybody took him at his word. The '49 models proved it: only Chrysler called them "stylish." Introduced in the spring of 1949, the firm's first all-new postwar designs were new but hardly radical, fully restyled but still tall and boxier than before. By contrast, Ford Motor Company's 1949 cars looked sleeker, while GM's various lines—some of which had been redesigned for 1948—looked almost a generation fresher. As for the independents, Packard's 1948 facelift was more evolutionary than Chrysler's '49s, while Studebaker was still a good five years ahead of anything Highland Park had. Likewise, the Step-down Hudson, also introduced for 1948, and Nash's new '49 Airflyte were more advanced than Chrysler's newest, at least in the context of their time. The best one could say of Chrysler's Silver Anniversary 1949 products was that they just managed to be as modern as their Kaiser-Frazer rivals, which by then were three years old. Even so, K-F had integral fenders fore and aft, while rear fenders were still separate at Chrysler Corporation.

Not that streamlining and integral fenders hadn't been contemplated. The numerous clays and prototypes developed for the 1949 program suggested that Chrysler would do away with old-fashioned styling elements, but nearly all the proposals were sleeker and more contemporary than what ultimately emerged. For example, the experimental A109 DeSoto/Dodge, a running model of which was on hand as early as September 1946, had flow-through fenders, as did the A116, a similar experiment with Chrysler proportions. Though the two designs were quite close to the final 1949 shape, neither they nor their alternatives ever made it into production. The reason they didn't, say most of the people involved with Styling at the time, was K. T. Keller.

Though Oliver Clark was still running Chrysler Art & Colour in the late Forties, he was an engineer first and a

1949 Chrysler New Yorker four-door sedan: $2726.

Chrysler's 1949 Royal wagon. Just 850 were built.

The $3206 Chrysler New Yorker convertible for 1949

1949 Chrysler Town & Country convertible: $3970.

1949 Chrysler Crown Imperial limousine. Price: $5334.

stylist second. Further, Clark reported to another engineer, Fred Zeder, the final authority on all body proposals. Keller was greatly influenced by the practical, objective engineer's approach, and although he did not specifically point any fingers at the competition, he bluntly told all that Chrysler would not rush pell-mell into streamlining at the expense of comfort. In a 1948 address at the Stanford School of Business, for example, he declared: "The buyer is proud of his car's symphony of line; its coloring and trim express his taste; he welcomes the applause of his friends and his neighbors. But he bought the car to ride in, and for his wife, and children, and friends to ride in.... Many of you Californians may have outgrown the habit, but there are parts of the country containing millions of people, where both the men and

1949 DeSoto Custom club coupe. List price was $2156.

DeSoto's first wagon was this 1949 DeLuxe woody model.

1949 DeSoto DeLuxe Carry-All four-door sedan: $2191.

the ladies are in the habit of getting behind the wheel, or in the back seat, wearing hats...."

Sic transit Chrysler for 1949. Its new cars were definitely wider than their predecessors and had a little more glass area, but their overall look was very "square," in both senses of the word. In fact, the '49s came to be identified with what some called "three-box styling"—one box piled on top of two others. And that basic shape permeated the line from Plymouth to Crown Imperial. The problem with this, of course, was that buyers were becoming much more style-conscious than Keller realized, and many were quite willing to put up with the extra entry/exit contortions required in a car styled more like a torpedo than a tank. Still, it was 1949, the seller's market was still there, and sales were good. This situation lulled several companies, including Chrysler, into a false sense of security.

Lacking any major distinguishing characteristics for their 1949 identities, Chrysler's various makes were set apart mainly by fractional differences in wheelbase and width and by surface embellishments, notably up front. Befitting its price, this year's Chrysler had the company's most ornate grille, two heavy tiers of chrome bisected by smaller horizontal and vertical bars—fewer pieces than the 1946-48 face, though it looked just as heavy. The main grille members wrapped around the front fenders and were joined by large parking lights. A similar ploy was used to identify Chryslers at the rear. Most 1949s bore unique taillights with tall, narrow, plastic lenses mounted on chrome bases and visible from three sides. They were like Cadillac's already famous tailfin lamps, which actually inspired them. Crown Imperials bore round taillights that did not rise above fender level. A massive deck "console" carried Chrysler stoplamp and backup lights, along with the license plate and trunk handle.

Mechanically, there was little change from 1948. Both Chrysler engines got higher compression, but though the six was up to 116 bhp, the eight remained at 135 bhp. Fluid Drive now required no use of the clutch except to downshift or to enter Reverse, and was renamed "Prestomatic." This made it sound more modern in the showrooms, where the transmission was meeting stiff competition from Hydra-Matic and Dynaflow. Ignition was now key-start, waterproofed to ensure damp weather reliability. In an age when manufacturers gave trick names to various mechanical features, Chrysler buyers soon became familiar with Safety-Level Ride, Hydra-Lizer shock absorbers, Safety-Rim wheels, Full-Flow oil filters, and Cyclebonded brake linings. The last three were especially important developments. The Safety Rim was a projecting lip around the perimeter of a steel wheel, which better gripped the tire casing and held it in place in the event of a blowout. The oil filter was mounted directly to the engine, without connecting lines. Cyclebonded linings were attached to the brake shoes without rivets, thus extending the life of the linings. These features were promoted as standard equipment for all the company's 1949 models.

This year's Chrysler line displayed noticeable changes in model offerings aimed at upgrading the make's image.

The limousine, brougham, and coupe disappeared from the Royal series, but a wagon was added at mid-model year. Coupes and broughams also vanished from the Windsor, Saratoga, and New Yorker lines, the theory being that two-door customers were adequately served by the new club coupe. The two long-wheelbase Crown Imperials returned. A newcomer was an Imperial sedan on the New Yorker wheelbase, more luxuriously trimmed and priced nearly $2000 higher, which theoretically gave dealers a glorious profit on unit sales. Unfortunately, the theory didn't pan out, and only 50 of these cars were built.

The 1949 Town & Country, which only entered production on July 8 of this year, appeared only as a convertible, still with Di-Noc decals between the white ash planking.

A T&C Newport hardtop was announced, but only one experimental was built. Curiously, Chrysler decided to offer the T&C Newport for 1950, dropping the convertible. Lack of buyer demand, said the company, was the main reason for the demise of the Town & Country sedans for '49. They were less practical than steel-bodied cars, less glamorous than convertibles. As a substitute, the conventional station wagon came back as a woody on the Royal chassis, with the Di-Noc and white ash combination but initially without the T&C name. Late in the model year, Town & Country convertibles began coming through with the Di-Noc portions eliminated and the spaces painted body color, a further step away from the original T&C concept. Standard 1949 wheelbases were longer: 125½ inches for the Sixes, 131½ inches for the Eights.

1949 Dodge Wayfarer coupe sold for $1611 in base form.

Dodge's natty 1949 Wayfarer roadster (late-year model)

Dodge's 1949 Coronet wood-body wagon. Price was $2865.

The first new postwar Dodge pickups appeared for '49.

The 1949 Dodge Coronet four-door sedan cost $1927.

1949 Plymouth DeLuxe two-door fastback sedan

1949 Plymouth Special DeLuxe convertible: $1982.

Plymouth's 1949 Special DeLuxe wood-body wagon

1949 Plymouth DeLuxe Suburban all-steel wagon (prototype)

The Six and Eight long-wheelbase cars remained at 139½ and 145½ inches, respectively.

DeSoto continued for 1949 as essentially a detrimmed, six-cylinder Chrysler powered by a smaller engine. However, the familiar 236-cid flathead six got a compression boost and now yielded 112 bhp. As usual the line was small, broken into DeLuxe and Custom series. The latter included a long-wheelbase eight-passenger sedan and

nine-passenger Suburban woody sedan. Standard models shared the six-cylinder Chrysler wheelbase. Fluid Drive with "Tip-Toe" hydraulic shift was standard on Customs and optional (at $121) for DeLuxes. DeSoto retained its vertical-bar grille motif, which set it off adequately from Chrysler but made it appear very upright. The DeSoto taillight was similar to Chrysler's but had a smaller lens. The old DeSoto hood ornament was replaced with a circular device containing a bust of Hernando DeSoto. Like all proper 1949 hood ornaments, it glowed brightly when the headlamps were switched on.

DeSoto's most significant new model for the year was the all-steel DeLuxe Carry-All, similar to the Suburban but mounted on the standard-wheelbase chassis. This sedan's rear seat folded down to provide a long cargo bed, much like that of the pioneering Kaiser Traveler and Vagabond of this same year. The difference was that the Kaisers had a double opening "clamshell" rear hatch, while the DeSoto had a conventional trunklid. The Suburban continued to offer enormous cargo space, abetted by a rooftop luggage rack, and nine-passenger capacity, thanks to its jump seats. Of DeSoto's three utility models, the Carry-All pointed the way to the future, selling 2690 copies. Woody wagon production was only 680; Suburban volume was just 129. The Suburban was dropped after 1952 and the wood wagon continued only until 1950. DeSoto then put all its utility-car emphasis on the Carry-All.

Dodge and Plymouth Divisions also ran reserialed '48s through April before bringing out their "true" '49s. Both makes bore the new corporate look, offered standard- and long-wheelbase models, and retained their previous flathead sixes with slightly more horsepower. Both also acquired eggcrate grilles, Dodge having the more elaborate one, but each make had its own rear-end treatment, Dodge receiving prominent vertical taillamps capped by tiny reflectors. Although this description isn't very exciting, the fact is that both Dodge and Plymouth had some interesting innovations. Of all the '49 Chrysler products, theirs were the most historically significant.

The Dodge line included a new longer-wheelbase standard series called Coronet, with a slightly detrimmed four-door dubbed Meadowbrook. More interesting was the 115-inch-wheelbase Wayfarer series. Along with an ordinary sedan and coupe, the junior line offered a novel roadster, the last of this body type in American mass production. The winsome, open Wayfarer had a manual soft top and snap-on plexiglass side windows. It sold for $1727, and 5420 examples were built. Dodge retained the roadster for 1950-51 as the "Sportabout," marked by conventional roll-down side windows. Collectors today agree that the 1949 is the most desirable vintage.

Another well-designed Dodge was the Coronet Town Sedan, fitted with fine broadcloth upholstery and priced $85 above the ordinary Coronet. There was also a Coronet woody wagon, but Dodge sold only 800 of them. After manufacturing 600 more for 1950, the division banished its woody in favor of steel-bodied wagons.

Speaking of steel wagons, Plymouth made history with one for 1949. It arrived in the short-wheelbase DeLuxe series under the Suburban name, a two-door model priced at $1840. Close to 20,000 were sold—a solid hit compared to the slow-moving woodies. DeSoto probably didn't like the name, but the Suburban set a trend not only at Chrysler but throughout the industry. Though Plymouth usually gets credit for the first "modern" wagon, Olds and Pontiac also offered all-steel models this year. Still, the Suburban cost much less than the GM cars, and it convinced buyers that wagons didn't have to rely on a traditional material that required annual maintenance and couldn't stand up to wet weather. Willys also offered a steel wagon beginning in 1946, but that was so heavily derived from the wartime Jeep that it's regarded more as a truck than a car. So Plymouth probably deserves the recognition it gets for convincing the market about a body style that, in a few short years, would become one of the most popular in history.

By any account, the Chrysler organization had a fine year on its Silver Anniversary. Sales were up for all divisions save DeSoto. The corporate model year total was close to a million units, some 110,000 more than in 1948.

1950

Model year 1950 was even better than 1949 for Chrysler Corporation. The company built 1.27 million cars and 125,000 Dodge trucks, an all-time record achieved despite a three-month strike by the United Auto Workers. K. T. Keller claimed that the total might have

been 1.6 million had the factories kept working. Material shortages were overcome (usually by throwing money at them), and plant expansion continued with a new DeSoto body shop, in operation on Warren Avenue by August. Employment was on the rise: 12,000 at Plymouth, 4000 at DeSoto, and 34,000 at Dodge (whose Hamtramck assembly plant built castings, stampings, motors, and bodies for other divisions as well). Dodge Truck accounted for another 5000 workers.

The boxy body design initiated for '49 seemed more popular than ever and, make for make, changed this year only in detail. In general, the cars were neater, cleaner, more cohesive in form, and exhibited fewer of 1949's excesses.

The Chrysler line received a simpler, full-width, egg-crate grille, much cleaner than the previous one. The obtrusive '49 taillights gave way to simpler units faired into the rear fenders, and the gaudy, all-purpose stop/backup light and trunk handle/light unit were removed. Eight-cylinder models used ornate front fender moldings, but the total impression was one of grace and refinement. An identifying feature on closed models was a three-piece rear window, and glass area increased by 27 percent.

For the first time, Chrysler offered hardtops in volume. Appearing in Windsor, New Yorker, and Town & Country trim, the new body style was called Newport. Interiors on the New Yorker and T&C versions were beautifully finished in green or tan leather and nylon cord or in black leather with silver-gray nylon cord. The Town & Country did not have Di-Noc on its door panels, but was decorated with the customary white ash. A new all-steel Royal Town & Country wagon appeared along with a true woody version decked out in Di-Noc. Though it outsold

1950 Chrysler Windsor Newport hardtop coupe: $2637.

Chrysler's 1950 Windsor convertible listed at $2741.

The 1950 Chrysler Imperial DeLuxe four-door sedan

Newport hardtop was the sole 1950 Chrysler Town & Country.

The novel 1950 Chrysler Windsor Traveler sedan: $2560.

1950 DeSoto Custom four-door steel-body wagon

DeSoto's first hardtop was the 1950 Custom Sportsman

1950 Dodge Wayfarer Sportabout roadster: $1727.

The 1950 Dodge Coronet convertible was priced at $2329.

the steel model six to one, the woody was in its final year. The steel wagon would have done much better had it not been introduced late in the season, but the model caught on and Chrysler would build more than 3000 of them for 1951. The division revived its interesting Traveler from 1947, again in the Windsor series. Unlike the previous offering, the '50 had a folding rear seat with no partition between it and the trunk.

As before, Imperials were grouped within the New Yorker series, designated C-49-2 for 1950. There were standard and Deluxe models, the difference being in the grade of upholstery. The lushly furnished Crown Imperial sedan and limo returned on their own 145½-inch wheelbase, and Derham offered the last of its padded-top customs on this chassis.

The 1950 Town & Country and Crown Imperials featured a novel innovation: four-wheel disc brakes, built by Auto Specialties Manufacturing Company (Ausco) of St. Joseph, Michigan, under the patents of inventor H. L. Lambert. Unlike today's caliper disc systems, the Ausco-Lambert brakes employed twin discs that spread apart to rub against the inner surfaces of a cast-iron drum, which served as a brake housing. They were "self-energizing" in that some braking energy contributed to braking effort. When the disc made initial contact with the friction surface, small balls set into oval holes leading to the surface were forced up the holes, moving the discs even further apart to augment braking energy. The effect was lighter pedal pressure than caliper discs, plus less fade, cooler running, and more friction surface than comparable drum brakes. Because of its high production cost, the all-disc system was standard only on the 1950 T&C and on Crown Imperials through 1954. It was a $400 option on other Chryslers, and thus rarely ordered. Current owners of cars so equipped consider the A-L brakes reliable and very powerful, but grabby and oversensitive.

The 1950 DeSoto was essentially a 1949 carryover, with minor styling revisions but no change in dimensions or specifications. Its main distinguishing feature was a lower, less bulky grille that better complemented the body lines. DeSoto, too, was expanding its model lineup; offering station wagons for 1949 (both wood and steel) for the first time since the war. A new entry in the Custom series was DeSoto's first pillarless hardtop, called Sportsman. Like the Newports, this was an obvious graft-on modification of the convertible, with new sheetmetal above the beltline. The body was, in fact, shared with the Windsor hardtop. DeSoto sold 4600 Sportsmans for 1950, which was a fair showing for a $2500 car but only a fraction of Chrysler's 14,000 Newports. As with its sister division, DeSoto wagons arrived late in the season, the steel version last of all. The DeLuxe Carry-All and the long-wheelbase Custom Suburban and eight-passenger sedans returned from 1949.

Dodge also came in for a design clean-up this year. It shed the upright taillights, and also dropped the eggcrate grille for a simple two-bar affair with a medallion in the middle. The 1949 model group was bolstered by the addition of two new body styles in the top-line Coronet series, the Diplomat hardtop and the steel-bodied Sierra wagon. The Sierra held the same production ratio to the woody

1950 Dodge Wayfarer two-door sedan. It cost $1738.

Plymouth's Special DeLuxe four-door sedan for 1950

New to Dodge for 1950: the Coronet Diplomat hardtop coupe

1950 Plymouth Special DeLuxe convertible: $1982.

Dodge's final woody wagon was this 1950 Coronet four-door.

The Plymouth Special DeLuxe club coupe for 1950: $1603.

wagon (100:600) as its Chrysler and DeSoto counterparts. Dodge would also drop woody wagons for 1951. The Diplomat was a good looker but a slow seller, accounting for only 3600 units this year.

Plymouth changed its front end with a single-bar grille, shifted rear-end styling, and retained its 1949 lineup intact. A pillarless hardtop for the company's low-price line was still a year away.

1951

With sales soaring and Chrysler Corporation financially healthy, K. T. Keller began entertaining the idea of a successor. After he was appointed to head the U.S. missile program following the outbreak of the Korean War, his need to hand over operational management became even more pressing, so in the autumn of 1950 he duly moved up to board chairman. Assuming the presidency was Lester Lum "Tex" Colbert (pronounced Cull'-bert). "Stand by," *Motor Trend* magazine predicted. "There's going to be some big action, and a lot sooner than you think." The changing of the guard brought no wholesale management clean-out, as many had expected, but change did occur by attrition. "As older men retired there was new blood waiting to be used," as the Detroit *News* put it.

Colbert's first association with Chrysler had come in 1929, when he graduated from Harvard Law School and joined the firm that advised Walter Chrysler. He moved to Chrysler Corporation as resident attorney in 1933. For two years he attended night school to learn how to read blueprints, and soon became an important aide to K. T. Keller. During World War II he headed the Chicago Dodge plant, then turning out B-29 aircraft, and he ran it so skillfully that Keller made him Dodge Division president after the war. Keller soon made it plain that Colbert was being groomed to succeed him as company president, and that appointment was formally announced on November 3, 1950.

1951

Colbert thought that Chrysler was getting too big for an old-style centralized operation, and favored more divisional input. He also took a serious interest in product planning, and favored an early and complete redesign of all of Chrysler Corporation's passenger cars, as he didn't care for Keller's three-box styling. At the same time, he laid plans for ambitious plant expansion and hard-hitting sales programs. A really thorough product overhaul would require the three-year lead time customary in Detroit, but the man who would create it was already in Highland Park when Colbert took over. His name was Virgil Exner.

Exner was one of the earliest members of the styling profession. He trained under Harley Earl at General

1951 Chrysler New Yorker four-door sedan. Price: $3378.

The $3916 Chrysler New Yorker convertible from 1951

1951 Chrysler New Yorker Indy 500 pace car (with Loretta Young)

1951 Chrysler Imperial Newport hardtop coupe: $4042.

1951 Chrysler Imperial convertible. It sold for $4402.

1951 DeSoto Custom convertible. Base price was $2840.

1951 DeSoto Custom Sportsman hardtop coupe

DeSoto's 1951 Custom four-door sedan listed at $2438.

144

Motors in the late Twenties and early Thirties, and headed Pontiac design from 1934 through 1938 before joining the Raymond Loewy team at Studebaker. Exner played a vital role in the design of Studebaker's landmark 1939 Champion and its all-new '47 line, but differences with Loewy prompted him to leave South Bend in 1949. It was then that K. T. Keller signed him to a contract. Initially, Exner headed an advance design studio at Chrysler and was relatively independent of Henry King, who was then in charge of production design.

Exner's main work at Chrysler through 1953 was a remarkable group of show cars built by the Ghia coachworks in Italy around Chrysler mechanical components. These served to showcase the firm's design capabilities during an era of stodgy production styling. Exner was experienced and imaginative. A student of industrial design from all countries, he considered the Italians to be the best when it came to automobiles. When he became company styling director in 1953, it was the most promising sign yet that Chrysler's "three-box" age was at an end.

Besides design, Tex Colbert encouraged further development of the hemi-head V-8, though the engine was already in production when he became president (see sidebar). He also spurred three other important engineering innovations: ventilated drum brakes, the company's first power steering system, and electric window lifts, the last appearing first on the 1950 Imperial (the '50 Crown Imperial had hydraulics). The new power steering system, called "Hydraguide," was standard on Imperials and New Yorkers and optional on Saratogas and DeSotos for 1951. It was fully hydraulic, and eliminated 80 percent of the steering effort required with the normal unassisted setup. Though a genuine automatic transmission was now nearing completion, Engineering still managed a few refinements of the old Fluid Drive. One was Fluid-Matic, a fluid coupling with a four-speed. Fluid-Torque (Chrysler), Gyrol (DeSoto), and Gyromatic (Dodge) utilized the concept with a torque converter mounted ahead of the clutch (the clutch pedal was used to select range, and you shifted by lifting your left foot).

Along with these changes, the Chrysler line underwent another facelift for 1951. At the front was a simpler grille, capped by a curious "ring and wing" mascot devised by Ed Sheard. Imperials used a chrome bullet instead, and also received the division's chief model changes with three new body styles—coupe, convertible, and hardtop. Elsewhere, the Imperial DeLuxe was dropped, the Royal became a Windsor, and the old Windsor was now titled Windsor DeLuxe.

It wasn't until July that Chrysler rocked the industry with the hemi-powered Saratoga. Cleverly, Chrysler hung its powerful, efficient V-8 on the lighter Windsor chassis, which had never been motivated by more than a flathead six. This was really the same concept that Oldsmobile had pioneered the previous year by slotting its own V-8 into the lighter 88 chassis to create the Super 88, and the result here was just as remarkable. In its lightest, club coupe guise, the Saratoga could sprint from rest to 60 mph in 10 seconds flat (against about 14 for a hemi New Yorker) and run the standing quarter-mile in about 18.5

seconds. These cars competed with the Olds 88s and Hudson's six-cylinder Hornets on the NASCAR Grand National circuit, where they impressed just about everybody. *Road & Track* magazine, which has never been bowled over by big Yank tanks, admitted that its test Saratoga had outgunned a Muntz Jet and even beat the vaunted Jaguar XK-120 up to 60 mph. The *R&T* crew

1951 Dodge Coronet convertible. Base price: $2568.

Dodge's top-line Coronet Diplomat hardtop from 1951

1951 Plymouth Cranbrook convertible sold new for $2222.

1951 Plymouth Concord two-door fastback sedan: $1673

On Designing the Hemi

The 331.1-cubic-inch FirePower V-8, introduced on Chrysler's 1951 senior models, had actually been in development since 1935. It had the same displacement as Cadillac's V-8, which had arrived for 1949, but produced 20 percent more horsepower. Specifically, the hemi packed .544 bhp per cubic inch against only .484 for Cadillac, .457 for Lincoln's 1951 V-8, and .455 for the Oldsmobile Rocket engine. Two sets of rocker shafts, arms, and pushrods allowed the valves to be large and inclined, and the engine ran cool thanks to the large, unobstructed, low-turbulence ports that contributed to its high volumetric efficiency. The spark plugs were mounted in the exact center of the hemispherical combustion chambers, providing less chance of pre-ignition.

Though the hemispherical cylinder head was developed independently of the block, their union was no accident. Chrysler engineers were striving for high compression. Compression ratio expresses how much the fuel/air mixture is squeezed in the cylinder before being ignited. Thus, a CR of 7:1, for example, means that the mixture is compressed to one-seventh its original volume. Chrysler wanted higher compression because it was the most obvious way to increase power and efficiency, but the CR could only be raised to the point of knock, which is caused by the mixture exploding wastefully instead of burning smoothly. One goal of the engine development program was to raise output for a given displacement without resorting to higher-octane fuels. When hemi research started, before the war, there was no sign that the octane ratings of readily available motor fuels would be high enough to make higher compres-

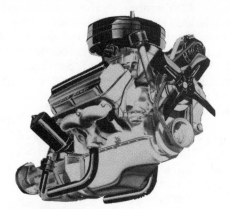

The 1951 Chrysler "Fire Power" hemi V-8

sion possible any time soon.

After a period of basic research in the late 1930s, the hemi V-8 entered its development stages under W. E. Drinkard, assisted by M. L. Carpentier. Originally a military project, it got attention during the war, but its civilian applications were obvious and the program continued after V-J Day. As at Cadillac and Oldsmobile, Chrysler decided that oversquare bore/stroke dimensions and a well-damped, five-main-bearing crankshaft were key elements of future V-8s. Also like Cadillac, Chrysler developed a "slipper" piston that was hunkered down between the crankshaft counterweights at the bottom of the stroke, which afforded smoother running, less friction, and slower wear. Choosing a bore of 3.81 and a stroke of 3.63 inches, Chrysler engineers achieved lower piston speeds and less cylinder and ring wear within a compact, rigid, and relatively light block.

Chrysler had evaluated a variety of valve and head designs in 1937, including two-strokes, sleeve valves, and rotary valves, none of which was a practical improvement on the conventional poppet valve. This led to development of the hemispherical combustion chamber. According to James C. Zeder (brother of

Fred), "The hemispherical combustion chamber consistently developed the highest efficiency of the many designs tested. It put to work more of the heat energy available in the fuel than any other production car engine." The engineers also found that the hemi would accept fuel with a much lower octane rating than previously had been anticipated, so the compression ratio of the initial production unit was set at only 7.5:1, lower than that of GM's 1949 V-8s. This gave Chrysler tremendous scope for improvement once higher octane fuels did become available during the middle Fifties. In fact, the firm demonstrated that a few modifications to camshaft, carbs, and exhaust would boost hemi output to upward of 350bhp. Drag racers would later get as much as 1000-bhp from the original hemi's 426-cid descendant.

The hemi was not without disadvantages. It was much more complex than conventional overhead-valve V-8s, requiring four instead of two rocker shafts and eight different sets of intake and exhaust pushrods and rockers. Though the initial 331-cid unit weighed less than the old Chrysler straight eight, it was heavier than comparable ohv V-8s. Two hemi heads weighed 120 pounds, compared to only 94 pounds for 1949 Cadillac heads. The hemi was thus expensive to build, and would become more so as time passed. But it quickly became world famous, the darling of racing folk, and a legend in its own time. It still is.

The hemi would continue in one form or another into the 1970s, an impressively long production run for any engine design. It was ultimately done in by a combination of factors that would have seemed unbelievable in 1951. These included inflation and a sharp rise in gasoline prices that combined to tilt buyers toward economy and away from high performance.

was genuinely taken with the big Chrysler: "While it has faults, and some of them are serious, we feel that it is outstanding among local efforts." The editors were equally impressed by its safe, sure, vacuum-assisted brakes, but suggested that power steering would be a cure for the high-ratio standard setup that needed almost five turns lock-to-lock. *Motor Trend* took a similar view, but gave its 1952 Engineering Achievement Award to Chrysler on the basis of 13 objective comparisons, nine of which the Saratoga either won or tied.

The Saratoga was favored to win the 1951 running of the Mexican Road Race, that treacherous, 2000-mile marathon car-basher from Juarez to the Guatemalan

border—and it did. Bill Sterling drove a minimally modified machine to first place in the stock class, crossing the finish line less than eight minutes behind Alberto Ascari's Ferrari to take third overall. There were few finishers, as the Mexican badlands claimed most of the cars. Of the 14 Chryslers that started, six finished, a higher percentage than most makes.

DeSoto had a hemi-head V-8 coming, but for 1951 the division had to make do with its old flathead six, slightly enlarged and putting out four more horsepower. The inevitable facelift this year was a useful one. It was marked by a more sloping, rounded nose and a shorter grille opening filled with the big chrome teeth that were to be a

Plymouth's first hardtop was the 1951 Cranbrook Belvedere.

1952 Chrysler Saratoga club coupe was a bomb with the hemi.

1951 Plymouth Concord business coupe, a $1537 buy.

1952 Chrysler Saratoga Town & Country wagon (ambulance)

1952 Chrysler New Yorker Newport hardtop coupe: $3969.

The '52 Chrysler New Yorker convertible listed at $4093.

DeSoto trademark for several more years.

Though there is considerable fuzziness on the subject, the smoother lines of Chrysler products in the early Fifties were probably influenced by Virgil Exner. Though he couldn't greatly change the overall shapes that had been locked up before he arrived, he could attend to ornamentation. One of his best efforts was this year's Dodge, which became smoother and sleeker without any change in wheelbase. A lower grille opening, cleaner flanks, and faired-in taillights freshened up appearance. Model offerings were unchanged.

For the '51 Plymouth, Exner retained the clean 1950 rear end but reworked the grille dentistry and hood. Like Dodge, the perennial breadwinning Chrysler make acquired a more horizontal appearance without any change in physical dimensions. Model designations were revised this year, with the short-wheelbase price-leader now called Concord, mid-models dubbed Cambridge, and the standard-wheelbase DeLuxe line relabelled Cranbrook. In the last group was Plymouth's first pillarless hardtop,

the Belvedere, distinguished by two-tone paint, with the contrast color applied to the roof, trunklid, and inboard portions of the rear fenders. Both Belvedere and Dodge's Diplomat were a year behind their GM opposition, but they proved popular and scored combined sales of about 50,000 units for the model year.

1952

The nation spent much of its time in 1952 worrying about Korea. President Truman said it looked like a prolonged war. Eisenhower succeeded Truman, promising that he would personally go to Korea to help settle things. Despite his optimism, however, the auto industry had to cut back production. Chrysler, which had enjoyed record volume of 1,233,294 units in calendar year 1951,

1952 Chrysler Imperial Newport hardtop coupe. Price: $4224.

The Chrysler C200 show car comes to America, 1952.

Ghia's 1952 Chrysler Special, an Exner-styled show car

1952 Chrysler D'Elegance, another 1952 Ghia/Exner project

1952 DeSoto Firedome Sportsman hardtop coupe: $3078.

The DeSoto Firedome four-door sedan for 1952

1952 Dodge Coronet Diplomat hardtop coupe: $2602.

Dodge's 1952 Coronet four-door sedan sold at $2256.

leveled off this year to just over 950,000. Ford Motor Company also saw sales plateau, though by a smaller amount. And for the first time in nearly a generation, Ford out-produced Chrysler this year, gaining an advantage that it hasn't relinquished since.

The 1952 downturn, which appalled Chrysler president L. L. Colbert, was due to several factors other than Korea. The great postwar seller's market had long been satisfied, and buyers were now becoming more choosy. This year they tended to choose Dearborn's cars, all of which received sleeker new styling for '52, over the boxy, upright Chrysler products. Another problem was that

1952 Dodge Coronet Sierra four-door wagon: $2908.

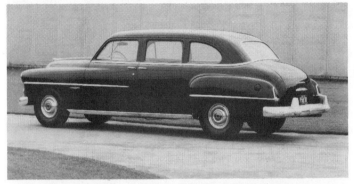

Dodge's last long sedan was this 1952 Coronet 8-passenger.

1952 Plymouth Concord two-door fastback sedan. Price: $1753.

Plymouth's 1952 Cranbrook Belvedere hardtop coupe: $2216.

Highland Park lagged in gadgetry. Ford and Chevy were selling fully one third of their production cars with fully automatic transmissions. Plymouth didn't have one yet. Neither did Dodge, DeSoto, or Chrysler. And most Chrysler Corporation divisions wouldn't have one until 1954. Yet another problem was Ford's all-out sales

challenge to Chevrolet. Ford shipped huge numbers of cars to dealers above their order levels, creating an oversupply that caused a massive price war between GM and Ford, which hurt Chrysler and the independents.

Chrysler Corporation's lineup this year had little new to offer. The war effort in Korea virtually assured there would be no major restyling, and the firm's '52s were so much like its '51s that the factory didn't even bother to list separate model year production figures. Physical changes were small. Plymouth had only a new hood badge, plus a revised decklid with the make name carried in the license plate bracket. Dodge got different hubcaps and a revised dash finish. DeSoto acquired a hood scoop. Chrysler had larger taillights incorporating the backup lamps.

About the only significant technical advance for the year was a hemi V-8 for DeSoto, a 276.1-cubic-inch unit labelled "FireDome" and introduced in February. Based on the larger Chrysler FirePower engine, it developed 160 bhp and accounted for nearly 50,000 installations. Even so, DeSoto sales dropped by 20,000 units for the model year.

Things were beginning to look just a little bit grim.

1953

Virgil Exner wielded more authority over Chrysler Corporation design for 1953 than he had before. An extensive sheetmetal reskinning made all models more shapely, though almost anything would have been easier on the eye than the upright boxes that the firm had been turning out since 1949. There was emphasis on more glass this year, with one-piece curved windshields across the board, and wrapped backlights replaced the formal closed rear rooflines. Hoods were drawn further down. Overall, the cars tended to be less bulky and somewhat lighter, which improved their performance.

Modest changes were seen on Chrysler's top-rung Imperials this year. The unique Imperial grille was a 1951-52 carryover, but a sloping eagle hood mascot was a unique new touch for '53. The Imperial dash still dated back to '49, as did the "chair high" seats. The New Yorker was reduced to the Windsor's 125½-inch wheelbase and appeared in standard and DeLuxe versions, thus rendering the Saratoga superfluous. A convertible replaced the club coupe in the Windsor Deluxe line. *Motor Trend* magazine's view of the '53 Chryslers was summed up by the headline, "Quality First." The editors noted an improved ride, but Cadillac, Lincoln, and Buick had now surpassed the hemi for horsepower. Lincoln also swept the stock classes in the 1952-54 Mexican Road Race, which disappointed Chrysler partisans.

With its hemi V-8 proving popular, DeSoto condensed its six-cylinder models into a single series for 1953. Called Powermaster, it offered all the body styles found in the V-8 Firedome group except the convertible. DeSoto continued to sell largely workaday cars, and the low volume

1953 Chrysler New Yorker DeLuxe four-door sedan: $3293.

1953 Chrysler Custom Imperial four-door sedan: $4225.

Chrysler's 1953 New Yorker club coupe listed at $3121.

1953 Chrysler New Yorker DeLuxe Newport hardtop coupe

DeSoto's V-8 Firedome convertible for 1953. Price: $3114.

1953 DeSoto Firedome 8-passenger sedan: $3529.

1953 Chrysler New Yorker Town & Country wagon: $3898.

1953 DeSoto Powermaster four-door wagon sold at $3078.

Modified Chrysler Special from 1953 (for C.B. Thomas)

The 1953 DeSoto Sportsman hardtop in Powermaster trim

of this year's convertible (1700 units) and Sportsman hardtops (6170) make these models extremely scarce today. Chassis lengths were unchanged, but styling was more curvy and glittery. Interiors were brighter thanks to more colorful fabrics and vinyls. DeSoto sales were up dramatically in 1953, better than the industry average (which also rose this year), and the make moved from 13th to 11th place in the production standings. Though it was still without an automatic transmission, DeSoto did have its standard three-speed stick, overdrive, and "Tip-Toe" shift with Fluid Drive and Fluid-Torque Drive. Power steering was a $177 extra this season, wire wheels $290. The latter, incidentally, were offered by all Chrysler Corporation makes for '53, including Plymouth, and were chrome plated, though painted wires were also ostensibly available. Chrysler Airtemp air conditioning came to DeSoto in January for the first time.

The greatest excitement from Highland Park this year was a totally redesigned Dodge, apparently the best Dodge since the war. Wheelbases were shorter (long sedans vanished), and bodywork was undeniably stubbier. But if it wasn't the most exciting restyle ever seen, it was miles better than what had gone before. There were "Space Saver" doors hinged to open wider, a wrapped backlight, straight-through fenderlines, and a lower hood bearing a streamlined ram mascot. Better yet, Dodge now had its first V-8, another, still-smaller version of the exciting hemi. It had all the well-known attributes of its bigger brothers: smooth manifolding and porting, large valves set far apart, high thermal efficiency, lots of room for water passages. It was mounted in what Dodge called a "Road Action" chassis, a rugged double-channel platform with new coil-spring independent front suspension.

The result of all this was a car that not only looked good but performed better than any Dodge in history. Red Ram V-8s broke 196 AAA stock car records at Bonneville, and Danny Eames drove one to 102.62 mph at El Mirage, California. Yet another "Red Ram" Dodge scored 23.4 mpg in the 1953 Mobil Economy Run. A clean, restyled dash and a variety of new interior colors rounded off a very desirable package, and Dodge sales soared by well over 100,000 units for the model year. Some 20,000 of those were convertibles and Diplomat hardtops, indicating Dodge's new appeal in the sporty car market. In fact, 1953 marked the beginning of Dodge's emergence as Chrysler Corporation's "performance" make.

Plymouth's 1953 offerings were redesigned along Dodge lines, but there were now fewer of them. Fastbacks were dropped, the Cambridge name supplanted Concord on the lower-priced series, and all models were built on a single 114-inch-wheelbase chassis. Although Plymouth still had neither a V-8 nor an automatic transmission, it rallied smartly with its newly styled cars and sold 640,000 of them for the model year. It also pulled away from Buick, which had gotten close to ousting Plymouth as number three in 1952.

Overall, Chrysler Corporation built 1.27 million cars for the model year, its best on record. Tex Colbert rejoiced, saying that Chrysler's bad days were now far behind. They weren't.

1953 Dodge Coronet convertible with the new Red Ram V-8

1953 Dodge Coronet Diplomat hardtop with continental kit

Plymouth's $2216 Cranbrook Belvedere hardtop for 1953

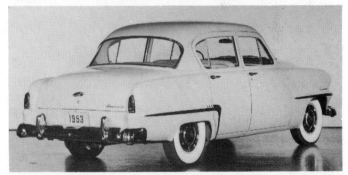

1953 Plymouth Cranbrook four-door sedan: $1914.

1953 Plymouth Cambridge Suburban two-door wagon

1954

1954 Chrysler New Yorker DeLuxe Newport hardtop coupe

With model-year sales that failed to top 800,000 units, 1954 was the worst year for Chrysler Corporation since World War II. Plymouth just managed to out-produce Buick on that basis, but it was overwhelmed in calendar year output by not only Buick but by Olds and Pontiac. The long-running policy of "bigger on the inside, smaller on the outside"—Keller's determination to build comfortable cars with lots of height and visibility, unchecked by Colbert—now ran smack into a public that seemed to prefer land yachts of the sort produced by General Motors. Chrysler's 1953 models were better looking but no larger—and in some cases they were actually smaller. The corporation's market share, formerly around 25 percent, was now down to 20 percent. Ford's dealer overstock "blitz" had begun in earnest the previous July, and naturally GM reacted vigorously. Each continued to take increases not from each other but from Chrysler and the independents.

On the surface, the '54 Chrysler line was one of the best the division had fielded since the early Thirties. The Windsor was dropped, and all models but the Windsor DeLuxe now had standard PowerFlite automatic and V-8 power, with up to 235 bhp on the New Yorker Deluxe and Imperials. The new, fully automatic transmission

(see sidebar) was fitted to 98 percent of Chrysler Division cars by the end of 1953, and air conditioning installations were higher than ever. Yet despite a nice facelift and fully redesigned dash and interior, the '54s just didn't sell. Against such flashy competitors as Buick and Olds, which now had a number of styling tricks including the wraparound windshield, these Chryslers seemed downright stodgy.

So did the DeSotos, now with V-8s in the strong majority. They were the best-looking DeSotos since the war, but they just didn't have enough flash. The '54s were marketed with the "DeSoto Automatic" (referring mainly to PowerFlite) and as "The Car with the Forward Look"

1954 Chrysler New Yorker DeLuxe club coupe: $3406.

The $4560 Chrysler Custom Imperial Newport for 1954

The Chrysler Windsor DeLuxe convertible for 1954

1954 Chrysler Crown Imperial limousine: $7044.

DeSoto's 1954 Firedome four-door wagon cost $3381.

1954 DeSoto Firedome Sportsman hardtop coupe: $2923.

(a term later to become more famous), but sales were down by almost 50 percent compared to 1953 despite prices that held closely to previous levels.

Dodge swam against the tide once again in 1954. Sales weren't great, but they should have been. The division increased horsepower on both its six and V-8, introduced a lush V-8 Royal series, and debuted a limited-production Royal 500 convertible at midyear. The latter was named for the Indianapolis 500, where a Dodge served as pace car this year. In a way, it was the first "Indy pace car replica." Priced at $2632, the 500 carried standard Kelsey-Hayes chrome wire wheels, a Continental-style rear-mount spare tire, special ornamentation, and the newly upgraded 150-bhp hemi-head Red Ram V-8. You could also specify a dealer-installed Offy manifold with a four-barrel carb, which must have made this car a screamer, though Chrysler never quoted actual horsepower. Of the 2000 Royal convertibles built for 1954, the 500 accounted for only about a third (701), but its real value was in furthering Dodge's reputation as Chrysler's performance outfit. And indeed, the division continued to rack up stock car victories. While Lincoln again dominated this year's Mexican Road Race, Dodge overwhelmed the Medium-Stock class in the same event, taking 1-2-3-4-6-9.

If Dodge's 1954 sales performance wasn't great, Plymouth's was poor. Cosmetic corrections consisted of a busier grille, new bright trim and interiors, and more color-keying inside and out. A three-series model line was reinstated, now bearing the names of great hotels—Plaza, Savoy, and Belvedere. Promotion called these cars "Hy-Style," but they were as stodgy a group as the industry produced for '54. Plymouth had the new PowerFlite in March and, with it, a slightly larger and more powerful six. It also got power steering for the first time, and dealers installed a few power brake boosters. Even so, sales took a beating. Ford and Chevy, each of which had been outselling Plymouth two to one, made it three to one in 1954. This was a serious setback because Plymouth was the Mopar breadwinner, and trouble here spelled real trouble for the entire company.

Despite the gloomy sales figures, Chrysler did have a

Airtemp: Chrysler's Airy Solution to the Long, Hot Summer

Chrysler Corporation was an early advocate of air conditioning. The Chrysler Building in Manhattan was the first fully air-conditioned skyscraper, and Airtemp had been invented specifically for it. Airtemp Division products also cooled Pullman cars on the nation's railroads in the Thirties, but Chrysler was late in applying what it had learned to automobiles. Packard fielded a pioneer air conditioning unit for 1940, and Cadillac followed for 1941. Though Chrysler ostensibly offered Airtemp cooling on some 1941-42 models, none are known to have been sold that way.

Air conditioning had become more widely available throughout the industry by 1954, and Chrysler's was brilliant compared with the complicated and cumbersome rival systems of the day. It was the most efficient, and it had the highest capacity available on any automobile.

Like Chrysler's PowerFlite automatic, the Airtemp system was disarming in its operational simplicity. A single switch—marked Low, Medium, and High—selected fan speed. High was capable of cooling a big DeSoto or Chrysler from 120 to 85 degrees in about two minutes, and also completely eliminated humidity, dust, pollen, and tobacco smoke. Since Airtemp relied on fresh air, drawing in 60 percent more than any other system, it avoided the staleness associated with more primitive rigs. It was also silent and unobtrusive. Instead of the awkward plastic tubes mounted on the package shelf, as on GM and other setups, Airtemp employed small ducts that directed cool air toward the ceiling of the car, the air then filtering down around the passengers instead of blowing directly at them. (This, incidentally, is a feature that today's cars—including Chrysler products—have lost due to cost considerations.)

On the outside, air-conditioned Mopar products used flush-mounted air intake grilles instead of clumsy-looking scoops like the competition. Airtemp Division also made notable progress in miniaturization. Its unit took up little trunk space, and the compressor took up only one cubic foot under the hood. The condenser panel was mounted out of the way, diagonally, in front of the radiator, where it received adequate fresh air without blocking the cooling system.

This '54 Chrysler New Yorker heralds the advent of PowerFlite.

Better Late: Chrysler's PowerFlite Transmission

Chrysler Corporation was the last major manufacturer to offer a fully automatic transmission, a delay that cost the company sales in the early 1950s. But when it finally appeared as PowerFlite in the autumn of 1953, it proved to be another Chrysler engineering success.

Initially offered on the firm's 1954 senior V-8 models, PowerFlite combined a torque converter with a two-speed planetary gearbox. Unlike GM's Hydra-Matic, it did not have a correct gear for every traffic situation. But unlike Packard's Ultramatic, it didn't hamper get up and go. PowerFlite "adjusts automatically to any power requirement and to every situation," promotions stated, "...gives you, in effect, an infinite number of gear ratios... without any mechanical lag or 'jerkiness' in the shifting. Unlike most other automatic transmissions, PowerFlite will not be damaged when the car is started by pushing. And, with as much as 110 fewer parts than the most complicated of competitive transmissions, the Chrysler PowerFlite is built to maintain its superior performance..."

PowerFlite's planetary gears had a torque ratio of 1.72:1, while its torque converter ratio was 2.6:1, giving a multiplication of 4.47:1 when starting from a complete stop. The Drive position started the car in first gear, then shifted smoothly to second at about 25 mph. The transmission could also be held in Low, or kicked down via the accelerator, all the way up to 65 mph. In normal use the second-to-first downshift occurred at 11 mph. The driver could downshift manually using the selector lever, but Low was not required in most situations.

PowerFlite's external controls evidenced thoughtful design. The selector lever, for example, was "gated," with strong detents that indicated the range selected by feel. The lever also needed a firm effort to move. The driver didn't have to go through a forward range to reach Reverse as with Hydra-Matic, and the transmission's smooth shifting characteristics allowed Chrysler to advertise "the right power for any road condition." Indeed, PowerFlite provided excellent acceleration. On the negative side, the transmission had no Park position and did not lock up in Reverse, so you had to rely on the parking brake instead, which often was not enough on steep hills.

couple of things to celebrate in 1954. One was its takeover of Briggs Manufacturing Company. Recently a supplier to Ford and Packard as well as Chrysler, Briggs had been in business since 1909. Its first Chrysler contract was for Plymouth bodies in 1930, which it continued to supply right into the Fifties. Briggs-built Chrysler bodies were always well made and durable, though it's interesting that this reputation didn't last after Chrysler assumed production. When founder Walter O. Briggs died in January 1952, inheritance taxes made it impossible for his family to retain the business, so they sold out to Chrysler, their biggest customer, for $35 million in December 1952. Briggs continued its relationship with Packard through 1953, but by mid-1954 it was a totally Chrysler operation.

The second thing worth celebrating in 1954 was the

Firedome Coronado sedan was DeSoto's 1954 spring special.

1954 Dodge Coronet Sierra wagon (styling prototype)

Dodge's convertible in the new 1954 Royal V-8 series

1954 Dodge Royal four-door sedan sold at $2373.

1954 Dodge Royal V-8 included this $2349 club coupe.

Plymouth's '54 four-door in new top-line Belvedere trim.

Dodge pickups were "Job-Rated" in the Fifties.

1954 Plymouth Belvedere four-door was priced at $1953.

opening of the Chrysler Proving Grounds at Chelsea, Michigan. The facility was built on 4000 acres laboriously acquired between 1947 and 1952. Company front men quietly tried to buy up all the necessary property, but the locals caught on and the company wound up spending a lot more than it had expected. Chelsea was dedicated at midyear, in time for 1955 prototype testing. Its main feature was a 4.71-mile banked-oval track, said to be designed for speeds up to 140 mph. In fact, Jack McGrath broke it in with a few laps at nearly 180 mph in a racing car, so it looked perfectly adequate for any stock road car. Don MacDonald of *Motor Trend* thought the whole thing was laughable because Chrysler didn't have anything anywhere near that fast. But he was wrong. Though he couldn't know at dedication time, there would soon be some very different cars in Chrysler showrooms, and MacDonald would not be alone in reappraising the company. Fighting back from its 1954 decline, Chrysler was about to experience its second postwar rebirth.

1955

People sometimes misunderstand automotive history's causes and effects, mostly because of lead times. In 1954, for example, numerous business articles blamed Tex Colbert for Chrysler's woes. In fact, he had taken over the presidency just in time to start Chrysler's cure, but that wasn't evident until model year 1955.

Colbert had recognized the need for decentralization, but in a staid corporation that word was anathema to old-guard managers. So he called it "divisionalization," and the managers went along with it. Divisions were told to take whatever talent they needed from Highland Park to tackle their respective problems. They did. Division purchasing agents studied and challenged their budgets. Division engineers studied ways to keep ahead of the

1955 Chrysler New Yorker DeLuxe Town & Country wagon

1955 Chrysler New Yorker DeLuxe St. Regis hardtop coupe

Chrysler's 1955 Windsor DeLuxe convertible sold at $3090.

1955 Chrysler New Yorker DeLuxe four-door sedan: $3494.

competition and even other Chrysler divisions. There was talk about division production and engineering staffs, too.

Chrysler's acquisition of Briggs Manufacturing Company was also largely Colbert's doing. Though it seemed a step away from divisionalization, it realized immediate savings that made short-term sense. Colbert also negotiated a $250 million loan from Prudential Insurance, which critics immediately said became Chrysler's "*de facto* owner," but Colbert put it to work. He also put Virgil Exner to work on his first full production assignment, the corporation's 1955 passenger-car line.

Exner had shown the styling direction he favored in a remarkable series of specials and show cars, most of them built with the active connivance of Ghia, the Italian coachbuilder. The K310, C200, and their successors showed that European design ideas could be applied successfully to Detroit automobiles. Exner fancied large, full wheel cutouts and extroverted classic grilles, and he liked "continental" spare tires, especially the kind that laid semi-sunken in the deck. Generally speaking, he didn't go for gimcrackery, although one notable exception was the "gunsight" taillight on the K310/C200, a feature applied to the production 1955 Imperial. But the overall result of his styling influence at Chrysler was positive, and for the first time since the glorious Chryslers and Imperials of the early Thirties, the company began reaching for design leadership.

The 1955 program didn't start with Virgil in charge. According to his son, Virgil Jr., "K. T. Keller asked dad what he thought of the initial Henry King plans, and dad replied, 'Lousy.' Keller told him to put the '55 line together—it had to be done within 18 months." This was in the winter of 1952-53.

Styling for the senior makes—DeSoto, Chrysler, and the now-separate Imperial—was inspired by Exner's 1952 Imperial Parade Phaetons, three of which were built on a stretched wheelbase. These huge show cars were designed from scratch in Exner's home studio to carry VIPs around New York, Detroit, and Los Angeles. Later they were reworked with 1955-56 Imperial front and rear sheetmetal. But while the Parade Phaetons closely influenced the design of the larger '55s, the totally revamped Dodge and Plymouth evolved separately and in their own way, largely under the direction of Maury Baldwin, one of Exner's young protégés.

The most obvious descendant of the Parade Phaetons was the new Imperial, one of the classic designs of the Fifties. It had a large, divided eggcrate grille, gunsight taillamps derived from those of the K310/C200, and Parade Phaeton sides, long, clean, sleek, and marked by raised rear fenders. The Chryslers had their own look, with huge "twin tower" taillights out back and a shorter pair of eggcrates surmounting a horizontal bar up front. DeSoto retained its toothy grille, got an ornate eagle hood badge, and used appropriately less imposing taillamps. Its most radical design feature was a "gull-wing" dashboard, housing instruments under the left wing and glovebox/radio speaker under the right.

Two-toning, by now very popular, was deftly handled in keeping with each make's image. Exner basically didn't

1955 Chrysler Windsor DeLuxe Newport hardtop for spring

1955 Chrysler C-300, first of "The Beautiful Brutes."

Imperial became a separate make for '55. Here, the sedan.

1955 DeSoto Firedome convertible listed at $2824.

"Gunsight" taillamps marked the '55 Imperial Newport hardtop.

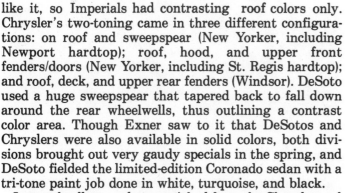
DeSoto's top 1955 sedan was this Fireflite four-door.

like it, so Imperials had contrasting roof colors only. Chrysler's two-toning came in three different configurations: on roof and sweepspear (New Yorker, including Newport hardtop); roof, hood, and upper front fenders/doors (New Yorker, including St. Regis hardtop); and roof, deck, and upper rear fenders (Windsor). DeSoto used a huge sweepspear that tapered back to fall down around the rear wheelwells, thus outlining a contrast color area. Though Exner saw to it that DeSotos and Chryslers were also available in solid colors, both divisions brought out very gaudy specials in the spring, and DeSoto fielded the limited-edition Coronado sedan with a tri-tone paint job done in white, turquoise, and black.

Long-wheelbase sedans vanished from the Chrysler and DeSoto lines for 1955, being effectively replaced by comparable Imperials on a 149½-inch chassis. DeSoto and Chrysler shared a 126-inch wheelbase, while the standard Imperial rode a 130-inch span. Aside from convertibles, all two-door models under these nameplates were hardtops, and Chrysler and DeSoto offered a pair of wagons.

There's no doubt that the 1955 Imperial, Chrysler, and DeSoto were handsome cars, not only in their day but in ours. They still look clean and stately, particularly in solid colors. Overlooking some of the garish ornamentation and the inevitable two-tones, they were well executed, especially compared to this year's Olds, Buick, and Mercury. It was in 1955 that Chrysler began to wrest the design leadership so long held by General Motors. By 1957, GM was hastening to catch up.

Before the '55s appeared, Tex Colbert had said that the six-cylinder Chrysler was "dead as a dodo." Accordingly, there wasn't a six available in any of the senior lines this year. DeSoto relied on a bored-out FireDome hemi, while Chrysler's Windsor Deluxe (there was no base series) had a smaller, 300-cid V-8 called "Spitfire." This was not a hemi but a "poly-head" engine, as were the new 1955 V-8s at Dodge and Plymouth. Unlike the hemi, the poly's intake and exhaust valves were placed diagonally across from each other rather than directly opposite, an arrangement that allowed the use of a single rocker shaft for each bank of cylinders instead of two, thus making spark plugs more accessible. Also, poly heads weighed less than hemi heads and the entire engine was much less costly to manufacture, yet the poly retained most of the hemi's desirable breathing qualities.

The hemi was standard for the 1955 Imperial and Chrysler New Yorker, and gained 15 horsepower (for a total of 250bhp) through higher compression and a redesigned four-barrel carb with vacuum-controlled secondary throttles. Dual exhausts were standard on these cars, along with PowerFlite automatic. PowerFlite remained optional for DeSoto and the Chrysler Windsor but, curiously, was not often ordered. An attempt to be different was a selector lever relocated from the steering column to the dash, but the feature was short-lived: pushbutton PowerFlite was being readied for '56.

All 1955 Chrysler Corporation cars were said to bear "The Forward Look," the firm's term for styling that leaped past that of its rivals. It certainly seemed to do just that, particularly in the case of the Chrysler 300, but this car won fame for a lot more than its handsome looks.

Introduced in February 1955, the 300 was the most powerful full-size car built anywhere in the world that year, the first production automobile with 300 horsepower. Tom McCahill called it "a hardboiled, magnificent piece of semi-competition transportation, built for the connoisseur." If fact, a connoisseur was behind it: Chrysler Division chief engineer Robert M. Rodger. Born in 1917, he had graduated from Clarkson with an M.E. degree in 1939, and received a masters degree from Chrysler's Institute of Engineering in 1941. He'd been part of the team that developed the hemi, and became Chrysler Division chief engineer in 1952. He later served as chief Product Planning engineer (1960) and special car manager for competition (1964). He died of leukemia in 1971, leaving a host of friends.

Early competition success with the hemi-engine Saratoga had interested Chrysler in a spirited stock car capable of not only out-dragging the Mercurys and Olds 88s but of destroying them on NASCAR ovals and reaping attendant publicity. Engineers knew they had all the power they needed, and Virgil Exner, knowing he had some terrific styling, encouraged Bob Rodger. The design chief teamed with Cliff Voss and Tom Poirier to create a unique hybrid package consisting of a New Yorker hardtop shell, Windsor rear quarter panels, and Imperial grille, parking lights, front bumper, and wire wheels. Rodger created a 331-cid hemi with a special cam, solid lifters and twin four-barrel carburetors, which put out an even 300 brake horsepower on the dyno. A tight competition suspension was designed to go with it. McCahill called the result "as solid as Grant's Tomb, and 130 times as fast." At Daytona Beach he ran 0-90 mph in 16.9 seconds and hit 130 mph on the straights.

Chrysler built 1692 of the 1955 C300s (plus 32 others and a bare chassis for export), and sold them for just over $4000 apiece. Radio, heater, and power steering were the only significant options. Air conditioning was not available. Colors were limited to monotone white, red, or black—no two-tones available either—and all cars had tan leather upholstery.

1955 DeSoto Firedome wagon sold new for $3170 basic.

1955 Dodge Coronet Lancer hardtop coupe: $2281 with V-8

1955 Dodge Custom Royal Lancer convertible. Price: $2748.

Dodge's 1955 Coronet Suburban four-door wagon with V-8

The 300 didn't run in Mexico, but it was nearly unbeatable in NASCAR. It won the Grand National crown at a 92-mph average, sped through the Daytona flying-mile at over 127 mph, set the class record for the standing-start mile at 76.8 mph, and won 37 NASCAR and AAA races of more than 100 miles. It was a truly stupendous Chrysler, and suddenly the idea that the Chelsea proving ground could handle 140-mph laps didn't seem so silly.

1955 Dodge Royal four-door sedan. Base price was $2310.

1955 Plymouth Belvedere convertible, a V-8-only model

1955 Plymouth Plaza two-door with optional two-toning

1955 Plymouth Belvedere Suburban V-8 wagon: $2425.

motoring that made 1955 one of the firm's most historic years.

Dodge touted its 1955 styling as "Flair Fashion." The front was marked by two large horizontal bars that wrapped around from the front fenders into a divided grille cavity. A dummy scoop appeared at the front of the hood and flared outward back toward the cowl. On some models it continued back to the rear fenders as an upper body molding with a "dip" in the rear quarters. It was a clever idea by Maury Baldwin—who was mostly responsible for the new design under Dodge/Plymouth exterior stylist Henry King—and made the still rather high-sided body seem much lower. Cheaper models, which were two-toned at the beltline in the usual way, looked a lot chunkier. Baldwin also came up with an asymmetrical and very stylish dash, with instruments and controls clustered on the left. Upper-priced models carried slim, chrome-plated tailfins, the embryonic expression of another Exner idea that would have vast repercussions in coming years.

All Dodges rode a longer, 120-inch wheelbase for 1955. The model lineup was simplified: Coronet sixes and V-8s, Royal and Custom Royal V-8s. Two-door hardtops were subtitled Lancer along with the Custom Royal convertible, which topped the line at $2748. Dodge upped V-8 displacement to 270 cubic inches. The base 175-bhp Royal and Coronet V-8 employed poly-head construction, as on the Windsors, while the Custom Royal unit retained hemi heads and offered 193-bhp in "power-pack" D-500 trim. Dodge also gave in to three-tone paint as an option for the Custom Royal series, which included a specially trimmed Lancer hardtop called "La Femme." Intended to attract female buyers, it had umbrella holder, compact, and a dazzling pink-and-white color scheme. (Women's versions of just about everything were a patronizing mid-Fifties phenomenon.)

Like Dodge, Plymouth grew slightly for 1955, though only by an inch in wheelbase and a few inches in length. More important was its completely new look, again along Dodge lines but less elaborate and flashy. Front and rear fenders were pointed, bodysides were curved and clean, and proportions were more pleasingly ample. The dash was redesigned with the glovebox centrally located, another mid-Fifties design fetish, which left two minor gauges over on the far right in front of the passenger. Again there were Plaza, Savoy, and Belvedere series, with Suburban wagons in the top and bottom lines and a convertible in the Belvedere range. Like all 1955 Chrysler products, Plymouth boasted a wraparound windshield for the first time, plus a colorful array of interior trims. It was a fine-looking car that could boast of fine performance thanks to Plymouth's first V-8, built along poly-head lines like the new Chrysler Windsor unit but sized at just 260 cubic inches. With a bore and stroke of 3.56 × 3.25 inches, it produced 167 bhp in base tune or 177 bhp with "power pack" (dual exhausts and four-barrel carburetor). Its outstanding features were lightweight aluminum pistons, an aluminum carb, and chrome-plated top piston rings for longer life and better oil control. Optional dashboard-controlled PowerFlite, suspended foot pedals, tubeless tires, and front shocks enclosed by

The astonishing transformation of DeSoto, Chrysler, and Imperial for 1955 should not eclipse the remarkable improvement in this year's Dodge and Plymouth. Both were so vastly altered they didn't seem at all related to their predecessors, which now seemed antique. Both enjoyed enormous buyer approval, although Plymouth, remarkably enough, built fewer '55s than it had '54s. Like the senior makes, both Dodge and Plymouth represented the 180-degree turnabout in Chrysler's approach to

coil springs were other engineering features new to Plymouth, and buyers could order air conditioning, power windows, and power front seats for the first time.

Plymouth's 1955 model year production record is misleading, because demand increased steadily throughout the calendar year, peaking when the '56 models were announced. Plymouth actually built 742,991 cars for calendar 1955, a record. The '55 was billed as "a great new car for the young in heart," which it was in addition to being the most exciting Plymouth that anyone could remember.

Chrysler Corporation recorded the highest dollar volume and unit sales in its entire history for 1955. Its cars represented 17 percent of American retail sales, compared to only 13 percent in calendar 1954. Dealer doubts were washed away, and confidence returned as the '56s were introduced.

1956

Chrysler Corporation unveiled its '56 models for dealers through a series of 27 meetings that began in mid-September 1955. The theme for these sessions was "conquest," as of GM and Ford, naturally. But 1956 proved anticlimactic for Chrysler and the industry as a whole. The total market declined by almost two million cars compared to record-setting '55, and production was down throughout Chrysler Corporation. With Imperial now counted as a separate make, Chrysler Division volume was only 95,356, and DeSoto surpassed Chrysler for the first—and last—time. Relatively speaking, however, the corporation held its own. Plymouth moved from sixth to fourth place in the model-year production race. Dodge and Imperial retained their previous positions. While Cadillac and American Motors squeezed past Chrysler, DeSoto built almost as many cars as it had in 1955, moving from 13th to 11th place.

The '56 Chrysler Corporation cars were basically facelifted versions of the '55s—or rather "taillifted," as each make now featured finned rear fenders, a Virgil

Exner styling fillip that would become the *ne plus ultra* for late-Fifties Detroit cars. Exner adamantly insisted that fins improved high-speed stability, which may have been true above 70 mph, but their real purpose was novelty. It's fair to say that taillfins had a stronger impact in their day than the "classic" radiator grilles and stand-up hood ornaments of more recent years. By 1957, everybody was trying to "out-fin" each other, and Exner had wrested the design initiative from GM's Harley Earl.

At Chrysler Division, 1955's "Hundred Million Dollar Look" was replaced by something called "Powerstyle," and a four-door hardtop appeared in the Windsor, New Yorker, and Imperial lines. Chrysler wheelbases were unchanged, but overall length went up via stretched rear quarter panels and larger bumpers. Imperial's chassis was lengthened by three inches between wheel centers, and there were similar gains in overall length. The division's hemi-head V-8 was bored out to 354 cubic inches for 280 bhp in standard form. A 12-volt electrical system, redesigned intake manifold, and a higher-winding PowerFlite were also touted. The Windsor's poly-head V-8 was also bored out, to the hemi's former 331 cid. Now called "Center Plane," the brakes were improved via molded-lining construction with floating shoe action, which gave a self-centering effect and uniform shoe-to-drum contact. Many of these mechanical innovations showed up throughout the corporate lineup.

This year saw a turning point for DeSoto, one that did not bode well for the make's future. The Colbert regime had considered dropping the Chrysler Windsor for '56, thus leaving more room for DeSoto in the lower-medium field. But the idea was greeted with a chorus of groans from Chrysler-Plymouth dealers, the more independent organization that Colbert himself had fostered. Divisionalization, it seemed, was breeding intramural rivalries. And as the Windsor accounted for nearly two-thirds of Chrysler's volume, it seemed foolhardy to drop it. Besides, the '56 Windsor was a terrific automobile. Tom McCahill rated it the best buy in its class: "Here is a full-bred, full-powered, big Chrysler V-8 that'll satisfy a lot more pocketbooks than will the New Yorker." With the power-pack 250-bhp version, he timed 0-60 mph in 10.5 seconds and recorded an actual top speed of 111

The Imperial sedan's price was up to $4832 for 1956.

1956 Imperial Southampton hardtop coupe: $5094.

1956 Crown Imperial 8-passenger sedan: $7603.

1956 Chrysler New Yorker Newport hardtop coupe

'56 Crown Imperial sedan rode a 149.5-inch wheelbase.

The $4243 Chrysler New Yorker convertible for '56

The 1956 Chrysler 300B hardtop coupe. Price: $4419.

1956 Chrysler Windsor Newport hardtop coupe: $3041.

mph. The die was cast, and it would have inevitable repercussions for DeSoto a few years hence.

The 1956 Chrysler 300B was a refinement of the '55 C300. This year's larger hemi pumped out 340 horsepower on 9:1 compression in this model; special 10:1 compression heads delivered 355 bhp. This would be the only 300 to ever exceed one horsepower per cubic inch,

and McCahill loved it, calling it the "mastodon of muscle." It could also be more personalized than the '55. For example, there were available rear axle ratios ranging from 3.08 to 6.17:1 (the latter must have delivered 0-60 mph times of around five seconds) and buyers could specify three-inch dual exhausts. Modified to advantage, the 300 again dominated NASCAR racing. Tim Flock's

1956 Chrysler New Yorker Newport hardtop sedan: $4102.

DeSoto's Firedome Sportsman hardtop coupe from '56

DeSoto's 1956 Fireflite Sportsman hardtop sedan

1956 DeSoto Fireflite convertible. Base price: $3544.

DeSoto's first Adventurer was this 1956 hardtop coupe.

The 1956 Custom Royal Lancer convertible from Dodge

1956 Dodge Coronet Suburban V-8 two-door wagon: $2599.

Kiekhafer Racing Team 300B won this year's 160-mile Grand National race at an average of over 90 mph, coming close to 140 mph on the straightaways. Yet the roadgoing 300B was highly civilized, available with tinted glass, power everything, air conditioning for the first time, and something called "Highway Hi-Fi."

Highway Hi-Fi was the distant ancestor of today's cassette tape and compact disc players for cars, and was aimed at those who wanted to hear their own kind of music instead of whatever the local DJs were spinning. Built for Chrysler by RCA, it was a compact phonograph that mounted under the dash and played through the normal radio speaker. To avoid frequent record changing, the system was designed around special platters that were about the same size as a 45 rpm "single" but ran at $16\frac{2}{3}$ rpm. These were inserted at the front of the unit. A special tone arm was supposed to stay "in the groove" over bumpy roads, though it usually didn't. Clumsy and inefficient, Highway Hi-Fi was available throughout the corporate line for '56, but it wasn't very popular.

DeSoto followed Chrysler for '56 in retaining its previous wheelbase and enlarging its hemi-head engine. Now at 330 cid, the V-8 produced 230 horsepower in the Firedome series or 255 in the upper-level Fireflite cars. The toothy '55 grille gave way to a glittery mesh affair, the new tailfins housed triple lamp clusters, and two-toning was more radical. Talking points included a 12-volt electrical system, the improved brakes, Highway Hi-Fi, and a gas interior heater. Bowing in February was the limited-production Adventurer, a lavishly appointed two-door hardtop marked by anodized-gold wheel covers and side trim and available with gold, black, or white paint. For this model, the hemi was again bored out, to 341 cid, good for 320 bhp. Although a prototype hit 137 mph at Daytona, the Adventurer never established itself as the racer the 300 was. One reason was the Auto Manufacturers Association decision in early 1957 to de-emphasize competition and to remove all factory support for racing. Only 996 of the '56 Adventurers were built. DeSoto paced this year's Indy 500 and tried to cash in on the honor with about 100 "Pacesetter" convertibles. All were painted white, carried most of the division's power options, and sold at $3615 a copy. The four-door hardtop body style, new to all Mopar makes this year, was available at DeSoto as the Firedome and Fireflite Sportsman and as a slightly detrimmed Firedome model dubbed Seville. (Cadillac, which at the time had an Eldorado called Seville, probably protested, because DeSoto used the name only once more , in 1959.)

Aside from modest tailfins, the '56 Dodge was generally little altered from the successful 1955 design. The division was right in the thick of the horsepower race this year with yet another hemi, a bigger-block, 315-cid unit named Super Red Ram and packing up to 260 horsepower in D-500 tune. The "La Femme" trim package was back for the Custom Royal Lancer (it wouldn't come back again, though) and there was a new special called the Golden Lancer, a two-door hardtop done in white and gold and carrying the hot D-500 mill. Four-door hardtops, also bearing the Lancer surname, appeared in all three Dodge series.

1956 Dodge Custom Royal Lancer hardtop coupe cost $2693.

Plymouth's 1956 Belvedere convertible. Price: $2478.

1956 Dodge Royal Lancer hardtop sedan: $2697.

1956 Plymouth Belvedere V-8 club sedan sold for $2170.

The Golden Lancer was the Dodge equivalent of Plymouth's hot Fury, which debuted at mid-model year. Considered a separate model like the DeSoto Adventurer (the Golden Lancer was technically a trim option), the Fury cost less than $3000 and came only as a two-door hardtop with white paint set off by gold-anodized bodyside sweepspears. Power was supplied by a 303-cid version of the Hy-Fire V-8, with 9.25:1 compression, solid lifters, heavy-duty valve springs, dual exhausts, and four-barrel carb, all of which added up to 240 horsepower. On test at Daytona Beach a prototype Fury approached 145 mph. The street version could hit 60 mph from rest in 10 seconds flat and had a top speed of 111 mph. It contributed greatly to Plymouth's emerging performance image. Only 4485 were sold, but that wasn't bad considering it cost $600 more than the equivalent Belvedere. Like the Adventurer, the Fury would continue for another two years as a limited-production performance special, disappearing for 1959 in favor of a regular series bearing its name.

In other respects, Plymouth still took its cues from Dodge for '56. There was a similarly mild "taillift," but

Hot Plymouth Fury arrived for '56 with 240-bhp V-8.

1956 Plymouth Custom Suburban V-8 four-door wagon

The Chrysler New Yorker Town & Country wagon for '57

Plymouth added only one of the new four-door hardtops, in the Belvedere line. Station wagons were now grouped in a separate Suburban series and sold mainly in four-door guise. Plymouth's pair of V-8s swelled to 270 and 277 cid for up to 200 bhp. And as on other '56 Chrysler makes, Plymouth's optional PowerFlite automatic now featured pushbutton range selection (via a small four-button panel on the far left of the dash). Plymouth was one of the few U.S. makes to score higher model year production in 1956 than 1955, chalking up 553,000 units and handily outpacing Oldsmobile and Pontiac, neither of which broke a half million. Good styling, the more potent V-8s, and high roadability had again made Plymouth a serious competitor in the low-price field.

1957

Many people still have fond memories of 1957. A lot happened that year. The Everly Brothers went to the top of the song charts with "Bye, Bye Love." In January, President Eisenhower took the oath of office for his second term, promising to erase the government's shocking $4 billion budget deficit. Appearing in bookstores was Jack Kerouac's semi-autobiographical novel *On The Road*, which introduced a new word to America: beatnik. Chrysler Corporation was also making introductions in 1957: "Torsion-Aire" ride, three-speed TorqueFlite automatic, more powerful engines, and "Flite Sweep" styling, the latest expression of "The Forward Look." Plymouth ads now proclaimed, "Suddenly, it's 1960!" And General Motors truly wished it were, for GM was suddenly far behind Chrysler in styling.

At the end of 1957, Chrysler president Tex Colbert could look with pride at a company reborn—a transformation, relatively speaking, every bit as remarkable as the one Lee Iacocca would work over two decades later. Starting with an undistinguished product line in 1950—mundane styling, old-fashioned engines, mushy suspension—Chrysler had made a sensational recovery with vivid new styling, the hemi- and poly-head V-8s, and

the best roadability in the industry.

It was generally conceded at the time that '57 was Chrysler's year. GM's market penetration was down to 45 percent, a five-year low, while Chrysler's share was 19 percent, higher than at any time since 1951. In 1957 model year production Plymouth rocketed upward by over 200,000 units. Dodge was up by 37,000, moving from eighth to seventh place. Chrysler and DeSoto held 10th and 11th, respectively, at about their 1956 volume. And Imperial production stood at nearly 40,000, a record that was equal to almost one-fourth of all Chrysler Division sales. Chrysler products also swept victories in every category of the Mobil Economy Run, with an Imperial the sweepstakes winner at 64.5153 ton miles.

Colbert made some important decisions in 1957. Early in the year, Chrysler adopted the GM plan of including dealer cooperative advertising charges in car pricing, which boosted local publicity efforts. Chrysler also issued a new, continuous franchise agreement for its dealers that spelled out the causes for which they might be terminated, thus bolstering dealers' sense of security. New, too, was a Service Responsibility Plan, designed mainly to protect the consumer but also, Colbert admitted, to define dealer territories more precisely. His "divisionalization" policy had perhaps gone too far by this time, with strong competition especially between Chrysler-Plymouth and DeSoto-Plymouth agencies.

Why did the 1957 Chrysler products do so well? Much of the answer lies with Virgil Exner. His tailfins really looked right this year, and in their overall cleanliness of line, crisp surface development, and balance, his cars simply had it over everybody else's. Chrysler and Plymouth were arguably the best-looking of the bunch. Both had gracefully swept and canted fins, taillights neatly integrated into the rear fenders, clean grilles, and enormous glass areas, including the first compound-curve windshields in regular production. Though its "shark fins" were a bit prominent, Plymouth had a daringly low beltline and the sleekest two-door hardtop in the industry. Compare the styling on these two makes with 1957 Olds/Buick and Chevrolet design, hulky and dated by comparison, and you realize just how much all the new Chrysler Corporation cars appealed to the "newest-is-best" mind-set of 1957.

It's true that the fins got out of hand after 1958. Exner

Chrysler's 1957 Windsor hardtop sedan sold at $3217.

The '57 Chrysler was very clean from the rear.

stayed with the concept too long, and by 1960 Chrysler had again taken a design back seat to GM. But in 1957 the fins seemed entirely functional, "fully aerodynamic," according to Exner colleague Maury Baldwin. "Wind tunnel tests proved conclusively that they aided stability at speeds over 60-70 mph," he said. "Later on, they did become a styling thing, with one company striving to out-do the other. But they were never *conceived* as a gim-mick. And I think that's important."

One of the many caveats that traditionally governs Detroit thinking is that radical styling should not be introduced at the same time as radical engineering. To its credit and benefit, Chrysler violated that rule for 1957. Of the year's significant engineering advances, torsion-bar front suspension has to rank near the top.

The main reason Chrysler began using torsion bars was to improve handling with no penalty in ride comfort. American cars had been criticized for generally sloppy handling for a generation. This led some Detroit engineers to begin rethinking suspension geometry, and anti-sway bars started to become more common. Though found on some prewar European models, torsion bars weren't tried in America until the stillborn 1946 front-drive Kaiser, and the first such production suspension was Packard's four-wheel "Torsion Level" setup intro-duced for 1955.

While a conventional leaf or coil spring tends to trans-mit road shocks directly into a car's structure, a torsion bar absorbs most of them by winding up against its anchor point with a twisting motion. This and greater

1957 Chrysler New Yorker hardtop sedan: $4259

$4202 bought the Chrysler New Yorker hardtop coupe for '57.

1957 Chrysler New Yorker convertible, a $4638 beauty

1957 Chrysler 300C convertible. Base price: $5359.

compactness are the torsion bar's two main advantages. (Indeed, the bar can be thought of as nothing more than a tightly wound coil spring that has been stretched out into a long, thin rod.) To these, Packard's system added a special touch: the bars linked front and rear wheels longitudinally as reaction points for each other (one bar per side). Torsion Level also had an electric load-leveler to compensate for the weight of passengers or cargo. Unfortunately, it was a complicated device consisting of no fewer than seven electrical switches, solenoids, and a control box, and it was susceptible to dampness and corrosion.

Chrysler had originally intended to switch to front torsion bars for 1955 or '56, but held off. One Mopar stylist noted that Packard might have claimed "that their system was twice as good!" Torsion Level was literally that, since it affected both front and rear wheels, but it was also trouble-prone and really didn't do all that much for handling. By contrast, Chrysler's much simpler front-only Torsion-Aire made its 1957 cars the best handlers in America, aided by more conventional improvements such as a wide lateral spring base, a lower center of gravity, higher spring rates, a higher front roll center and, improved rear-steer. Torsion-Aire Ride sent GM and Ford scurrying back to their drawing boards, where they produced notorious air suspensions that didn't work half as well and were quickly canned.

Torsion-Aire wasn't Chrysler's only mechanical marvel for 1957. A new automatic transmission, introduced the previous spring for Imperial, was extended to all the company's '57 models. Called TorqueFlite, it was a three-speed unit with manual selection for first and second, via

'57 Imperial's big fins carried new "gunsight" taillamps.

pushbuttons as on the '56 PowerFlite. It was standard on the big Chryslers, Imperials, and the DeSoto Fireflites and Adventurers, and optional elsewhere at $220 extra. Normal starts with TorqueFlite were made in first (2.45:1 ratio). The upshift to second (1.45:1) and into third was made via a direct torque converter unassisted by planetary gears. The converter provided up to 6.62 torque multiplication on take-off, which produced astounding acceleration and allowed rear axle ratios to be lowered numerically for improved fuel economy in moderate driving. Pushbuttons labeled "1" and "2" could be used to hold these gears up to 25 and 70 mph, respectively, and a "safety" prevented first from being accidentally engaged at too high a speed, thus overrevving the engine. Torque-

1957 Chrysler 300C hardtop coupe: $4929

The base 1957 Imperial four-door sedan, priced at $4838.

The new Imperial Crown Southampton hardtop coupe for '57

1957 Imperial Crown convertible. It sold for $5598.

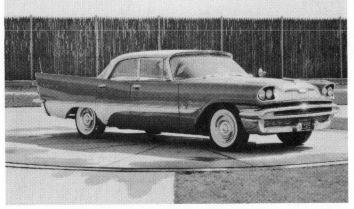

DeSoto's 1957 Fireflite convertible: $3890.

1957 DeSoto Firefite Sportsman hardtop sedan: $3671.

Flite skipped second on deceleration, thus avoiding lurch (an overrunning brake prevented transmission torque during the downshift).

Chrysler Division fielded a raft of new models for 1957. The Saratoga series was revived and a big 300 convertible appeared along with new Imperial Crown and LeBaron series. The only deletions were the Windsor Nassau and New Yorker St. Regis hardtop coupes and the Windsor convertible. Prices went up some $200-$300 across the board, and doubled in the case of the long-wheelbase Crown Imperial limousine, now built by Ghia. The bottom-line Windsor looked clean and sleek, but that wasn't adequate in 1957. So, Chrysler soon offered an optional "Flite-Sweep" color insert for the bodysides, a dart-shaped panel running from mid-body to tail, painted to match the roof. An "observation package" appeared in May for the New Yorker and Windsor Town & Country wagons. This comprised a rear-racing third seat inspired by that on the Plainsman show car of 1956, plus an electric tailgate window and four "Captive-Air" tires (the third seat left no storage space for a spare, a contretemps that would be resolved for 1958 with a Plainsman-style rear fender spare tire well). Chrysler's huge new windshield was an impressive improvement, and its A-pillars intruded less into the entranceway than the "doglegs" on this year's GM, Ford, and AMC products. Exner had seen to every detail. Even the license plate housing was streamlined, a "shadow box" set into the trunklid.

1957 DeSoto Fireflite Shopper 6-passenger wagon

DeSoto's 1957 Fireflite hardtop coupe listed at $3614.

Limited-edition muscle: 1957 DeSoto Adventurer hardtop

'57 Fireflite rear view emphasizes "tri-tower" taillamps.

Dodge's 1957 Sierra four-door station wagon

1957 Dodge frontal styling was busily glittery.

Chief stylist Virgil M. Exner, circa 1957

The 1957 Dodge Coronet Lancer hardtop sedan: $2665.

The 1957 Chrysler 300C, technically a part of the New Yorker line, appeared at the New York Auto Show in December 1956. Ornamentation was kept to a minimum: a simple chrome strip on the lower rear body, terminating in a red-white-and-blue 300 medallion (a badge that would last through the end of the letter-series 300s in 1965). The 300 now got its own grille, a trapezoidal honeycomb affair flanked by intakes that channelled air to the front brakes. The C was the first 300 available with stickshift, and it had Mopar's most heroic V-8, 392 cubic inches and 375 bhp, with 390 bhp optional via a higher-lift cam. "Uncle Tom" McCahill, now thoroughly in love with the big performer, ran 0-60 mph in 8.4 seconds with TorqueFlite and the standard engine. With the right gearing, it would do 150 mph. The AAA's "anti-racing edict" was now in force, which prevented the 300 from defending its stock-car title in 1957, but the C did take the standing- and flying-mile championships at Daytona early in the year. It was "motorized dynamite," McCahill said, "not for the faint of heart."

The 1957 Imperial sold well because it was now so different from Chrysler and a more obviously upmarket car. The new Crown set the sales pace at close to 18,000 units. Styling was the most "formed" of any Chrysler make this year. All models bore curved side glass, contoured bodysides, and front fenders with rounded "lids" over dual or quad headlamps. The Imperial grille was an important-looking affair, with five vertical bars ahead of alternating heavy and light horizontal bars. Out back were massive but gracefully curved fins containing restyled "gunsight" taillamps in their upper trailing

edges. The rear deck sloped down gently to a massive bumper with a broad oval either side of the license plate, and looked best without the phony spare tire embossing, which was optional. The Southampton name was carried over from 1956 to denote hardtop coupes and sedans, marked by a landau-style roof with heavily sculptured rear quarters that could be two-toned. Pillared sedans were topped by a more elegant "six-window" greenhouse.

DeSoto also saw a modest sales improvement for 1957, largely because of its new Firesweep line, built on the 122-inch Dodge wheelbase, versus 126 for Adventurer, Firedome, Fireflite, and Chrysler Windsor. Firesweep was DeSoto's natural reaction to competitive pressure from the Windsor, an attempt to expand at Dodge's

Dodge's $2580 Coronet hardtop coupe for 1957

1957 Dodge Custom Royal Lancer convertible: $3146.

1957 Plymouth Belvedere four-door sedan

1957 Plymouth Belvedere Sport Coupe hardtop: $2349.

This Plymouth paced the 1957 Daytona Speed Weeks.

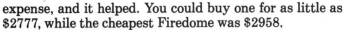

expense, and it helped. You could buy one for as little as $2777, while the cheapest Firedome was $2958.

DeSoto styling was quite attractive for '57, almost as good as Chrysler's. The two upper series wore a broad bumper/grille, with a full-width oval jutting out above a rectangular mesh panel. Headlamps were sunk into nacelles sized to accept either the usual two-lamp system or the new "four-eyes" arrangement legalized by some states this year. Firesweep used the same grille, but achieved a different look with heavy "eyebrows" above the headlamps, as on the '57 Dodge. All DeSotos continued with vertically stacked triple taillights, and oval dual exhaust outlets protruded directly below, thus forming a "base" for the new fins. Bodyside contrast color

panels were shaped roughly the same as in '56.

DeSoto came as near as it ever did to passing Chrysler in production in 1957, ending up about 7000 units behind. These were big, heavy, powerful cars. An enlarged hemi with up to 290 bhp was standard Fireflite/Firedome fare, while the limited-edition Adventurer displayed yet more cubic inches and 345 bhp. There was also a new Adventurer convertible. The Firesweep used a less potent wedge-head engine offering up to 260 bhp. The Adventurer was the most aggressive and lavishly trimmed '57, but only a handful built, 1650 hardtops and just 300 convertibles.

Dodge continued to be Chrysler's "performance" line for '57, a group of relatively light cars packing relatively

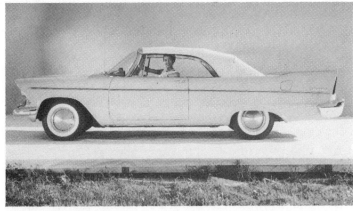

The '57 Plymouth Belvedere convertible listed at $2638.

1957 Plymouth Savoy club sedan

The hot 1957 Plymouth Fury hardtop. Just 7438 were built.

1957 Plymouth Savoy club sedan. Base price was $2147.

big engines. The 354-cid hemi now produced 340 horsepower in D-500 trim, and even the old flathead six got a horsepower boost. Dodge had the busiest styling at Chrysler this year, marked by a heavy twin-bar grille, a flat hood, wild two-toning, and the only hood ornament still fitted by Highland Park. The unique D-500 option was still available for any model in the lineup, even the plain-Jane Coronets, which must have been veritable Q-ships. All D-500 cars automatically got stiffer shocks and springs rates, so their torsion-bar front suspension gave what *Motor Trend* called "close liaison with the road." Undoubtedly, Dodges were among the hottest of the hot 1957s. Even the mild 245-bhp V-8 could produce 0-60 mph times of less than 10 seconds, and the D-500s were simply astounding off the line.

But Plymouth was Chrysler's greatest success story for 1957. To demonstrate the magnitude of its sales recovery, consider Plymouth in relation to league-leading Chevrolet:

Model Year Production

	Chevrolet	Plymouth	Plymouth Pct. of Total
1953	1,346,475	650,451	32.6%
1954	1,143,561	463,148	28.8%
1955	1,704,667	401,075	19.0%
1956	1,567,117	552,577	26.1%
1957	1,505,910	762,231	33.6%

It's hard to recall how revolutionary this Plymouth seemed at the time. Its hardtop coupe, for example, had a roof so clean and delicate-looking that it hardly appeared to serve any structural purpose, yet it was very strong. The grille was composed of slim, graceful bars, its height reduced at the center by a bumper raised over a separate

stone shield. At a time when most cars were garishly two-toned, Plymouth settled for a slim contrasting bodyside color spear for the top-line Belvedere, a modest low-set panel on lesser models, simple full-length chrome moldings, or nothing at all. Glass was plentiful, interiors were colorfully upholstered in jacquard cloth and vinyl, and the dashboard grouped instruments in a bolt-upright pod in front of the driver. Suburbans saved space with a Plainsman-inspired spare tire well in the left rear fender. Model offerings remained as per 1956 until mid-model year, when a hardtop sedan joined the Savoy series. Power was up. A new 301-cid V-8 arrived, and a 290-bhp 318 was optional for the rapid Fury, still a limited-production item available only in white (actually cream) and bearing gold-anodized bodyside sweepspears. It was about the most slippery-looking car in the 1957 field, and one of the quickest.

These Plymouths were fine cars in every way but one: they were serious rusters. Somewhere along the way to the '57 redesign, Plymouths in particular and Chrysler products in general lost the relative corrosion resistance they'd had through 1956. This problem, along with deteriorating construction quality, would become an increasing sales handicap for Chrysler Corporation in the years ahead.

1958

Aside from mild facelifts and certain series adjustments, model year 1958 saw few changes in Chrysler Corporation cars. Chrysler Division stood mostly pat. The Windsor was downsized to the 122-inch DeSoto Firesweep/Dodge wheelbase, and again put pressure on DeSoto with prices only about $300 higher than equivalent Firesweeps. Detail styling changes brought busier grilles, standard quad headlights, and taillights inexplicably shrivelled to fill only part of the rear fender cavity. Side trim was reshuffled, and interiors now often featured metallic-colored vinyl combined with jacquard cloth in various patterns. Imperial changed even less than Chrysler, but did boast two new innovations: the industry's first automatic speed control (Auto-Pilot) and the first integrated electromechanical door-locking system on an American car.

The AMA "racing ban" continued to prevent the Chrysler 300 from returning to the track, but this year's edition, the 300D, was a stormer on the street. For $400 you could order it with Bendix Electrojector fuel injection, born of Chrysler's desire to answer similar options at Chevy and Pontiac the previous year. Chrysler's "fuelie" gave more problems than performance: it made tune-ups difficult and was generally unreliable. It was also very rare: only 16 cars were so equipped, and nearly all were later converted to dual-quad carburetors. On one of its few competitive outings, the 300D set a 156.387-mph speed record in Class E at Bonneville. At Daytona, Brewster Shaw ran a 16-second quarter-mile at 84 mph.

1958 Chrysler Windsor hardtop coupe sold at $3214.

The high-performance Chrysler 300D hardtop for 1958

The $4761 Chrysler New Yorker convertible for '58.

Imperial's 1958 Crown four-door sedan

Chrysler Windsor "Dartline" hardtop sedan for spring 1958

1958 Imperial Crown four-door sedan: $5632.

1958 Chrysler New Yorker four-door sedan: $4295.

DeSoto's Fireflite four-door sedan for '58: $3853.

DeSoto, too, made only minimal styling alterations, mainly a more complicated grille and the quad headlights. At $4369, the Adventurer convertible was the most expensive DeSoto in history—and one of the rarest, a mere 82 produced. The '58 could be extremely quick, and it was a pleasure to drive thanks to fast-shift Torque-Flite and the torsion-bar front suspension. DeSoto joined this year's corporate movement away from the hemi, offering a wedge-head 350-cid V-8 for the Firesweep and four 361-cid units with 295 to 355 horsepower for senior models. A Fireflite with the standard 305-bhp engine could accelerate from 0 to 60 mph in 7.7 seconds and from rest to 80 mph in 13.5 seconds. Top speed was an easy 115 mph. The Adventurer was even quicker.

Both Dodge and Plymouth entered '58 with only the most basic changes. A badly needed front-end rejiggle cleaned up Dodge looks considerably, with less prominent grille bars set against a mesh background. Plymouth

1958

essentially wore its '57 clothing, with standard quad lights, a revised front stone shield, and "lollipop" taillights set into the lower portions of the "shark" fins. V-8s were bored out again. Dodge acquired the 361 wedge as its top-line powerplant. Plymouth offered up to 350 cubic inches and 315 bhp with fuel injection.

Despite fine styling, Dodge and Plymouth, like other Chrysler makes, saw sales fall alarmingly for 1958. The national economy had been hit by a severe recession, which naturally increased buyer demand for economy

1958 DeSoto Fireflite Explorer 9-passenger wagon

Plymouth's mid-line 1958 Savoy Sport Coupe hardtop

1958 DeSoto Adventurer hardtop with fuel injection

1958 Plymouth Belvedere Sport Sedan hardtop: $2528

1958 Dodge Custom Royal Regal Lancer hardtop coupe

The $2457 Plymouth Belvedere Sport Coupe hardtop for '58

Dodge Custom Sierra wagon cost $3087/$3215 for '58.

1958 Plymouth Fury hardtop coupe. Base price: $3067.

imports and cheaper domestics like Rambler. But Chrysler was also plagued by work stoppages that seriously curtailed production during peak-demand periods. The corporation reported a $33.8 million loss for the year against its 1957 profit of almost $120 million. Tex Colbert could not take comfort from the general industry decline, for the firm's market share was down from 19 to 15 percent (he had predicted taking 25 percent). Colbert was forging ahead on other fronts, however, such as breaking into the European market by acquiring a 25-percent interest in Simca of France. The corporation recovered enough to record an $11-million profit in the last quarter of the year, so management wasn't unduly worried.

Plans were now afoot to further separate Imperial from Chrysler. Imperial had been built at Jefferson Avenue ever since the first one back in 1926. Commencing in 1959, production would shift to a separate operation on Warren Avenue in Dearborn, the facility formerly occupied by declining DeSoto. Despite low 1958 sales, Imperial still accounted for over 20 percent of Chrysler Division production, but volume was down by almost two-thirds this year. Division manager E. E. Quinn was replaced by former sales vice-president Clare Briggs.

In general, 1958 was a year that Chrysler would rather forget. The Chrysler marque dropped to 12th place in industry production on just 63,681 sales for the model year. Similar declines showed up at Plymouth (down by over 300,000, though still in third place overall), at Dodge (off by over 50 percent, dropping from seventh to ninth), and at DeSoto (down by 67,000 units, falling from 11th to 13th). Now, the firm could only hope that better times were just around the corner. They weren't.

1959

Model year 1959 promised to be better than 1958 for Chrysler Corporation and the U.S. auto industry as a whole. It was and it wasn't. Chevy and Ford saw sales increases of about 50 percent, but Chrysler Corporation scored only modest gains (DeSoto actually fell again), and its market share dropped to the 12-13 percent range, a mere dollop compared with banner 1957. Chrysler's continuing problems in 1959 were due largely to its having very little that was truly new, while Ford and GM had both restyled, the latter fielding almost incredibly exotic finned designs for Cadillac, Buick, and Chevrolet.

Styling revisions for this year's Imperial and Chrysler were slight: gaudier grilles, heavier trim, another ill-fitting taillight for Chrysler, revised two-toning. More significant was an array of wedge-head V-8s to replace the hemis in both lineups. The Chrysler Windsor introduced what would become one of Mopar's most popular engine sizes, the 383, while New Yorker and Imperial packed 413-cid versions. Front suspension was revised with widely variable cam adjustments and new torsion bars, anchor point seals, and ball joints. An Imperial

option was automatic self-leveling, a response to the GM airbag suspension, consisting of a compressor acting on flexible nylon-reinforced rubber air springs. Like the GM system, though, it was not very popular.

This year's high-performance Chrysler, the 300E,

1959 Chrysler New Yorker hardtop coupe: $4476.

Chrysler's 1959 Windsor four-door sedan: $3204.

1959 Chrysler New Yorker hardtop coupe

Chrysler's 1959 Windsor hardtop coupe. Price: $3289.

A fleet of "Lion-Hearted" '59 Chrysler police cruisers

The letter-series Chrysler for '59, the 300E: $5319.

1959 Imperial LeBaron Southampton hardtop coupe (not built)

1959 Imperial Crown Southampton hardtop sedan: $5647

DeSoto's 1959 Adventurer hardtop coupe sold for $4071.

retained the distinctive squared grille and clean flanks of previous editions, but wore the standard models' restyled taillights, fins, rear bumper, and deck. These did nothing to improve appearance. Rumors floated that the E had lost its predecessors' punch. Dual four-barrel carbs remained, but the 413 wedge (here with 380 bhp) lacked the hemi's wild cam, hydraulic valve lifters, and optional fuel injection. Chrysler further damaged the 300's image by promoting it more as a luxury car and offering it with New Yorker options. Among these was a corporate-wide innovation for 1959, swivel front seats, which swung outward as the doors were opened. They looked great in the ads, but in practice they were expensive and unnecessary, and relatively few were ordered.

This sort of fluff naturally made many enthusiasts begin to question the 300E, but there was no need. It topped the 300D's performance in most road tests, and even Chrysler Engineering's own Chelsea proving grounds tests showed that it was three seconds faster in the 0-90 mph sprint. Yet only 690 of these cars were built, making this the rarest letter-series 300 until 1963.

DeSoto Division had a dismal year in 1959, the most discouraging since 1954. One reason had to do with styling, which was much busier and more ornate, especially up front, without giving the buyer anything really new. Firesweep moved up to the 361 wedge as standard power. Senior models got 383s, and the wedge-heads gave away little to the previous hemis in acceleration. There was a wide choice of hardtops, wagons, sedans, and convertibles in four series, including a new Adventurer line. But model year production was down to about 46,000 units, so DeSoto had the dubious distinction of being one of the few makes to suffer lower sales in '59 than in '58.

Though fins were growing on Chrysler's senior '59 models, they remained modest on this year's Dodge. Frontal styling was all-new if a bit odd, interiors were revised, and several interesting options appeared, including the corporate swivel front seats. Dodge's most potent engine was now the 383 twin-four-barrel D-500 unit, but it cost $304 extra, which made many buyers think twice. As in recent years there was only one wheelbase, the 122-inch Windsor/Firesweep platform, and the model array was as comprehensive as ever: Coronet, Royal, and Custom Royal, plus Sierra and Custom Sierra wagon series. Dodge moved about 20,000 more cars than it had the previous season to inch past Mercury in sales, but overall results were pretty disappointing.

Plymouth's 1959 line was good enough for another third-place finish and 15,000 more sales—though that looked grim compared to the near half-million increase for Ford and Chevy. Tailfins became more prominent, while the front end was reworked with a garish eggcrate grille, flatter hood, and sculpted headlamp "brows." The more expensive Plymouths used anodized-silver side trim panels. The Plaza range vanished, and other model names moved down a notch as Fury became a regular series, consisting of two- and four-door hardtops and a four-door sedan. Moving in at the top of the line was the high-performance Sport Fury, a two-door hardtop and convertible in the $3000-$3300 bracket. A 260-bhp version of the 318 V-8 was standard for Sport Fury, and a new 361

1959 DeSoto Adventurer hardtop coupe

Finned utility: 1959 Dodge D-100 Sweptline pickup

The 1959 Dodge Custom Royal Lancer convertible: $3422.

1959 Plymouth Sport Fury convertible with swivel seats

A 1959 Dodge Coronet ready for taxi service

Plymouth's $2814 Belvedere convertible for 1959

1959 Dodge Custom Royal Lancer hardtop sedan: $3270.

1959 Plymouth Fury hardtop sedan. Base price: $2771.

"Golden Commando" unit with 305 bhp at 4600 rpm was available for just $87 extra.

Overall, 1959 had to be a major disappointment for the Highland Park folks. The predicted comeback didn't happen, mainly due to the continuing shrinkage of the middle-priced field so important to Dodge, DeSoto, and the Chrysler Windsor. The Edsel, product of untold millions in Ford market research, was fast proving to be that company's biggest mistake since the war, and it suffered the same problems that hurt the mid-range Chrysler products.

At the same time, the public was eagerly turning to imports and domestic economy cars. Mainly on the strength of the new Lark, Studebaker sales shot up by 150,000 units for 1959. Rambler, which had come literally from nowhere, soared from 12th to seventh place in 1958, and was a close fourth to Plymouth in 1959. "An anticipated rising level of retail demand" was promised for 1960, which would see Chrysler's own compact enter the lists to do battle with Lark, Rambler, the imports, and the forthcoming Ford Falcon and Chevy Corvair. But Rambler would forge past Plymouth in 1960 sales, while the senior Chrysler lines continued to lose ground. A revolution was in the making: the "foreign invasion" that Chrysler scoffed at as late as 1957 was in full flood.

This was the year Chrysler lost its role as industry styling leader, so hard-won by Exner with the 1955 and 1957 models. "By 1959," he later observed, "it was obvious that I'd given birth to a Frankenstein. The fins were copied by just about everybody, rarely with good results." But Chrysler's results weren't that good either after 1958, and only Exner could take responsibility for that.

There were still certain people at Highland Park who refused to admit that Chrysler's marketing approach might be in need of readjustment. DeSoto had no plans for any immediate change in model orientation. And Chrysler-Imperial Division shrugged off the blatant proof that its old concepts were no longer viable. Said division chief Clare Briggs in 1959: "There will never be a small Chrysler."

1960

Generally, Chrysler Corporation chief executive officers have enjoyed long tenure, especially considering the company's many ups and downs over the years. Walter Percy Chrysler ran the firm for 15 years, K. T. Keller for 12. Tex Colbert had been in power for more than a decade when he handed over the presidency to friend and colleague William C. Newberg in early 1960. No one suspected that Newberg would last only 64 days. Colbert, now board chairman, then reassumed the post, but he himself was forced out by the end of July 1961.

Some observers view 1960-61 as the turning point in the company's postwar history. To be sure, these were critical years that brought lightening-fast changes not only at the top but also in middle management, not to mention the firm's automobiles. The early Sixties saw the continuing decline and eventual departure (in 1964) of Virgil Exner, who had shaped Mopar products for the past decade. They also brought the end of DeSoto and, with it, consolidation of the firm's four car divisions into two. Finally, there were sales catastrophes for both Dodge and Plymouth, and a bold new step into small cars with the Valiant and Lancer. Yet at the same time, the company declared that "there will never be a small Chrysler." It was a time of advanced schizophrenia in Highland Park.

A Chrysler executive of this period noted that the "never-a-small-Chrysler" aphorism summarized the company's basic conservatism in the early Sixties. Interviewed in 1976, he wondered, "Can you imagine what might have happened if we'd taken the initiative? Suppose, for example, we'd have surrendered to the inevitable and built a small Chrysler—a 1962 Cordoba. Or we could have called it DeSoto—with the big DeSoto gone, the name was available. We were still riding on the crest of our engineering and styling leadership; we could

have pulled off the greatest coup of the decade. We'd still be riding high today. But it didn't happen. And a radical approach like that will not happen [this is 1976, remember] in the foreseeable future...After Colbert and Exner left, a sort of hibernation set in."

While a smaller car bearing the Chrysler badge might have gone nowhere, indications are that the company missed an important chance. The all-new 1961 Ford Thunderbird and the 1963 Buick Riviera were two landmark designs that sold well themselves and brought in many derivative sales for their linemates. Of course, Chrysler did take a shot at small cars with the Valiant, but it soon became obvious that compacts were only a passing fad and less preferred than what we would come to know as intermediates. And the public overwhelmingly wanted "full-size" cars to *be* full-size. When Chrysler fielded a smaller standard Dodge and Plymouth for '62, it took a terrific beating, and Exner, who had originated the concept, soon left. With hindsight, it's much easier to explain what must have been extremely baffling to management at the time, so let's look at what actually happened.

Bill Newberg had risen fast in the corporate hierarchy, largely because his mentor was Tex Colbert. Soon after joining Chrysler as a test driver in 1942, Newberg was appointed to run the B-29 engine plant in Chicago. He was so successful in that job that he was named president of Airtemp Division in 1947. In 1951, Colbert became vice-president of Dodge Division, then a corporate vice-president in 1953. In 1959, Colbert made Newberg executive vice-president, the first time anyone at Chrysler had held that rank. Newberg looked like a perfect choice to take over the president's chair from Colbert. But revelations that Newberg had personal financial interests in several of Chrysler's outside suppliers surfaced soon after he assumed that office and, facing conflict-of-interest charges, he resigned in disgrace two months later. He became a bitter opponent of his former friend (who reassumed the presidency on July 2, 1960) and stirred up enough trouble to put Colbert on the defensive. A lackluster 1960 sales year did the rest.

By the time stockholders met in April 1961, Colbert was in deep trouble. First-quarter 1961 shipments were down 57 percent from the same period in 1960, and

The Chrysler Windsor hardtop coupe for 1960: $3279.

1960 Chrysler New Yorker hardtop sedan sold for $4518.

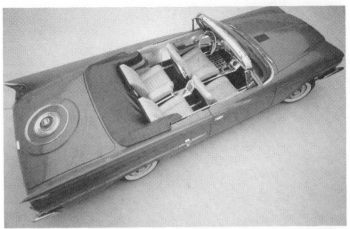

The $5841 Chrysler 300F convertible for 1960

1960 Chrysler New Yorker Town & Country 9-seat wagon

The 1960 Chrysler 300F in hardtop form listed at $5411.

almost 7000 salaried employees had been laid off. When Colbert said, "If we'd been able to combine our progress in cost reduction with a comparable improvement in sales...," all hell broke loose. One stockholder stood up holding a letter from Newberg that read: "We cannot ever again have a strong Chrysler under the czarist rule of Mr. Colbert." The firm's market share hadn't approached 20 percent in years, said the letter; in the past three years, Chrysler had lost $7 million on sales of $8 billion. Colbert snorted, "It's unfortunate that [Mr. Newberg] didn't see fit to be here." A stockholder answered that Newberg's selection as president in 1960 "doesn't reflect very well on your judgment." Colbert shot back, "Mr. Newberg concealed his interests," which

brought a welter of boos. Another stockholder asked how much the Newberg investigation had cost. Colbert didn't know. "Don't you know *anything* about your company?" someone shouted. Then a former executive, Karl Horvath, stood up: "Who are you trying to fool, Mr. Colbert? You've got your head in the sand...You do all the planning with one hand on the panic button and the other in the till."

Colbert carried the votes, but word went out quickly that Chrysler was in the market for a new president, though Colbert might stay on as board chairman. Chrysler was, Colbert didn't. On July 27, 1961, he was replaced as president by former administrative vice-president Lynn A. Townsend, and George H. Love became chairman.

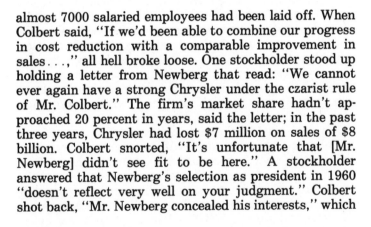

Imperial's only 1960 convertible was this $5774 Crown.

1960 Crown Imperial limousine by Ghia. Just 16 were built.

1960 DeSoto Fireflite hardtop coupe. Price: $3102.

DeSoto charged $3017 for the '60 Fireflite sedan.

1960 Dodge Dart Pioneer four-door wagon

1960 Dodge Dart Phoenix hardtop sedan (prototype)

1960 Dodge Dart Phoenix hardtop coupe. Price: $2618.

The Colbert era was typical of Chrysler's turbulent history. However controversial his last years, and despite the scandal attached to his temporary successor, it should be recognized that Colbert managed to keep surprises coming: Exner's trend-setting style, the hemis and polys and wedge-head V-8s, pushbutton TorqueFlite, torsion bars, unit construction. In design and engineering, his was the last interesting period for the corporation as a whole until Lee Iacocca created a new Chrysler Corporation for the 1980s.

From 1960 to 1964, Chrysler could claim a gradually improving position, blithely building cars that were, in retrospect, oversized, overweight, fast yet dangerously slow to react to the driver and, at times, horrendously styled and finished. These cars flew in the face of ultimate reality, but this was not evident to management at that time. They had their hands full trying to shore up the rickety financial and sales situation they inherited at the end of the Fifties.

Chrysler's most important engineering development for 1960—the last under L. L. Colbert—was unit construction, adopted for all models except Imperial. Engineers were now confident that the "unibody," as they called it, would offer significant advantages in mass production, resulting in tighter, more rattle-free cars without added weight or expense (see sidebar).

Detail improvements throughout this year's corporate lineup included the first four-way hazard flashers, as well as an automatic version of the 1959 swivel seat. Standard on Imperial and optional elsewhere, this seat pivoted outward through a self-activating latch release when either front door was opened. Appearing on this year's Chrysler was electro-luminescent "Astra-Dome" instrumentation, which used electrical current that passed through conductive surfaces to light a layer of phosphorescent ceramic material. A sprayed-on coating covered an opaque plastic film containing the dial markings, which made them stand out brightly.

Imperial aimed at greater driver comfort for 1960. A high-backed driver's seat with extra foam padding, adjustable "spot" air-conditioning beneath the steering column, six-way single-control power seat, Auto-Pilot cruise control, and automatic high-beam headlamp dimmer were new innovations. Base models were now named Custom and were upholstered in crown-pattern nylon. The Crown series had more conservative nylon and vinyl, wool broadcloth, or leather upholstery, and the top-line LeBaron featured wool broadcloth. Ghia continued to supply long-wheelbase Crown Imperial limos in miniscule numbers. Exner's unique two-tone roof finishes proliferated. Southampton hardtops were available in solids, two-tones, and combinations with brushed-finish stainless steel.

The Chrysler 300 made a comeback for 1960 with the F, the last resurgence before a succession of styling and marketing decisions watered down the 300 name. With its restrained styling and handsome blacked-out crossbar grille, the big F wore the flamboyantly finned 1960 Chrysler shell better than most other models. And it was plenty hot, thanks to its ram-induction 413-cid V-8 and the first four-speed gearbox offered on a Chrysler since

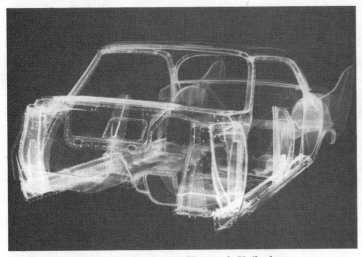

Structural plastic model for the '60 Plymouth Unibody

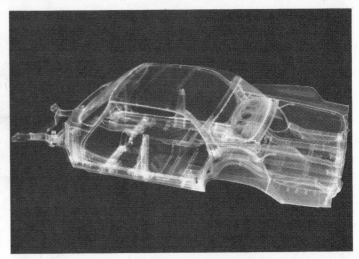

A similar model of the 1960 senior Dodge Unibody

Chrysler's Unibody: Blessing or Curse?

The first production unit body/chassis appeared in 1922 from Lancia of Italy. By 1960, unitized construction had long been a feature of American Motors and its predecessor companies, Nash and Hudson. Inspired by aircraft industry practice, the so-called "monocoque" principle offers weight and material savings over conventional body-on-frame construction and the additional advantage of being able to absorb stress throughout its structure. Unit construction also simplifies assembly in that it eliminates the traditional method of attaching body to frame with flexible mountings, then increasing frame stiffness by reinforcing the body.

Chrysler's approach to unit construction was called "Unibody." Its structure consisted of a stamped steel bodyshell welded to a box- or channel-section steel frame to form a single unit. The lower half of this had to be particularly stiff to support the body and drivetrain, but rigidity was also enhanced by the integral attachment of the upper half. Welding replaced nuts and bolts as the main means of piecing the car together, eliminating the chance of bolts working loose through time and mileage. The lack of an underframe aided stylists by making it easier to lower the floor and hence the body lines.

Until recently, unit construction was not widely seen in the U.S. auto industry because of several drawbacks. Structural stress distribution, for example, was often a matter of hit or miss, and it wasn't known until the job was done whether or not good results had been achieved. Often, it was necessary to shore up the unit shell, which added more weight and expense and made the resulting structure more complicated and expensive than a separate body and frame. Unit construction is also much more susceptible to the type of corrosion that would do little long-term damage to a conventional frame. And once rust sets in, it demolishes the rigidity of a unitized structure with startling rapidity. Nash, especially, had suffered from this problem.

Chrysler's theory on corrosion was that, no matter what, its cars had to improve. Premature rust was one of the leading complaints about the firm's 1957-59 models, possibly the result of Chrysler's relative inexperience in building its own bodies (these had been supplied by Briggs Manufacturing Company through 1954). Some former executives held that Chrysler's sales problems in 1960-62 were due to the 1957-59 models, which had sold well but rusted in equally impressive numbers.

To forestall rust, American Motors began dipping its unibodies in pools of zinc chromate in 1958, and Chrysler elected to do the same when it introduced unit construction for 1960. Although engineers thought that a dip of 18-22 inches would be sufficient, the shells passed through seven baths in the Chrysler process, including cleaners, rinses, phosphate coatings, and Bonderite (the last providing a better painting surface). The result was a structure that resisted rust rather better than AMC's.

Chrysler engineers solved stress calculations by reducing them to mathematical equations that were checked by computers, then just coming into their own. It was a typical Chrysler Engineering feat—accomplishing hitherto unreachable technical goals with apparent ease. Its Unibody cars were definitely quieter, more solid, and less apt to rust out quickly than any Chrysler products since the old Briggs-bodied models. But unit construction was also much more expensive than body-on-frame, and the annual facelifting vogue meant comparatively more elaborate changes or all-new body jigs that increased tooling and production costs further. It was one problem even Chrysler couldn't overcome entirely.

Some companies had rejected unit construction for a variety of compromises. The '51 Kaiser, for example, employed bolted-up sub-assemblies to which body panels were attached, an arrangement that Kaiser-Frazer engineers thought gave the best of both worlds. The Chrysler Unibody was also something of a compromise in that it relied on a separate front sub-structure to support engine and suspension. It was anchored at 10 spots to a boxed, longitudinal frame section that led to the rear to support driveline and rear suspension. However, structural twist tests on four-door sedans indicated a 100-percent improvement in rigidity and a 40-percent gain in beam strength compared with conventional body-on-frame construction.

Today, unit construction is all but universal, especially in small-car engineering where it's taken for granted. Because it's no longer such a big deal, Chrysler doesn't play up the Unibody the way it did in the Sixties, but you can't buy a K-car or any of the firm's other new-wave models without it.

Dodge's top-line Polara convertible for 1960: $3416.

1960 Dodge Matador hardtop coupe. Price: $2996.

Companion 1960 Dodge Polara hardtop coupe was $3196.

World War II. The four-speed was the Pont-a-Mousson unit as used in the French Facel-Vega, for which Chrysler had been supplying a stream of hemi engines since 1954. The ram manifolds were optional for Plymouth, Dodge, DeSoto, and other Chryslers but were standard on the 300F, the first seen in a passenger automobile.

Ram-induction technology had been applied in racing for some time, and experiments designed to measure its effectiveness in production cars had been going on since 1952. Engineers found it possible to calculate optimum intake manifold lengths by using telescoping tubes and an engine dynamometer, concentrating on the mid-range area of 2000-3500 rpm, where they expected to reap performance gains. A length of 30 inches proved the optimum for each tube, one per port. The left-hand cylinder bank tubes were routed over the top of the engine aft of the carb, while the right bank tubes criss-crossed after leaving the left-hand carb. Placing carbs on the ends of the tubes, rather than somewhere in the middle, gave a steady power increase all along the torque curve, eliminating pulsations. The side-mounted carburetors were, incidentally, quite easy to work on, positioned somewhat lower than conventional mid-manifold carburetors, which left room for effective air cleaners under lower hoodlines. They also ran cooler, which reduced the chance of fuel starvation during hot weather. Adjusting the length of the ram tube inner runners made it possible to produce peak torque at almost any rpm. The smaller ram engines, for example, developed peak torque at 2800 rpm, but shortening the inner tubes raised the peak to 3600 rpm for the 300, which gave more pull in the 3000-5000 rpm range.

Motor Trend magazine tested a 300F with the 375-bhp, ram-tuned engine and recorded a standing quarter-mile of 16 seconds at 85 mph, terrific for a big bruiser weighing over two tons. Though the car handled well and was comfortable to boot, the editors thought the 300F had "traded a measure of its brute, racy feeling for that of a sporty, personal-type car, like the four-seater Thunderbird."

The F was apparently a much more potent road machine than the preceeding E. It was also generally better designed for its purpose, except for the standard tachometer. Letter-series Chryslers had never had one up to now, and the only place an owner might have fitted one was in the hole for the clock between the speedo and combination gauge. There was no room for it in the F's wild Astra-Dome instrument cluster, so it was installed on a new full-length center floor console. Unfortunately, this put it almost on the floor, but then it was hardly essential with TorqueFlite. On a more positive note, the F was the first 300 with four bucket seats, a feature that proved to be so popular that it would inspire similar interior styling throughout the Mopar lineup in the years immediately ahead.

Though buyers couldn't know it in 1960, DeSoto was in its last full model year. The now 32-year-old make would see sales of only about 25,000 cars this year and exactly 3034 of its 1961s, the last of the line (the name would persist on trucks in certain export markets, however). The Firesweep and Firedome were dropped for '60, leaving only Fireflite and Adventurer series, both built on the 122-inch Chrysler Windsor platform, shorter by four inches than the 1959 chassis. Each line offered hardtop coupes and sedans and a four-door sedan at prices ranging from about $3000 to $3800, but there were no station wagons, a first since the early Fifties. Costing little less than a Windsor, DeSoto could hardly compete on equal terms. Still, it looked better than it had since perhaps 1955, with a clean, trapezoidal, Chrysler-like grille and soaring fins housing the taillights. The problem was that no one was much interested in a DeSoto when a Chrysler only cost about $50-$100 more. Not surprisingly, Chrysler outsold DeSoto by a 3 to 1 margin in 1960, even though it wasn't a particularly good year for Chrysler either. Toward the end of the year, Colbert's divisionalization collapsed. DeSoto was merged into a new Chrysler-DeSoto-Plymouth Division (Dodge soldiered on alone). The three-make combine was short-lived, however, and by 1962 there would be only Chrysler-Plymouth and Dodge Divisions, plus Dodge trucks and the non-automotive companies. The same, relatively compact breakdown persists to this day.

After a poor 1959, Dodge bounced back as one of the few bright spots at Chrysler Corporation for 1960, completing nearly 370,000 cars for the model year. A major redesign brought flashy new styling, the lineup split into the junior Dart and the senior Matador and Polara series, and there were powerhouse engine options ranging up to a mighty 383 V-8 with ram induction and 330 horsepower.

Relatively speaking, Plymouth did far worse than Dodge, selling about 10,000 fewer cars than in model year 1959 and barely holding onto third place. Its main line was a repeat of the 118-inch-wheelbase Savoy, Belvedere, and Fury, with a half-dozen Suburban wagons on a 122-inch wheelbase. The '60s were even more heroically finned than the '59s and wore a much more grotesque face—in all, a highly overstyled, retrograde design that looked backward rather than forward. Indeed, you could reverse Plymouth's successful slogan of three years before, and some said of the '60 that "Suddenly, it's 1957." Against strong competition from an improved and defined Chevrolet, a swoopier Ford, and a still-surging Rambler, this year's Plymouth was not very attractive in any sense. Though the 305-bhp Golden Commando V-8 still provided good go, oddly shaped contrast color panels on the front fenders and a "Sky-Hi" hardtop rear window that baked the necks of back seat passengers were not very helpful. But the big Plymouth was set for a complete design overhaul in a couple of years. Meanwhile, the division had something brand new to entice buyers into its showrooms.

The big newsmaker for 1960 was the compact Valiant—"Nobody's Kid Brother," as the ads said. Styled by Exner, it had begun life in May 1957 as experimental project A907. The corporation had been playing with the idea of a "compact" since at least 1935, and one had come close to production in the early postwar years. But Chrysler kept delaying. However, it realized as early as GM and Ford that it would eventually need a smaller car, and Colbert deserves credit for giving the green light to the 907 at the height of the big-car boom in 1957. The

1960 Plymouth Fury hardtop coupe: $2599.

The 1960 Plymouth Fury hardtop sedan cost $2656 new.

1960 Plymouth Sport Suburban wagon, a V-8-only model.

program involved over 30 hand-built prototypes and 57 experimental engines, which racked up over 750 million test miles. Management might have called it Falcon, ironically enough, after a two-seat 1955 show car, but Chrysler had traded that name away to Ford in 1958. The ultimate choice came from the usual raft of ad agency proposals, and it was a good one. Valiant was quickly recognized as the best engineered—and strangest-looking—of the Big Three compacts. Technically, the debut edition was not a Plymouth, but Valiant officially became part of the Plymouth line beginning with the 1961 model year.

At the heart of Chrysler's new compact was a new engine, the so-called Slant Six, nicknamed for its canted block. The product of a decade's research, this powerplant was destined to be reliable and extremely long-lived, continuing in production for well over 20 years.

1960

Displacing 170 cubic inches in its original Valiant application, it provided 101 bhp in standard tune or 148 bhp with optional "Hyper-Pak." Available only as a dealer option through 1961, "Hyper-Pak" consisted of an extended intake manifold utilizing the ram-induction principle, capped by a four-barrel carb. Dual exhausts were included, along with a milled head that upped compression from the normal 8.5:1 to 10.0:1. A highly understressed 225-cid Slant Six with 145 bhp served as the new base power unit for the big 1960 Plymouths, thus replacing at last the old L-head six. (With the right tuning, the 225 was good for at least one bhp per cubic inch, as demonstrated by the XNR show car, which had a claimed 250.) Valiant's standard transmission was a three-speed manual unit with floorshift, and pushbutton TorqueFlite was optional, of course. As expected, it had torsion-bar suspension at the front and leaf springs (set asymmetrically) at the rear.

Riding a 106.5-inch wheelbase, shorter than both Corvair's and Falcon's, the Valiant premiered as a four-door sedan and wagon in base V-100 and pricier V-200 trim levels. The wagon had seating for six or, with extra-cost third seat, nine (really eight). Entry-level prices were about $75 more than the opposition's. Exner's styling was distinctly different, if not odd. The sedan was a semi-fastback along the lines of certain Ghia specials, with a longish hood and drop-off deck. A "toilet seat" spare tire outline broke up the trunklid and added interest, if not

entertainment. The grille cavity was squared off *a la* 300F and prominent compared to Falcon's plain stamping and Corvair's grilleless nose. The wagon had wrapped rear side windows and drop-down tailgate glass, and with the second seat folded down it could hold 72 cubic feet of cargo, more than rival compact wagons. Valiant was generally considered the quickest of the domestic small cars. It was unitized, of course, but there was no sign of a tailfin. Exner was now thinking along other lines.

Plymouth built about 185,000 Valiants for the 1960 model year, which was pretty good. Though less than half the Falcon total, it was only about 50,000 units behind Corvair, which GM had hoped would sell 400,000. Considering Chrysler's smaller production facilities and dealer network, Valiant took a fair slice of the compact market, and sold far better than the big Plymouths.

In retrospect, the 1960 Valiant looks better now than it did when new. It forsook long-standing styling fetishes for a fresh approach that was distinctly its own. It definitely had more flair than the dowdy Falcon. And while its engineering hadn't started completely from scratch like the Corvair's, it was solidly built and out-performed both Corvair and Falcon. It also handled and rode better than its Big Three rivals, not to mention Rambler and the poor Studebaker Lark. It was a good basic package that would live a long time. Virgil Exner's mistake was in trying to apply Valiant-like styling to the whole Chrysler Corporation line over the next two years.

The 1960 Valiant V-100 four-door sedan: $2053 basic.

1960 Valiant V-100 wagon

The 1960 Valiant sedan in upper-level V-200 trim: $2130.

1961

Chrysler Corporation generally stood pat for 1961. The company fielded its last finned Imperial, Chrysler, DeSoto, and Dodge, and shaved the fins off the standard Plymouth. It also introduced a Valiant clone called Lancer in the Dodge line, as well as a new Valiant/Lancer hardtop and two-door sedan. Imperial lost its pillared sedan body style. Chrysler shuffled series, going from the familiar Windsor-Saratoga-New Yorker trio to a new Newport-Windsor-New Yorker arrangement.

In sales, Chrysler-Plymouth Division didn't do badly. Chrysler racked up 100,000 sales for the calendar year, better than any 12-month period since banner 1957. Plymouth declined, but didn't fall off much more than the industry as a whole. This was quite an achievement, really, because this year's Plymouth was a far-out blob, with a front end that *Motor Trend* magazine later said "sparked a whole generation of Japanese sci-fi monsters."

The pairing of Chrysler and Plymouth in one division meant that the Chrysler badge could go on being applied to big cars only, with Valiant generating small-car business for dealers. Company president Lynn Townsend and his team thought that compacts like the Buick Special, Mercury Comet, Pontiac Tempest, and Olds F-85 might do to Chrysler what the One Twenty had done to Packard: fatally damage its image. "Instead of risking the Chrysler image in any car-size contest," said division general manager Clare Briggs, "we have made capital of our car's tradition. The Newport was promoted as a lower-priced [$200 below the '60 Windsor] but full-sized Chrysler that offered a tempting alternative to buyers exploring the upper strata of the low-price field." It was true and it worked: Newport sales totaled 57,000 for the model year against only 41,000 for the baseline 1960 Windsor.

But Chrysler's upsurge was one of the few bright spots for the corporation in 1961. With Imperial production moved to the former DeSoto plant in Dearborn, output was sporadic and the assembly line worked only on alternate weeks. DeSoto was discontinued before the end of 1960 after a brief run of 1961 models with just two body styles (hardtop coupe and sedan), no series names, and an awful two-grille puss. DeSoto dealers now became Chrysler dealers, intensifying rather than reducing their traditional rivalry with established Chrysler outlets.

In the most crucial market sector, Plymouth had tailed off to a poor seventh in the calendar-year production race, while Dodge, which had built over 400,000 cars to finish sixth in calendar 1960, built 221,000 units for ninth place in 1961. But though the model year standings looked a little better, both Dodge and Plymouth actually declined for the calendar year because of very slow 1962-model sales. Even as Colbert's and Newberg's heads rolled, stockholders had no inkling that the '62s would spell even more trouble.

1961 Chrysler New Yorker hardtop sedan: $4261.

The Chrysler New Yorker Town & Country wagon for '61

The convertible in Chrysler's new-for-'61 Newport series

1961 Chrysler 300G hardtop coupe. Base price: $5411.

Imperial's 1961 LeBaron Southampton hardtop sedan

1961 Imperial Crown convertible. Price: $5774.

One of the last DeSotos, the '61 hardtop sedan

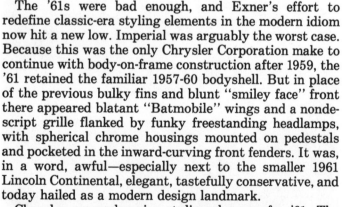

Hardtop coupe was the only other '61 DeSoto offered.

1961 Dodge Polara hardtop sedan. It sold at $3110.

Dodge's 1961 Dart Phoenix hardtop coupe: $2618 basic.

1961 Dodge Dart Phoenix convertible: $2988 with V-8

The '61s were bad enough, and Exner's effort to redefine classic-era styling elements in the modern idiom now hit a new low. Imperial was arguably the worst case. Because this was the only Chrysler Corporation make to continue with body-on-frame construction after 1959, the '61 retained the familiar 1957-60 bodyshell. But in place of the previous bulky fins and blunt "smiley face" front there appeared blatant "Batmobile" wings and a nondescript grille flanked by funky freestanding headlamps, with spherical chrome housings mounted on pedestals and pocketed in the inward-curving front fenders. It was, in a word, awful—especially next to the smaller 1961 Lincoln Continental, elegant, tastefully conservative, and today hailed as a modern design landmark.

Chrysler escaped major styling damage for '61. The only significant changes wrought on the all-new 1960 platform were an inverted-trapezoid grille (the previous year's shape turned upside down), matched by vertically stacked and slanted quad headlamps as on recent Lincolns. Fins became clumsier and chromier and taillamps moved down to the back panel just above the bumper, but the "toilet seat" rear deck embossing was mercifully absent.

When the finless 1961 standard Plymouth appeared, it seemed like an almost cynical rebuke to the make's recent styling past. "Howitzer-shell" taillamps were thoughtlessly stuck on the sides of scalloped rear fenders, and the swollen nose was marked by extensions of a heavy front fender bulge swept forward over the headlamps and inward, thus outlining a grille of almost indescribable ugliness. Only slightly less bizarre were this year's senior Dodges, the full-size Dart and Polara, which used the Plymouth's basic structure with different sheetmetal fore and aft. The front was conventional enough—strongly peaked fenders and a concave checked grille with horizon-

Mid-1961 Dart Phoenix hardtop. Note extra taillamps.

Dodge's D-100 Sweptline half-ton pickup for 1961

The oddly styled 1961 Plymouth Fury hardtop coupe

The 770 hardtop in Dodge's new '61 Lancer compact line

1961 Plymouth Fury hardtop coupe listed at $2599 basic.

1961 Dodge Lancer 770 four-door sedan: $2164.

The 1961 Plymouth Valiant V-100 two-door sedan: $1955.

tal quad headlamps—but the rear was something else. Oddball "reverse" fins kicked up sharply just aft of the C-pillars, and tapered rearwards to terminate in elliptical creaselines that ran forward on the bodysides. The Polara had higher, more ungainly fins than the Dart, and its taillights were set into the ellipses instead of in the back panel, thus looking like ingrown toenails. If the treatment seemed merely offbeat on hardtops and sedans, it was positively hideous on station wagons.

By far, Chrysler's best-looking '61s were its compacts, especially Dodge's new Lancer. It was slightly less busy than the Valiant (which changed only in detail), bearing a smooth, 1960 Pontiac-style grille and no rear deck embossing. The new two-door hardtop was the sportiest and cleanest of all. Unfortunately, Lancer did not sell well, doubtless because of its obvious close kinship with the Valiant and strong competition from GM's new "B-O-P" (Buick-Olds-Pontiac) compacts. But it was only a holding action anyway. A "proper" Dodge compact was in the works for 1963.

Plymouth's "Sonoramic" ram-induction 361 V-8 for '61

1961 Plymouth Valiant V-200 hardtop coupe. Price: $2137.

1962

Design work on Chrysler Corporation's 1962 models began in 1958-59. Even then it was obvious that the age of tailfins was waning. Virgil Exner and his team desperately wanted to retain the styling initiative that they'd wrested from GM, and they knew they couldn't do it with higher fins. The '59 Cadillac had the grossest in industry history and was roundly criticized for it. (GM severely cut back on fins for 1960.) Neither could they do it with bulk. The medium-priced Buick, Olds, Chrysler, and Mercury suffered large sales drops in the late Fifties, and Ford Motor Company's similarly pitched new Edsel was proving a monumental flop. The public was increasingly attracted to economy imports, and the VW Beetle,

which had Big Three dealers laughing back in 1950, was now a formidable rival to the lower-priced domestics. All of these factors came together in 1962 model planning at Highland Park, but the planning went awry and catastrophe ensued. The only consolation was that it might have been much worse.

Exner had prepared a whole fleet of finless, downsized Chrysler Corporation cars for 1962, everything from Valiant to Imperial. All these proposals were derived from a single "theme car," created secretly in an off-limits studio and known only to Exner, exterior chief stylist Cliff Voss, and a small group of modelers. Exner was an unabashed classic-car enthusiast. He'd demonstrated that with squared grilles as early as the 1951 K-310 show car and as recently as the 1960 Valiant, with "toilet seat" spare tires, and with the '61 Imperial's clamshell-like front fenders and bizarre freestanding headlights and taillights. Now he wanted to incorporate

1962 Chrysler New Yorker hardtop sedan: $4263.

Chrysler's 1962 Newport Town & Country wagon

Chrysler's 1962 New Yorker Town & Country wagon

1962 Chrysler 300 hardtop sedan (production prototype)

The $3027 Chrysler Newport hardtop coupe for 1962

1962 Chrysler 300 hardtop sedan (production prototype)

classic styling themes throughout the line, with long hoods, short decks, and close-coupled passenger compartments. The formula would have been exactly right in 1965, but he was, again, ahead of his time.

Exner assigned his best people to sculpt the different bodies: Fred Reynolds for Chrysler and Imperial, Don Kopka for DeSoto, Maury Baldwin for Dodge and Plymouth, all supervised by Voss. Historian Jeff Godshall, himself a Chrysler stylist, recalled: "Exner welcomed anything different, so the bumpers were V-shaped when every other car had straight pieces of chrome, the wheelwells showed unusual curves, and the rear window sill carried a quirky jog. Exner's car looked like nothing Chrysler—or anyone else—had ever built....Curious front fender blades stretched from canted, forward-thrusting headlamp pods back into the doors. The rear quarter panel was known as the 'chicken wing' to the junior stylists, and highlighted a rear deck that sloped

sharply off....In startling contrast, the center body section was a continuous, graceful curve, with the window glass set [nearly] flush for an uninterrupted sweep."

Bill Newberg had approved this basic look for the entire 1962 corporate line. But after he left, Colbert came back, made his own review, and had second thoughts. The official end for the DeSoto marque was announced on November 18, 1960, which killed that truncated variant before it appeared. Management also decided that the proposed Chryslers and Imperials were too chunky, and ordered Exner to come up with an alternative. His solution was simply to shave the fins from the 1961 shells, though freestanding lights and clamshell front fenders were retained for Imperial. The 1962 Chrysler was gorgeous, however—one of the best-looking Chryslers of the postwar period.

The '62 Chrysler would last only a year, since a new design was being readied for 1963, but it had all the good

A '62 Chrysler Newport sedan for Milwaukee's fire chief

1962 Dodge Lancer 770 four-door sedan. Base price: $2114.

1962 Imperial Custom Southampton hardtop coupe: $4920.

1962 Dodge Lancer GT hardtop coupe sold at $2257.

The Imperial LeBaron Southampton hardtop sedan for '62

Dodge's 1962 Dart 440 9-passenger wagon

Downsized Dodge: 1962 Dart 440 hardtop sedan

Dodge's low-range 1962 Dart 330 hardtop coupe: $2463.

1962 Dodge Dart 330 sedan police car

Smaller "full-size" '62 Dodges made fine police cars.

styling features of the recent past and none of the bad. The front end was a carryover from 1961, with slanted quad headlamps and an inverted trapezoidal grille (still carrying a different insert for each series). The flanks were now beautifully clean and logical, and roofs lost their contrasting color panels. The model lineup was revised once more to capitalize on the sporty image of the

letter-series 300. Newport had replaced the Windsor at the bottom of the order for 1961. Now the mid-range Windsor became the "non-letter" 300, a sort of glorified version with optional bucket seats. Powertrain offerings were mainly unchanged.

To be fair, this mass-market 300 wasn't necessarily a toothless tiger. It was available with many of the performance options from this year's 300H, including the big 380-bhp 413 V-8, heavy-duty suspension, and manual transmission. Likewise, body styles were restricted to convertible and two-door hardtop, plus a hardtop sedan—no wagons or four-door sedans to cloud the image. And these cars were certainly good-looking. It was a successful ploy: the non-letter series scored 25,020 model year sales, while the 300H count was a mere 435 hardtops and 123 convertibles. The letter-series 300 continued with minimal chrome trim, four big bucket seats, console, black-out grille, and a 413-cid V-8 with 380 or 405 horsepower. The 405-bhp unit made the H moderately more potent than the 1961 300G, though there is mixed opinion about just how great a road car the H really was.

If many of Exner's touches remained, the Imperial was much cleaner for 1962. The gross 1960-61 tailfins were banished in favor of elongated "gunsight" taillights, riding in their traditional place atop the newly planed rear fenders. The model line still comprised Custom, Crown, and LeBaron series, but the Ghia-built Crown Imperial was absent this year.

Where Exner got his way was on the design of the junior makes. The 1962 Dodge and Plymouth were smaller in every dimension than their '61 counterparts, and sales fell disastrously. Dodge had a wider model mix, however, and coped better. Besides a modestly facelifted encore edition of its Lancer compact, Dodge added a genuine full-size line on the 122-inch Chrysler wheelbase at mid-model year. Called Custom 880, it combined the peaked-fender 1961 senior Dodge front end with the 1962 Chrysler's rear-end sheetmetal. The results were predictable: despite its abbreviated selling season, the Custom 880 outsold the truncated '62 Dart/Polara by a margin of 3 to 2. Plymouth had nothing comparable, though, so it had to rely on its shrunken Savoy, Belvedere, Fury, Sport Fury, and Suburban, none of which were as large as the full-size Ford and Chevy. A smaller standard Dodge/Plymouth may have seemed like a good idea at the time, but it didn't work, even though small car sales were still growing. Chevy had launched a more conventional compact, the Chevy II, to shore up the Corvair, and Ford had a new mid-size car called Fairlane that was roughly equivalent to the downsized Chrysler products. When big-car buyers compared the Exner-styled Dodge and Plymouth with this year's flashy Galaxie and Impala, however, they found there was no comparison.

The upshot was that Plymouth fell to eighth place in model-year production for 1962, its lowest ranking ever. Dodge held onto ninth, not too far off its 1961 pace, thanks to its more comprehensive model range. Dodge also reacted more swiftly to adversity, punching out its mid-size wheelbase to 119 inches for 1963, while Plymouth was forced to stick with its stubby 116-inch-wheelbase platform for its "full-size" offerings through 1964.

Dodge's bucket-seat Polara 500 convertible for 1962

1962 Plymouth Valiant V-200 four-door sedan: $2087

1962 Dodge Polara 500 hardtop sedan, a midyear addition

Plymouth's 1962 Valiant V-100 wagon

1962 Plymouth Sport Fury hardtop coupe: $2851 basic.

1962 Plymouth Fury convertible. Base price: $2924.

Plymouth's 1962 Fury hardtop coupe sold at $2585 with six.

Companion '62 Sport Fury convertible sold for $3082.

Both makes came back in the improved market of 1963-65, but Plymouth would not see third place again until the Seventies, and then only twice. Model year 1962 spelled the ultimate humbling of what once had been America's third most popular make.

Off the record, Exner was not enthusiastic about the downsized Dodge/Plymouth and the finless senior makes.

"He always referred to them as the plucked chickens," Virgil Exner, Jr., recalled. But hardly anyone likes to admit to failure. Fred Reynolds, who designed the stubby, stillborn '62 Chryslers, once said that the 1962 DeSoto prototype had lost its appeal for him only six months after it reached steel-model stage. If so, Fred couldn't have liked the Chrysler and Imperial very much either.

It was during 1962 that Exner was dethroned as vice-president of design in Highland Park. His successor was Elwood Engel, lured away from Ford to lead Chrysler Corporation along a more conventional styling path. Exner continued as a consultant through 1964, after which he had no further involvement. In retrospect, his Chrysler career can be viewed in two ways. When he was good, he was very, very good. But when he was bad....In a 1976 interview, Exner's son admitted that "it *was* time for a change. Their image needed changing....But it's still his design section that is operating there. He built it up from 17 to what it basically is today, whatever it is today." Exner also left a legacy of styling originality and vivid imagination at Chrysler. The quality of his work was surpassed only once before he arrived, by Ray Dietrich. And after Exner left, it would be a long time before the company's cars were as innovative and noticeable again. He was undoubtedly the greatest single influence in making Chrysler what it came to be in the Fifties and early Sixties.

Lynn Townsend relieved L. L. Colbert with a vengeance in mid-1961, and moved quickly to usher in new and much more hard-nosed leadership. He created an Administrative Committee of top decision-makers to guide the firm, among whom was administrative vice-president Virgil Boyd. An accountant by training like Townsend, Boyd had been a vice-president at American Motors since that company's creation (out of Nash and Hudson) in 1954. Also in the new guard was "Flamethrower" John Riccardo, whose nickname was built on his reputation as a tough guy. Riccardo came to Townsend's attention as an accountant, and he came to Highland Park in 1959 as financial staff executive for International Operations. Later, he was Export-Import Division manager, a Chrysler Canada vice-president, and manager of Dodge Sales, Chrysler-Plymouth, and Corporate Marketing. He would succeed Boyd as president in 1970. He moved up to chairman in 1975, a job he would hand over to Lee Iacocca four years later.

As the dust settled and Townsend's team took control, business improved and stockholders heaved a sigh of relief. The days of turmoil and uncertainty were over—or so they thought. But on the product front, the influence of Tex Colbert and Virgil Exner was still present, and it wouldn't be entirely washed away until 1965.

1963

The most talked-about Chrysler Corporation feat of 1963 was the "Engelbird," the Ghia-built "production" turbine car designed to test consumer reaction to the unfamiliar engine (see sidebar). Meanwhile, a revolutionary five-year/50,000-mile warranty was featured for the first time throughout the corporate line, a piece of marketing genius that took competitors by surprise and sent them scrambling to announce similar plans. It covered all engine and powertrain parts against defects in

1963 Chrysler New Yorker Town & Country wagon

Chrysler's 300 convertible for 1963: $3790.

1963 Chrysler New Yorker hardtop sedan. Price: $4118.

materials and workmanship for five years or 50,000 miles, whichever came first. It was also transferable to a second owner within this time/mileage limit.

The "Crisp, Clean, Custom Look" made its debut on this year's Chrysler, the first to be styled under the direction of Elwood Engel. Several Exner trademarks remained, however: sharply creased bodysides; large, inverted trapezoidal grilles; big, open wheel wells; slightly bulging headlamp housings. Though still huge, the New Yorker dropped to a 122-inch wheelbase, the same as on the Newport and 300 (as well as the Dodge 880). All models wore wider rear roof pillars that cut down on visibility, and the rear deck was shortened and recontoured, sloping gradually to the fenders with no sign of a tailfin, shaved off or otherwise. Body styles were unchanged. The Newport again carried 265 bhp standard, the non-letter 300 series had 305 bhp, and the New Yorker 340 bhp. The letter "I" would have been confusing, so the '63 edition of the letter-series 300 was the J. It had a

The $5782 Imperial Crown convertible for 1963

Dodge sold its '63 Polara convertible for $2963.

Imperial's 1963 Custom Southampton hardtop sedan

1963 Dodge Dart 270 convertible. Base price: $2385.

Ghia built only 13 of the '63 Crown Imperial limousines.

The bucket-seat Dodge Dart GT hardtop coupe, new for '63.

390-bhp version of the New Yorker's 413-cid V-8, but looked and acted more than ever like a standard Chrysler. The letter series was still promoted more on creature comforts than on-road performance, and only 400 of the 300Js were sold, a record low.

For Imperial, 1963 styling revisions were modest. There was a new grille, with a pattern of elongated rectangles, and Engel redesigned the basic 1957-62 roofline to give the above-beltline area the look of the Lincoln Continentals he'd previously done at Dearborn. He also did

1963 Dodge Polara 500 hardtop coupe (styling prototype)

Dodge's A-100 compact pickup (prototype)

A Tale of Turbines

Chrysler's interest in gas turbine engines dated to before World War II, and developed in the postwar years through aircraft applications. With a grant from the Navy Bureau of Aeronautics, the firm built a turbo-prop engine with fuel economy equal to that of a piston aircraft powerplant. Company engineers then returned to automotive turbine development in the early Fifties.

Though the turbine engine is not complex in its design, it does present problems in automotive applications when it comes to production feasibility. Its main element, of course, is the turbine, a wheel with a ring of blades around its circumference. A fuel mixture flows past the blades, causing the wheel to rotate and thus produce power. The turbine engine works best at constant rpm, so it's ideal for aircraft, which usually fly at steady speeds. But a car changes speed constantly and needs good acceleration for standing starts and passing, plus engine braking to assist in slowing. Thus, an automotive turbine must be designed somewhat differently from its aircraft counterpart in order to provide the requisite performance. Also, it must run cooler and quieter, and it should not produce exhaust emissions above a certain level, though the last had yet to become an engineering criterion in the Fifties.

To meet these requirements, Chrysler engineers developed a rotating heat exchanger, also known as a regenerator, to recover heat from exhaust gases, thus keeping running temperatures low and fuel mileage acceptable. The problems of flexibility in automotive applications and the need for high-temperature alloys

able to withstand the turbine engine's greater heat were also investigated early on. The company's first turbine test car was a near-stock 1954 Plymouth Belvedere hardtop fitted with a turbine rated at 100 horsepower. It ran successfully at the firm's Chelsea, Michigan proving grounds. Its successor was a 1956 Belvedere sedan, which was driven cross-country in a durability/performance test. The car ran satisfactorily, but returned a disappointing 13 miles per gallon. Both these turbine experimentals were powered by "first-generation" engines that were expensive to build compared to those that would follow.

A "second-generation" turbine developing about 200 bhp was first seen in a 1959 Plymouth hardtop on a run from Detroit to New York. This engine featured new materials for some internal parts, and was more efficient than the 1954-56 versions. Metallurgical research had now produced "buildable" heat- and oxidation-resistant alloys for engine construction, thus bringing the turbine a step closer to production reality.

A "third-generation" design was tried in three vehicles: a stock-looking 1960 Plymouth, a 2½-ton Dodge truck, and a unique show car designed by Maury Baldwin and called TurboFlite. "We incorporated a lot of interesting things in it," Baldwin says. "Entrance-wise, the whole cockpit above the beltline lifted to admit passengers. Mounted between the fins was a deceleration flap, such as now used on racing cars. The headlights were retractable. The car was built by Ghia. We did a ⅜-scale model and then full-size drawings. It was probably one of the best engineered show cars we ever did."

By 1962, Engineering had developed the CR2A turbine, first installed in a Dodge Dart four-door hardtop that made an endurance run from New York to Los Angeles. (A '62 Plymouth Fury

George Huebner in '62

two-door hardtop was also modified around this engine.) The CR2A returned better gas mileage than the conventional piston engine in the Dodge control car traveling alongside. It differed from earlier turbines in having a new fuel nozzle mechanism that varied the angle of the jet stream to the turbine blades, thus providing real engine braking, improved performance, and reduced lag. Earlier turbines took seven seconds to go from idle to full output, while the CR2A needed only 1.5-2.0 seconds. Encouraged by this progress, Chrysler decided to build a small fleet of turbine-powered cars for consumer evaluation.

Aside from its mechanical novelty, the "production" Chrysler turbine car, unveiled in May 1963, was strikingly beautiful. Designed by Elwood Engel, it bore more resemblance to recent Thunderbirds than any Chrysler product—no surprise, as Engel had been involved with the 1961 Thunderbird design before he left Ford to work for Chrysler. For this reason, it has often been referred to as the "Engelbird." A bucket-seat, four-passenger two-door hardtop, it was painted Turbine Bronze and equipped with full power assists, auto-

1963 Dodge Custom 880 hardtop sedan. Price: $3109.

away with Exner's freestanding headlights and gunsight taillamps. The model lineup was unchanged except for reintroduction of the Ghia-built Crown Imperial, which had been absent for 1962.

Moving rapidly to lengthen and enlarge its standard cars, Dodge Division put everything except 880s, compacts, and wagons on a 119-inch wheelbase for 1963. It also kept almost all base prices under $3000 for this line, which continued 330, 440, and Polara nomenclature from 1962. The 225-cid Slant Six and 318 V-8 were the standard powerplants, though the Polara 500 trim package came with a 305-bhp 383-cid V-8. The top performance engine, and a formidable dragstrip competitor this year, was the Dodge Ram Charger, a 426-cid wedge-head V-8 with

1963 Chrysler Turbine, built by Ghia

Only 50 of the '63 turbine cars were completed.

matic transmission, and other luxury equipment. Headlight and backup light bezels were styled with a rotary-blade motif to emphasize the car's unusual power source, and there were massive "boomerang" horizontal taillights set into steeply angled rear fenders. Under the hood was a "fifth-generation" turbine with twin regenerators that rotated in vertical planes, one on each side, with a central burner. It was quieter, lighter, and smaller than the CR2A, and its acceleration lag was cut to only 1.0-1.5 seconds. Maximum-output engine speed after gear reduction was 4680 rpm, compared to 5360 rpm for the CR2A, and the new engine had 20 percent fewer moving parts than a conventional piston powerplant. While it was down slightly on horsepower compared to its predecessor, this new turbine had more torque, 425 lbs/ft versus 375. It was the closest thing to a production-ready turbine engine that Chrysler had yet produced.

Because of the limited number planned and the expense involved, Chrysler contracted with Ghia of Italy to build 50 of the "Engelbird" turbine cars. They were loaned to "consumer representatives" chosen from some 30,000 inquiries Chrysler received after announcing the public evaluation project. Each "owner" had use of the car for about three months. In all, 203 people from 48 states and ranging in age from 21 to 70 drove these cars from 1963 to 1966. According to one surreptitious test by motoring writer John Lawlor, the "Engelbird" was quick, capable of 0-60 mph in under 10 seconds. Unfortunately, fuel economy was disappointing, about 11.5 mpg, and in the end this proved to be the biggest stumbling block to mass marketing.

The report on the testing program, issued in 1967, noted that the turbine engine required little or no maintenance compared with a piston powerplant. One out of every four consumer testers complained about gas guzzling despite the engine's ability to run on kerosene, jet fuel, or diesel fuel in addition to ordinary gasoline. One out of three disliked the acceleration lag. The main compliments centered around the car's vibrationless operation and the snazzy styling. Writing in 1973, Lawlor commented in retrospect about his experience: "Getting 11.5 mpg out of a 4100-pound car that can go from zero to 60 in 11 seconds has begun to look like an attractive proposition, particularly when you consider that the fuel used could be a much cheaper one than today's gasoline." One wonders if he wouldn't have changed his mind a year later in the wake of the first energy crisis.

Chrysler's turbine engine could again be a very attractive alternative. Considering the amount of weight-cutting and downsizing that has gone on since the early Sixties (and continues to go on as we move through the 1980s), it is not hard to imagine the same kind of engine powering a more efficiently designed automobile at close to 20 mpg on diesel fuel.

The beautiful Ghia turbine cars suffered a sad fate: all but 10 were cut up before the watchful eyes of U.S. Customs. Since they'd been built abroad, Chrysler would have been charged import duty had it kept them all, an enormous expense given their construction cost. However, Highland Park did pay duty on the 10, and they were dispersed to museums such as Harrah's in Reno and the Chicago Museum of Science and Industry. Two were retained at the Chelsea proving grounds.

Plymouth's Sport Fury hardtop coupe for 1963

425 bhp, courtesy of aluminum pistons, high-lift cam, and dual four-barrel carburetors.

Part and parcel of Dodge's sales blitz in this comeback year was an all-new compact to replace the Lancer. Borrowing the Dart name from the downsized 1962 standard line, it differed significantly from this year's restyled Valiant. Riding a five-inch-longer wheelbase (except wagons, which shared the Valiant's 106 inches), the Dart was a cleanly styled package priced only a few dollars above comparable Valiants. It was also part of an industry trend toward larger, more luxurious, and often sportier compacts, the last exemplified by the bucket-seat Dart GT hardtop and convertible, of which about 35,000 were built. Led by the volume 170 and 270 series, Dart

The $2924 Plymouth Fury convertible for 1963

Plymouth's first Valiant convertible appeared for '63.

1963 Plymouth Valiant V-200 four-door sedan: $2097.

Plymouth's 1963 Valiant Signet 200 hardtop coupe: $2230.

1963 Plymouth Valiant V-200 wagon. Base price: $2392.

was handily outselling the big Dodge by spring of 1963.

Dodge continued to go after some of DeSoto's old business with the Chrysler-based 880, now offered in an expanded line of base sedan and wagon and a full range of Custom-trim body styles. Fewer than 30,000 were sold, however, as people apparently preferred to pay a little more for a Chrysler Newport and its more prestigious name. The 880 persisted because the two-division structure dictated parallel model lines for both Dodge and Chrysler-Plymouth dealerships. This policy worked fine in the good years, but would create competition when times were leaner. The days when Chrysler products progressed in a logical size/price sequence from Plymouth to Imperial were over, and the two surviving divisions were slugging it out with one another harder than they'd ever done before.

Plymouth also unloaded its Exner-designed compact for 1963, but the Valiant's stubby replacement was not as stylish as the Dart. Other Plymouths were stuck with the truncated Exner styling from 1962, though Engel did a good job in making it more conventional and "important." Quad headlamps within a full-width checked grille, plus sharper-edged fenders and a squared-off Thunderbird-like roofline were on hand this year. Plymouth began to fight its way back in the sales standings and built half a million cars for the model year. It would do even better in 1964.

1964

Pulling out of its chilling 1962 nosedive, Chrysler Corporation made money in both 1963 and 1964 and remained stable. Corporate net earnings in 1963 broke a record at $161.6 million, and worldwide sales for the year of $3.5 billion were second only to 1957. Lynn Townsend said the improvement stemmed from the "5/50" warranty, a strengthened dealer organization (some 462 new outlets had been added), and broader market coverage. Stock split four-fold, and passenger-car production broke the one-million mark for the first time since 1960 (at 1,047,722). In a move that it would later regret, the firm acquired a controlling interest in Simca of France, and began negotiations for a similar deal with the Rootes Group of Great Britain. Cummins, a British diesel engine manufacturer, had been added in 1963. Chrysler was now striving to be a multi-national outfit like Ford and GM, a bit of corporate puffery for which it would pay dearly.

Plymouth continued to fight back from its recent dismal sales, retailing nearly 600,000 units for 1964. This year's standard models wore a Chevy-like grille and more side decoration than the '63s. The familiar lineup—Savoy, Belvedere, Fury, and Sport Fury—returned with added horsepower, and any model could be ordered with the 365-bhp 426 wedge-head V-8.

Since 1962, the Valiant line had been topped by a sporty bucket-seat hardtop called Signet, and a convertible version was added for '63. This year, Plymouth attempted to expand its share of the sporty compact market (uncovered by Chevrolet with its 1960 Corvair Monza) by introducing the Barracuda. This was a fast-back coupe that some called a "glassback" because of the huge curved backlight that made up most of the tapering roof. Though the Barracuda was recognizably a Valiant with a trendy superstructure, it was different enough to be interesting. The 225-cid Slant Six was standard, and a

new 273-cid V-8 (derived from the long-running 318) was a desirable option. With oversquare dimensions (3.62×3.31 inches), this new small-block arrived for '64 as the top engine for the Valiant and Dodge Dart as well. It delivered 180 bhp in standard form. The Barracuda offered a combination of sporty looks, good performance and handling, room for four, and unusual utility (the back seat and a "security panel" trunk partition folded down

1964 Chrysler New Yorker Salon hardtop sedan: $5860.

The Imperial Crown convertible for '64. Price: $6003.

The 1964 Imperial Crown Coupe hardtop sold for $5739.

The Chrysler 300 hardtop coupe for '64. Price: $3443.

1964 Chrysler Newport Town & Country wagon

The 1964 Dodge Polara hardtop coupe. Note "V" roofline.

1964 Chrysler 300K convertible. Only 625 were built.

Dodge's 1964 Dart GT convertible listed at $2536.

to create a long cargo deck). Plymouth sold 23,443 of them through the balance of the 1964 model year.

For Dodge, this was a year of minor styling revisions and a continuing emphasis on high performance. Cars with the wedge-head 426 still ruled the dragstrips. One of the most famous of these was "Color Me Gone II," driven by Roger Lindamood, which was Top Eliminator at the 1964 NHRA Winternationals. More exciting was the return of the hemi V-8 as a low-production item intended strictly for racing, mainly NASCAR stockers. Bringing back a fabled engine was a canny move, and it was more powerful than ever, with at least 425 bhp (estimates and claims varied) from 426 cubic inches. The hemis dominated the NASCAR circuit. They swept in first, second,

Concave grille, new rear deck marked all '64 Dodge 880s.

The 1964 Dodge Custom 880 convertible: $3264.

Dodge's compact A-100 panel van from 1964

1964 Dodge Dart GT hardtop coupe. Base price: $2318.

An early Plymouth Barracuda on the paint line. Sports fastback hardtop was a clever Valiant derivation.

1964 Plymouth Sport Fury hardtop coupe: $2864.

The mid-range Plymouth Belvedere four-door sedan for '64

Plymouth charged $2947 for its '64 Fury convertible.

1964 Plymouth Valiant Signet 200 convertible

and third in this year's Daytona 500, though the victory went to Plymouth, not Dodge, as a young driver named Richard Petty scored the first of his many wins at the Florida supertrack.

A facelifted Dodge 880 continued to woo big-car customers for '64. At the other end of the line was a mildly reworked Dart, still with GT hardtop and convertible. They were spritely and low-priced, but Dodge would never get its own version of the Plymouth Barracuda. On the strength of a half-million total sales, Dodge moved back into sixth place on the industry production list, the spot it had held in its best years.

A cosmetic touch-up was ordained for this year's Chrysler, and it was hardly more than a tinsel shift because an all-new design was coming for '65. Wheelbases, models, and drivetrains were unaltered. Grilles, badges, wheel covers, and trim moldings were shuffled, however, and the backlight on closed models was enlarged a bit. Both letter and non-letter 300s continued to feature a black mesh grille with bold crossbars, plus a new paint-filled side stripe. Chrysler had revived its practice of issuing midyear specials to spark the spring selling season beginning with the 300 Pace Setter hardtop and convertible and the New Yorker Salon hardtop sedan for '63. All came with extensive luxury equipment and were, of course, commensurately priced. This year's offering was the Silver 300, a loaded two-door hardtop with metallic silver paint, "canopy" vinyl roof treatment, and an individual bucket-seat interior with reclining front passenger seat. Like other 300s, the Silver variation could be ordered with a four-speed manual as well as TorqueFlite automatic. The letter series continued for 1964 as the 300K, equipped with a mild 360-bhp version of the 413

engine, though 390 bhp was available at extra cost. The K sold much better than the J, a record 3647 units. Altogether, 1964 was a much better year for the Chrysler marque than '63.

Elwood Engel drastically revised the Imperial for 1964. The old silhouette was gone completely, and the car now

1964 Plymouth Valiant V-200 wagon. Base price: $2388.

Plymouth's 1964 Valiant Signet 200 hardtop coupe

looked more like his square-edged Lincoln Continental. A divided grille, unadorned bodysides, and a clean rear deck complete with Continental-style vertical tire bulge were the main design elements. The Custom was dropped and Crown became the base series, with prices starting at $5581. Upmarket was a lone LeBaron hardtop sedan and the Ghia Crown limo. All models rode a specific 129-inch wheelbase except for the limo, which retained its usual 149½-inch chassis.

Things got only better for Chrysler Corporation in 1964, especially at the upper end of the size/price spectrum. Chrysler production was up 10.3 percent for its best total since 1955, and Imperial output saw a colossal 65-percent gain over 1963. The corporation as a whole enjoyed another encouraging year. Plymouth was back in the groove, Dodge was strong, and the company hadn't built more new cars for a single model year in a decade. "We actually feel," said Chrysler-Plymouth general manager P. N. Buckminster, "that we can set a production record next year, surpassing Cadillac." He was right. Chrysler was again riding high.

1965 Chrysler New Yorker 6-window town sedan: $4104.

1965 Chrysler New Yorker hardtop coupe. Price: $4161.

1965 Chrysler 300L convertible. Just 440 were produced.

1965

Former Chrysler Corporation chairman K. T. Keller died of a coronary in January 1966, just short of his 85th birthday. He departed with the respect of many, not only for his achievements at Chrysler but also his civic activities, including 21 years on the Detroit Arts Commission. "We have lost one of the industry's great men," said Lynn Townsend. Keller had been a constant reminder of the glory days of Walter Percy Chrysler, and it was hard to imagine the auto world without him.

Though inactive in company affairs after retiring as chairman in 1956, Keller had made several predictions in 1958 about the industry in general and Chrysler in particular. As he chain-smoked filter cigarettes in his office on the 12th floor of the Fisher building, he had told the press that the age of tailfins and increasing car size wouldn't last. "The present trend in cars has about another year or two to go," he said. "Then we'll get back to design for function, and there'll be more stress on utility. It takes more than styling to make a successful car. The car must be a good, dependable product. Right now we have quite a bit of gingerbread design—lots of jigsaw work. We'll go back to simplicity of design, you wait and see." He would be proven correct, though his words weren't noticed much at the time.

He was right about his old company too, and the Detroit *Free Press* eloquently quoted him in its obituary: "There is one thing that bothers me as I look back. I wonder if we are counting too much on security as against individual enterprise . . . I have an uneasy feeling that we as individuals are not as spunky as we used to be. We seem not to take the personal chances, without which our common American goal is in danger of being medioc-

rity." Chrysler Corporation was certainly not as spunky as it had been, and it appeared to become even less so. But conservative managers could point to the extremes of success and failure the firm had experienced since the war and insist that it was now time to settle back with conventional products that reacted to industry trends instead of starting them.

New ideas had emerged through the Forties and Fifties under Keller, Exner, Colbert, and Zeder, but Chrysler Corporation just didn't seem to be trying anymore as the Sixties wore on into the Seventies. Still, there was hardly anything a big automaker could do wrong as long as sales were good, and Chrysler's sales were very good indeed during the latter half of the Sixties. For example, when the 1965 totals were in, Chrysler production between January and December was 224,061, a monumental 54 percent increase over 1964. That total also marked a new high for the make, surpassing by a fourth the previous record of 176,000 units set in calendar 1955. Chrysler was

1965 Chrysler Newport 6-window town sedan. Price: $3146.

The Imperial Crown convertible for 1965. Price: $6194.

Chrysler's '65 Newport Town & Country wagon

1965 saw the last of the Ghia Crown Imperial limos.

1965 Chrysler Newport convertible (styling prototype)

1965 Imperial Crown convertible. Only 633 were built.

now outselling Cadillac, just as Clare Briggs had predicted. Plymouth and Dodge also came bouncing back in 1965, with Plymouth coming close to its record output of 1957 and Dodge building another half-million units. Only the low-volume Imperial seemed to be faltering. Compared to about 24,000 units for the 1964 model year, 1965 saw only about 18,400 for the corporation's prestige make.

Despite low sales, Imperial was not greatly altered for '65, since a full redesign had been made only the year before. The only serious change was a new grille with glass-covered dual headlamps.

The Chrysler line was fully redesigned for 1965, and Elwood Engel did an excellent job. Edged with brightwork, an Engel trademark, fenders swept cleanly from front to rear in an unbroken line, with slightly arching body sculpture between the belt and lower body. Side glass was curved, bumpers were molded in at each end, and a new, wider grille enclosed the headlights (with glass

covers on 300s and New Yorkers). Inside, a column lever replaced the familiar TorqueFlite pushbuttons, a development shared by all Mopar makes this year.

At midyear the New Yorker's white-finished taillight lenses were replaced by conventional red units. The novel lenses, which lit up red when the brakes were applied, were apparently dreamed up to blend better with the rear brightwork, but had a high scrappage rate in manufacture.

The last of the letter-series 300s appeared this year, the 300L. The once-brutish performers had long been rendered almost as ordinary as standard Chryslers and were thus selling better, the L's total of 2845 units being second only to that of 1964's 300K. The non-letter 300 line, improving equally well, had a higher profit margin than the letter series, which explains the latter's demise, curiously just as the industry was on the verge of new performance heights. But the really hot cars that were now selling in volume were the big-inch intermediates

From Dodge, the new '65 Coronet 500 hardtop coupe

1965 Dodge Coronet 500 convertible. Base price: $2894.

Dodge's big, bucket-seat '65 Polara 500 convertible.

Top-line elegance: 1965 Dodge Monaco hardtop coupe.

1965 Dodge Custom 880 four-door sedan. Price: $3010.

that came to be known as "muscle cars," not standard-size cruisers like the letter series.

Dodge Division fielded another broad lineup for '65 yet didn't do quite as well in model year terms as it had the year before. Still, its cars were exciting, good-looking, and often fast, which was what consumers wanted. The Dart was facelifted, with a brash eggcrate grille and an interesting partial vinyl roof option for hardtops. There were now 10 basic models, ranging from around $2100 to about $2600 basic. The 170-cid Slant Six continued as standard fare, while the optional 273-cid V-8 could be ordered with either 180 (2-bbl) or 235 (4-bbl) bhp. Further up the scale, the old Coronet name was revived for a restyled version of the 1962-64 intermediate platform. Now on a 117-inch wheelbase, two inches shorter than the '64s (wagons still measured 116), they were priced from about $2200 to $2900. Replacing the previous Polara 500 was a Coronet 500 hardtop and convertible, which enjoyed an encouraging 32,745 sales. Standard equipment included bucket seats, console, and the 180-bhp 273-cid V-8.

Above Coronet were three standard-size Dodge series on a new 121-inch wheelbase. Joining the familiar Polara and Custom 880 was the Monaco, a luxury hardtop coupe with a $3355 base price. Though sharing basic structure with the new Chrysler, the full-size Dodge looked somewhat different, with bold vertical-bar grillework and "pie-wedge" taillamps. A trim option created the buckets-and-console Polara 500 package, but Monaco was the division's main entry in the burgeoning personal-luxury field. Designed in the image of Pontiac's Grand Prix, a prime competitor, the Monaco sported standard 315-bhp 383-cid V-8, Thunderbird-like full-width taillights, front buckets, console, special wheel covers, and unusual rattan-like inserts on door panels and seatbacks. The corporate 413 V-8 came to Dodge this year as a big-car option, with the 365-bhp 426-cid wedge at the top of the engine chart.

There was more performance news from Dodge, as the 426 hemi became a semi-production item for a special altered-wheelbase Coronet dubbed Hemi-Charger. Built on the Plymouth Belvedere's 115-inch wheelbase (there was also an even wilder 110-inch-wheelbase version), this was nothing less than a factory-built drag racer for winning the National Hot Rod Association's Super Stock (S/S) and Factory Experimental (F/X) classes. The deceptively ordinary two-door sedan bodywork was lightened considerably over standard issue, with aluminum and fiberglass panels (plus a few undisclosed tricks). Underneath were a special super-heavy-duty frame and driveline components. Dodge had been putting these "altereds" together in very small numbers since 1962, and reaped enormous sales benefits from their dragstrip exploits. Naturally, none of these cars carried the 5/50 warranty.

Dodge hardtops came in different styles for 1965: a formal T-Bird style with a squared-off roofline, a semi-fastback, and a glassy style with a V-shaped C-pillar. Multiple hardtop styles followed a practice also in vogue at Ford, and it was an interesting way of making a lineup appear quite a bit more varied than it really was.

Plymouth at last got a genuine full-size offering to supplement its intermediate-size models for 1965, and the resulting "full-line" model range had a great deal to do with the make's near-record sales. The 116-inch-wheelbase platform, which had been a loser as a full-size contender in 1962-64, was ideal when promoted as a mid-size. Plymouth now did so, like Dodge, marketing it under the Belvedere label. (As model names go, Belvedere was turning into a real survivor. It had been around since 1952.) There were Belvedere I and II series, plus a top-line bucket-seat hardtop and convertible called Satellite, bereft of Belvedere badges but officially part of the same production grouping.

The new big Plymouth was the Fury, a structural twin to this year's Chrysler and Dodge Custom 880/Polara and available in the same body styles save the four-door six-window sedan. Plymouth had an exclusive, though, in its pillared two-door. The model lineup progressed in price and posh from Fury I, II, and III to the top-of-the-line Sport Fury hardtop and convertible. All rode a 119-inch wheelbase (121 for wagons) and were available with a wide choice of engines from the 225-cid Slant Six to the wedge-head Commando 426. As on the equivalent Dodge Custom 880/Polara, styling was resolutely blocky but pleasantly inoffensive and handsome in its way. Vertically stacked quad headlamps flanked a wide mesh grille on all models (the Dodges used horizontal headlamps), bodyside sculpturing was tastefully modest, and back panels were done Chevrolet-style, with taillamps denoting series rank (one for Fury I and II, two for Fury III and Sport Fury).

The compact Valiant changed little for 1965. Barracuda was now ostensibly a separate model, at least in advertising, though it still bore a big "V" emblem below the huge backlight and "AV" series nomenclature. An important development was the "Formula S," a Barracuda package option denoted by racing stripes and special emblems. It included notable roadability features such as heavy-duty front torsion bars and rear springs, firmer-than-stock shock absorbers, and a front anti-roll bar. It also gave you the 273-cid Commando V-8, which was now up to 235 bhp via 10.5:1 compression and a four-barrel carburetor, plus high-lift, high-overlap camshaft, dome-shaped pistons, solid lifters, dual-contact breaker points, an unsilenced air cleaner, and low-restriction exhaust system. The Formula S sounded sweet and flew like a bird. The Barracuda itself was still earning criticism for its "glassback" body style, but in any form it offered a fine combination of good handling, performance, and room. It was the most single popular model in the 1965 Plymouth line, with production totaling close to 65,000 units.

A milestone was reached amidst general rejoicing over Plymouth's fine sales year. As the '66 models were entering production, the 14-millionth car to bear the Plymouth name came off the line. That worked out to an average of close to 370,000 cars per year since the first one in 1928.

Plymouth unveiled a novel show car in 1965, one of Elwood Engel's first. Named the XP-VIP, it was conceived as a posh executive express, with two-door styling and a sloping roof rather than limo proportions and square-cut lines. The roof was composed of two huge

The Dodge Custom 880 wagon for 1965

1965 Plymouth Barracuda fastback hardtop coupe: $2487.

Barracuda boasted a big backlight. Striping cost extra.

1965 Plymouth Fury III hardtop coupe. Base price: $2691.

No-frills full-size: 1965 Plymouth Fury I two-door sedan

Plymouth's new 1965 Satellite hardtop coupe: $2649.

1965 Plymouth Valiant 100 wagon. It cost $2361 basic.

Plymouth's 1965 Valiant Signet convertible

pieces of glass divided by a longitudinal support bar, and each piece (except for side window sections) could be fully retracted into the trunk area. The glass was of the new photochromic type, automatically darkening in bright sunlight and lightening again under clouds. Interior fittings were apropos: telephone and tape recorder in front and TV, stereo, and traveling bar in the rear. The VIP name would be used for a new top-line production series commencing in 1966, but that's about the only thing that survived from this experiment.

After a quiescent period following the AMA "racing ban" of 1957, Plymouth had pursued Ford and Dodge in the hot-car stakes by making the corporate wedge-head 426 V-8 available as its top power option in 1963. Around this, Plymouth conceived its "SuperStock" drag racer, a 3200-pound flyer with aluminum front fenders and hood, and a "426 II" SuperStock for NASCAR, with improved head, racing cam, special carbs, and manifolds. Richard Petty won 14 Grand National events with his NASCAR rig during the '63 campaign and Plymouth won 19 in all,

second only to Ford's 23. Petty came back in 1964 with the Hemi and won the NASCAR Grand National title, the first ever for a Plymouth driver. These racers could hit 175 mph on the big ovals, a good 5 mph faster than anyone else. For 1965 you could buy Plymouth's answer to the Dodge Hemi-Charger, the Belvedere I SuperStock hardtop, priced at $4671. With a standard 365-bhp wedge or optional 425-bhp hemi, it was tremendous performance value for the money.

1966

Though everyone expected 1966 to be a somewhat quieter year than blockbusting 1965, Chrysler Corporation was pleased to record almost the same high production and very little change in its industry ranking. The company's market share actually rose a point, to 16.6 percent, thanks to improved Imperial and Chrysler volume.

This year's Chrysler was still a determinedly big car in every dimension. Since the '65 had done well with two more inches of wheelbase and three inches greater length, designers followed the same philosophy for '66. Though wheelbases were unchanged, overall length went up, and a mild facelift brought the usual grille and tail-end revisions. The sporty 300, now without a letter series, had a more angular roofline and lost its traditional black-out grille. Generally, the '66 Chryslers were busier than the '65s, which had set a styling benchmark that was hard to top.

Styling chief Elwood Engel also reworked the Imperial for '66, and the result was one of the most beautiful designs for that make in years. The previous split grille was replaced by an oblong affair containing multiple rectangles, but the rear deck still bore Exner's eagle emblem and a more subdued "toilet seat" spare. Wheelbase and length were unchanged. This body/frame design was now in its last year, as Imperial would be switched to the unibody Chrysler platform for 1967, thus bringing the prestige marque in line with the lower-echelon makes. The decision contributed to the end of the Ghia Crown Imperial.

Ghia had been building the Crown Imperial under contract since 1957, using bare "kits" furnished by Highland Park. The first-year output of 36 would be the record. After 31 units in 1958, production never rose above 10 per model year, and there were none at all in 1962. Production resumed thereafter, but the tally was only 13 for 1963 and 10 each for 1964 and 1965. The '65 proved to be the last of the line. The main reason was that construction costs by that time had risen 54 percent since 1957, which led Chrysler to think that it could probably get what few limousines it needed at a much lower price by switching to a domestic supplier. Also, the old personal relationship that had brought Chrysler and Ghia together in the late Forties was no more. Exner was gone, and Ghia's Luigi Segre, who had worked closely with him,

Chrysler's New Yorker hardtop sedan for 1966. Price: $4233.

The Imperial Crown Coupe hardtop for 1966. Price: $5887.

The 1966 Chrysler New Yorker hardtop sedan

The 1966 Imperial Crown Coupe hardtop from the rear

The $3583 Chrysler 300 hardtop coupe for '66

1966 Dodge Polara hardtop coupe. Base price: $2874.

1966 Chrysler 300 hardtop coupe

The companion '66 Dodge Polara convertible sold at $3161.

had died in 1963. Thus, Crown limo tooling was shipped from Italy to Spain, where 10 more examples bearing 1966 Imperial grilles and rear decks were completed. After this, Chrysler just barely remained in the limousine business, with 12 "LeBaron" conversions carried out by the Stageway Coach Co. of Fort Smith, Arkansas in 1967-68. Constructed on a 163-inch wheelbase, they were the largest luxury cars in the world. Stageway built 15 more from 1969 through 1972, and Hess & Eisenhardt converted two 1972 standard models (with 1973 grilles). The Imperial make would vanish for a time after 1975, and Ghia would become a Ford subsidiary.

Dodge's new 1966 Monaco hardtop sedan: $3170.

1966 Dodge Coronet 440 four-door sedan

The '66 Dodge Monaco wagon listed for as low as $3436.

1966 Dodge Coronet 500 hardtop coupe: $2705 with V-8.

The Coronet 440 wagon from Dodge for 1966

Dodge's 1966 Coronet 440 convertible cost $2672 basic.

The pert and punchy 1966 Dodge Dart GT convertible

Though the Ghia Crown Imperial was gone, 1966 saw several interesting design exercises from Chrysler. This year's flagship show car was the Chrysler 300X, a sleek, production-based convertible with a sharply raked windshield and lever steering instead of a steering wheel. Also, Stageway built a big limo called the "Mobile Executive," which prefigured its 1967 "production" limousines. As displayed at the 1966 Chicago Auto Show, this car featured a custom interior with telephone, dictating machine, typewriter, TV, stereo, writing table, and reading lamps.

The Chrysler make maintained 10th place in the 1966 model year production race. Imperial remained 14th, but in unit volume it was farther than ever behind Lincoln. Under the Colbert regime, Imperial had moved away

from Chrysler to become a separate make with its own identity. Now it was moving back toward greater commonality with Chrysler both structurally and mechanically. Practical-minded Lynn Townsend told stockholders that Imperial had failed to conquer Cadillac or Lincoln. A likely contributing factor was that no matter how the company referred to it, the public still largely thought of it as the *Chrysler* Imperial.

One reason why the corporation as a whole maintained volume in 1966 was the resurgence of Dodge. In a determined effort this year to maximize its performance appeal and to shrug off its time-honored aura as the "retiree's special," the division launched a dynamic ad campaign that implored customers to "Join the Dodge Rebellion." It also fielded a wide assortment of new prod-

Dodge's base 1966 Dart wagon. Base list price: $2436.

1966 Dodge Dart two-door sedan. It sold at $2094.

Plymouth's new Fury VIP hardtop sedan for 1966.

'66 Plymouth Fury VIP hardtop sedan listed at $3133.

ably Ford's Mustang 2+2, probably because it was based on a smaller car with already graceful proportions, instead of an upright intermediate. But the Charger was a good, solid styling job. It was previewed by the Charger II show car of 1965, and similarly featured hidden headlamps, wall-to-wall taillights, four bucket seats, and full-length center console, plus every available Coronet engine from Slant Six to hemi. Base price was just over $3000, but free use of the option book could get that up to about $5000. Like Barracuda, the Charger arrived with almost wagon-like cargo-carrying versatility, though neither was a hatchback. It employed a similar load deck conversion arrangement, except that instead of a one-piece fold-down rear seatback it had twin foldable backrests, since each rear seat was a bucket. Though the Charger lacked a compound-curve backlight like the Barracuda, that piece of glass was still pretty big. Overall, it was a successful fastback conversion of the Coronet. More importantly, it avoided the Marlin's dumpy short-nose proportions and ungainly rear roof styling.

The hot-selling Dodge for 1966 was the full-size Polara/Monaco, a strange combination of conventional four-square sedans and rakish hardtops and convertibles. The hardtop roofline was neat and crisp, one of the few that really looked better with a vinyl cover than without. The best of this line was the Monaco 500, a blatant, limited-production (10,840) challenge to the personal-luxury Pontiac Grand Prix. Available only as a hardtop coupe, the 500 had a four-barrel 383 V-8, posh trim inside and out, vinyl top, and a $3600 price tag. It led the line well, and brought almost as many people in to see the "Dodge Boys" as the new Charger. However, many prospects settled for the plainer, less-expensive sedans, wagons, and hardtops in the Monaco series, the facelifted, renamed continuation of the Custom 880 built on the same 121-inch wheelbase.

Plymouth volume was down for 1966. Most of the losses went to Pontiac and intramural rival Dodge, both of which had formidable competition for the upper reaches of the Plymouth line. As at Dodge this year, Plymouth had little truly new, though the mid-size Belvedere/Satellite got an extensive and attractive facelift. For the final year of a four-year styling cycle, Valiant was treated to an outer sheetmetal redo that made it much more rectilinear. The usual lineup of body styles continued in 100, 200, and Signet trim, minus the 200 convertible. Barracuda drew even farther away from Valiant for '66, acquiring its own grille (a split eggcrate design) and exchanging Valiant emblems for miniature barracuda fish. Drivetrain specifications were unchanged. The Formula S option package was still available and fairly popular.

Plymouth's mid-size line continued for '66 minus the SuperStock "funny car." But that was okay, because performance fans had real reason to rejoice: the fabled hemi returned as a full production option for any Belvedere/Satellite as well as Dodge's intermediate Coronet and Charger. The exciting Satellite "Street Hemi" combined the awesome 426-cid powerplant with some of the cleanest, sweetest styling in Plymouth history. The mighty engine added $1105 to the Satellite's base price of about

ucts: the mid-size Charger fastback derived from the Coronet, a full range of Monacos, and a bucket-seat Monaco 500 hardtop. The result was one of the best sales years in the marque's history: 632,658 cars. That was good for a fifth-place finish, only 50,000 units behind Plymouth and far ahead of Olds, Buick, and Mercury volume. It was a truly impressive performance considering that Dodge had not seriously restyled, so credit must go to the vivid sales campaign and the spirit created by the image of cars like the Charger.

Trying to make a sporty fastback coupe out of an ordinary sedan is tricky business aesthetically. Plymouth had been only partly successful with the Barracuda, and Rambler had been underwhelming with its Classic-based Marlin. The best transformation of this sort was prob-

Plymouth's 1966 Sport Fury hardtop coupe: $3006.

1966 Plymouth Belvedere II convertible

Plymouth's 1966 Satellite hardtop coupe: $2695.

1966 Plymouth Barracuda fastback with Formula S option

1966 Plymouth Valiant Signet hardtop coupe. Price: $2261.

$2600, and few were sold for under $4500. So equipped, the car could reel off a quarter-mile in 14.5 seconds and 0-60 mph in about seven, which was really reeling. All production 426 hemis had twin Carter AFB four-barrel carbs mounted in line, a relatively mild 10.25:1 compression ratio, and a milder cam than the racing versions.

The competition hemi was now formally available to special order, so NASCAR reinstated it for Grand National events after a one-year hiatus. Richard Petty took eight of Plymouth's 16 victories this year on the stock car circuit, though part of the reason he did so well was a boycott by Ford, which was piqued at the hemi's return to the ovals.

Plymouth and Dodge shared honors in drag racing during 1966, the hottest entries being their lightweight intermediates. Some of those running under Plymouth's colors carried the initials "GTX," a designation that would appear on the make's hottest production mid-size for 1967.

One other '66 Plymouth that should be mentioned is the VIP, a new top-line full-size offering distantly related to 1965's show car of the same name. The series comprised two- and four-door hardtops priced at $3069 and $3133, respectively, and was aimed straight at Chevy's Caprice and Ford's posh LTD in the lower end of the luxury class. Like its rivals (which had appeared for 1965), the VIP was not so much for very important people as it was for upwardly mobile types with extra cash. For their money they got walnut-grain vinyl inserts on bodyside moldings, special VIP badges, an optional vinyl-clad roof, and a cushy interior with cloth or tufted-vinyl upholstery, swiveling aft-cabin reading lamps, and woodgrain dash trim. Sales were high enough to encourage Plymouth to retain the series for a few years, but in its debut season the VIP was roundly outsold by the Caprice, on the order of something like 25 to one.

1967

The Chrysler marque rose to ninth place in the industry's calendar 1967 production standings. It was a height the make had rarely reached, and it came largely at the expense of American Motors, whose sales were dropping. Rambler and Studebaker had pioneered the compact car in the late Fifties. Now, in the words of one historian, they had "elephant footprints all over them." Chrysler, by contrast, had steadfastly remained the big highway cruiser it had always been, and was less affected by the competition in the booming national economy of the mid- to late Sixties. In fact, Chrysler was doing very handsomely, building about a quarter of a million units per year through 1968. But this surge would be only temporary. Chrysler-Plymouth Division would suffer from strikes and the general economic decline at decade's end, and Chrysler would build only 158,614 cars in 1970.

Chrysler model offerings in the late Sixties reflected what planners saw as the temper of the times. The New Yorker wagon was quietly dropped for '66 after hardly more than 3000 of the 1965 models had been sold. The Newport wagons catered to the medium-price utility market through 1968, after which wagons were consigned to a separate Town & Country series, with a shorter wheelbase than other body styles. There had not been a New Yorker convertible since 1961, while the old four-door sedan was making a comeback against the four-door hardtop. There were two sedan styles for 1965, a conventional four-window version and an airier six-window variation of nice proportions, but the latter disappeared for '67. New this year was the Newport Custom, a three-model series sandwiched between Newport and 300 on the price and equipment scale. Though all models were more cluttered in appearance than the '66s, the Custom was also saddled with unpleasant bright moldings on the bodysides. A new two-door hardtop roofline with wide triangular C-pillars appeared for '67. It had a serious blind spot but was very stylish. Called a "semi-fastback," it would continue until 1969, when it was erased by that year's new "fuselage" styling. Annual model changes at least broke even, destroying about as many nasty body styles as good ones.

A new Imperial derived from the Chrysler platform appeared for 1967, and was carried over into the '68 model year with little change. Body-on-frame now gave way to unit construction on a 127-inch wheelbase, three inches longer than Chrysler's, all of it ahead of the cowl. Styling was conservative and not very distinguished.

Chrysler-Plymouth Division kept on building muscles for 1967, probably the peak of the muscle car era in America. This was also the last year before serious government emissions and safety regulations took effect, and it produced a memorable batch of cars. Plymouth's were among the most celebrated. The high-performance GTX hardtop and convertible appeared at the top of the Belvedere line, sporting Chrysler's big-block 440-cid V-8 first seen in the company's full-size cars for 1966. It was a showroom extension of what was being used in NASCAR, where Richard Petty was quickly earning the nickname "The King." Driving hemi-powered Belvederes, he racked up 27 Grand National victories (out of Plymouth's total of 31), 10 of them in a row. He won the Grand National championship hands down, and both his skein of victories and 10-straight record have yet to be surpassed.

While the intermediates ran up stock car and drag racing successes, Chrysler-Plymouth Division was giving both Valiant and Barracuda a long-needed restyle. The latter was now entirely divorced from Valiant stylistically, though both rode the same 108-inch wheelbase. Barracuda's assignment was to compete with the new Camaro that Chevrolet was launching this year, as well as Ford's top-ranked Mustang, Mercury's new Cougar, and Pontiac's Firebird. It was a tall order, but the '67 Barracuda was a gem: sleek and clean, gracefully curved in all the right spots, and now with a convertible and notchback coupe to accompany the fastback. Significantly, the new styling brought more room under the hood for physically larger engines, and Plymouth obliged by offering a 383 V-8 with 280 bhp as the Barracuda's top power option. Over 60,000 of the '67s were sold, a good run aided by deletion of hardtops and convertibles from the

1967 Chrysler New Yorker hardtop sedan: $4339.

The $3407 Chrysler Newport Custom hardtop coupe for '67

Chrysler's 300 convertible for '67 sold at $4289.

The '67 Chrysler body drop at the Jefferson Avenue plant

1967 Imperial Crown convertible. Just 577 were built.

1967 Dodge Polara 500 hardtop coupe: $3155 basic.

The $5733 Imperial Crown hardtop sedan for 1967

The Dodge Monaco hardtop sedan for 1967. Price: $3275.

1967 Dodge Coronet R/T hardtop coupe: $3199.

Furious fastback: the '67 Dodge Charger

The '67 Dodge Coronet 500 hardtop coupe with hemi V-8

Valiant line to avoid intramural competition. But there was also no Valiant station wagon for '67, which helped to lower Plymouth compact sales from previous levels.

The big Plymouths acquired a mild but handsome face-lift, with the same chiseled styling as before. Series lineups stayed the same. The 1967 ad slogan was "Plymouth's Out to Win You Over This Year," but sales tailed off for the second year in a row.

Dodge sales tailed off even more, down by more than 170,000 units from banner 1966 to put the make back in seventh place again, behind Buick and Oldsmobile. Exactly why this happened is hard to say, because this year's line was one of the best in Dodge history. Most of the 1967 restyle revolved around a "delta" theme, with wedge taillights and similarly shaped grilles, plus low sweeping rooflines. The two big-car lines, Polara and Monaco, continued with sedans, hardtops, and wagons, plus special sports sub-models, the Polara and Monaco 500s. All rode a 122-inch wheelbase and shared Chrysler structure, including the blind-quarter two-door hardtop roof.

The Charger continued almost unchanged in 1967, still a derivative of the mid-size Coronet. A new power option was a fortified 375-bhp version of the 440, which Dodge dubbed Magnum. This powerplant was standard for a hot and beautiful Coronet hardtop coupe and convertible called R/T (Road/Track). Heavy-duty suspension, wide tires, and oversize brakes were included. Right out of the box, an R/T could do 0-60 mph in 7.2 seconds. Despite that racy designation, Dodge didn't rely on the R/T for NASCAR, where its big gun was the Hemi-Charger. But nobody could touch Richard Petty this year, and the Chargers won only five major races in 1967.

Dodge's compact Dart was fully restyled for '67. As with the Valiant, wagons were scrapped, reducing the model count from 18 to 12. Base, 270, and GT series continued, the latter still confined to hardtop coupe and convertible. Styling was better than ever, with a nicely curved mid-section, clean grille, and delta taillights to match the rest of the Dodge family. There was the usual array of 170- and 225-cid slant sixes and 273-cid V-8s in 180- and 235-bhp versions. Dodge was calling its dealers "The White Hats" this year, so for spring it issued fancy trim and dress-up packages for Dart, Coronet, Charger, and Polara called—what else?—the "White Hat Specials."

Chrysler had established ties in the early Sixties with Rootes Group, the British manufacturer of Hillman, Humber, Singer, and Sunbeam cars and Commer trucks. In retrospect, it was a move that Chrysler may prefer to forget. The firm bought controlling interest in Rootes for $56 million, while the British government invested $4.2 million in order to retain a small say in its affairs. Rootes was one of Britain's traditional "Big Four" automakers, but always a distant third to British Motor Corporation and Ford of England. Its individual makes had been gathered together between the Depression and 1955 by Lord William Rootes, a dynamic entrepreneur who was one of the first Britons to recognize the potential of the American export market. Unfortunately for Chrysler, this amalgamation was already in serious trouble by 1967, facing a cash flow crisis created by sagging sales of

1967 Dodge Dart convertible. Its base price was $2700.

The companion '67 Dodge Dart GT hardtop coupe: $2417.

Plymouth's 1967 Sport Fury "fast top" hardtop coupe

1967 Plymouth Fury VIP hardtop sedan: $3117.

1967 Plymouth Barracuda hardtop coupe, new this year

The $2449 Plymouth Barracuda hardtop coupe for '67

1967 Plymouth Barracuda Formula S fastback coupe

Plymouth's hot one for '67: the Belvedere GTX hardtop coupe

1967 Plymouth Satellite hardtop coupe with hemi V-8

1967 Plymouth Valiant Signet four-door sedan: $2308.

a generally aging product line.

For the time being, Chrysler allowed continued production of the rapid Sunbeam Tiger. An Anglo-American hybrid, it was basically the neat Alpine sports car, a design that dated from 1960, powered by the potent 289 Ford V-8 instead of the usual asthmatic four. Chrysler-Plymouth dealerships sold the Tiger briefly in 1967, but when it became obvious that the corporate 273-cid V-8 would not fit the engine bay, the Tiger was dropped. An abortive Sunbeam fastback based on the ordinary Hillman Hunter sedan was brought to the U.S. for 1968-70, but it failed to sell and was likewise dropped. Then Chrysler tried a federalized version of the subcompact Hillman Avenger. Called the Plymouth Cricket, it was a dreadful little buzz-box that rusted with abandon and suffered severe reliability problems. Predictably, C-P canned it after 1973. Meantime, the corporation had strengthened ties with Mitsubishi of Japan, which by 1970 was supplying Dodge dealers with a group of much more saleable small cars marketed under the Colt badge. The Oriental products were far more successful than the British ones ever hoped to be, a forecast of the future.

1968

In 1968, the Viet Cong launched its Tet Offensive at the cost of many lives to convince the world that it was a viable force in strife-torn Vietnam. In the spring, Martin Luther King, Jr., and Robert Kennedy died by assassins' hands. In late autumn, the North Koreans seized the USS *Pueblo*, holding its crew for "spying." It was a forbidding year, and Americans were divided in their choice for president. Richard Nixon won by a hair. But the year's events didn't affect the auto industry, which just kept rolling. That included Chrysler: Plymouth had its best 12 months since 1957 and Chrysler and Dodge matched their big 1966 volumes. Only Imperial suffered a production decline.

By 1966, Chrysler engineers had had enough experience with unit construction to confidently apply it to the prestige Imperial. Vast technological improvements had been made in noise isolation, the chief reason luxury-car makers had shied away from unit structures, and the art of computer stress-testing had been honed to a fine science. But decisions were in the offing that would lead to further retrenchment for Mopar's finest. In a far-reaching move, product planners concluded that the Imperial would share more Chrysler sheetmetal as well as its basic structure from model year '69 on. It was this key decision, perhaps more than any other, that doomed Imperial to its eventual, though temporary, passing as a separate make after 1975. By that time, it just wasn't "different" enough to cause many buyers to opt for one instead of a New Yorker, and the make had resolutely failed to make inroads into the sales territory of either Cadillac or Lincoln. The marque would be resurrected for another try in 1981, but would again be dropped following very slow sales.

1968 Chrysler 300 hardtop coupe. Price: $4010.

1968 Chrysler Newport "Sportsgrain" hardtop coupe

Chrysler's 1968 Newport Custom hardtop coupe

1968 Imperial Crown Coupe hardtop. Base price: $5722.

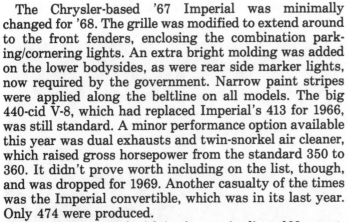

1968 Chrysler Newport Town & Country wagon

1968 Dodge Coronet 440 hardtop coupe

The Chrysler-based '67 Imperial was minimally changed for '68. The grille was modified to extend around to the front fenders, enclosing the combination parking/cornering lights. An extra bright molding was added on the lower bodysides, as were rear side marker lights, now required by the government. Narrow paint stripes were applied along the beltline on all models. The big 440-cid V-8, which had replaced Imperial's 413 for 1966, was still standard. A minor performance option available this year was dual exhausts and twin-snorkel air cleaner, which raised gross horsepower from the standard 350 to 360. It didn't prove worth including on the list, though, and was dropped for 1969. Another casualty of the times was the Imperial convertible, which was in its last year. Only 474 were produced.

Chrysler continued with its four-series line of Newport, Newport Custom, 300, and New Yorker at base prices ranging from about $3400 to $4500. Town & Country station wagons of both six- and nine-passenger capacity were included in the standard Newport line. Both New-

port series continued with the sound, smooth-performing 383-cid V-8 as standard power, while 300s and New Yorkers used the Imperial's 350-bhp 440-cid engine. Chrysler wheelbases were as before: 124 inches for all models save wagons, which were two inches shorter. Mid-season specials this year included Newport hardtops and convertibles with a sprightly throwback to the original Town & Country: simulated wood panels for the bodysides in the same style and material used for wagons. Called "Sportsgrain," this $126 trim option made these the first woodgrain non-wagon Chryslers since the Town & Country Newport was dropped back in 1950. The panels looked flashy on the clean-sided '68 body and added some appeal during the spring selling season, though these were by no means unabashed luxury cars like the original T&C. Again this year, Newport specials were fielded with unique color schemes—in turquoise this time—in two- and four-door hardtop body styles. This trim package was later extended to the 300 series.

Elsewhere at Chrysler-Plymouth, the Belvedere/Satel-

The handsome, all-new 1968 Charger was easily the most exciting Dodge of the decade. Sales zoomed.

lite was handsomely reskinned for 1968. The hot GTX returned, but the performance spotlight now focused downmarket on the first "budget" muscle car. Plymouth chose a whimsical name for it, Road Runner, after the popular Warner Brothers cartoon character who always baited the scheming coyote. The idea was to pack the best of Plymouth performance into a low-cost package that anyone with a decent income could afford. By most standards, Plymouth succeeded. The base price was only $2900, which included a 335-bhp version of the 383 V-8, four-speed manual transmission, heavy-duty suspension, special Road Runner decals, and a plain vinyl interior. A

novel touch was the horn, which mimicked the cartoon character's unmistakable "beep-beep" and probably mortified a fair share of Super Sport Chevy owners. Chrysler-Plymouth sold a startling total of 44,799 Road Runners, which was phenomenal for a muscle car (and compared to only about 19,000 GTXs). An RR two-door hardtop was added in the spring, but the coupe outsold it 2 to 1. Although built to a price, the Road Runner coupe was a very good-looking car—almost European, with thin roof pillars and flip-out rear quarter windows. And it could really run, which was the whole idea.

The full-size Plymouths got an exterior tinware shuffle

Dodge's hot '68 Coronet R/T hardtop listed at $3379.

1968 Dodge Dart GTS hardtop coupe: $3189.

Plymouth's posh Fury VIP hardtop sedan for 1968

for '68, continuing on the 119-inch wheelbase (wagons 121). There was the usual lineup of Fury I/II/III, Sport Fury, VIP, and Suburban. All were big, rather garish, and thoroughly forgettable, but America still preferred big cars and the standard-size Plymouths accounted for nearly half of the make's total sales this year. The big Furys' success underlined the lack of foresight that had produced the "plucked chickens" back in 1962-64, and Plymouth remained determined to have full-size cars in its lineup for the forseeable future.

For keen drivers, the Barracuda was far more interesting. Happily, Plymouth's entry in the burgeoning pony-car field didn't change during its three-year second-generation design. There were only minor trim changes for '68, notably a vertical-bar grille insert. More significant was an expanded engine lineup. A new "small-block" 340 V-8 appeared, derived from the long-running 318 that itself became the base Barracuda V-8 this year. The 383 returned with 300 bhp for the Formula S package. Though fast on the street, the big-block Barracudas fell short at the dragstrips, so Plymouth released a limited number of hemi-powered models to back them up. The most successful of the dragstrip stars was the team of Ronnie Sox and Buddy Martin, factory blessed (if not backed) in the National Hot Rod Association's Super/Stock category.

Dodge had a really bang-up year in 1968. No wonder: once again the Dodge Boys had decided to race hard and sell performance. This time they caught the eyes of enthusiast buyers with a model grouping called the "Scat Pack": Chargers, Coronets, and Darts wearing "bumble-bee" racing stripes around their tails and equipped with beefy drivetrains, wide tires, and hot engines.

The restyled and sleekly beautiful 1968 Charger was easily the most exciting Dodge of the decade. Though still based on the Coronet platform, it had a smashing new "Coke-bottle" shape that curved in the right places without looking bulbous. The pure fastback of 1966-67 now gave way to a "flying buttress" notchback style, with C-pillar sail panels extended rearward either side of a near-vertical rear window. Up front was a simple loop grille, with fine vertical bars and hidden headlamps, above a simple bumper. The Charger's styling transformation was so dramatic that one magazine was moved to say that it made the 1966-67 look like shipping crates for the new model. The '68 was definitely lean and muscular. And the R/T version with standard 375-bhp, 440-cid V-8 performed accordingly. The hemi was still optional. Dodge sold nearly 100,000 Chargers for the model year, with far more R/Ts than ever before. If the '68 looked less slippery than the 1966-67 version, it was in fact more aerodynamic. When it lapped Daytona at about 184 mph, elation blew off the roof in Hamtramck. Unfortunately, Ford had been burning the midnight oil too, and the Ford Torino/Mercury Cyclone fastbacks proved capable of nearly 190 mph. Dodge won only five NASCAR Grand National events in 1968, so it was determined to come back with something slicker for the '69 campaign.

The performance king of the Coronet line was no slouch, either. Called Super Bee, it was, predictably, a Road Runner for the Dodge Boys, announced at about

1968 Plymouth Fury II two-door sedan. Price: $2715.

Fury III hardtop sedan was a popular Plymouth for '68.

1968 Plymouth Sport Satellite hardtop coupe

1968 Plymouth Satellite four-door sedan: $2572.

Plymouth Road Runner hardtop was a mid-1968 entry.

The 1968 Plymouth Barracuda Formula S fastback coupe

The '68 Plymouth GTX hardtop coupe sold at $3355 basic.

1968 Plymouth Barracuda Formula S hardtop coupe

Companion '68 GTX convertible saw just 1026 copies.

1968 Plymouth Valiant Signet four-door sedan: $2447.

mid-season. Dodge dipped into its parts bins for the standard four-speed, a rock-hard suspension, and the 335-bhp Magnum 383, but spent a few more dollars on the interior than Plymouth had with the Road Runner. The Bee's $3138 base price included the Charger instrument panel with its complete complement of gauges, plus Coronet 440 upholstery, which was in sharp contrast to the Jeep-like starkness of the Road Runner. Although it didn't have the Runner's cute graphics and far-out horn, the Super Bee was more car.

The Scat Pack also included a hot version of the compact Dart, clean-cut, light, and fast. This was the bumblebee-striped GT Sport or GTS, a two-door hardtop and convertible powered by the 340 or 383 V-8s from the Barracuda Formula S. As at Plymouth, GTS drag racers weren't fast enough, so Dodge ran off a few hemi-powered Darts that competitors could buy for just over $4000. The price seems unbelievable today, but it works out to

only about $11,250 when you factor in inflation—and, of course, there's nothing like the Hemi-Dart being built now. NHRA approved it for the Super/Stock "B" class. A few Darts were also run with Magnum 440 V-8s.

The other member of 1968's Scat Pack was the Coronet R/T, again listing hardtop coupe and convertible but powered by the 375-bhp Magnum 440 from the Charger R/T. Like this year's mid-size Plymouths, the Coronet came in for a completely new look that was very much inspired by GM's 1966-67 intermediates. Notable were the "hippy" rear fender contours, and front fenders laterally tapered up slightly from a flat hood to give the front end a "double-delta" shape per current division practice. The Coronet lineup continued as revised for '67, with Deluxe as the base series, followed by the mid-range 440 and the top-of-the-line 500. The latter still included a four-door sedan and two wagons in addition to the traditional convertible and hardtop coupe. Interestingly, combined Coronet R/T and 500 sales were barely half the total for the new Charger, 50,998 versus a smashing 96,108.

The full-size Polara and Monaco continued as the Dodge Boys' big bruisers for '68, still on the 122-inch wheelbase unique to this line. Styling was a rehash of '67, with three-element grilles, wedge-shaped taillamps (full-width on all but wagons), and rearranged exterior ornamentation. As before, there were bucket-seat Polara 500 and Monaco 500 offerings for the sporty crowd, but that crowd was shrinking rapidly. Only 4983 Polara 500 convertibles and hardtops and just 4568 Monaco 500 hardtops were sold for the model year.

1969

Chrysler Corporation was riding high at the end of the Sixties—high enough to tell the public bluntly that the 1969 Chrysler was "Your Next Car." Years before, Virgil Exner had pioneered the combination bumper/grille on his XNR show car. Now here it was in production courtesy of Elwood Engel. The bumper formed an oblong frame across the front of the car and, as on the XNR, encompassed radiator opening and headlights. Unlike Exner's special, though, it announced a body with "fuselage styling" free of creases, wrinkles, asymmetrical humps, and tailfins. The '69 Chryslers and Imperials were smooth, good-looking, and very luxurious. They would have a very good sales year.

While Dodge and Plymouth emphasized performance in the late Sixties, Chrysler and Imperial downplayed it. The letter-series 300 had been lopped off after 1965, and mildly tuned 383s and 413s were used that same year. The big 440 was adopted for 1966 mainly in anticipation of emissions standards that would take effect for '68. Wheelbase remained at 124 inches, but the '69 Chrysler was a whopping 225 inches long and nearly 80 inches wide, about as mammoth as it would ever get. Model names were all familiar, but Town & Country wagons were now broken out as a separate series. Engines again revolved around 383 and 440 V-8s, the smaller units assigned to Newports, with 290 bhp standard and 330 bhp optional. New Yorkers and 300s carried the 350-bhp 440 as standard, with 375 bhp optional. All but the 375-bhp engine were available for Town & Country.

At the corporate level, Lynn Townsend's regime labored away to achieve permanent profitability. What else was there to worry about? Highland Park was turning in one good year after another. K. T. Keller's tightly centralized corporate structure had been decentralized under Tex Colbert. Townsend recentralized it, but still left many operations to the two car divisions. However, both Dodge and Chrysler-Plymouth were more centrally controlled than the former Plymouth, Dodge, DeSoto, and Chrysler Divisions. Virgil Boyd had become president on January 1, 1967. On January 9, 1970, he was relieved by John Riccardo, who promised continuity and progress. Chrysler Realty Corporation had been estab-

1969 Chrysler New Yorker hardtop coupe. List price: $4539.

Brawny beauty: 1969 Chrysler 300 hardtop coupe

The hardtop sedan in the 1969 Chrysler Newport Custom series

Chrysler's Town & Country wagon for 1969

1969 Chrysler Town & Country wagon

1969 Chrysler Newport Custom hardtop sedan: $3631.

1969 Imperial LeBaron hardtop coupe. Price was $5898.

1969 Dodge Polara 500 hardtop coupe. List price: $3314.

1969 Dodge Monaco hardtop sedan with optional "Super-Lite"

The $2692 Dodge Coronet 440 hardtop coupe for '69

lished by Townsend in 1967. Essentially, Realty grew out of the old Dealer Enterprises section, and was designed to help dealers to buy and build their operations by lending them the wherewithal to do it. Under Riccardo, the retail outlets were upgraded and company-owned dealerships multiplied. On the production line, quality control became an end in itself for the first time in postwar Chrysler history.

For a car that was now almost entirely a Chrysler, the '69 Imperial did pretty well. Production was up to 22,000 units—led by almost 15,000 LeBaron hardtop sedans—an improvement of nearly 7000 from 1968. The LeBaron was no longer a $7000 semi-custom but a more conventional model priced down toward $6000, which obviously helped sales. Stylists had done a good job with the long, low, "fuselage" bodyshell, here carrying a simple, full-width eggcrate grille with concealed headlamps (the latter shared with the Chrysler 300), faddish sequential turn signals at the rear, and—for air-conditioned coupes—ventless side glass. Although the 127-inch wheelbase was held over from '68, the new body was stretched by about five inches, yet Chrysler managed to engineer about 100 pounds off the curb weight. Coupe and sedan body styles were now available in both Crown and LeBaron trim, and a pillared sedan appeared for the first time since 1960, a Crown model priced identically with its hardtop sedan counterpart. The LeBaron's lower prices enabled the upper series to beat the Crown in sales for the first time. Overall, 1969 was the third best year in Imperial history. It seemed that sharing Chrysler's body hadn't hurt—but, then again, it was a tremendous year for the industry as a whole.

Plymouth's production level of 720,000 units for 1969 was almost as good as its previous year's output. However, 1970-model sales late in the year were slow, and Plymouth actually fell to sixth place again for calendar 1969. The compact Valiant saw little change, still on a 108-inch wheelbase and offering two- and four-door sedans in base 100 or plusher Signet trim as it had since 1967. Styling hadn't changed much since then either. Barracuda retained its fine styling in hatchback, convertible, and notchback hardtop body styles, and now had something extra for performance fans. Called the 'Cuda, it was a package option built around the 340- and 383-cid engines, developing 275 and 330 bhp gross, respectively. Later there was a 375-bhp 440 option.

Plymouth's strong push of the past several years in hot intermediates cooled somewhat for model year '69, and there was little new except for a Road Runner convertible. The Super Commando 440 claimed 15 more bhp, thanks to a trio of two-barrel carburetors on an Edelbrock intake manifold. Dubbed the 440-6bbl., it was easily identified by a fiberglass hood that sported a large scoop. Unfortunately, the hood showed up mainly in rearview mirrors on the race track. Richard Petty had quit campaigning Plymouths after he'd failed to prosper with them in 1968, and signed on with Ford for the NASCAR wars of '69. Plymouth won only two Grand National races this year, but it wasn't quite ready to give up on NASCAR or Petty. Chrysler-Plymouth Division was also watching Dodge closely—which was worth doing.

1969 Dodge Coronet Super Bee hardtop coupe: $3138.

1969 Dodge Coronet R/T hardtop coupe sold for $3442.

1969 Dodge Charger hardtop coupe with 426-cid hemi V-8

1969 Dodge Charger R/T hardtop coupe listed at $3592.

1969 Dodge Charger 500

Flush backlight marked the '69 Dodge Charger 500.

The big Plymouths, still reacting to their opposition, also came in for the "fuselage" look this year and an inch more wheelbase, now measuring 120. The familiar Fury I/II/III line continued, with the upper end shared again by Sport Fury and VIP. The latter were available as hardtop coupes with or without formal roofline, and as a hardtop sedan. Engine offerings were unchanged because of the expense of the restyling plus the money that Chrysler was spending to meet government mandates—$365 million for the '69 models alone.

The most exciting Chrysler Corporation car for 1969 had to be the Dodge Charger Daytona, built especially for the Daytona 500 and similar stock car enduros, a determined effort to win back the NASCAR laurels so recently lost to Ford. The Daytona was instantly recognizable—from a block away—by its wind-cheating bullet-shaped nose, hidden headlamps, front spoiler, flush-backlight full-fastback roof and, most of all, a pair of towering rear deck fins supporting a huge airfoil/stabilizer. Compared with the new '69 Charger 500, the Daytona was about 20 percent more aerodynamically efficient, an incredible

gain that leapfrogged Ford and gave the winged warrior a theoretical advantage of 500 yards per lap. Dodge built 505 Charger Daytonas in all, just enough to exceed NASCAR's stipulated 500-unit limit to qualify as a "production" model. The 440 was standard, the hemi optional.

The Daytona's first outing came at Talladega, a piece of one-upmanship designed to embarrass Ford, which had named its most torrid Torino after the Alabama track. Dodge driver Richard Brickhouse won handily, but it was an empty victory because a drivers' strike kept all the Ford pilots away. Further, the late-season arrival (in April) coupled with the mandatory waiting period before its first race kept the Daytona from really dominating the circuit. Dodge won 22 Grand Nationals, but Ford won 26 and repeated as NASCAR champion.

Like Plymouth, Dodge also offered a tri-carb 440 V-8 at mid-year but called it "Six-Pack." The six-throat setup was a first for both makes. Coronets so equipped were fitted with a fiberglass hood displaying a prominent scoop, as on the Plymouth version. The Coronet Super Bee added

The 1969 Dodge Charger Daytona, photographed at Chrysler's Chelsea Proving Grounds. Production was just 505.

a two-door hardtop to its existing pillared coupe style *a la* Road Runner, and likewise retained the 383 V-8 packing 335 bhp as standard. Coronets were the sleepers in the Dodge line, outshone in press and racing by the Charger Daytona but nevertheless among the smoothest, quickest intermediates money could buy. They wore a facelift of the 1968 redesign, still blessedly uncluttered, and came in Deluxe, 440, 500, and R/T series, plus the Super Bee. The 440 did not necessarily refer to engine size. Coronet's

base V-8 was a 273-cid unit, and the 440 Magnum continued as standard only for R/T.

Up in the standard-size arena, Dodge dropped the Monaco 500 for 1969 but continued the Polara 500 hardtop and convertible, priced around $3500. Still on a 122-inch wheelbase, all big Dodges shared "fuselage styling" with Chrysler and the Plymouth Fury, but somehow appeared cleaner and more aggressive, perhaps because of their big, clean, three-section rectangular grille and

1969 Dodge Coronet Deluxe Police Pursuit

The "formal roof" '69 Plymouth Fury VIP hardtop coupe

1969 Dodge Dart Swinger 340 hardtop coupe: $2836

Plymouth's 1969 Sport Suburban wagon: $3651-$3718.

deft two-toning along the lower bodysides.

Dodge continued its four-pronged compact line for '69, with base Dart, Custom, GT, and GTS models as before, plus one new entry, the Swinger 340. This was a low-bucks ($2836) muscle mini to compete with the likes of Chevy's Nova SS. A good-looking sportster available only as a hardtop coupe, Swinger 340 had the bumblebee-striped tail that had become a Scat Pack trademark, and came with the 340-cid V-8, a four-speed manual transmission, heavy-duty suspension, and D70 tires. With 275 bhp for a shade over 3000 pounds, it was fast off the line and competent on twisting back-country roads, a very attractive package indeed. Dodge sold nearly 200,000 of the mildly restyled '69 Darts, which represented a fine improvement—and a healthy contribution to its success this year.

Chrysler Corporation entered the Seventies in much better shape than it had entered the Sixties. Plymouth, though out-produced by Pontiac for third place, was cranking out about 700,000 cars a year for a solid fourth in the standings. Dodge was long established as the hot car in the Chrysler camp, not only with intermediates but with compacts and full-size cars too, and it had enjoyed several tremendous years. Chrysler was running neck and neck with Cadillac, running up about a quarter-million sales every 12 months. Imperial had generally been a commercial disappointment, but its 1967 and 1969 body-sharing with Chrysler had realized production cost savings, and it remained a producible and saleable product.

By the dawn of the Seventies, the trauma of Colbert's

Bargain buy: 1969 Plymouth Valiant 100 two-door sedan

last years and the brief reign of Bill Newberg were ancient history, and the firm had established a presence both in Europe (with Simca and Rootes) and Japan (via Mitsubishi). Even that fascinating plaything of corporate engineers, the turbine engine, had surfaced again, this time due to the government's newfound concern with clean-burning engines, and Chrysler enjoyed at least a three-year lead in turbine research over General Motors.

Scanning the field of their vision, the Townsend team could hardly be displeased. They had only to keep on doing what they were doing, Riccardo said. Or so it seemed...

The 1969 Plymouth GTX hardtop coupe: $3416.

1969 Plymouth Barracuda fastback with 'Cuda 383 option

1969 Plymouth Barracuda hardtop coupe. Base price: $2780.

The '69 Barracuda Formula S fastback with 383 V-8

1970

From among Lynn Townsend's many accomplishments at Chrysler, anyone who loves the automobile must acknowledge his greatest gift to posterity: the Chrysler Historical Collection. It was established in 1969 under the direction of Cliff Lockwood, who'd been with the firm since the days of Walter P. Chrysler himself. As the name suggests, it is a repository of company memorabilia and material—everything from a complete set of shop manuals for every Chrysler Corporation model ever built to the office furniture of the founder. Lockwood was relieved in 1971 by John Bunnell, who upon his own retirement passed the guardianship to C. R. Cheney. Each of the Collection's directors was enthusiastic in recording and preserving Chrysler history. It is unfortunate that, as the Seventies unfolded and business worsened, management's interest in the archives declined. During particularly bad times, the big rooms in the main Highland Park complex were simply locked up and placed off limits to researchers and historians. One can virtually chart the ups and downs of Chrysler in the Seventies—and there were many—by listing the dates when the Historical Collection was fully open, partly open, or completely closed.

While looking back with the Historical Collection, the Townsend team also looked forward, approaching the Department of Transportation to promote further work on the gas turbine. In 1970, company research director George J. Huebner made an analysis of alternate power sources: electric, steam, and the Chrysler turbine engine, which by now had reached its sixth-generation design. To no one's surprise, Huebner concluded the turbine a better alternative than either rival. Its on-road performance had been much improved, with reduced throttle lag and fuel consumption compared to 1966 levels. While its high manufacturing costs and exhaust emission levels were problems still to be resolved, Huebner felt sure that they could be licked, especially with an ample transfusion of government money. In late 1972, the newly created Environmental Protection Agency (EPA) awarded Chrysler a $6.4 million contract to investigate the engine's cost and emission problems. Chrysler, said the EPA, would provide "gas turbine automobile engines for use as 'test beds' to establish baseline gas turbine performance and emission levels."

Had it not been for growing federal concern with emissions, the turbine program might have expired well before the Seventies. But this engine has yet to become a production reality at Chrysler or anywhere else. And although research continues sporadically, it doesn't look like it ever will. General Motors, after an expensive investment in tooling, abandoned its Wankel rotary project when prototype engines proved unacceptably heavy on fuel and high in emissions. The Chrysler turbine continued to demonstrate similar problems. Still, it's interesting that Chrysler was pushing a concept so ecologically enlightened, particularly during a period of dirt-cheap gas and 18-foot-long whalemobiles.

Mid-model year 1970 saw Chrysler introduce the first car to bear the Cordoba name, but Ricardo Montalban

The Chrysler Newport Custom hardtop sedan for 1970

Chrysler's 1970 Town & Country wagon listed at $4738/$4824.

1970 Chrysler Newport Custom hardtop sedan: $3861

1970 Chrysler New Yorker hardtop coupe. Base price: $4681.

Chrysler's 1970 "spring special" was the Cordoba, a specially trimmed Newport hardtop. Just 1868 were built.

could keep his Ferrari a while longer: this was anything but a "small Chrysler." Instead, it was a two- or four-door Newport hardtop with gold paint, color-keyed wheels and grille, special vinyl roof and bodyside moldings, and an "Aztec Eagle" interior design. Newports of all varieties could be ordered this year with the corporate 440-cid V-8, which had been designed to cope with government emissions mandates. A special Newport 440 hardtop was also offered, complete with TorqueFlite, vinyl roof, and special interior trim and accessories.

Another flashy newcomer for 1970 was the 300-H. Despite the designation, this was not a revival of the letter series (which had ended at L) but a collaborative effort with Hurst Performance Products, which had worked similar deals with Olds and Pontiac. A floor-mounted Hurst shifter controlled the usual TorqueFlite, and the package included special road wheels, H70 × 15 white-letter tires, heavy-duty suspension, and the 440 V-8. The 300-H was highlighted by the gold-and-white paint job typically seen on Hurst-sponsored specials plus a

1970 Chrysler New Yorker hardtop sedan sold at $4761.

1970 Chrysler New Yorker hardtop sedan

Companion 300 version listed at $4313 for 1970.

Chrysler sold the 1970 New Yorker four-door sedan at $4630.

Limited-edition Chrysler 300-Hurst appeared for mid-1970.

Note special hood and deck styling.

customized hood, rear deck spoiler, special grille paint, a custom interior, and pinstriping. Production was restricted to just 501 copies.

Alongside the Concept 70-X show car seen this year, Chrysler plugged the Cordoba de Oro, an Engel design exercise on the 124-inch wheelbase. It featured the strongest wedge profile since Virgil Exner's XNR of 1960, though it looked rather heavy near the back. Another feature harking back to the Exner years was a cantilevered roof *sans* A-pillar, just like on the old Ghia-built Norseman that had sunk aboard the *Andrea Doria*.

The Imperial convertible had vanished after 1968. This year marked the end of the open Chryslers, with just 1124 Newports and 1077 of the 300s. All models wore a mild facelift of the "fuselage" 1969 styling, and were arrayed as before in Newport, Newport Custom, Town & Country, 300, and New Yorker series. Engine specifications were mainly unchanged. What did change was volume, and in a big way. This was a declining year for the industry as a whole, but Chrysler's decline was huge: only 180,000 units for the model year, 159,000 for the calendar year. This was about 80,000 units off the 1969 pace, and marked the first time since 1964 that fewer than 200,000 Chryslers had left the factory. The only consolation was

Imperial production fell sharply for 1970. Shown: the $6095 LeBaron hardtop coupe. Production was just 1803.

1970 Imperial LeBaron hardtop sedan. Base price: $6328.

1970 Dodge Challenger R/T convertible listed at $3535.

1970 Dodge Challenger hardtop coupe

The 1970 Dodge Challenger R/T convertible

that everybody else was ailing, too. In calendar year production, Chrysler slipped below Cadillac again.

Imperial's situation was just as bad—actually worse on a percentage basis. Fewer than 12,000 were built for the model year, a loss of better than 50 percent and large enough to give management second thoughts about the marque's future. Whatever magic the 1969 model had, the almost unchanged 1970 didn't. Perhaps the market for expensive Chryslers had now been exhausted. A heavier eggcrate grille and reshuffled trim certainly wasn't enough, nor was "standard everything." One upshot of this debacle was the demise of the Crown after

1970, leaving Imperial with just a single, two-model LeBaron series for 1971 and beyond. An incidental casualty was the Stageway-built LeBaron limousine. The last half dozen of the 163-inch-wheelbase haulers were built this year, selling for $16,500 apiece. Thus, Imperial lost its limousine-class aura and a proud "carriage trade" tradition dating back some 40-odd years.

The state of the industry considered, Chrysler's divisional partner fared well in 1970. Plymouth retailed some 685,000 cars for the model year, and came within 5000 units of Pontiac in the race for third place. Although public interest in performance cars seemed to be slacken-

Smaller backlight and padded roof marked the 1970 Dodge Challenger Special Edition hardtop.

The 1970 Dodge Challenger R/T hardtop shows off its handsome lines. Hood scoop identifies 440 "Six Pack" V-8.

1970 Dodge Challenger R/T hardtop. Base price: $3226.

The bumblebee-striped '70 Challenger R/T

Twin scoop hood identified 1970 Dodge Challengers with the 440 Magnum V-8. R/T hardtop is pictured.

ing, Plymouth's emphasis on hot ones seemed to help. Even the full-size line got an overt performance entry, notably a new GT version of the Sport Fury two-door hardtop, with standard 440-cid V-8, heavy-duty suspension, and long-legged rear axle ratios (as high as 2.76:1). Another novel package, though not in the GT's league, was the S/23. Standard power here was the tame 318, but there was a well-tuned suspension plus trendy "strobe stripe" bodyside decoration. Plymouth continued to woo the luxury class. Though it dropped the Fury convertible and VIP series this year, it added the plush Gran Coupe in February. This was essentially a Fury II two-door sedan with just about every convenience, comfort, and appearance feature available in the big-car line as standard equipment except air conditioning. It sold for $3833. The price was $4216 with a/c.

1970 Dodge Charger hardtop coupe (styling prototype)

1970 Dodge Charger hardtop in $3711 R/T form

All 1970 Dodge Chargers (R/T shown) continued with the successful 1968-69 styling. Note scoops on doors.

The 1970 Dodge Charger hardtop coupe with optional "500" appearance package. Luggage rack was a separate item.

But it was the intermediates that were more equal than other Plymouths for 1970. The star performer was the new Superbird, set within the Road Runner series as a continuation of the 1969 Dodge Charger Daytona. The droop-snoot front end and huge tailfins carrying a stabilizer wing high above the rear deck were similar to but not exactly the same as Daytona pieces. No matter: the Superbird looked as fast as it was. Racing versions recorded over 220 mph. The stock street drivetrain was the four-barrel 440 with TorqueFlite automatic, but a six-barrel 440, a racing hemi, and a four-speed manual gearbox were options. NASCAR thought it could stop Plymouth from repeating the "Dodge cheat" with this car by raising the production minimum from 500 to 1500 units. But Plymouth simply built what it took to qualify the Bird and then some. Altogether, 1920 left the factory.

A rather oddly shaped new grille marked Dodge's mid-size 1970 Coronet. Shown: the 500 hardtop coupe.

Though the car was intended strictly for racing, dealers were finding their sales floors flooded with young bloods holding cash, and the division happily raised production to meet demand.

The Superbird's great moment came at Daytona, when Pete Hamilton romped to victory at a near-150-mph average ahead of every Ford and—perhaps more poignant —every Dodge. Of the 38 Grand National events won by Chrysler products this season, 21 belonged to the Super-

bird. It was enough, incidentally, to tempt Richard Petty back into the fold. And for good measure, Plymouth signed up Dan Gurney as well.

If Dodge could have the "Scat Pack," Plymouth could have the "Rapid Transit System," which is what it called its 1970 powerhouse cars. In addition to Superbird, the System included the hot GTX hardtop (but not the convertible, which was dropped this year), and a trio of Road Runners. The heyday of muscle cars was fast drawing to

1970 Dodge Coronet 500 hardtop coupe. Base price: $3048.

1970 Dodge Coronet 440 hardtop coupe sold at $2805 basic.

1970 Dodge Coronet 440 four-door sedan

1970 Dodge Coronet 440 sedan cost $2783 basic.

The 1970 Dodge Coronet R/T convertible, still with "Scat Pack" bumblebee rump stripes. Price: $3785.

a close, however, so Runner sales were off by 50 percent in 1970. For 1971, both Road Runner and GTX were merged back into the basic Satellite lineup. The last year for the GTX was 1971, while the Runner ran through 1974.

For the first time in years, Plymouth moved to shore up its position in the compact market. Its weapon was the Duster, a pretty little fastback coupe based on the Valiant two-door sedan, which it replaced. Though offered only in that body style (a Duster 340 was fielded as a counterpart to Dodge's Swinger 340), cute "whirlwind" graphics, snazzy paint, and sharp interiors combined to help Duster run up over 217,000 sales for the model year against only 51,000 Valiant four-doors.

Likewise, Plymouth increased its appeal in the ponycar segment with a new third-generation Barracuda, built on the existing 108-inch wheelbase. Oddly, the fastback body style that had originally suggested the fishy name disappeared, but the convertible and notchback hardtop coupe returned with burly new styling. They certainly looked good—two inches lower, three inches wider overall —but they weren't as fleet or agile as the lovely 1967-69s. Interestingly, though, Chrysler beat Ford to market with a bigger pony by a full year. In addition to base and performance 'Cuda versions of each body style there was the Barracuda Gran Coupe, which, confusingly, was also offered as a convertible. Both were intended to compete with luxury ponycars like the Mercury Cougar XR-7 and Ford's Mustang Grandé. As a whole, Barracuda sales were well up in 1970—which was encouraging, because ponycar demand was generally falling off.

After several years of sitting on the sidelines, Dodge finally got into the ponycar fray for 1970 with its aptly named Challenger. Inspired by the Cougar and also aimed at the more affluent end of the sporty compact market, it was planned alongside the third-generation Barracuda and shared its new E-body unitized structure. Though drivetrain and chassis components for both were borrowed from Mopar's mid-size cars, the Challenger was intended as a deliberately beefier package. It thus emerged riding

a two-inch longer wheelbase (110 inches) and was longer and heavier overall than Barracuda.

Dodge studio chief Bill Brownlie suggested not only the Challenger's name but its styling. This differed from the Barracuda's in having a venturi "mouth" grille instead of a split affair, quad instead of dual headlamps, a bodyside creaseline (missing on the Plymouth) artfully hopped up to match rear fender curvature, and a smoother back panel with horizontal instead of square

1970 Dodge Coronet 500 four-door sedan: $3082.

Dodge's 1970 Coronet Super Bee in two-door hardtop form. With standard 383 V-8 as shown, it listed at $3074.

1970 Dodge Coronet Super Bee hardtop coupe

Production of this model totalled 11,540

taillamps. Model offerings consisted of base hardtop and convertible and bumblebee-striped R/T editions of both. Optional for hardtops was a Special Edition package similar to the Gran Coupe. It comprised a vinyl roof with a smaller "formal" backlight and SE emblems on the sail panels, plus leather seat facings, woodgrain dash trim, and an overhead console with warning lights for "door ajar," "seat belts," and "low fuel." As with the Barracuda, virtually every engine in the Mopar stable was available for the Challenger, from the thrifty Slant Six to the big-block 440 and—for an extra $1227.50—the awesome hemi.

With base prices ranging from $2900 to $3500 and a

broad range of options, the Challenger sold very well, partly because it was the only new ponycar for 1970. About 84,000 went out the door for the model year, which was good volume for any ponycar this season.

Elsewhere, 1970 Dodge specs and dimensions generally duplicated those of 1969, but all model lines came in for several styling changes. Dart and Coronet both received new split grilles. The mid-size line looked rather oddly misshapen up front, but the Dart was well-executed, with a longer hood and new rear styling too. The Charger, still closely following its 1968-69 look, reverted to a full-width grille (the '69 had a split one) surrounded by a massive loop bumper, and was available with six-cylinder power

1970 Dodge Dart Swinger hardtop coupe. Base price: $2261.

1970 Dodge Polara hardtop coupe with "Super Lite" option

The Dodge Monaco hardtop sedan for 1970: $3743.

1970 Dodge A-108 Custom Sportsman window van

The Dodge D-100 Adventurer pickup for 1970

1970 Plymouth Barracuda convertible. Base price: $3034.

for the first time. The exotic Daytona, having proven its point, was dropped. The big Polara and Monaco were facelifted along general corporate lines, with loop bumpers surrounding grilles and taillights. Ignition/steering column locks, fiberglass belted tires, dual-action wagon tailgates, and a long list of federally mandated safety equipment completed 1970 refinements.

One interesting feature would not return on the full-size Dodge. This was the predictive Super-Lite, an auxiliary driving lamp mounted on the left side of the grille. First offered for 1969, it used a European-style quartz-iodine bulb and special optics to throw a long-range "pencil beam" to increase nighttime driving safety. Unfortu-

nately, Super-Lite proved controversial and was ruled illegal by some states, which prompted Dodge to withdraw it after 1970. It would be another dozen years before Washington would liberalize U.S. automobile lighting standards to permit more powerful lamps like this.

Chrysler Corporation finally got officially involved this year in the Trans-American Challenge, the road racing series for production "sedans" inaugurated in 1966 by the Sports Car Club of America (SCCA). The Trans-Am had quickly turned into a battleground for ponycar manufacturers, with competition heating up as the market for the production models expanded. By 1969, the series had spurred development of the Chevrolet Camaro Z-28 and

Dodge's 1970 Monaco wagon sold at $4110/$4242 basic.

1970 Plymouth 'Cuda hardtop with 426-cid hemi-head V-8

1970 Plymouth Sport Fury GT hardtop coupe: $3898.

Fat tires, wider stance marked the 1970 Plymouth Hemi-Cuda.

Plymouth's 1970 Sport Fury S/23 hardtop coupe

Ford's Mustang Boss 302, highly specialized machines sold to the public only in limited numbers solely to legalize their racing counterparts.

The advent of the new Challenger and the third-generation Barracuda made it imperative for Chrysler to establish a formal Trans-Am presence, so the company fielded not one but two teams for the 1970 campaign. Dan Gurney was signed on to prepare a Barracuda for driver Swede Savage, who ran under the colors of Gurney's All-American Racers. Dodge partisans could root for Sam Posey, whose Challenger was prepared by Ray Caldwell's Autodynamics firm. Unfortunately, neither effort was very successful: Mustang won the 1970 championship

despite a strong showing by AMC and its Roger Penske-prepared Javelin driven by Mark Donohue. Not surprisingly, Chrysler's Trans-Am adventure ended as quickly as it began. However, the program did spawn two limited-production ponycars that are avidly sought-after by collectors today.

Dubbed AAR 'Cuda and Challenger T/A, they arrived at midyear sporting all the "right stuff." Power in each case was supplied by a special version of the 340-cid small-block V-8, with a beefier bottom end and an Edelbrock aluminum intake manifold mounting a trio of two-barrel carburetors, plus appropriate exhaust manifolding that terminated in large, chrome "megaphone"

1970 Plymouth Fury III hardtop sedan. List price: $3246

1970 Plymouth Fury Gran Coupe sold for as low as $3833.

1970 Plymouth GTX hardtop coupe. List price: $3535.

1970 Plymouth Sport Satellite hardtop coupe

1970 GTX production was down to 7748 units.

Plymouth's Sport Satellite four-door sedan for 1970

1970 Plymouth Road Runner with 440 6-bbl. V-8 option

The amazing, winged 1970 Plymouth Superbird was a Road Runner for NASCAR racing. Exactly 1920 were built.

The Valiant-based Plymouth Duster coupe, new for 1970

Duster sold close to 217,000 copies in its first year.

1970 Plymouth Valiant Duster coupe with optional vinyl roof

side-exit pipes protruding from below the rocker panels ahead of the rear wheels. Rear spoilers and scooped fiberglass hoods were also featured, as was a noticeable front-end rake, created by fitting jumbo G60 × 15 rear tires (versus E60 × 15s at the front). The AAR 'Cuda carried American flag decals behind distinctive "strobe" bodyside stripes. The Challenger T/A (the initials were necessary because Pontiac had already copped the Trans Am name for its hottest Firebird) wore wide upper body striping and "340 Six Pack" lettering. Both cars were finished off with competition-style hood tie-downs and lots of matte-black paint to contrast with the "psychedelic" body colors then in vogue.

The AAR 'Cuda and Challenger T/A marked the zenith of Chrysler ponycars, the firm's most blatant high-performance sportsters ever. With their mellow exhaust system, they sounded neat. And with the tuned 340, they were very fast: the T/A, for example, could reel off 14.5-second standing quarter-miles at trap speeds of over

95 mph, which was close to hemi performance. Unfortunately, both these models are rarities today because of very low original production, a little more than 2100 of the T/As and about 2500 of the AAR 'Cudas. And with Chrysler's withdrawal from Trans-Am after just this single season, neither of these "homologation specials" would be back for 1971.

1971

Model year 1971 was the last in which Detroit would advertise gross horsepower. For 1972, the industry would switch to the more realistic SAE net measurement, a numerical distinction that underlined the public's drift away from performance in the early Seventies. Newly imposed insurance surcharges had all but killed the muscle market in 1969-70. Now, smaller engines with less horsepower—at least on paper—were not only fashionable but far more affordable, and "performance" began to be equated less with tire-burning acceleration alone and more with a balance between straightline go and improved cornering ability.

A further blow came during the winter of 1973-74, when an embargo by Middle East oil producers precipitated an unprecedented national energy crisis. Suddenly, gasoline was in short supply, prices skyrocketed and, in some areas of the country, service stations resorted to rationing, which led to long lines at the pumps. The result was a large-scale consumer shift from Detroit's traditional out-size products toward smaller, more economical models, chiefly imports.

Ironically, big-car sales would recover once the embargo ended and gas started flowing again. But the damage had been done: Americans had "discovered" small cars, and things haven't been the same since. In particular, they discovered Japanese cars, which realized huge sales gains in the mid-Seventies by combining American-style appearance and engineering with boring reliability in well-made smaller models that offered far more economy than anything available from domestic automakers. This and the public's heightened energy consciousness sent Detroit scurrying back to its drawing boards. Though the results wouldn't be seen until fairly late in the decade, a design revolution was underway. Today we know it as "downsizing." In retrospect, the turbulent events of the early Seventies prompted a renaissance in American automotive design. Happily, it's still with us.

Chrysler Corporation's path through the perilous Seventies would be a rocky one. Of course, the firm had to contend with the same problems that made life difficult for all U.S. automakers in these years: ever-stricter safety and emissions standards, plus new fuel economy mandates devised in the aftermath of the energy crisis. Yet of all the Big Three companies, Chrysler was perhaps least prepared for what lay ahead. Its 1971 fleet was chockablock with full-size heavyweights pushed by thirsty V-8s.

The Imperial LeBaron hardtop sedan saw improved production for 1971, with 10,116 built. Base price was up to $6864.

The Chrysler 300 put in its last appearance for 1971. Shown is that year's hardtop coupe, priced at $4608.

All 1971 Chryslers bore a minor facelift of the 1969-70 "fuselage" look. Newport hardtop coupe shown sold for $4265.

To be sure, its Plymouth Valiant and Dodge Dart continued to lead the compact field, but the firm would be increasingly handicapped by too many dinosaurs that it allowed to hang on too long. While GM released the small Chevy Vega this year and Ford debuted its subcompact Pinto, Chrysler staunchly refused even to consider fielding anything smaller than Dart/Valiant, relying instead on "captive imports." This strategy, which reflected the ever-present "never-a-small-Chrysler"

philosophy among company managers, was only partly successful. Dodge moved quite a few Japanese-made Colts, even if dealers weren't particularly eager to push them due to low profit margins, but the British-built Plymouth Cricket was a disaster. And in the really high-volume intermediate and full-size segments, where car company fortunes are won or lost, the lack of anything truly new would nearly cost Chrysler its very existence by decade's end.

The hardtop sedan continued to lead Chrysler New Yorker sales for '71. Base price was now up to $5041.

To a large degree, the history of Chrysler Corporation in the Seventies involved the same sort of downward spiral that had killed Studebaker in the Sixties and periodically threatened American Motors with a similar fate. An automaker that experiences several years of declining sales—or that sinks to a sales level consistently below its breakeven point of profitability—has less money with which to develop newer, more competitive products and to keep older ones fresh. This only aggravates the sales problem, which leads to further losses, and so on. This is exactly what happened to Chrysler. In addition, quality control or workmanship deteriorated noticeably as the decade wore on. This reflected the firm's declining fortunes, but it only made matters worse.

Signs of the trouble ahead were evident in 1971, though they were faint. The sales year was, as a whole, underwhelming. Though Plymouth managed to regain third place in the model year production standings, it came on greatly reduced volume. Chrysler and Imperial trundled along at about their 1970 level. Dodge was a bright spot, but not very bright, with production up only a few points from the previous year.

Having gone to all the trouble of introducing its own ponycar for 1970, Dodge curiously seemed to back away from the market this year. The Challenger returned for '71 with only minor changes to battle Ford's much bigger new Mustang and GM's striking second-generation Chevrolet Camaro and Pontiac Firebird. The R/T convertible was canned, leaving the R/T hardtop and the two base models. A new arrival was the Deputy, a strippo

This 1971 Dodge Charger SE in "Hot Apricot" toured the auto show circuit that year. Note sunroof.

coupe with fixed rear side glass, priced $121 less than the standard hardtop. All models were marked by a reworked front, with a one-piece plastic grille frame and a rather awkward two-piece plastic-and-aluminum insert, painted black on R/Ts, silver on other models. The R/Ts also got color-keyed bumpers, simulated brake cooling slots on the rear quarters, and revised tape striping. The SE

package was unchanged from '70, but was now limited to base models. Interiors stayed the same except for minor trim revisions. There were no major mechanical changes either, although the 383 V-8 that was previously optional across the board was now restricted to the R/T.

Though outputs stayed the same, engines seemed much punier when rated by the SAE net method. The Dodge

Three of the six models in the expanded 1971 Dodge Charger line (from top): Super Bee, 500, and SE.

A minor facelift marked the encore-edition 1971 Dodge Challenger. Shown: the $2848 standard hardtop coupe.

1971 Dodge Charger Special Edition boasted rakish new styling and a $3422 suggested base retail price.

1971 Dodge Charger Super Bee. Base price was $3271.

1971 Dodge Demon 340 fastback coupe. Base price: $2721.

The R/T continued as the hottest production Dodge Charger for 1971. Scat Pack stripes were gone now.

383 Magnum, for example, came down from 335 bhp gross to 250 bhp net, and there were similar paper losses throughout the corporate stable. However, Chrysler Corporation did not drop compression this year like GM, so Challengers with the big 440 and hemi engines were still stunningly fast. A footnote to the Trans-Am caper was the appearance of a '71 T/A in this year's Scat Pack ads. Of course, it never made it to the street.

Total Challenger sales fell dramatically for '71, down by almost 60 percent from the 1970 level. Four Dodge

dealers attempted to spur interest in the car by agreeing to supply Challengers for the 1971 Indianapolis 500. Accordingly, 50 "Hemi-Orange" convertibles, all with white interiors, were prepared for use during pre-race festivities. Two of these were equipped with heavy-duty equipment, one as the actual pace car, the other as a backup. This promotion artist's dream turned into a nightmare when the pace car—loaded with dignitaries—went into a skid as it was leaving the track after the warmup lap and crashed into a press box, injuring several

1971 Dodge Coronet Brougham four-door sedan: $3232.

The Dodge Dart Swinger hardtop coupe for '71: $2561.

1971 Dodge Polara Brougham hardtop sedan, top-of-the-line full-size luxury for $3884.

1971 Dodge Charger 500 listed at $3223 basic.

1971 Dodge Demon fastback coupe in $2343 standard form

reporters. Reportedly, the car was later rebuilt for use in data-gathering tests prompted by numerous lawsuits resulting from the accident. Dodge dealers could apparently order decal sets this year to make their own pace car replicas, though the idea likely seemed fairly ludicrous in view of the accident.

A similar round of changes attended the '71 Barracuda. Styling was only mildly altered, the Gran Coupe convertible was scratched, and a fixed-pillar coupe was added. The smaller 198-cid Slant Six became base power for

hardtops, with the 225 standard on convertibles and the Gran Coupe hardtop. The 318 was still the base V-8, and two 383s remained optional. Standard power for the 'Cuda was a four-pot 383, while 340, 440 4bbl., and the hemi all returned as options. Along with its Challenger counterpart, the Barracuda convertible was now the last ragtop still in production at Chrysler Corporation. Production wasn't very high, however: just 1388, of which 374 were the high-performance 'Cuda species. The open Challenger saw just 2165 copies.

1971 Dodge Dart Custom sedan sold at $2609 basic.

1971 Dodge Colt hardtop, a "captive import" from Japan

The Mitsubishi-built Dodge Colt wagon for 1971

1971 Dodge Colt four-door sedan: a robust budget buy

If Dodge and Plymouth let their ponycars languish, it was because new market realities had forced a shift in the performance action from intermediates to compacts. Both divisions were ready. Plymouth's fastback Duster returned in base and hot 340 guises with few mechanical changes and only a mild grille redo. Adding spice to the line was the "Twister," an optional appearance package

consisting of flat-black hood, bodyside tape stripes featuring the cute "whirlwind" cartoon character, Rallye wheels, and a 340-style black grille. Also new this year was the Gold Duster, an appearance package consisting of color-keyed paint, trim, and pebble-grain vinyl roof, plus special identification. Dodge got a duplicate of the Duster this year and called it Demon. It took over for the Swinger hardtop as the division's performance compact. Engine offerings paralleled Duster's as did appearance, apart from appropriate badges and a Dart grille.

As was proving to be the case elsewhere, compacts were again gaining sales strength at Chrysler Corporation. The base Duster saw production of close to 174,000 units for the model year, bolstered by about 13,000 of the 340 variants. The Demon's performance was less spectacular, about 70,000 standard models and another 11,000 Demon 340s. Divisional rivalry had given Dodge a Duster clone, so Plymouth got a Valiant version of the 111-inch-wheelbase Dart Swinger hardtop to calm C-P dealers. Called Scamp, it was the first pillarless Valiant since 1966.

Chrysler Corporation's big product news for 1971 was four new mid-size model lines, two each for Dodge and Plymouth. What actually happened was a model realignment around two different wheelbases, 115 inches for two-doors and 117 inches for four-door sedans and wagons, following a practice begun by GM back in 1968.

At Dodge, the Charger line was expanded by taking in all the previous Coronet two-doors, including the Super Bee. There was now a base pillared coupe offered alongside standard, 500, and R/T hardtops. A new entry was the Special Edition, a luxury hardtop with hidden headlamps and extra-wide rear roof panels. Coronets were arrayed in base and Custom sedans and wagons, plus a high-trim Brougham sedan and a brace of woody-look Crestwood wagons.

Plymouth similarly split up its Satellite series. Two-door models now bore Sebring, Sebring Plus, GTX, or Road Runner identification. Sedans and wagons were available in base and Custom form, the fancy sedan was called Brougham here, too, and the top wagons were given the odd name of Satellite Regent.

Styling for new mid-size Mopar crop was the latest expression of the "fuselage" look, with markedly tucked-under bodysides, massive loop bumper/grilles, and hefty back bumpers. It was a good-looking group, even if these cars were no longer so "intermediate" in size. With their more rakish rooflines and tighter dimensions, the coupes were naturally more exciting to look at. And with the right equipment, they were pretty exciting to drive, too. The Road Runner and Super Bee were motivated by a regular-gas 383 V-8 with 300 bhp (gross), and the premium-fuel hemi and six-barrel 440 were optional. The Plymouth GTX and Dodge's Charger R/T started with a 370-bhp four-barrel 440, and were available with the same step-up engines. A midyear option took the Runner into small-block territory for the first time, a 275-bhp version of the 340 V-8.

It's almost a shame that Chrysler restyled its intermediates when it did. With their curvy new contours, the muscle models looked a lot meaner than their blocky

Facelifted Plymouth Barracuda adopted four headlamps for 1971 only. Shown is the snazzy 'Cuda 340 hardtop.

The 1971 Plymouth 'Cuda convertible saw just 374 copies. List price was $3412.

Along with Dodge's Challenger, the Plymouth Barracuda was the last ragtop in production at Chrysler for 1971.

1971 Plymouth Satellite four-door sedan: $2734.

1971 Plymouth Satellite Sebring Plus hardtop coupe

The 1971 Plymouth Sport Fury non-formal hardtop coupe saw production of only 3912 units. List price: $3677.

1971 Plymouth Road Runner hardtop coupe: $3147.

1971 Road Runner production was 14,218 units.

Plymouth's new-look 1971 Road Runner still packed a standard 383 V-8. The 440/6 shown here was optional.

1968-70 forebears, yet the "faster" styling arrived just as interest in old-style performance cars was tapering off. Production totals were discouraging for all the hot Mopars. At Dodge, the Super Bee tally was just 5054 units, and the Charger R/T saw a mere 3118. The Charger SE did far better at 15,811 units, a clear sign of where the market was going. Plymouth retailed 14,218 of the '71 Road Runners, but that was still 2000 units below Sebring Plus production. The GTX was down to 2942.

Individual intermediates weren't the only 1971 Chrysler Corporation models to suffer low production, and a look at figures for the full-size lines suggested that some model rationalization was clearly overdue. This year's unnecessarily broad and complex Dodge Polara/Monaco line, for example, saw these numbers: 2487 Polara two-door hardtops, about 4600 Polara Brougham two- and four-door hardtops, and 5500 Monaco wagons. In retrospect, it's clear that the swing to smaller cars was well under way long before the first energy crisis. Dodge and Chrysler-Plymouth didn't get the message. Both could have had smaller big cars in production by 1974. In fact, neither would have any before 1979.

All the company's 1971 big cars changed mainly in cosmetics, with mechanical alterations made where necessary to meet federal requirements. "Fuselage" styling was still the order of the day, with the same high beltline

The standard Plymouth Duster fastback coupe for '71

1971 Plymouth Duster 340 fastback coupe: $2703.

Duster 340 was Plymouth's "whirlwind compact" for 71.

Splashier graphics marked the '71 Duster 340.

1971 Plymouth Duster with optional "Twister" decor option

British-built Plymouth Cricket continued unchanged for '71.

Indifferent workmanship kept Cricket sales low.

that made all these cars look as heavy as they were. Dodge instituted a minor facelift for the Polara/Monaco. Plymouth did the same with its Fury, and also shuffled model offerings. The VIP was cancelled, leaving Sport Fury as the luxury series. The burly Sport Fury GT hardtop returned with its standard 440 V-8, but found only 375 buyers. The S/23 was dropped.

The Chrysler line was also rejuggled slightly. The old Royal name returned at mid-model year for a trio of Newports priced right around $4000, about $200-$300 less than the standard issue. Despite this, there were some rather serious price increases taking place. This was the first year that the least expensive Chrysler listed above $4000, yet the Newport four-door of only two years before carried an advertised base price of $3414. There were several reasons for the hikes. Government mandated safety and emissions equipment added to production costs, as did popular accessories that had been made standard equipment, and inflation was beginning to take a toll.

Once again, Chrysler Corporation's outlook was decidedly cloudy.

1972

Chrysler Corporation had acquired a 15-percent interest in Mitsubishi Motors Corporation of Japan in 1971, and further acquisitions of 10 percent per year were scheduled for 1972 and '73. Contrary to the previous Simca and Rootes deals, this foreign investment would pay off for the company, especially Dodge. Various Mitsubishi models now became "captive imports" under the Dodge banner, and these well-built subcompacts gave the division a significant presence in what would soon become the hottest sector of the market. Most of these cars would appear with the Colt moniker, which would lead to considerable confusion in some years.

The first of the Dodge-badged Mitsubishis had arrived at mid-model year 1971, and they continued virtually unchanged for '72. This Colt was built on a diminutive 95.3-inch wheelbase and was powered by a 1.6-liter (95.7-cid) inline four-cylinder engine—with hemispherical combustion chambers. Offered in coupe, two-door hardtop, four-door sedan, and five-door wagon body styles, it was exactly the kind of package that was proving so successful for makes like Toyota and Datsun. In future years, the powers in Highland Park would thank their lucky stars for having a Japanese connection.

Dodge made only detail changes to its domestic compacts and intermediates for 1972, but its full-size cars were more fully restyled. These were good-looking giants, with grillework built low into the front end and a minimum of fancy trim to clutter up the bodies. The revised sheetmetal concealed the basic 1969-71 understructure on the customary 122-inch wheelbase. Monaco and Polara series continued, the latter including Custom sub-models as before. All together, they accounted for

New Yorker Brougham became the top-line Chrysler for 1972. This hardtop sedan retailed at $5350.

about 100,000 of Dodge's total half-million unit sales for '72—which tells you just how important compacts and intermediates had become. Big-inch engines were still around, and Polara/Monaco shoppers could opt for two versions of a new corporate 400-cid V-8 as well as the 440 in four different power ratings.

Like other automakers, Chrysler Corporation was forced to lower compression and generally detune all its 1972 engines for compatibility with low-lead gasoline, in line with tightening emissions requirements. With SAE net horsepower now quoted in car advertising, the differences in specifications between 1971 and '72 engines

1972 Chrysler New Yorker hardtop coupe: List price: $4915.

Chrysler Town & Country wagon was as impressive as ever for '72.

Newport Royal ousted the standard Newport as the base Chrysler for '72. Shown: the $4124 hardtop coupe.

Imperial LeBaron hardtop sedan production went up to 13,472 units for 1972. Base list price was $6778.

1972 Imperial LeBaron hardtop sedan

1972 Imperial LeBaron hardtop sedan

were somewhat masked. For example, the company's hottest 440, previously rated at 385 bhp gross, was down to 280 bhp net this year. A more accurate indicator of what was happening to all Detroit powerplants was torque output, which in this case fell from 490 to 375 lbs/ft, though that comparison is between the '71 tri-carb unit and the single four-barrel '72 engine. Compression was also being cut to accommodate the standards, and the company's ratios now hovered at around 8.2:1. They'd been as high as 10.3:1 only a year before.

The new 400-cid V-8 powered the bulk of this year's rearranged Chrysler line. The 300 series was dropped along with the plain Newport, and the Newport Royal became the new low-end offering below Newport Custom.

A new entry was the New Yorker Brougham, basically fancier versions of the regular New Yorker hardtops and sedan. All Chryslers remained on a 124-inch wheelbase except Town & Country wagons, which continued to share the 122-inch-wheelbase Dodge platform. Like its sister division, Chrysler also backed away from "fuselage styling" this year, though it too retained the 1969-71 full-size corporate bodyshell. Appearance was still clean-limbed, even if easy-change items like grilles, taillamps, and side trim were a shade more tacky.

Imperial's fortunes continued their steady decline, and the New Yorker Brougham proved it. The new top-line Chrysler offered much the same sort of luxury for $1200-$1500 less than Imperial. Not surprisingly, it out-

"Sad mouth" grille marked the 1972 Dodge Challenger.

The standard 1972 Dodge Challenger hardtop: $2790.

The 1972 Dodge Charger hardtop coupe kicks up its heels.

1972 Dodge Charger hardtop coupe. Base price: $2913.

The 1972 Dodge Charger in another pre-announcement press pose at Chrysler's Chelsea Proving Grounds

sold the prestige make by almost 2 to 1 despite price reductions intended to spark Imperial sales. They didn't spark, of course, and the LeBaron two- and four-door hardtops scored production of just 2332 and 13,472 units, respectively. As before, power was supplied by the New Yorker's 440-cid V-8, now rated at 225 bhp net, but Imperial had an exclusive in its newly standardized "Sure-Brake," an anti-skid system supplied by Bendix and first offered for 1971 as a $250 option. As on the big Dodges and Chryslers, outer skin was retouched to achieve a bulkier, more imposing appearance, so bodyside curvature was reduced and fenderlines squared up. Massive vertical parking/turn signal lamps were integrated into a reshaped bumper/grille.

Plymouth greatly rationalized its offerings for 1972, not so much for retrenchment as for reorganization. In fact, the make was on the verge of three very good sales years and would set a new model year production record for 1973, with 882,000-plus units. The full-size Fury came in for the same sort of styling changes applied to Chrysler's other big cars for '72: visibly lower beltlines, blockier fore and aft sheetmetal, fewer curves. A new double-loop bumper/grille appeared, and costlier models retained hidden headlamps. At the top of the line, the Sport Fury name was retired after 10 years in favor of the "Gran" series, consisting of Gran Coupe two-door hardtops with formal and less formal rooflines and the Gran Sedan four-door hardtop. As at Dodge, fresh fronts were ordained for

1972 Dodge Coronet Custom four-door sedan

Dodge Coronet Custom four-door sold at $2998 for '72.

The 1972 Dodge Polara Custom hardtop sedan (foreground) and Monaco hardtop coupe

The popular Mitsubishi-built Dodge Colts returned with few changes for '72. Wagon and hardtop are shown.

Two members of Dodge's 1972 compact clan, the Demon coupe (foreground) and Dart Swinger hardtop coupe

1972 Plymouth Fury Gran Coupe two-door hardtop: $3941.

1972 Plymouth Fury Gran Sedan four-door hardtop: $3987.

The Sport Suburban continued as Plymouth's top full-size wagon for 1972. Note double-loop front end.

Plymouth's mid-size and compact models, but the GTX vanished and the Road Runner was demoted to a standard 340 V-8.

Detroit performance continued to wane in 1972, and there was graphic evidence on the Dodge/Plymouth engine chart and in this year's Challenger/Barracuda. The hemi disappeared as a regular production option, reverting to its former "competition-use-only" status, and the 440 was reserved strictly for full-size models. The 400-cid V-8 was now the largest powerplant available in intermediates, and the 383 V-8 was abandoned corporate-wide. For real interest value, the ponycars and the 340 versions of the Duster/Demon were the only items left. But Barracuda and Challenger surrendered their convertibles,

Plymouth's mid-size Satellite Sebring Plus hardtop bore few outward changes for '72.

1972 Plymouth Satellite Sebring Plus hardtop had a $3127 base price. Canopy vinyl roof cost extra.

leaving just base hardtops and the sportier 'Cuda and Challenger Rallye, the latter a replacement for the previous R/T. The 340, now rated at 240 bhp net, was the hottest power option for both. Interestingly, it was standard for the 'Cuda, while the Rallye made do with a tame 318.

The Challenger seemed to fare worse in this year's styling changes too, with a new eggcrate grille that curved downward at its outboard ends like a sad mouth. The Barracuda reverted to a 1970-style split grille. The brash 'Cuda was brasher than ever, sporting a unique "three-

1972 Plymouth Road Runner hardtop coupe: $3147.

The 1972 Plymouth Valiant Scamp hardtop coupe: $2561.

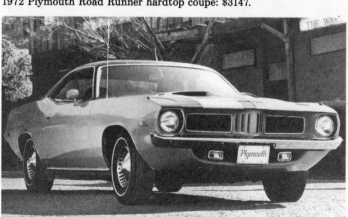

Sporty Plymouth 'Cuda hardtop returned for '72 with a fresh face, but its convertible companion didn't. Base price: $3029.

runner'' flat-black hood, with the area around its twin scoops painted body color.

Despite the general de-emphasis on dig, the 340-equipped ponys were still quite fast. The 'Cuda could turn a 0-60 mph time of 8.5 seconds and a 16-second quarter-mile, which was hardly unimpressive. The Rallye was equally capable, being much more than just a "decal performance" car. Unfortunately, though, that's what it looked like, with twin simulated air extractors on the front fenders and trailing black tape stripes. F70 × 14 tires were standard Rallye fare, along with a "performance" hood wearing NACA-style air ducts. The 340 engine brought dual exhausts with bright tips, and could be ordered with four-speed manual transmission and a Performance Axle option comprising 3.55:1 final drive, Sure-Grip limited-slip differential, and increased cooling capacity. Yet Dodge seemed almost apologetic in advertising the Rallye. Said one blurb: "The way things are today, maybe what you need is not the world's hottest car. Maybe what you need is a well-balanced, thoroughly instrumented road machine."

Maybe we did, but apparently a good many buyers didn't think this was it. The sales figures tell the story. On the Plymouth side, the Duster 340 easily outsold the 'Cuda by better than 2 to 1. The Challenger Rallye/Demon 340 contest was much closer, but the compact still won, if only by a few hundred units.

The market was definitely "thinking small" in 1972, at least Chrysler Corporation's market. Consider that the most popular single Dodge model was the stylish yet practical Dart Swinger hardtop, with close to 120,000 deliveries. The hands-down favorite at Plymouth was the plain, no-nonsense Duster coupe, which recorded better than 173,000 sales.

1973

The one-millionth car to bear the Chrysler nameplate came down the Jefferson Avenue line on June 26, 1973. It was a base Newport sedan (the Newport Royal series was dropped this year), and 54,146 others were sold for the model year. For the industry as a whole, 1973 was the bonanza year of the decade: over 11 million new cars were sold, an all-time record that would stand for quite a while. But with the Middle East oil embargo that hit late in the year, neither the world nor the auto industry would ever be the same again. Chrysler made critical decisions based on its pre-embargo success, and it would take a long time for the company to change direction.

The '73 Chrysler line again listed Newport, Newport Custom, Town & Country, New Yorker and New Yorker Brougham series. The *grande luxe* Brougham continued

Note the cute "whirlwind" cartoon on the side striping of this 1972 Plymouth Duster 340 fastback coupe.

1972 Plymouth Duster 340 fastback coupe. Base price: $2742.

1972 Duster 340 production was 15,681 units.

The four-door sedan was the least loved 1973 Chrysler New Yorker Brougham. Production was 8541.

A little-known Chrysler show car, the Newport-based "Mariner" was displayed during the 1973 season.

about $500 upstream of the standard New Yorker but a good $1000 downstream of Imperial. It would ultimately ring down the curtain on Imperial, because it grew increasingly like the super-luxury offering while selling for much less. Engines were down to two: 185-bhp 400 and 215-bhp 440 V-8s, the latter standard for T&C and New Yorkers, optional for Newports. Styling for both Imperial and Chrysler was little changed, the former continuing with its full-width grillework and hidden headlamps, the latter wearing a more blunt face with a smaller, oblong grille flanked by exposed headlamps. Overall length was up—to 231 inches for New Yorker/Imperial—thanks largely to the 5-mph front bumpers newly mandated by Congress. They cost owners about twice what body shops had charged for repair work on previous bumpers. Imperial retained its 127-inch wheelbase, though this was the last year it would do so, and still included all power accessories as standard. New

Yorker adopted standard air conditioning and retained options like the four-wheel anti-skid braking system and vinyl roof, along with the sliding sunroof introduced on hardtops for 1971 as a sop to lovers of the now-vanished convertibles.

Plymouth half-heartedly plugged the Rootes-built Cricket subcompact for the last time this year, while its domestics notched a 20 percent sales gain. The compacts continued to carry the make, the Valiant sedan and Scamp hardtop on the 111-inch Dodge Dart wheelbase, the Duster and Duster 340 coupes continuing on the 108. The new 5-mph front bumpers dictated more upright fronts for intermediates. Eggcrate grilles appeared on the 115-inch-wheelbase Sebring, Sebring Plus, and Road Runner coupes, while a less integrated loop style graced the 117-inch-wheelbase Satellite sedans and wagons. The 318-cid V-8 was now the base powerplant for the Runner, but up to 440 cubes and 285 horsepower were still

Imperial was mildly restyled for '73, its last year on the 127-inch wheelbase. LeBaron hardtop sedan is shown.

Though this '73 Chrysler Newport bears "Royal" fender script, that name officially disappeared this year.

Another look at the '73 Chrysler Newport hardtop sedan

Base price for the model was now up to $4316.

available at extra cost.

Senior Plymouths retained their 120/122-inch wheelbase for '73 and also bore more blunt frontal styling plus a reworked rear end. As before, there was a single price leader Fury I four-door sedan. The Fury II was now reduced to a sedan and wagon, and the Fury III lost its formal hardtop coupe style. Gran Fury offerings contin-

ued, again minus the formal hardtop. The best-looking big Plymouth was the midyear Fury Special, a trim package featuring dark metallic chestnut paint, parchment vinyl roof, color-keyed interior and bodyside moldings, stand-up hood ornament, plus shag carpeting and "tapestry" cloth seat inserts.

In contrast to the poor sales of the British-built

1973 Dodge Challenger Rallye hardtop coupe

Rear-quarter louvers marked the 1973 Dodge Charger SE.

The '73 Dodge Charger SE shows off its new canopy vinyl roof

1973 Dodge Coronet Custom four-door sedan: $3017

1973 Dodge Dart Swinger hardtop coupe. Price: $3077

Plymouth Cricket, the Japanese-made Dodge Colt was a fair success. Coupe, hardtop, sedan, and wagon continued as before, with minor trim changes. A new entry was the Colt GT, basically a sportier version of the regular two-door hardtop, with a different grille insert, racing stripes, and slotted road wheels.

Dodge's domestics naturally came in for heftier front bumpers, but 1973 styling changes were not major. Compacts acquired a new front-end cap with a pointed nose and grille, the latter with a texture that recalled 1946-48 appearance. Bowing to pressure from certain groups that objected to the devilish connotation of the Demon name, the fastback coupes were renamed Dart Sport. A new option for them was the "Convertriple,"

Dodge's Duster double became the Dart Sport for '73. Shown is the spiffy 340 version, priced at $2853.

1973 Dart Sport 340 displays the new grille treatment used for all of Dodge's compacts this year.

1973 Dodge Dart Sport coupe with "Hang 10" option

Japanese jazziness: 1973 Dodge Colt GT hardtop coupe

matched at Plymouth by the "Space Duster." Both referred to a fold-down rear seatback and optional sliding sunroof, the latter also a new item for this year's Scamp/Swinger hardtops. The 198-cid Slant Six continued as the base engine for Plymouth/Dodge compacts, with the 225-cid version and 318/340 V-8s optional. The Duster/Dart Sport 340 continued with the high-winding small-block, plus the requisite "boy racer" striping.

The mid-size Dodges got revamped front ends and

minimally reworked taillamps for '73. New to the two-door Charger line was a Rallye package option, available in either hardtop or pillared coupe form. It consisted of loud bodyside tape striping, hood tie-downs and "power bulge," plus front and rear anti-roll bars, fat raised-white-letter tires, and more complete Rallye instrumentation. Curiously, customers could still order a big-block Coronet—the 280-bhp (net) 440—but only for the plain-vanilla four-door sedan or wagon. However, the 440 was

Dodge Monaco (hardtop coupe shown) acquired larger front bumper guards to meet 1973's new impact standard.

1973 Dodge Monaco hardtop coupe. Base price: $4276.

1973 Dodge Polara Custom hardtop sedan: $4001.

Dodge built 8839 of its 1973 Polara Custom three-seat station wagons.

optional for any of the two-doors. This year's Charger Special Edition acquired a revised rear roof treatment, with louvered quarter windows that helped relieve an enormous over-the-shoulder blind spot.

The full-size Polara and Monaco adapted to "crash" bumpers in different ways. The former retained its exposed headlamps from 1972, but they now flanked a rather dull, square, cross-hatch grille. Monacos continued their '72 hidden-headlamp design, but with beefier front bumper guards adorned with large, black rubber blocks.

Chrysler Corporation's two ponycars carried on with only minimal changes, but managed to score higher sales. The Slant Six was dropped as the base engine for both Dodge Challenger and Plymouth Barracuda, leaving the 318 V-8 as standard and the 340 optional. The latter was replaced at mid-season by the corporate 360 V-8 that had been around since 1971. Each line continued with base

continued on page 273

1973 Plymouth Fury Gran Sedan four-door hardtop

Plymouth's 'Cuda hardtop coupe for 1973

1973 Plymouth Fury Gran Coupe two-door hardtop: $4064.

The $3258 Plymouth Satellite Sebring Plus for '73

The 1973 Plymouth Road Runner kicks up a little dust. Base price this year was up to $3115.

Woody-look side trim was featured on Plymouth's top-line Satellite Regent station wagon for 1973.

Plymouth's popular Duster coupe for 1973

1973 Plymouth Duster with optional "Gold Duster" package

Plymouth's two best-selling compacts for 1973 were the standard Duster coupe and the Valiant four-door sedan.

1973 Plymouth Valiant Scamp hardtop coupe: $2617.

1973 Plymouth Cricket five-door wagon

Looking little different from the 1964 "letter-series" 300K, the convertible version of Chrysler's "non-letter" 300 (top). Above left: Again from '64, the Plymouth Sport Fury two-door hardtop. Above right: Styling became more rounded on the mid-size Dodge Polara for '64, as this two-door hardtop illustrates. Right: Plymouth's sporty compact in the early '60s was the Valiant Signet 200. Here, the 1964 two-door hardtop. New 273-cid small-block V-8 was the top power option.

The 1962-64 Plymouth became the mid-size Belvedere for 1965. Bucket-seat Satellite (two-door hardtop shown above left) was top of the line. Above right: The true big Plymouth Fury returned for '65 on a 119-inch wheelbase. Here, the Sport Fury convertible. Right: A prototype for Dodge's big 1965 convertible sans identifying Polara or Custom 880 badges. Below: The mid-size Dodge was called Coronet for '65. This is the bucket-seat 500 two-door hardtop. Opposite page, top left: 1966 Plymouth Valiant Signet two-door hardtop. Top right: The Formula S version of the facelifted 1966 Plymouth Barracuda. Center left: Plymouth's luxurious 1966 VIP two-door hardtop. Center right: 1966 Chrysler 300 two-door hardtop. Bottom: 1966 Dodge Coronet 500 convertible.

Again in like-new condition is this 1967 Chrysler New Yorker two-door hardtop (top). Above: The '67 Plymouth Barracuda Formula S fastback had definite Italian overtones. Right: Small front fender badge signals the presence of the mighty 426 hemi under the hood of this 1966 Plymouth Satellite two-door hardtop. Below right: Ditto on this '67 Dodge Coronet 500 two-door hardtop. Opposite page, top left: The big and brawny '67 Plymouth Sport Fury convertible. Top right: The hottest mid-size Dodge for '68 was the Coronet R/T (two-door hardtop shown). Center left: The Chrysler 300 two-door hardtop from '68. Center right: The elegant 1968 Dodge Charger R/T two-door hardtop. Bottom: 1968 Plymouth Sport Fury standard and "fastroof" two-door hardtops.

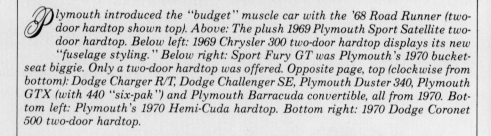

*P*lymouth introduced the "budget" muscle car with the '68 Road Runner (two-door hardtop shown top). Above: The plush 1969 Plymouth Sport Satellite two-door hardtop. Below left: 1969 Chrysler 300 two-door hardtop displays its new "fuselage styling." Below right: Sport Fury GT was Plymouth's 1970 bucket-seat biggie. Only a two-door hardtop was offered. Opposite page, top (clockwise from bottom): Dodge Charger R/T, Dodge Challenger SE, Plymouth Duster 340, Plymouth GTX (with 440 "six-pak") and Plymouth Barracuda convertible, all from 1970. Bottom left: Plymouth's 1970 Hemi-Cuda hardtop. Bottom right: 1970 Dodge Coronet 500 two-door hardtop.

This lovingly preserved hemi-engine 1970 Plymouth Road Runner (above) is a prime collector car today. Right: Dodge's 1970 Challenger hardtop with "Plum Crazy" paint. Below: 1971 Dodge Charger 500 hardtop coupe. Below right: 1972 Dodge Demon 340 coupe, a hot little devil. Opposite page, top left: 1972 Plymouth Road Runner two-door hardtop. Top right: The Dodge Polara Custom four-door hardtop from '72. Center: Louvered rear roof and greater luxury marked the 1973 Dodge Charger S.E. Bottom: The Road Runner put in its final appearance on Plymouth's mid-size platform for 1975. Power and performance were both well down on those of earlier models due to federal mandates.

Aspen arrived during model year '76 to replace the Dodge Dart. Shown above are the SE coupe (left) and Custom sedan. Right: The big Dodge Royal Monaco hardtop for 1977. Below: Plymouth's equivalent was the Gran Fury, here in Brougham trim. Below right: The post-1975 Chrysler New Yorker Brougham was a continuation of earlier Imperials. Here, the '77 four-door hardtop. Opposite page, top: 1978 Omni marked the start of the front-drive revolution at Dodge. Center: 1977 Plymouth Volare coupe with Road Runner package. Bottom left: Plymouth's Fury Sport hardtop for '78. Bottom right: 1979 Dodge St. Regis sedan.

Slick coupe version of the front-drive Dodge Omni bowed for '79 as the 024 (right). Below: The downsized Chrysler Cordoba for 1980. Below right: The 1980 Chrysler LeBaron coupe in sporty LS dress. Bottom: After a seven-year hiatus, the Imperial was revived for '81 as a plush coupe built on the Chrysler LeBaron/Dodge Diplomat platform. Opposite page, top: 1981 New Yorker Fifth Avenue sedan, one of the last big Chryslers. Center left: The R-body 1981 Plymouth Gran Fury. Center right: 1981 Chrysler Cordoba LS evoked memories of the fabled letter-series 300s. Bottom left: The 1981 Dodge Aries-K wagon. Bottom right: Dodge's personal-luxury Mirada CMX coupe for 1981.

*J*mperial for '82 (top) was little changed. Above: Chrysler's 1983 New Yorker Fifth Avenue Edition sedan. Above right: Dodge made a bid for the "Euro-sedan" market with the front-drive 600ES, new for '83. Right: Introduced in mid-1982, the Town & Country version of Chrysler's K-car-based LeBaron convertible is a collectible automobile of the future. Below right: Dodge's 400 convertible led Detroit's ragtop revival for 1983 while helping to stimulate Chrysler Corporation's comeback. Opposite page, top: The front-drive Chrysler Executive Sedan from 1983, a novel takeoff from the LeBaron. Center left: Plymouth's front-drive Horizon TC3 evolved by 1983 into the sprightly Turismo 2.2. Center right: Dodge fielded a genuine GT in the 1984 Daytona (Turbo shown). Bottom: The '85 version of Dodge's Shelby Charger gained over a third more power courtesy of turbocharging.

odge combined turbocharged excitement with open-air fun in the front-drive 600ES Turbo convertible, introduced late in the '84 model year. Shown above is the '85. Left: Both of Chrysler's K-car saviours received an "aerodynamic" facelift for '85. Here, the Plymouth Reliant wagon. Below: Chrysler Corporation's newest winners are the H-body sports sedans, offered as the LeBaron GTS (shown) and Dodge Lancer. Both are front drive, of course.

continued from page 255

pillared coupe and standard and sporty hardtop coupes, but the Challenger Rallye was now technically an option package and not a separate model. Rated at 240 bhp (net), this year's 340 V-8 could still propel the TorqueFlite-equipped Challenger over the standing-start quarter-mile in 16.3 seconds at 85 mph, which was fair going for the day. Challenger/Barracuda boasted new thin-shell bucket seats, but were otherwise little changed inside. Barracuda scored about 22,000 model year sales, while its Dodge counterpart managed to top 32,000. Still, that was pretty thin volume—too thin, really, to be profitable. And although ponycars seemed to be rebounding a bit, their long-term sales prospects seemed anything but bright in 1973.

Overall, this was destined to be the best model year that Chrysler Corporation would have for quite a while. Plymouth's near-900,000 units was far and away its best ever. Dodge recorded 665,000 units for one of the better annual performances in its history. Chrysler came up with some 234,000 cars, its highest production total since 1969.

1974 Chrysler Newport hardtop coupe

1974

A completely redesigned fleet of full-size Chrysler Corporation cars appeared for model year 1974—just in time for an energy crisis that all but wiped out big-car sales. In the wake of the Middle East oil embargo and the resulting fuel shortages that gripped America during the cold winter of 1973-74, auto writers were quick to con-

demn Chrysler for its incredibly poor timing. But the fact is that the new full-size lines were scheduled long before the Organization of Petroleum Exporting Countries (OPEC) decided to up-end the nation's oil-dependent economy. Perhaps Chrysler should have had more foresight. Then again, there was hardly an advance warning about the embargo from any quarter, though predictions about what an oil shutoff would do to the economy had been voiced, if faintly, for years.

While all U.S. automakers suffered from sudden sales drops in the full-size and intermediate segments, Chrysler suffered more than most. Total industry volume was down 24 percent for the year, but Chrysler's aggregate production fell 26 percent, though its market share stayed about the same. All the company's makes suffered losses. Chrysler retailed a mere 117,000 of its '74s and

Chrysler adopted a more forward-thrusting nose for '74. Shown is the $4752 Newport hardtop coupe.

'74 Chrysler New Yorker hardtop sedan sold at $5686. Body structure was all-new this year.

only about 14,500 Imperials. Together, they were out-produced nearly 2 to 1 by Cadillac, one of the few makes, curiously enough, to avoid out-and-out disaster this year. Plymouth and Dodge were down too, but their big-car losses were offset by strong demand for their still-popular compacts. For the model year, a total of nearly 740,000 units enabled Plymouth to move up from fifth to third place in the industry, the second and last time it would hold that position in the Seventies. Dodge ran off nearly a half-million cars, but again finished seventh.

Aside from buyers' sudden new concern with fuel economy, spiraling prices were putting a damper on sales of all cars, not just the larger ones. Chrysler decided to raise its prices for '74 against solemn promises by Ford and GM to hold the line, if only Washington would go easy on the extent and timing of safety and emissions requirements. In the end, the other manufacturers followed Chrysler's lead. The Cost of Living Council called the

Imperial became more Chrysler-like than ever for '74. Shown: the LeBaron hardtop sedan, priced at $7804.

price hikes "an act of consummate gall." Chrysler chairman Lynn Townsend replied by raising prices another one percent.

The corporation's 1974 full-size models were recognizably new, with crisper superstructures, lower beltlines (a high waist had made the "fuselage" generation seem fat and ungainly to some eyes), and generally more massive sheetmetal contours. Imperial lost more status by adopting Chrysler's 124-inch wheelbase, and both lines were given pseudo-classic square grilles of the sort they'd studiously avoided. Thus, Chrysler was again late in catching on to an industry styling trend. Model lineups and drivetrains were largely untouched, though engines were appropriately retuned for this year's emissions requirements.

Dodge abandoned the Polara nameplate and marketed its biggies under the Monaco moniker. The single series comprised base, Custom, and top-line Brougham variations, the latter two having extra trim and equipment to go along with their stiffer sticker prices. Plymouth made no change in its full-size offerings, but its Furys now looked more like the big Dodges than ever. Sheetmetal was basically the same on both aside from a lower bodyside creaseline on the Monaco. Grilles were also similar, the Monaco having a slightly shallower opening with thicker horizontal bars and a more pronounced "sub-

The 1974 Imperial LeBaron hardtop coupe was a low-production item, with just 3850 built for the year.

Dodge's Challenger ponycar made its final bow for '74. This car carries the Rallye performance package option.

Luxury SE continued to lead Dodge Charger sales for 1974. Base price this year stood at $3742.

1974 Dodge Charger SE fixed-pillar coupe

1974 Dodge Charger hardtop coupe. Base price: $3412.

1974 Dodge Charger fixed-pillar coupe: $3212.

Dodge's 1974 Coronet Custom four-door sedan. Price: $3374.

1974 Dodge Dart Sport and Swinger hardtop coupe were little changed outside. Note hardtop's new sunroof.

1974 Dodge Dart Sport coupe. Base price was $2878.

1974 Dodge Dart Special Edition four-door sedan: $3837.

The Dodge Monaco Custom hardtop sedan for '74.

Dodge's 1974 Monaco Custom hardtop sedan: $4539.

Dodge Colt GT hardtop was newly restyled for 1974.

The 1974 Plymouth Barracuda hardtop coupe. Price: $3067.

Like the Dodge Challenger, the Plymouth Barracuda would be out after '74. Shown is that year's 'Cuda hardtop.

1974

grille" under the bumper. The close kinship was especially evident in station wagons and in the modest "blade" fins on the rear fenders of other models.

Otherwise, there was little new at Chrysler Corporation for '74. The two compact lines assumed vital commercial importance in the wake of the oil embargo, and continued to sell well despite barely discernible appearance alterations. Recognizing that some compact-car buyers wanted both luxury and good fuel economy, both Dodge and Chrysler-Plymouth released more poshly trimmed versions of the 111-inch-wheelbase two-door hardtop and four-door sedan. Dubbed Dart Special Edition and

Valiant Brougham, they were distinguished by standard vinyl roof, standup hood ornaments, special name script, bodyside pinstriping, full wheel covers, and lush velour cloth interiors, plus "standard extras" like TorqueFlite, power steering and power brakes. Each was available with the Slant Six or 318 V-8, and together they helped broaden the already wide appeal of Chrysler's mainstay compacts.

The Challenger and Barracuda ponycars took their final bows for 1974, little loved now and little mourned when production ceased in March. Changes were confined to bulkier back bumper guards in line with this year's re-

1974 Plymouth Fury Gran Sedan four-door hardtop: $4675.

1974 Plymouth Fury Gran Sedan four-door hardtop

1974 Plymouth Fury Suburban 6-passenger wagon

Plymouth's Fury Gran Coupe two-door hardtop for '74

1974 was the last year for the Plymouth Road Runner as a separate model. Production was 11,555 units.

quirement for 5-mph impact protection at the rear, plus the barest of trim changes. A shade under 12,000 Barracudas and some 16,400 Challengers were built for the model year. The ponycar market was just about gone, and AMC's Javelin would also disappear after 1974. Demand would pick up again later in the decade, but the Chevrolet Camaro/Pontiac Firebird would be the only genuine ponycars around to take advantage of it.

Chrysler's intermediates stayed with their basic 1973 design for a second year. Fronts were blunted on the 117-inch-wheelbase sedans and wagons, while trim was hardly even shuffled on the 115-inch-wheelbase coupes.

The rather contrived Special Edition continued as the most popular Dodge Charger, and the Satellite-based Plymouth Road Runner was in its last year as a separate model. Chrysler still relied on "spring specials" to perk up sales. The Plymouth Satellite Sebring didn't have customers beating down dealership doors, so it came in for a mid-year package option called "Sundance." Available with Aztec Gold Metallic or Spinnaker White body, it boasted a canopy vinyl roof, "premier" wheel covers, ornate gold/black/white upholstery, and upper body/roof striping with a sunburst motif. Some things never change.

Plymouth's mid-size popularity champ for '74 was the $3329 Satellite Custom four-door sedan.

1974 Plymouth Duster with "Gold Duster" option

1974 Plymouth Duster coupe listed at $2829 basic.

1974 Plymouth PB300 Voyager Sport window van

Plymouth's 4WD Trail Duster, new for 1974.

1975

1975 Chrysler Cordoba coupe with optional vinyl roof

Prospects for recovery in the U.S. car market didn't seem too rosy as model year 1975 opened. Though the oil embargo was about to be lifted, it had touched off a severe national recession and a worrisome inflationary spiral that only aggravated the industry's rising production costs. Detroit reacted to the worsening economy and the latest round of federal mandates by instituting massive price increases. America's car buyers were about to encounter "sticker shock."

Once again, Chrysler Corporation's fortunes took a tumble. Initial 1975-model sales dropped to 1970 levels, and a two-month inventory piled up in Highland Park. Company chairman Lynn Townsend brashly refused to slash prices. Instead, he slashed production. By November 1974, the firm's aggregate car sales were down 34 percent. Though that was admittedly less than GM's 43-percent decline, Chrysler felt its loss more acutely because its fixed costs were spread over much smaller volume than either GM's or Ford's.

The next step was inevitable: Chrysler was forced to lay off 18,000 employees in an attempt to eliminate $120 million in fixed costs. Again, Washington and Detroit pointed fingers at each other. Politicians claimed the automakers had caused their own problems by raising prices. Townsend replied that the Administration had failed to stimulate new-car sales, and chided President Ford for suggesting that consumers should spend less. In early 1975 he raised prices again—and the backlog swelled to 300,000.

Something had to give, and something did. Chrysler instituted a cash rebate plan, the first time in history that an auto company actually paid people to buy its prod-

ucts. For once, rival firms had to follow Chrysler's lead. Meantime, Townsend began planning for drastically reduced production and for a new company structure that would enable Chrysler to survive in a long-term market of only six million units annually, compared with the typical industry-wide average of nine to 10 million. It was a gamble—an industry recovery might leave Chrysler short of capacity—but he took it: "We are not going to permit ourselves to go on rosy forecasts of the future."

Such a sweeping reorientation in Chrysler's way of doing business implied equally sweeping changes on the product front. Coincidentally, 1975 brought the first of these. Ironically, it was the long-shunned "small Chrysler." Called Cordoba, it was really just a more luxurious Plymouth Satellite with Jaguar-like frontal styling, but it was appealingly handsome. Built on the corporate 115-inch mid-size platform, it had the shortest wheelbase of any Chrysler since the war—and it was only 2½ inches longer than the very first Chrysler of 1924. There was just a single body style, a fixed-pillar coupe usually decked out with vinyl roof covering to accentuate

The new-for-'75 Chrysler Cordoba scored over 150,000 sales in its first year on the market.

Chrysler's 1975 Newport Custom four-door sedan: $5254.

1975 Chrysler New Yorker Brougham hardtop sedan

the small vertical rear quarter windows styled in the then-trendy "opera" idiom. Ricardo Montalban was asked to abandon his Ferrari to tout the Cordoba's virtues as a "road car" in numerous magazine ads and television commercials. Though standard equipment included radial tires and anti-roll bars at each end, the Cordoba was really a personal-luxury car of the Ford Thunderbird/Buick Riviera/Chevy Monte Carlo stripe. Interiors were beautifully upholstered in crushed velour or a combination of brocade and vinyl, and leather seat coverings were optional. If the Cordoba was a frank copy of other maker's products, it was a clever copy. More importantly, it was a genuine success, just the shot in the sales arm that Chrysler needed. In its debut year, Cordoba ran up 150,105 deliveries, almost two-third's of the nameplate's total 1975 volume.

Except for higher prices, the rest of the Chrysler line was little changed for '75. The standard New Yorker series disappeared, leaving three Newports (two-door hardtop and four-door sedan and hardtop at $4854-$5008), three Newport Customs (same body styles but priced at $5254-$5423), two Town & Country wagons (six- and nine-seater, $6099 and $6244), and a trio of New Yorker Broughams (as per Newport, $6277-$6424). Unfortunately, only the Newport four-door sedan, the least expensive model in the line, sold better than 20,000 units.

When a Washington, D.C. talk show host was asked to name an extinct dinosaur from that area, he replied "Chrysler." As dinosaurs went, the '75s were quite attractive. Their emphasis, as *Road & Track* magazine noted, was "off performance and on luxury and economy ...guns and butter." The Broughams were as luxurious as the name implied, with standard leather, velour, or brocade upholstery; shag carpeting; simulated burled walnut panels and filigree moldings on dash and door panels. With a nod toward the new consumer emphasis on fuel economy, Chrysler numerically lowered final drive ratios and offered a new option called the Fuel Pacer, which consisted of an intake manifold sensor connected to a warning light that glowed whenever the driver's right foot was too heavy on the gas pedal. (The Fuel Pacer would be revived 10 years later for a somewhat different

Imperial bid a temporary farewell after 1975. Shown is that year's LeBaron hardtop coupe, priced at $8698.

Dodge's new 1975 Charger SE was closely allied with Cordoba in structure, appearance, and running gear.

Cordoba-like nose graced the '75 Dodge Charger SE.

1975 Dodge Charger SE was base priced at $4093.

1975 Dodge Coronet Custom four-door sedan: $3754.

Dodge's 1975 Coronet Custom wagon, a V-8-only entry

economy aid: an indicator light for signalling the driver when to move to the next higher gear in a *manual* transmission car.) Other engineering changes were modest: a 50,000-mile battery for 440 V-8 models (optional with the 400 engine), similarly long-lived spark plugs, and extra-cost load-leveller rear shock absorbers. In line with the rest of the industry, all Chrysler Corporation cars adopted catalytic converters for emission control this year. Company engineers had opposed the "cat con," fearing it wouldn't last more than 50,000 miles and

would be ruined by a few tankfuls of leaded gas. Their fears were well-founded, but there was no other way to meet the government's mandated exhaust cleanup.

After fewer than 9000 were built, Imperial was retired. The final 1975 off the Jefferson Avenue line was a LeBaron four-door hardtop, completed on June 12th. It carried serial number YM43-T5C-182947 and sold for $10,403. If you can find this car, you will have an artifact of some note. For 1976, the same basic design, complete with split waterfall grille and hidden headlamps, would

1975 Dodge Coronet Brougham hardtop coupe: $4154.

The Dodge Dart Custom sedan for '75 listed at $3444.

1975 Dodge Dart Custom four-door sedan

return with New Yorker Brougham badges and a $2000 lighter base sticker price.

Though total industry volume this year was off eight percent from 1974 levels, Chrysler Corporation nosedived by a whopping 24 percent. Plymouth's percentage drop was even greater than that, and the make had not had such a bad season since 1962, the year of the "plucked chickens." Buyers were now getting used to gas that was twice as costly as it was before the energy crunch—and accustomed to higher new-car prices. With typical fickleness, the market began turning away from compacts, which were Plymouth's stock-in-trade. This year's Valiant/Duster line had only minor styling changes (a smoother grille was the main one) and the same model offerings as before. They were the strength of the ticket, but they weren't strong enough. Dearborn had a new luxury compact, the Ford Granada/Mercury Monarch, to supplement its aging Maverick/Comet, and both Ford and GM had much greater depth in their intermediates than Plymouth. In a vain attempt to convince buyers it really had downsized its big cars, Plymouth transferred the Fury label to what had been the Satellite line and applied new front and rear sheetmetal. Nobody was fooled

by the "small Fury," and despite what the ads said, this was *not* "the car a lot of people have been waiting for." To avoid confusion with the newly named intermediates, Plymouth retagged its full-size line Gran Fury and adopted the 1974 Dodge Monaco lineup of base, Custom, and Brougham models. All Gran Furys except wagons

1975 Dodge Dart Sport fastback coupe. Base price: $3297.

The 1975 Dodge Dart Special Edition hardtop coupe

rode a slightly longer 121½-inch wheelbase, though probably no one noticed. Brougham had its own grille treatment and a fixed-pillar "hardtop" with opera windows, a sign of the times.

Dodge was having similar problems, but it had one weapon Plymouth didn't: a new Cordoba-based Charger

SE. Priced at about $5000, it didn't sell as well as the Chrysler, likely because buyers preferred that name's greater prestige, but its 30,000-unit run was the best recorded this year by any Dodge model save compacts. The full-size line was rejiggled into Monaco, Royal Monaco, and Royal Monaco Brougham offerings, with

1975 Dodge Royal Monaco Brougham pillared hardtop coupe

Less than 18,000 Fury Sport hardtops were built for '75.

1975 Plymouth Fury Sport hardtop coupe: $4105 with V-8.

1975 Plymouth Fury Sport hardtop coupe

Plymouth's Road Runner was reduced to an option package for the 1975 Fury hardtop coupe. Few were sold.

hidden headlamps and a very heavy-looking front-end treatment on Royals. The advent of the Charger SE returned pillarless hardtops to the Coronet line, which got an uninspired two-piece square grille and the small Fury's rear-end sheetmetal. The Dart/Swinger compacts were distinguished by a cleaner, thin-bar grille insert but had little else new. In all, Dodge had to settle for model year sales of 377,000 units, its worst showing since 1962, and eighth place in the production standings.

Mopar performance fans had little to cheer about for '75. Ponycars and high-power engines were history, the Dodge Charger was nothing like its namesake of five

1975 Plymouth Fury hardtop with Road Runner option

1975 Plymouth Gran Fury Brougham pillared hardtop coupe

1975 Plymouth Gran Fury Brougham pillared hardtop coupe

1975 Plymouth Gran Fury Custom hardtop sedan: $4837.

Plymouth's 1975 Gran Fury Sport Suburban wagon

'75 Gran Fury Sport Suburban listed at $5455/$5573.

1975 Plymouth Duster 360 coupe. Only 1421 were built.

Plymouth's 1975 Duster coupe in new Custom trim: $3418.

1975 Plymouth Valiant Brougham sedan. Base price: $4139.

years earlier, and the Road Runner suffered the indignity of being reduced to a mere appearance package for Fury hardtops. The Dart Sport/Duster with small-block V-8 was still around and still interesting, though the engine now measured 360 instead of 340 cubic inches and was somewhat tamer. Still, it can be reasonably argued that these were more balanced "performance" cars and perfectly right for the times, as only die-hard speed freaks wished to waste their wallets on 1975's much more expensive gasoline.

On October 1st of this year, Lynn Townsend retired as Chrysler Corporation chairman at the age of 56, nine years before mandatory departure. John Riccardo moved up to succeed him, while Riccardo's replacement as president was Eugene A. Cafiero, who came out of a strong production background at Dodge. "It certainly is a fair statement that any chairman would like to retire during a profitable year," Townsend admitted. But he insisted that he had been under "absolutely no pressure" from stockholders to step down and that the decision to retire was his alone: "The automobile industry is entering a new era in which it is going to have to change substantially . . . There are going to have to be new methods . . . Even if I were to stay on to age 65, I would not be here to see the culmination of many decisions being made at the present time. My early retirement is for the benefit of our management team and our company."

Riccardo emphasized that there would be no dramatic changes in marketing strategy or dealer relations, in a way undermining Townsend's statement. But Cafiero's appointment was seen as a considerable injection of new blood. There was more of that in the Administrative Committee, the company's main decision-making body since 1961, which was now composed of Riccardo, Cafiero, and four new executive vice-presidents with an average age of just over 50, quite young for such a high post. Just to emphasize its strong leadership role, the group changed its name to Operations Committee.

1976

A once-proud marque, Imperial, was gone for 1976. Said Chrysler-Plymouth Division vice-president Robert McCurry: "We won't be participating in the luxury segment, but we will upgrade the appearance and appointment levels of the New Yorker Brougham and Newport entries to the point that they will be a much better value in the marketplace."

Singer Jack Jones warbled in TV commercials, "What a beautiful New Yorker. It's the talk of the town." What it was, in fact, was the 1975 Imperial with a "wide-stripe" grille and few other changes. Brougham offerings were reduced from three to two (the four-door sedan disappeared) and now carried "Imperial-level" trim, though they had already been pretty plush. Yet the strategy worked as McCurry had hoped. Nearly 40,000 Broughams were retailed for the model year against

The Chrysler Newport Custom hardtop coupe for 1976: $5479.

Chrysler's personal-luxury Cordoba was little changed for '76.

25,000 of the '75s and just 9000 of the last Imperials.

The personal-luxury Cordoba returned, sporting an optional 60/40 split front seat (shades of Virgil Exner!) and metric readings on gauges set into a simulated Brazilian rosewood dash. It again performed yeoman duty, outselling all other Chryslers combined and seven out of its eight class rivals (only Chevy's much less expensive Monte Carlo bested it).

An important engineering innovation that showed up throughout the 1976 corporate lineup was an Electronic Lean Burn System, fitted to the big 400- and 440-cid V-8s. Basically, it consisted of an electronic microprocessor, called a "spark control computer," which received data from sensors about a variety of engine operating conditions, including throttle position, manifold vacuum,

rpm, and coolant temperature. In response to sensor signals, the computer continuously adjusted spark timing so that the engine would run at the leanest mixture possible at any given moment, thus burning less fuel. It was a significant feature, even if it did somehow seem trifling in the heavy, big-block full-size cars. However, the technology would find its way onto other engines in the immediate years ahead. And it offered proof—if any be needed—that Chrysler Corporation was still very much a company that took pride in engineering "firsts."

The year's main new-model introduction came at midseason with the arrival of two new compacts to replace the aging Dodge Dart and Plymouth Valiant. Built on the new corporate F-body platform (the Dart/Valiant's A-body dated back to 1967), they were near-identical

1976 Chrysler New Yorker Brougham hardtop sedan (left) and Newport Custom hardtop coupe.

Dodge Aspen Special Edition coupe from mid-1976

The base Dodge Aspen five-door wagon, also from mid-1976

Mid-1976 Dodge Aspen Special Edition four-door sedan

Mid-1976 Dodge Aspen Custom coupe. Base price: $3518.

twins differing only in grille treatments, badges, and trim. Dodge called its version Aspen, after the famous Colorado ski resort, while Plymouth went Italian with the name Volare. Base, mid-range Custom, and a top-line luxury series appeared under each nameplate, the last named Premier if Volare and Special Edition if Aspen. Body styles comprised the expected four-door sedan, a semi-

fastback coupe with large triangular rear quarter windows, and a four-door station wagon with a large, one-piece rear liftgate that many people thought of as a door. The wagon was a significant entry, as Chrysler had been without compact haulers since 1966. As with the Dart/Valiant, coupes rode a shorter wheelbase than the four-door models, but the measurements were longer in

Dodge's 1976 Charger SE coupe retailed at $4763. Styling was not greatly altered from the previous year's.

1976 Dodge Charger SE production was 42,168.

1976 Dodge Charger Daytona coupe

1976 Dodge Charger SE coupe. Note revised taillamps.

The $4059 Dodge Coronet Custom four-door sedan for '76

each case, 108.7 and 112.7 inches, respectively. Though they were only marginally larger outside than their predecessors, the Aspen/Volare was carefully designed to make maximum use of available interior space. The upright styling helped, particularly on the sedan and wagon, being pleasantly conservative and yet not too square.

Though orthodox in most every way, the Aspen/Volare

had great sales appeal thanks to its inoffensive looks, good performance/economy balance, and the top-line models' unexpected luxury. About the only thing unusual about them from an engineering standpoint was the mounting of their front torsion bars. Chrysler felt it important to maintain this feature rather than switching to coil springs, so the bars were mounted crosswise

1976 Dodge Charger Sport was more closely related to the Coronet than the higher-priced Charger SE.

1976 Dodge Dart Swinger hardtop coupe: $3510 basic.

1976 Dodge Dart Swinger hardtop coupe

The Dodge Dart Custom four-door sedan for '76

1976 Dodge Dart Custom four-door sedan

The economy-oriented 1976 Dart Lite coupe

The $4763 Dodge Royal Monaco four-door sedan for '76

Dodge dinosaur: the 1976 Royal Monaco Brougham pillared hardtop coupe saw only 4076 copies for the model year.

1976 Dodge Royal Monaco Brougham wagon: $5869.

4WD fun: Dodge's 1976 Ramcharger SE sports/utility

instead of longitudinally. The ostensible reason for this was to better isolate the suspension from the body and thus provide a smoother, quieter ride, but the more likely reason was lack of space in the new platform for positioning the bars fore/aft. A "big-car ride" was claimed for the arrangement, but most critics said the "Isolated Transverse Suspension System" simply made for mushier handling.

Predictably, the Aspen/Volare carried unitized body/chassis construction. In later years the cars would be

notorious for rust problems that would make them the most recalled models in the history of such government doings, at least before GM's front-drive X-cars. The real problem was shoddy workmanship and not any inherent design fault, however.

Power was supplied by two familiar and reliable engines, the 225-cid version of the near-bulletproof Slant Six and a mildly tuned 318 V-8. Most Aspen/Volare customers ordered the optional TorqueFlite automatic, but a four-speed manual was available and seemed par-

Mitsubishi-built Plymouth Arrow hatchback coupe was new for '76. Shown is the top-line 200 version.

Plymouth's Gran Fury Brougham four-door sedan carried a base retail price of $5162 for 1976. It sold poorly.

1976 Plymouth Fury Sport pillared hardtop coupe: $3988.

ticularly well-suited to the Aspen R/T and Volare Road Runner. Offered only in coupe form, these two were actually package options, and they weren't just for show. Besides the 318 V-8, each included a heavy-duty suspension, three-speed floorshift manual gearbox, plus sportier interior trim. A two-barrel 360 V-8 was optional across the board, offering 155 bhp against 145 for the 318 and 100-110 for the Slant Six.

In all, the Aspen/Volare made an auspicious debut, with production of almost 300,000 for the Plymouth ver-

sion and 220,000 for the Dodge. Despite their well-publicized troubles in later years, they provided a timely bridge between the Dart/Valiant and the first-generation front-drive cars of 1978. And as events would quickly prove, the basic F-body platform was versatile enough to spin off an even plusher compact that's still with us at this writing, albeit in greatly modified form.

Aspen/Volare did not immediately replace Dart/Valiant, which continued to be available for the entire model year. Naturally, the older compacts weren't changed much for their final season but, except for the 360 variants, the entire model complement was continued, including the plush Special Edition/Brougham hardtops and sedans. And there was an interesting new twist, a lightweight economy package for the fastback coupe. Whimsically dubbed Dart Lite and Feather Duster, it was built around a special version of the 225-cid Slant Six with an aluminum intake manifold, and an overdrive manual transmission with aluminum case and a long-legged final drive ratio was available. Paring weight further were aluminum bumper reinforcements and aluminum hood and rear deck inner panels. Options were deliberately limited to discourage buyers from piling on weighty, economy-robbing accessories.

Big-block engines began to disappear this year. Dodge

1976 Plymouth Volare Premier coupe. Base price: $4402.

Plymouth's $3976 Volare Premier wagon for 1976

Plymouth's top-line Volare for 1976 was called Premier. It's shown in each of the three Volare body styles.

1976 Plymouth Volare coupe with Road Runner option

'76 Volare Road Runner option included heavy-duty chassis.

was down to one 440, an option for the full-size Monaco, and Plymouth's largest V-8 was the 400-cid unit. The Monaco and Gran Fury were stylistically unchanged for '76, a reflection of their continuing sales declines despite a general rebound in big-car demand. The mid-size Plymouth Fury and Dodge Charger/Coronet were basically reruns too, but Dodge confusingly transferred coupes back to the Charger line. Each division's intermediate series was now down to a single pillarless two-door hardtop, fixed-pillar styles with opera windows substituting

as this year's top-trim offerings. Dodge tried to recapture some of the Charger's lost glory by issuing a tarted-up Cordoba-based SE bearing the Daytona name, but it amounted to little more than jazzy two-tone paint.

At the end of 1975, the Operations Committee had looked at the market and made two key decisions: dump the full-size Plymouth and Dodge by 1978, and charge ahead full steam on development of a front-wheel-drive subcompact. To some company veterans, these moves had worrisome overtones of 1962, when the "plucked chickens" had

The lightweight, aptly named 1976 Plymouth "Feather Duster"

Plymouth's 4WD Trail Duster sports/utility for '76

1976 Plymouth Voyager Sport extended-body window van

dislodged Dodge and Plymouth from their traditional industry positions. But Riccardo, Cafiero, and McCurry were convinced that the traditional big car really was doomed this time. As if to confirm their view, General Motors released a squadron of newly designed full-size models shrunk to intermediate proportions for 1977. By the time Chrysler would get around to doing the same, its situation would be very grave indeed.

1977

New-model developments at Chrysler Corporation for 1977 focused on two new "senior" compacts, the firm's reply to the growing market for more luxurious smaller cars uncovered by the Ford Granada. They bowed at mid-model year as the Chrysler LeBaron and Dodge Diplomat. Both were built on the new corporate M-body platform, a derivative of the F-body Aspen/Volare and riding the longer 112.7-inch wheelbase used for the four-door models in the "junior" compact lines. Two body styles were initially offered, a four-door sedan and a fixed-pillar two-door coupe, each available in standard trim and as an upper-level version called Medallion. Styling on the seniors was appropriately more formal than on the juniors. The coupes were particularly attractive, with longer door windows than Aspen/Volare two-doors and correspondingly smaller rear quarter lights. Another interesting design touch was a rear window slightly vee'd at the center, something that GM had used on various personal-luxury cars since the 1967 Cadillac Eldorado. LeBaron achieved distinction at the front with square quad headlamps positioned just above the bumper and surmounted by twin, rectangular parking/turn indicator lamps on each side. This positioning was reversed on the Diplomat, which carried a finely checked square grille with three vertical bars. LeBaron had a shinier frontispiece with large rectangular sections.

Aside from their more conservative lines and plusher cabin appointments, LeBaron/Diplomat was much like the Aspen/Volare. Base power was supplied by the

1977 Chrysler Cordoba coupe. Base price: $5418.

1977 Chrysler Cordoba coupe with optional "Crown" roof

Cordoba (optional "Crown" roof shown) continued as the best-selling Chrysler model for 1977.

Arriving at mid-1977 was Chrysler's LeBaron "senior" compact. Medallion coupe shown was priced at $5436.

veteran 318 V-8, but transverse-torsion-bar front suspension, standard front disc brakes, leaf-sprung live rear axle, and unitized construction were all shared. The 225 Slant Six was a credit option available for buyers who wanted better economy, but either model could be loaded up with just about every comfort and convenience feature available in a full-size Chrysler Corporation car: vinyl roof, air conditioning, cruise control, electric rear window defroster, tilt steering wheel, sliding steel sunroof, and power seats, windows, and door locks. Standards included TorqueFlite automatic, power steering and brakes, and radial tires. LeBaron/Diplomat carried a more ornate instrument panel than Aspen/Volare, with a curved section in front of the driver to bring radio and heat/vent

1977 Chrysler LeBaron Medallion four-door sedan: $5594.

Chrysler's New Yorker Brougham hardtop sedan for '77

Still an Imperial continuation, the '77 Chrysler New Yorker Brougham hardtop sedan listed at $7215.

1977 Chrysler Newport hardtop sedan. Base price: $5433.

1977 Chrysler Newport hardtop sedan

controls closer to hand. This section had lots of holes that looked like places for instruments, but some of these were taken up by minor switchgear. However, alternator and coolant temperature dials were fitted along with the customary speedometer and fuel gauge.

Despite their mundane origins, both models sold well. The LeBaron tallied nearly 55,000 sales despite the abbreviated selling season, and Diplomat scored close to 38,000. Coupled with Cordoba deliveries, LeBaron made Chrysler a high-volume make for the first time in many moons. The marque's model year production total was nearly 400,000 units, an all-time record. The figure would hover at around the 350,000-unit level for both 1978 and '79.

Incidentally, curb weights on the M-body models ran around 3500 pounds, which made LeBaron the smallest

Dodge's compact Aspen wagon proved popular. Here, the little-changed '77 model in Special Edition trim.

1977 Dodge Aspen SE four-door sedan. Base price: $4366.

and lightest Chrysler in history. And, of course, it perpetuated a grand name, preserved by the now-departed Imperial but revered from the Thirties and Ray Dietrich's exquisite coachwork on Chrysler chassis. On the subject of tradition, it's too bad Dodge didn't revive the DeSoto name for its M-body, but Diplomat was an appropriate choice, a name associated with Dodge since 1950 and its first pillarless hardtop.

Aside from its well-received luxury compacts, Chrysler Corporation had little else to generate excitement for '77. In fact, there was a little less of everything at both Dodge and Chrysler-Plymouth Divisions. The Newport Custom was dropped from the Chrysler lineup, and Plymouth trimmed Gran Fury offerings from nine to seven while reinstating the 440 V-8. Neither would not last long. Styling and engineering changes were minute on all three full-size model groups. Dodge took a cue from Plymouth and produced a "downsized" Monaco by simply transferring the name to what had been the Coronet and calling all its out-size cruisers Royal Monaco. Dodge/Plymouth intermediates were more alike than ever. In fact, they were built nose-to-tail at the company's Lynch Road facility.

1977 Dodge Charger Daytona coupe

Both mid-size lines sported restyled fronts with square grilles between vertically stacked quad rectangular headlamps, but changed little in other respects.

The successful personal-luxury Chrysler Cordoba continued with its basic 1975 look, but there was now a choice of three different vinyl roof treatments, each suitably set off by small "opera lights" that glowed softly when the headlamps were turned on. Any of these could

1977 Dodge Aspen coupe with R/T performance package

1977 Dodge Aspen coupe with R/T and Super Pak options

The 1977 Dodge Aspen R/T could be a good goer when equipped with the optional 155-bhp 360 V-8.

1977 Dodge Charger SE with optional T-bar roof

Dodge priced the 1977 Charger SE at $5098 basic.

1977 Dodge Charger SE production was 42,252 units.

1977 Dodge Diplomat Medallion coupe. Price: $5313.

1977 Dodge Diplomat Medallion coupe

The $4146 Dodge Monaco Brougham pillared hardtop for '77

1977 Dodge Monaco Brougham four-door sedan: $4217.

The Dodge Monaco Brougham four-door sedan for 1977

be combined with a manually operated steel sunroof, and a new T-bar roof with removeable glass panels was now available for those who wanted even more in the way of a convertible's open-air feel. The Cordoba's double at Dodge, the Charger, returned in luxury SE and sportier Daytona forms, the latter still with gaudy two-toning and a plethora of pinstripes.

The T-top and manual sunroof also appeared as new options for the Aspen/Volare coupes, but the junior compacts were otherwise much the same as before. The sporty Aspen R/T and Volare Road Runner packages were still available, and could now be augmented by a new option group consisting of front and rear spoilers and wheel arch "spats" *a la* Pontiac's Firebird Trans Am. The optional

Dodge's 1977 Royal Monaco Brougham four-door sedan

Plymouth's '77 Fury Sport hardtop with special interior

1977 Plymouth Fury Salon four-door sedan

A 1977 Plymouth Fury sedan set up for police work

1977 Plymouth Fury Salon had a $4185 base price.

1977 Plymouth Gran Fury Brougham pillared hardtop coupe

1977 Plymouth Fury Sport pillared hardtop coupe

Two-door Gran Fury Brougham sold at $4963 for '77.

360-cid V-8 acquired Electronic Lean Burn technology, and a two-barrel version of the six-cylinder slant-block engine appeared as the "Super Six" (single-barrel carburetion was standard).

By this time, production cost pressures and declining profits were rapidly blurring the distinction between certain Dodge and Chrysler-Plymouth models. Even prices were the same in some instances. Dealers also had something to do with this "twinning" process, and management continued to issue parallel model offerings for both divisions' agents. Midway through the 1976 season, Chrysler-Plymouth franchises got a new captive import to match the Mitsubishi-made Colt being sold at Dodge outlets. Marketed as the Plymouth Arrow, it was a

1977 Plymouth Volare Custom coupe. Base price: $3752.

1977 Plymouth Volare Road Runner coupe with T-roof

The $4271 Plymouth Volare Premier wagon for 1977

'77 Plymouth Volare Road Runner coupe with "Super Pak"

'77 Plymouth Volare Premier sedan sold at $4354 base.

Plymouth's imported 1977 Arrow GT hatchback coupe

small (92.1-inch wheelbase) hatchback coupe, essentially a "federalized" version of Mitsubishi's home-market Celeste. Offerings consisted of base 160 and fancier GS and GT models, all powered by a 1.6-liter overhead-cam four. Engineering was resolutely conventional, with front-engine/rear-drive layout, live rear axle on leaf springs, and coil-spring/MacPherson-strut front suspension. More a 2+2 than a genuine four-seater, the diminutive Arrow was little changed for '77 and sold for as low as $3400, making it this year's least expensive Plymouth by far.

In future years, management would slap the Plymouth nameplate on other Mitsubishi-built small cars, in part to maintain the illusion of Plymouth as a full-line make. It would prove to be a good move, providing vital sales support, but it only served to downgrade a once-prominent marque even further.

1978

Despite what some critics would later suggest, Chrysler Corporation did not stand by helplessly in the turmoil of the Seventies. In fact, the Riccardo team doggedly attempted to meet changing buyer needs. Chrysler may have been slow to react to market changes under Townsend, but not under Riccardo: the '75 Cordoba/ Charger, '76 Aspen/Volare, '77 LeBaron/Diplomat, and this year's new front-drive Dodge Omni and Plymouth Horizon subcompacts were all correct and logical developments.

Chrysler's—indeed, the entire U.S. auto industry's—

A front-end facelift marked the 1978 Chrysler Cordoba, here with optional "Crown" roof treatment

Chrysler Cordoba coupe. Base price was now $5811.

Chrysler's 1978 Cordoba coupe

problems in the late Seventies went far beyond product decisions to the very heart of the relationship between business and government. Meeting federal safety and emissions standards was costly for automakers, which operate on a fixed product schedule with little flexibility for change in response to dramatic market fluctuations. The marketplace itself was gyrating more than ever, consumers jumping from large to small to intermediate cars, back to large and then back to small again, all in rapid-fire order. Confounding the industry's ability to predict such swings were vacillating gasoline prices and an inflation rate that continued to head skyward. Given the industry's traditional three-year lead times and the overwhelming expense of just a single all-new design, it's no wonder U.S. automakers tended to lag behind buyer preferences for most of the decade.

The frosting on this bitter cake was a new set of standards that took effect with the 1978 model year. Known by the acronym CAFE (for Corporate Average Fuel Economy), this legislation, born in the wake of the 1973-74 energy crisis, mandated that the fuel economy of all cars sold by a given manufacturer had to average at least 18 mpg on a "sales-weighted" basis; the target figure would then rise in steps, reaching 27.5 mpg for model year 1985. Failure to comply meant stiff financial penalties—$5 per car sold for each .1 mpg over the CAFE target of any given year. It was a costly and controversial act, but Washington had the last word as usual.

With all this, smaller automakers had the most acute problems. American Motors would not exist today were it not for a financial rescue in the early Eighties by Renault of France. Chrysler would not now exist were it not for

Chrysler LeBaron Town & Country wagon, new for '78

1978 Chrysler LeBaron Medallion four-door sedan: $5692.

The $5526 Chrysler LeBaron Medallion coupe for '78

1978 Chrysler New Yorker Brougham hardtop sedan: $7831.

Chrysler Newport hardtop coupe, priced at $5804 for '78

assistance from the federal government that precipitated the firm's crisis in the first place.

Too often in its history, Chrysler Corporation had introduced the right car at the wrong time, but this year it had a product that was absolutely right, a timely response not only to CAFE but also its own declining position in a topsy-turvy market. Designated the L-body, it was a state-of-the-art subcompact with front-wheel drive and a European style four-door hatchback sedan body. It arrived amidst much fanfare as the Dodge Omni and Plymouth Horizon, near-identical twins (only grilles and nameplates differed) that some wags quickly referred to as "Omnirizon."

Cut very much from the same cloth as Volkswagen's trend-setting Rabbit, the L-body was the first domestically produced front-drive small car and the first front-drive U.S. car of any kind since the Cadillac Eldorado of 1967. Like the Rabbit, it employed a compact power package, with a four-cylinder overhead-cam engine mounted transversely in the nose instead of longitudinally. In fact, the engine used a 1.7-liter enlargement of the Rabbit's 1.5/1.6-liter block. Carburetor and ancillaries were added ("dressed") by Chrysler. The Omni/Horizon also mimicked the VW with MacPherson-strut front suspension, a coil-sprung beam rear axle located by trailing arms and able to twist slightly under wheel deflection, plus rack-and-pinion steering and front-disc/rear-drum brakes. The five-door body was quite close to the Rabbit's in appearance, but the L-cars were slightly larger overall, with a longer 99.2-inch wheelbase.

Press reaction to the L-body twins was generally favorable. Most testers agreed that Chrysler's new mini wasn't as peppy or as much fun to drive as the Rabbit, which was something of a benchmark in this regard. But it was just as practical and almost as thrifty with fuel, and it had a little more room and a softer ride of the sort likely to appeal to Americans accustomed to much bigger, heavier transportation. Predictably, it sold like mad: close to 82,000 Omnis and nearly 107,000 Horizons.

If you'll pardon the pun, Chrysler had pulled a Rabbit out of its hat. But if the Omni/Horizon wasn't exactly original, it represented important new business for the company at a critical juncture. Suddenly, Chrysler had the lead in small cars among domestic producers, and the L-body made the Ford Pinto and GM's various Vega-derived models look clumsy by comparison.

It almost didn't work out that way. Company officials later admitted that the Omni/Horizon would have been delayed for at least two years had it not been for Volkswagen's willingness to supply engines. Moreover, the company saved not only time but a vast amount of money by not having to run up its own four-cylinder unit at this point. (Of course, the firm *was* working on a four of its own, but we wouldn't see it for a few more years.)

As the L-body neared release, Chrysler played down the Aspen/Volare, which hadn't been catching on with buyers the way the Dart/Valiant had. Both compact lines were ostensibly reduced to just a single series with the same three body styles as before, but the three trim levels were actually maintained as option packages rather than discrete models or series. A new option group for Aspen/

Volare two-doors was the Super Coupe, basically the R/T and Road Runner packages combined with the "Super Pak" body add-ons (spoilers and wheel arch spats) and swathed in gallons of matte-black paint. The Super Coupe also included special striping, heavy-duty underpinnings, and the four-barrel version of the ubiquitous corporate 360-cid V-8. Both divisions revised grille inserts and interior and exterior trim for the '78 season, but the compacts were little changed in other respects.

The Aspen/Volare station wagon was extended to the M-body twins for '78, with suitable styling modifications.

The big Chrysler wagon disappeared, but the new LeBaron inherited its Town & Country name and pseudo-wood bodyside trim. The Diplomat wagon was unadorned.

In a move reminiscent of fateful 1962, Plymouth deleted the full-size Gran Fury totally in 1978, leaving the mid-size Fury as the make's largest offering. Dodge carried on with its mammoth Royal Monaco in a reduced selection. The standard Chrysler was now down to just Newport and New Yorker Brougham series, each offering two- and four-door hardtops distinguished by minor tinware alterations.

1978 Dodge Aspen SE four-door sedan

Dodge's 1978 Aspen SE five-door wagon

1978 Dodge Aspen Custom coupe

1978 Dodge Aspen coupe with R/T option package

Dodge's front-drive Omni hatchback sedan, new for '78

$5368 bought Dodge's 1978 Charger SE coupe

The $5043 Dodge Diplomat Medallion coupe for 1978

Magnum XE was a new variation on the Dodge Charger theme for 1978. Model's base price was $5509.

1978 Dodge Monaco Brougham four-door sedan

Dodge's 1978 Monaco Brougham pillared hardtop coupe

The personal-luxury market got extra emphasis this year. Chrysler's Cordoba received a crisper rear roofline, a fine-checked grille, and stacked rectangular quad headlamps (replacing the former dual round units). There was also a new "S" model intended to woo budget-conscious buyers, priced $200 below the standard model.

Dodge left the Charger SE mostly alone, continuing the original Cordoba-like front-end treatment, but the hokey Daytona was cancelled in favor of a slick-looking new variation called Magnum XE. Advertised as "the totally personal approach to driving excitement," it was marked by modest bulges in the bodysides where the Daytona

Plymouth's 1978 Fury continued to be a close relative of Dodge's mid-size Monaco. Shown: the Salon four-door.

The mid-size Plymouth Fury was in its final year for 1978. Shown is the Fury Sport pillared hardtop coupe.

1978 Plymouth Fury Sport hardtop coupe. Base price: $4483.

1978 Plymouth Fury Sport in thin-pillar hardtop form.

had merely used paint, and a smooth, definitely un-formal nose with a simple three-bar square grille flanked by horizontal rectangular quad headlamps. The lamps were placed behind glass covers that automatically flipped up when the light switch was pulled, and they blended nicely into wraparound front fender side marker lamps.

Specifications and equipment paralleled Cordoba's, but styling differences and special colors set the Magnum apart. It outsold the rather staid Charger by a stunning margin, 55,000 to 2800, but the Cordoba was still the popularity champ, scoring production of close to 125,000 for the model year.

Plymouth's benchmark 1978 front-drive subcompact Horizon. It was nearly identical with Dodge's new Omni.

1978 Plymouth Horizon hatchback sedan with "woody" option

1978 Plymouth Volare Premier four-door sedan

The 1978 Plymouth Horizon's base price was $3976.

1978 Plymouth Volare coupe with Road Runner option

Plymouth's popular Volare Premier wagon for '78

Plymouth Sapporo hardtop, new from Mitsubishi for '78

The Mitsubishi-built Plymouth Arrow coupes for '78 (from left): GT, GS, and 160.

On the import front, Mitsubishi had sent over a new Colt sedan (based on the home-market Galant Lancer model) for 1977. This year, both Dodge and Plymouth got a conventionally engineered notchback coupe that was larger than anything they'd previously received from Japan. The Dodge version was more overtly sporty, so it was marketed as the Challenger, thus resurrecting the ponycar name of four years earlier. Plymouth's entry was tagged Sapporo and was trimmed more like a Cordoba, with landau vinyl roof and C-pillar opera lights. The Challenger had louvered rear quarter windows, bright two-tone paint, and no plastic top cover. Standard powerplant for both was a rather anemic 1.6-liter ohc four, but most buyers opted for the extra-cost 2.6-liter unit, with contra-rotating "Silent Shafts" to reduce the vibratory coupling forces inherent in a large four-cylinder engine. TorqueFlite automatic was an optional alternative to the standard five-speed overdrive manual gearbox for either model. The Mitsubishi 2.6 would loom large in Chrysler's future domestic model plans.

In all, 1978 was a dismal sales year for Chrysler Corporation. Plymouth finished a distant seventh in the production race, with 500,000 cars. Dodge was right behind in eighth position, recording 468,000 units. Despite the success of the new Omni/Horizon, these figures didn't look like much compared to past years. Worse, Ford, Pontiac, and Olds all had tremendous seasons, and Chevrolet and Buick were only slightly off their brisk 1977 pace. Perhaps the lesson to be learned in Plymouth's case is that you can't desert a market—here, the full-size field—without losing something.

Yet Chrysler Corporation would desert big cars entirely after '78. This year's Dodge Royal Monaco and Chrysler Newport/New Yorker would be the last of their breed—huge, opulent, heavy cars that had already been rendered anachronisms by the momentous events of recent years. Though Chrysler didn't immediately suffer from their demise, the make's total production would be cut by half for 1980, though for a very different reason.

1979

Under John Riccardo and Gene Cafiero, Chrysler had moved rapidly to dispose of losers, shore up winners, and revise its product lineup to meet market needs. By 1978 they had sold an unfinished Pennsylvania assembly plant to Volkswagen, sold Airtemp to Fedders, disposed of the Big Sky recreation facility in Montana, and secured British government assistance for its reeling UK subsidiary. Rebates were used whenever necessary, and they were necessary often except for the hot-selling Omni and Horizon. The car market just wasn't cooperating.

The Omni and Horizon sold well in their first year, and came back with an additional model in their second: a hatchback coupe on a shortened 96.7-inch wheelbase, called 024 and TC3, respectively. These slick twins were quick on their feet, good-looking, and well-built, and they won

Chrysler's 1979 Cordoba coupe with two-tone paint

1979 Chrysler Cordoba with "Crown" roof and sunroof

1979 Chrysler LeBaron Medallion coupe: $6017.

The $6425 Chrysler LeBaron Medallion sedan for '79

The elegant 1979 Chrysler LeBaron Town & Country wagon

R-body Chrysler New Yorker appeared for 1979. Shown is the top-shelf Fifth Avenue Edition.

1979 Chrysler New Yorker Fifth Avenue Edition sedan

Chrysler's 1979 Newport sedan, another new R-body model

some encouraging conquest sales from import buyers who wanted a sporty 2+2. Unfortunately, the TC3 was the only new 1979 offering from Plymouth, which was now without its entire intermediate Fury line. With only five body styles against Dodge's 14, the inevitable—yet unbelievable—happened: Dodge outsold Plymouth for the first time in history. The model year count was 404,266 units to 372,449. Dodge finished a typical

seventh in the production race. Plymouth ended up ninth, just ahead of Chrysler, and its volume was the lowest since the make's introductory year of 1929.

Of course, sales losses were more the result of model assignments within Chrysler-Plymouth Division than of any failing by Plymouth itself. Even so, the division's combined model-year total was only a shade over 700,000 cars, and Plymouth alone had done much better than that

1979 Chrysler Newport sedan. Base price was $6405.

1979 Dodge Aspen wagon with Sport Wagon option package

1979 Dodge Aspen coupe with R/T option package

The $5966 Dodge Diplomat Medallion coupe for '79

Dodge's 1979 Diplomat Salon wagon could be ordered with T&C-style wood-look side trim.

in the not-too-distant past. At only 1.1 million units for the '79 model year, Chrysler Corporation was well off its stride.

Elsewhere, the Dodge Diplomat/Chrysler LeBaron line-ups were somewhat expanded by a mid-range trim level called Salon, slotted between base and Medallion and offered for all body styles. The spirit of the great letter-series 300 was revived during the year with a special option group for the Cordoba. It comprised unique trim, bucket seats, and the familiar blacked-out cross-bar grille, and added some $1600 to the standard car's base price. Compared to the original article, this new "300" had everything except performance. Though it carried a 195-bhp 360-cid V-8, it had none of the blinding speed of the big hemi- and wedge-head monsters of the Fifties and Sixties. Dodge's counterpart continued to be the

1979 Dodge Magnum XE coupe. Base list price: $6039.

1979 Dodge Magnum XE with T-roof and two-tone paint

1979 Dodge Omni 024 hatchback coupe: $4864 basic.

1979 Dodge Omni hatchback sedan with optional roof rack

The '79 Dodge Omni 024 featured good aerodynamics.

The '79 Dodge Omni five-door listed at $4469 base.

Magnum XE, priced the same as the base Cordoba. Charger was dropped. So too was the entire mid-size Monaco line.

Dodge had a new 118½-inch wheelbase model for '79. Called St. Regis (an old Chrysler name), it shared body/chassis structure with the new R-body Chrysler Newport and New Yorker, all drastically downsized four-door sedans of trim proportions, considerably smaller and lighter (3500-4000 pounds) than the mastodons they replaced. However, stylists gave them a big, heavy look,

which may explain why they didn't sell all that well. Then, again, maybe not: it was damnably hard to predict the public's desires in 1979. R-body styling was clean if not terribly exciting. The St. Regis wore a Magnum-style nose with glass-covered headlamps and a large checkerboard grille. The Newport had a slightly different treatment with exposed headlamps, while the New Yorker had body-color headlamp lids and, oddly, opera windows built into the trailing edges of the rear doors. The significant thing about this new trio is that they were really just

John Riccardo on Government Regulations

(From a 1979 speech)

Side Guard Door Beams: "In 1970 the government proposed putting these in all cars. We said they would be a waste of money in many kinds of cars. After the public was forced to spend almost half a billion dollars for them, the General Accounting Office concluded that the beams provided 'little, if any, benefits in terms of reduced deaths and serious injuries...'"

Catalysts and Unleaded Gas: "In 1973, EPA said 'the public interest dictates that catalysts be phased into use,' and forced them on American cars. Chrysler

said there was a better way to do the job —through combustion in the engine; that unleaded gas would cost much more than leaded; that the catalyst would need exotic metals that can only be had from Russia and South Africa. It's 1979, and unleaded gas costs 4 to 8 cents more a gallon than leaded gas. That's almost $2 billion a year in needless inflation. The industry is importing more than 1.6 million ounces of platinum and rhodium a year from South Africa. By 1981 the cost of precious metals will add another $1.5 billion every year to inflation."

The Ignition Interlock: "In 1974 the government required the famous ignition interlock that prevented a driver from starting his car until he buckled up the bag of groceries on the passenger seat. I personally testified that it [would] create a consumer backlash against safety regulations. The government went ahead with this pinball approach to engineering and the outcry was so loud that within three months Congress told us to take off the interlock—after $250 million of the consumers' money had been poured down the drain."

Dodge's full-size R-body for '79 was dubbed St. Regis. Base list price was $6532.

Magnum-like nose graced the 1979 Dodge St. Regis sedan.

1979 Dodge St. Regis sedan

rebodied continuations of the previous mid-size Fury/Monaco, as the wheelbase dimension suggests. Typically, they were promoted as more socially responsible downsized big cars, and as such they served as well as a brand-new design—which is a good thing, because Chrysler was fast running out of money for new products of any sort.

Economic indicators had begun pointing to a major recession as early as 1977, and it hit in the spring of 1979 as oil prices headed upward again, triggering economic jitters among car buyers and fueling an already red-hot inflation rate. Chrysler Corporation experienced dismal 1979 model year sales, and its cash flow situation now went from serious to critical. In late 1978, the firm had arranged to sell off all its European subsidiaries to Peugeot of France, which instantly became Europe's largest volume automaker. In mid-1979, the corporation sold a solid money-maker, Chrysler Realty, a move that made it apparent just how grave the situation had become. Without income from its European subsidiaries and several domestic operations that had also been hied off, Cafiero said it was "like trying to survive after a 38 percent cut in our domestic car market." Another indication came from surveys that projected Chrysler would be flat out of money in three to eight years.

In August, the firm's Supplemental Unemployment Benefit fund (for workers with less than 10 years seniority) ran out, milked dry by the 27,600 layoffs made since the beginning of the year. Chrysler had lost $205 million in 1978. For 1979 the loss would be a staggering $1.1 billion. Inflation was now pushing interest rates to

unbelievable levels, which put a big damper on all new car purchases, yet Chrysler was the only U.S. producer to lose money this year. Its share of the market now stood at under 10 percent.

With income greatly reduced and shrinking ever faster, the company now found itself woefully short of money at a time when it urgently needed to develop new engines and drivetrains. Riccardo hoped to convert all the company's models to front-wheel drive by 1985-86, yet designers and engineers could not afford to experiment because waste could not be tolerated. Inexorable government regulations, requiring Chrysler to spend hundreds

Plymouth's new Horizon TC3 hatchback coupe for 1979

1979 Plymouth Horizon TC3 hatchback coupe with roof rack

1979 Plymouth Horizon hatchback sedan. Base price: $4469.

1979 Plymouth Volare coupe with Duster option group

1979 Plymouth Horizon hatchback sedan in two-tone trim

of millions to meet fixed deadlines for emission and safety standards, had to be amortized over relatively few cars compared to GM and Ford. Studies indicated the firm's costs for government regulations were $200 to $300 more per car than GM's and that average unit interest costs were $125 against GM's $10. "Chrysler has no choice but to seek temporary assistance," Riccardo said in 1979. As early as the spring of this year, he claimed the company needed $1 billion in advance tax credits and an immediate injection of $750 million in operating capital.

President Jimmy Carter had a facile answer to all this, which amounted to "Heal Thyself." The government would approach Chrysler's financial problems "very cautiously," he said. Aid, if any, would be minimal, confined to possible guarantees for loans made by private

sources. Earlier, Secretary of Transportation Brock Adams had blithely told the stricken industry to "reinvent the automobile." Carter said Chrysler's troubles were its own doing and suggested that its management be "reconstituted" to build more fuel-efficient cars.

The entire domestic auto industry was beset by the problems Chrysler cited. They were only more evident at Highland Park because of Chrysler's weaker volume position. Carter's own inflationary policies had caused the credit squeeze. Congress after Congress had imposed unbending regulations, requiring a company to spend so many dollars per year in order to comply with safety and emissions targets regardless of market conditions and under unyielding time schedules. According to the Bureau of Labor Statistics, these mandates added $593

1979 Plymouth Volare Premier five-door wagon

1979 Plymouth Volare wagon with Sport Wagon package

1979 Plymouth Volare coupe with Road Runner option

1979 Plymouth Champ, a new front-drive Mitsubishi mini

1979 Plymouth Volare Road Runner. T-roof was optional.

The sprightly 2.6-liter '79 Plymouth Fire Arrow coupe

to the cost of the average new car between 1968 and 1979. Inflation doubled this added cost. Chrysler had spent $300 million just to meet the standards for 1978, which didn't even count taxes and workmen's compensation for the 10,000 employees required to institute regulatory compliance.

By government measurements, Chrysler had the best corporate average fuel economy of the Big Three in 1979. It had more models rated at 25 mpg or higher than GM, Ford, Datsun, Toyota, or Honda. And its percentage of small-car to big-car sales was the highest among the Big Three: over 87 percent of its 1979 production consisted of mid-size models or smaller. The Omni/Horizon was on the market over a year before General Motors' front-drive X-body cars.

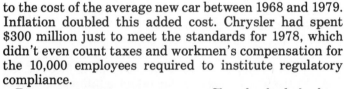

The Plymouth Volare Premier four-door sedan for 1979

Responding to Carter's criticism, Riccardo said, "We'll do whatever it takes to save this company." Nobody doubted him. But in the dismal spring of 1979, there were few around who thought of Chrysler Corporation as anything but terminal. The whole decade had been a gigantic game of Shoots and Ladders for Highland Park. Again and again it had been up the ladder, down the shoot. This time it looked as if Chrysler was on a shoot with no bottom.

1980

Throughout the late Seventies, Chrysler Corporation attempted to stay competitive by making a number of seemingly sensible, logical, market-oriented product decisions. Yet the company ended the decade with insurmountable financial problems. It asked the government for assistance, but the response was not encouraging, bureaucrats charging that the company had caused its own problems.

Obviously, many of Chrysler's woes were the result of outside factors. Yet there is no doubt that management had consistently displayed horrendously bad timing. Whether by plan or accident, Chrysler always seemed to be introducing the right cars at the wrong time. The L-body Omni/Horizon would have been splendid had it appeared in 1974, and it literally kept the company afloat in 1979. But when it first appeared in early 1978, people

The downsized 1980 Chrysler Cordoba. Crown model is shown.

1980 Chrysler Cordoba coupe. Base price: $6978.

Chrysler LeBaron Fifth Avenue sedan from mid-1980

Mid-1980 Chrysler New Yorker Fifth Avenue Limited Edition

1980 Chrysler New Yorker Fifth Avenue sedan

were still on the big-car binge to which they'd returned about mid-1975. The M-body LeBaron/Diplomat would have been fine in model year 1975, to compete with the new Ford Granada. But by 1977, it was simply another Mercedes look-alike. Chrysler delayed too long in replacing the Valiant/Dart and in thinning its wide full-size Plymouth and Dodge lineups. The company also allowed too much grass to grow under its managerial feet, hindering efficiency and smooth communications between major operating departments—as Lee Iacocca soon found out.

On November 2, 1978, the Detroit *Free Press* carried twin banner headlines that, together, had great irony: CHRYSLER LOSSES ARE WORST EVER...LEE IACOCCA JOINS CHRYSLER. "Great timing!" Iacocca would later write in his autobiography. "The day I came aboard, the company had announced a third-quarter loss of almost $160 million."

Long before he joined **Chrysler**, Lido Anthony Iacocca had acquired the enviable status of a living legend. The rarest of combinations in his age, he was both a businessman and a national hero. Born of Italian immigrants in 1924, Iacocca had risen with supersonic rapidity to become a Ford Motor Company vice-president at the age of only 35. Of course, he'd had a flying start. His father, Nicola, had settled in Allentown, Pennsylvania, where he built a Ford rental agency from scratch. It soon became the largest one in the area. Later, the elder Iacocca had expanded into real estate, and before the Depression the family's holdings had reached a net worth of over $1 million—a fortune they managed to keep mostly intact through those hard times.

Lee Iacocca breezed through high school with excellent grades, received his bachelor's degree from Lehigh and, on a scholarship, a master's in mechanical engineering from Princeton. Because of his father's influence, he had always wanted to work for Ford, so he whizzed through an 18-month company marketing course and then took a job in a small Ford sales outpost in Pennsylvania. Climbing the ladders at various regional sales offices, he came to the attention of Ford Division general manager Robert S. McNamara in 1956 through a successful promotion plan, "$56 a month for a 1956 Ford." McNamara applied Iacocca's strategy nationwide, and said it helped sell an additional 72,000 cars. From there, promotions came quickly as the cigar-puffing Iacocca boosted sales of any car or truck he ever touched.

Lee Iacocca had the habit of keeping little black books that he used to chart and plan his career. At one point he noted that by age 35 he intended to become a Ford vice-president. His 35th birthday came and went without the planned promotion. Later, he told a *Newsweek* magazine reporter that he was so disappointed that he thought to himself, "Hell, that's the end." But 18 days later he was called in by Henry Ford II and offered the vice-presidency of Ford Division. One year later, in 1960, Iacocca replaced McNamara as division chief.

Another entry in one of Iacocca's black books concerned a car he wanted to build. It would appeal primarily to young Americans, be small and sporty, and offer sharp looks and ample performance at a low price. It arrived in the spring of 1964 and went on to become the most successful single new model in industry history: the Ford Mustang. Largely on the strength of this dazzling feat, Henry Ford II named Iacocca president of Ford Motor Company in 1970.

As president, Iacocca gave Ford eight of its most profitable years, with fast-selling products like the new-generation Mustang II, the plush Ford Granada/Mercury Monarch, the big T-Birds and Continental Mark IV/V, and the German-made subcompact Fiesta. But in the end, he was just too successful, too popular to keep his job—particularly working for a strong personality like HF II. The outcome was inevitable: Henry told Iacocca to go. When Iacocca pressed him for the reason on July 13, 1978, all Henry would say is, "Well, sometimes you just don't like somebody." Later a Ford "family spokesman" said Iacocca had "lacked grace," was too "pushy," and that "the son of an immigrant born in Allentown, Pennsylvania, is a long way from Grosse Pointe." Iacocca thought that about said it all. But after back-to-back years of $1.8 billion profit for Ford, his firing was a case of bad timing that will forever haunt his old employers, especially in view of what would happen later.

Though he had been unceremoniously kicked out of the "Glass House," Iacocca was already too much of a folk hero for people to feel sorry for him. Instead, they speculated on what glittering prize he'd go after next. Suggestions ran right up to high political office, including President of the United States. But Iacocca wouldn't have it. He was still an automobile man, even though he'd never worked for anyone but Ford. John Riccardo and others in Highland Park wanted him badly, and had feelers out to him by the end of July 1978. On November 2 they made it official: Iacocca would be the new president of Chrysler Corporation. He was also to succeed Riccardo as chairman and chief executive officer on January 1, 1980. As it happened, Riccardo resigned in September 1979, and all Detroit saluted "Chairman Lee."

"What I found at Chrysler was a state of anarchy," Iacocca later wrote. "There were 35 vice-presidents, each with his own turf. There was no real committee setup, no cement in the organizational chart, no system of meetings to get people talking to each other. I couldn't believe, for example, that the guy running the engineering department wasn't in constant touch with his counterpart in Manufacturing. I took one look at the system and I almost threw up. That's when I knew I was in really deep trouble."

By February 1979, Iacocca realized Chrysler was running out of cash. He was thunderstruck: "Chrysler had no overall system of financial controls—nobody in the whole place seemed to fully understand what was going on when it came to financial planning and projecting. I couldn't find out *anything*. This was probably the greatest jolt I've ever had in my business career. I already knew about the lousy cars, the bad morale, and the deteriorating factories. But I simply had no idea that I wouldn't even be able to get hold of the right numbers so that we could begin to attack some basic problems.

"Over a three-year period I had to fire 33 out of the 35 vice-presidents. That's one a month!...I learned that Chrysler was in urgent need of first-rate financial people." Iacocca went back to his black notebooks,

The 1980 Chrysler Newport sedan listed at $7247 basic.

Mid-1980 Chrysler LeBaron Fifth Avenue Limited Edition sedan

Mid-1980 Chrysler LeBaron Fifth Avenue Limited Edition sedan

1980 Chrysler LeBaron Medallion sedan. Base price: $7329.

Chrysler's 1980 LeBaron Town & Country wagon: $7324.

The 1980 Chrysler LeBaron LS coupe was a one-year-only variation on the M-body.

wherein he'd tracked the careers of several hundred Ford executives. He proceeded to hire some out of retirement, coaxed others away from his former employer, and put the best brains he could find to work on improving quality and tightening controls on purchasing. Dealers and suppliers were given strong commitments of support.

Duplication was eliminated, expenses were cut, white- and blue-collar workers were fired in droves. Costs were reduced by $500 million, and the company's breakeven point in unit volume was cut by more than half. The United Auto Workers Union agreed its Chrysler workers would forego scheduled pay hikes and cost-of-living

1980 Chrysler LeBaron LS coupe

Dodge's 1980 Aspen Special Edition coupe

1980 Chrysler LeBaron Salon coupe, base priced at $6643

1980 Dodge Aspen Special Edition five-door wagon

increases to work for less than their GM and Ford counterparts. Riccardo had recently abandoned a separate Dodge and Chrysler-Plymouth divisional structure to try to economize. While the divisions would not formally return under Iacocca, separate Dodge and Chrysler-Plymouth district and zone sales managers were appointed in order to build a more competitive marketing and distribution organization.

Iacocca was just beginning to get a grip on the situation when the bottom dropped out of the market. The Shah of Iran was deposed in January 1979, which precipitated another round of big OPEC price increases that sent gasoline prices heading upward once more. Buyers again completely reversed themselves, switching from big cars back around to compacts. "In a period of five months in 1979, the small-car share of the market rose from 43 percent to nearly 58 percent," wrote Iacocca. "Never before in the history of the auto business had there been such a violent change...." Chrysler was building nothing larger than intermediates by 1979, but even they were too large to find many takers now, and the recreational vehicle (RV) market now dropped by half.

It is important to note that Chrysler didn't immediately turn to the government for a "bailout." Riccardo's first approach to Washington was a request for a two-year freeze on government regulations, so the industry could spend its money on tooling for smaller models to meet the sudden shift in buyer demands from which the Japanese were reaping huge profits and becoming an increasingly competitive threat. He got nowhere. Neither did a suggestion that U.S. antitrust laws be revised to allow the several Detroit producers to pool technology for meeting safety and emissions regulations, as in Japan. By midsummer, Riccardo and Iacocca had decided to ask for government loan guarantees. Iacocca said that it was the only way out but "...the last thing in the world I wanted to do. Ideologically, I've always been a free enterpriser, a believer in survival of the fittest. Once the decision was made, however, I went at it with all flags flying."

Iacocca believes the turning point in his loan guarantee campaign came on August 6, 1979, when G. William Miller left as chairman of the Federal Reserve to become Jimmy Carter's Treasury Secretary. Previously, Miller had told Riccardo that Chrysler should file for bankruptcy. Now he said the Administration would consider loan guarantees if Chrysler would submit a survival plan. Iacocca had one prepared in three months. Calling for $13.6 billion in spending, it was presented before all 535 members of Congress during the second week of December, complete with an unprecedented preview of Chrysler's proposed new models. "Here is the future of Chrysler," Iacocca proclaimed. "A 'yes' vote puts them into production in less than 10 months."

The five-year survival plan was not only ambitious but represented a revolutionary change in the shape of Chrysler products. For 1981: the "K-car," a front-wheel-drive compact to replace Aspen/Volare, comparable in size to the recently released GM X-body but more conventionally styled and including a compact station wagon that GM didn't offer. First-year production would be 600,000 units, all with four-cylinder engines. Also, a revived

Imperial, a high-profit personal-luxury coupe. For 1982: a higher-priced luxury version of the K-car, with Chrysler/Dodge rather than Dodge/Plymouth nameplates. Also designed for high profit margins, it would be built at Lynch Road in place of the R-body New Yorker/Newport/St. Regis. For 1983: a restyled LeBaron/Diplomat with an upmarket derivative likely called New Yorker, plus an in-house five-speed manual gearbox, a small front-drive pickup truck, and a possible diesel conversion of the Slant Six. For 1984: a front-drive M-body replacement on a shorter wheelbase, and a new sports car based on the K-body platform. For 1985: more body styles for selected front-drive model lines. Plans beyond 1985 were not firm, but included replacing Omni/Horizon with a smaller suc-

The Diplomat S-type coupe, a sporty 1980 mid-size Dodge

1980 Dodge Diplomat Salon five-door wagon

Family-oriented: 1980 Dodge Diplomat four-door sedan

cessor, a possible V-6, an all-new "H-car" in 1987, and another new LeBaron/Diplomat/New Yorker range in 1990.

Iacocca knew such an ambitious program would never fly if he didn't back it up personally. "Testifying before Congressional and Senate committees has never been my idea of fun and games," he wrote later. "But if we had even the slightest chance of getting Congress to approve the loan guarantees, I knew I would have to appear in person...Hour after hour I had to sit in the box and go on trial for all of Chrysler's so-called sins of management—both real and imagined. We were scolded for not having the foresight of the clever Japanese to build cars that get 30 mpg, even though American consumers had continually demanded bigger cars. We were lectured for not being prepared for the overthrow of the Shah of Iran. I had to point out that neither Carter, [former Secretary of State Henry] Kissinger, [Chase Manhattan Bank president] David Rockefeller, nor the State Department had anticipated that event."

Just about everybody came out against the Chrysler proposal, including GM chairman Thomas A. Murphy and most of the financial community. "For most of them," Iacocca wrote, "federal help for Chrysler constituted a sacrilege, a heresy, repudiation of the religion of corporate America. And other assorted bullshit!"

Iacocca and Riccardo fought back with double-page signed ads in automotive and general media: "Would America be better off without Chrysler?" they asked. Then they answered, "NO," stressing the 140,000 employees and 600,000 related jobs that would be lost, the decrease in domestic market competition, the recent Chrysler record of building more fuel-efficient cars, and the enormous sacrifices that they had already made to keep going. They also pointed to precedents: loan guarantees to Lockheed, five major steel companies, and the cities of New York and Washington—some $409 billion worth, they said, against Chrysler's own piddling billion. "We were a microcosm of what was going wrong in America and a kind of test lab for everybody else," Iacocca said. "Help now...or we can't continue." Chrysler won just before Christmas. It was some kind of present!

As ironed out between House and Senate conferees, the Chrysler survival package provided $3.5 billion in aid, including $1.5 billion in Federal loan guarantees. However, it required $475 million in wage concessions from the UAW and $125 million from management. In addition, Chrysler would issue $150 million in new shares under an employee stock ownership plan, and had to raise an additional $2 billion from the private sector to qualify for federal loan backing. The bill was passed 54-43 by the

1980 Dodge Omni 024 hatchback coupe with De Tomaso option

1980 Dodge Omni hatchback sedan. Base price: $5681.

New Cordoba-based Mirada replaced the Dodge Magnum/Charger for 1980. It's shown with the optional CMX package.

Senate and 271-136 by the House with only minor alterations. It is worth noting that the Lockheed aid package passed the House by only three votes, and aid to New York City by a mere 10.

The 1980 model year was already on when Congress approved the loan guarantee package, so this season's Chrysler Corporation cars were naturally not affected by it. In the main, new-model developments were what one would expect: more choices in those product lines that were selling, fewer in those that weren't.

The big Chrysler news for 1980 was a smaller second-generation Cordoba. Actually, this was a very heavily restyled LeBaron/Diplomat coupe, built on the M-body's 112.7-inch wheelbase and using many of its underbody panels. The camouflage job was a necessary expedient given Chrysler's cash-poor position in the late Seventies, but it turned out well. The familiar long-hood/short-deck proportions were retained, but with crisper body lines that imparted a more formal, almost razor-edge look.

Dimensional changes were significant and welcome. Compared to the first-generation design, the new Cordoba was some six inches shorter and more than four inches narrower overall, and curb weight was down by a useful 350 pounds. This made it possible to list the 225-cid Slant Six as the standard powerplant, with the trusty 318 V-8 still around for optional duty.

Several trim permutations were offered, distinguished mainly by roof treatment and interior trim grade. The most luxurious was the Crown Corinthian Edition, which must have pleased Ricardo Montalban after all his TV commercials extolling the previous Cordoba's "fine Corinthian leather." Though still available only as a coupe, the new Cordoba could be made to look like a convertible with the top raised by ordering the "cabriolet" option, a canvas-like material that covered the triangular C-pillar windows as well as the normal roof.

As before, Dodge continued to sell a Cordoba clone. This year's edition doubled as a replacement for the slow-selling Magnum XE, which along with the old Cordoba was all that had remained of the company's once-broad intermediate offerings. Called Mirada, it shared the new Cordoba's chiseled body but looked somewhat racier, thanks to a Magnum-style sloped nose with a simple horizontal-bar grille. Like its cousin, Mirada used large single rectangular headlamps instead of duals and shared a swept-away instrument panel borrowed from the R-body sedans. There were fewer exterior appearance options, so Mirada wasn't as busy as the Chrysler. It looked best perhaps with the CMX package, which added discreet bodyside tape stripes, handsome 10-spoke forged aluminum wheels and—regrettably—a chrome wrapover roof band. Mechanical specifications and equipment paralleled Cordoba's, of course. It was a striking car that earned praise from "buff book" editors not only for good looks but for good performance too. And the Mirada was surprisingly brisk with the optional 185-bhp 360-cid V-8.

Altogether, Dodge retailed close to 33,000 Miradas. The new Cordoba did even better at nearly 54,000. However, this was not the sort of volume Chrysler really needed despite the cars' hefty profit margins.

The R-body sedans didn't provide much help. The Chrysler Newport/New Yorker returned with only minor

1980 Dodge Mirada coupe in standard form: $6850.

Slow-selling Dodge St. Regis was little changed for 1980.

1980 Plymouth Horizon TC3 hatchback coupe: $5681 basic.

styling changes to record a disappointing 28,574 deliveries, against nearly 133,000 for '79. The Dodge St. Regis, likewise little changed, saw only 17,000 sales. An interesting development was the return of the Gran Fury name for an R-body Plymouth, which was hard to distinguish from the Newport. Sales totalled about 18,600, most of them to fleet customers, which was the intended market anyway. All this must have vexed company product planners as they watched Ford and GM do far better with their downsized big cars.

Among Chrysler's higher-volume lines, the M-body LeBaron/Diplomat was effectively facelifted with blockier rear rooflines on sedans and coupes, more sharply creased front and rear fenderlines, and bolder grilles. With the arrival of the new Cordoba/Mirada, the M-body two-doors adopted the shorter 108.7-inch wheelbase of the Aspen/Volare coupes, which gave them a more closely coupled appearance. Chrysler tried to sell them as semi-GTs by offering specially trimmed Diplomat S-type and LeBaron LS coupes with fancy wheels and bucket seats, but buyers much preferred the workaday sedans and

1980 Plymouth Horizon hatchback sedan listed at $5526.

Plymouth mainstay: the 1980 Horizon hatchback sedan

The revived 1980 Gran Fury was a Plymouth R-body variation.

1980 Plymouth Volare coupe with Duster option group

1980 Plymouth Volare Premier five-door wagon

End of the line: Plymouth's 1980 Volare premier coupe

wagons. Overall, LeBaron/Diplomat finished the year with production well down on 1979 levels, perhaps reflecting public wariness over Chrysler's worsening financial situation and the possibility of being stuck with an "orphan."

The L-body Omni/Horizon and their 024/TC3 coupe derivatives again accounted for the lion's share of Dodge and Plymouth sales in 1980. There was no money available for substantial design alterations, but none were really needed. The emphasis at each division was now on options and merchandising, including "a wide array of dress-up packages for economy-minded families and weekend rallyists to customize...to their tastes and needs." While families were no doubt satisfied with the plain-Jane models, the company catered to enthusiasts with a new package option for each L-coupe. The more tasteful was the Turismo, which added bright monotone

paint and black window moldings to the TC3, plus cast-aluminum wheels carrying larger steel-belted radial tires. Dodge's offering was the De Tomaso, named for Italian magnate Alessandro de Tomaso of Pantera and Mangusta fame. This got you an 024 with shocking red or yellow paint set off by black-finished rocker panels, rear spoiler, and vertical louvers over the rear side windows. It also included beefier springs and shocks and extra-wide Aramid-belted tires on ornate cast-aluminum wheels, plus a leather-covered shift knob and steering wheel and an upper-windshield "sun band" emblazoned with the De Tomaso name. Sad to say, no more horsepower came with it.

With their front-drive K-car successors waiting in the wings, the compact Dodge Aspen and Plymouth Volare came in for only minor styling changes in this, their final year. The main one was a full-width grille with a single rectangular headlamp at each end. The same three body styles were available as usual, along with the customary option packages. Plymouth revived the Duster name this year for a specially outfitted coupe, and Dodge continued its interesting Sport Wagon equipment group from '79, consisting of a front air dam, wheel arch flares, bucket seats, exterior tape striping, and styled road wheels.

In 1957, one of the glory years for what Iacocca now called the "old" Chrysler Corporation, there were 18 U.S. makes vying in the annual production race. Chrysler had five of them, holding third, seventh, 10th, 11th, and 15th places. Of the 12 makes still around in 1980, Chrysler had three, ranking seventh, eighth, and 11th. Dodge, again outselling Plymouth, was the corporation's top seller this year, at 308,638 units for the model year. These figures painted a pretty grim picture: 1980 was the worst year in the history of the American automobile industry, and Chrysler lost $1.7 billion.

Never mind, said Iacocca. Chrysler had turned the corner. If it hadn't, at least it had been given a reprieve. Less than a year after the loan guarantees were approved, the new K-cars appeared in dealer showrooms. It was a dramatic moment that Walter P. Chrysler himself would have appreciated, for with them rode the future of his company.

1981

Few new models have been more openly or thoroughly previewed than the K-cars. Virtually every important styling and engineering feature of Chrysler Corporation's vital new front-drive compacts was known almost a year before the formal announcement date. When the public got its first look at them, the Ks had been seen so much in newspapers and magazines that they almost seemed like last year's models. One can only wonder what would have happened to the Airflow under such circumstances.

Yet the massive, detailed pre-announcement publicity was inevitable and painfully necessary. Company president Lee Iacocca had been forced to show the K-car, as well as more advanced new-model plans, in open Congressional hearings in order to win approval for the federal loan guarantees without which production would not have been possible. Soon everyone knew Chrysler had staked its near-term future on public acceptance of the K-car, so the new model naturally became a part of the drama surrounding the company's touch-and-go existence in the summer and autumn of 1979.

This was Chrysler Corporation's darkest hour, though that "hour" was actually about 12 agonizing months long. The press, ever quick to recognize a good story, played up Chrysler's travails for all their worth. As a result, the K-car's actual appearance in dealer showrooms seemed almost anticlimactic. One newspaper may have inadvertently given a clue as to how the big event was viewed by many reporters, and also managed to poke fun

1981 Chrysler Cordoba Crown coupe with Special Edition roof

Imperial returned for '81 as this personal-luxury coupe.

The 1981 Imperial carried an $18,300 price tag.

1981 Chrysler LeBaron Medallion sedan. Price: $7656.

1981 Chrysler LeBaron Medallion four-door sedan

at the general high level of media hype about Chrysler's problems over the preceeding months. It came in the form of a caption to a widely circulated wire service photo that showed a smiling Iacocca standing beside the first K-car off the assembly line. Read the cheeky copy: "And if this one sells, we're gonna build another one right away."

The K-cars got off to a poor sales start despite all the ballyhoo and, considering how much was riding on them, this fact did not exactly go unreported. Neither did it go unnoticed among Chrysler's employees, suppliers, and bankers, and it must have given more than a moment's pause to a lot of folks in Washington. Iacocca said it was because "we had some unexpected problems with our new robotic welders in the factories, which led to production snags. And the sticker price was too high at first because we built cars [for initial delivery] with more options than buyers wanted to pay for." Fortunately for Chrysler, the K-cars stumbled only briefly. In just a few months they were, by all accounts, a solid success, just what Chrysler had needed—and had promised to deliver as its part of the bargain with the government. You could almost hear the collective sigh of relief in Highland Park.

The new models arrived with singularly appropriate names. Plymouth's version was called Reliant, which had the same noble ring as Valiant. Aries was a good choice for Dodge, the name for the zodiac sign of the ram, thus harking back to the days of the famous Red Ram V-8. Per long-standing company practice, the K-cars were divi-

sional duplicates, sharing the same square-cut styling and a trio of body styles. Two- and four-door notchback sedans and a five-door wagon were offered in Custom and spiffier Special Edition trim levels under each nameplate. The only major styling difference was in the grilles: a body-color horizontal-bar affair for Aries (and somewhat reminiscent of the Mirada's), a formal Mercedes-like face for Reliant.

As the building block for a new fleet of Chrysler Corporation products, the K-car's technical makeup merits more than a passing glance. None of it was truly innovative, but it was well-executed. The base engine, for example, was the company's first four-cylinder unit since the early Thirties. Dubbed "Trans-4" because of its transverse mounting, it was a newly designed overhead-cam powerplant with an aluminum cylinder head, cast-iron block, and—shades of the Fifties—hemispherical combustion chambers. Displacement was 2.2 liters (135 cubic inches), a little smaller than GM's and Ford's smallest powerplants but markedly larger than the engines in most small-capacity imports. In its initial form, the slightly undersquare 2.2 (bore and stroke 3.44×3.62 in.) was rated at 84 horsepower at 4800 rpm and 111 lbs/ft torque peaking at 2800 rpm, with a single two-barrel carburetor and mild 8.5:1 compression. Chrysler claimed the 2.2 had been subjected to more test miles than any other engine in its history, and that work would pay off in what would prove to be high durability and reliability. The only engine option was the Mitsubishi

1981 Chrysler LeBaron Town & Country wagon: $7740.

1981 Chrysler LeBaron Salon coupe

The Chrysler LeBaron Town & Country wagon for 1981

Base price on the '81 Chrysler LeBaron Salon coupe was $7017.

1981 Chrysler New Yorker Fifth Avenue Edition sedan

2.6-liter "Silent Shaft" four familiar from the Challenger/ Sapporo coupes. It was available only with three-speed TorqueFlite automatic, which was optional for the 2.2. Standard gearbox was a four-speed overdrive manual with floorshift.

K-car chassis engineering followed typical small-car practice. Construction, of course, was unitized for strength and light weight. The suspension consisted of MacPherson struts, lower A-arms, coil springs, and an anti-roll in front, and a flexible beam rear axle located by trailing arms and suspended on coils. Rack-and-pinion steering was chosen for its inherently greater precision and superior road feedback. Brakes were the by-now

expected front discs and rear drums, with standard vacuum assist.

At 99.6 inches, the K-cars were about five inches shorter between wheel centers than GM's competing X-body models, yet overall length was about the same. Because of the shorter wheelbase, the Aries/Reliant gave away some interior space to their GM rivals, but the differences weren't great. Handling was evenly matched too, though the Ks weren't as sporting even with their heavy-duty suspension compared to the more firmly suspended Xs. However, the K-cars had a clear edge in driving position and perhaps ride. More importantly, they would soon prove much more reliable than the GM products, which suffered the indignity of displacing the old Aspen/Volare as the most recalled cars in the industry.

Iacocca was right about sticker prices. Though the Aries/Reliant was advertised at under $6000 basic (pricing was identical regardless of nameplate), too many of the first cars carried heavy option loads that pushed that to well over $8000, which seemed shockingly expensive for a domestic small car. It is to Chrysler's credit that it got properly optioned cars out to customers as quickly as it did.

The result was a brilliant sales performance. For the model year, Reliant sold nearly 230,000 copies—better than half of Plymouth's total and more than any other single model line in the Chrysler fleet—and Dodge built over 180,000 Aries. While this wasn't the predicted 600,000 units, it was a lot better than some people

Fifth Avenue Edition package added $1535 to the '81 Chrysler New Yorker's $10,343 base price.

1981 Chrysler Newport four-door sedan: $7546.

1981 Chrysler Newport four-door sedan

The vital front-drive Dodge Aries for 1981. Special Edition wagon shown had a $7102 base price.

The $6192 Dodge Aries Custom coupe for 1981

1981 Dodge Aries Custom four-door sedan: $6325.

1981 Dodge Diplomat Medallion four-door sedan

'81 Dodge Diplomat Medallion sedan listed at $7542.

expected. By contrast, corresponding figures for the last Volare/Aspen were 110,000 and 85,000, respectively.

The subcompact Omni/Horizon continued to do well in 1981's depressed market despite few changes. Grille inserts were revised for the first time, and five-doors were now available with a new "Euro-Sedan" package option. This consisted of upgraded interior trim, extra instruments (the Rallye cluster from the 024/TC3 coupes), stiffer suspension, cast-aluminum wheels, stickier tires, and black-painted greenhouse moldings. The L-body coupes returned much as before, with a revised Turismo package for the TC3 and a less gaudy De Tomaso group for the 024. During the model year, the K-car 2.2 was phased in as an option for any L-body, and it did wonders for both the performance and refinement of the subcompact.

The full-size R-body might well have disappeared this year had it not been for pleas from fleet sales executives to keep them in producton, so the Plymouth Gran Fury,

1981 Dodge Diplomat Salon coupe with two-tone paint

Dodge's 1981 Diplomat Salon five-door wagon: $7407.

1981 Dodge Diplomat Salon coupe. Base price: $6919.

1981 Dodge Omni hatchback sedan retailed at $6018.

Charger 2.2 version of the Dodge Omni 024 was a mid-1981 release. Note reverse hood scoop and rear spoiler.

Dodge St. Regis, and Chrysler's Newport/New Yorker came back, minimally altered, of course. The only changes worth mentioning were different grille textures on the Chryslers and a high-bucks package option for the New Yorker. Called Fifth Avenue, it added about $1500 to the base price and included every extra in the Chrysler book save aluminum road wheels, a "carriage" roof treatment, and power sliding sunroof. Gas prices were still high, so the market for these cars still wasn't there.

Newport/New Yorker did about 13,000 sales, as did the Gran Fury. Dodge managed to move only about 16,000 St. Regis cars.

With most of the company's resources diverted to the K-cars, the mid-size LeBaron/Diplomat (for marketing purposes they were now considered intermediates) and the personal-luxury Cordoba/Mirada were virtual 1980 carryovers. The Mirada picked up Cordoba's convertible-look cabriolet roof, and a second Cordoba model was add-

1981 Dodge Omni 024 hatchback coupe. Base price: $6197.

Dodge's 1981 Mirada CMX coupe with "cabriolet" roof

1981 Dodge St. Regis sedan. Base price was now $7435.

Plymouth's 1981 Gran Fury sedan listed at $7181 basic.

1981 Plymouth Gran Fury sedan: fleet market favorite

ed, the LS, with less exterior gingerbread and a letter-series 300-style cross-bar grille as its main distinctions.

There was one other splash, of sorts, from Chrysler for 1981: Iacocca's promised revival of the Imperial. Coming from a company in such dire straights, there was, predictably, much less here than met the eye. Marketed as a fully equipped "one-price" car—at an eye-opening $18,300—the new model was available only as a two-door coupe derived from the Cordoba/Mirada, which in turn had originated with the LeBaron/Diplomat and, before that, the humble Aspen/Volare. The front suspension employed the same, curious transverse torsion bars, while the back end had an ordinary live axle suspended on simple leaf springs. However, Imperial did have an exclusive in the engine compartment: a new fuel-injected version of the venerable 318 V-8, with a mild 8.5:1 compression and a modest 140 horsepower at 4000 rpm.

Company publicists tried to capitalize on the downsizing craze by pointing out how much smaller the new Imperial was than the last 1975 model. Indeed, it was: wheelbase was about a foot shorter, overall length nearly 20 inches less. Still, the '81 weighed nearly two tons at the curb, so neither its performance nor fuel economy (16 mpg) were exceptional even for the heavyweight class, and its road manners were boring.

If the new Imperial was deadly conventional, at least it was lavishly equipped. The initial base price included clearcoat paint, Mark Cross leather or rich cloth upholstery, electronic instrumentation with digital readouts, full power, and the customer's choice of stereo system and steel-belted radial tires. The only option listed was power sunroof, at a hefty $1044. All Imperials were built at Chrysler's Windsor, Ontario facility, and special measures were taken to insure quality comparable with the world's best. Each car was subjected to a series of checks at a special factory Quality Assurance Center, plus a 5.5-mile road test and a final polish before shipment. Chrysler even boasted that first-year production would be limited to "just" 25,000 units to insure good build quality—not to mention adding an extra dash of snob appeal.

Despite all this, the reborn Imperial got lost in the urgency of Chrysler's well-publicized financial predicament and the importance of the K-car launch. There was precious little money to promote the new flagship, though singer Frank Sinatra, in a gesture to his friend Iacocca, helped by appearing in TV commercials. Apparently, potential buyers were either tuned to other channels or didn't realize Chrysler was back in the luxury market, because the car landed with a sickening thud: just 7225 sales for the entire model year. "It's Time for Imperial," blared the ads, but this car had been put in motion by the "old" Chrysler Corporation, and it arrived at anything but the right time.

Still, it had handsome styling, dominated by a classic vertical grille emphasized by hidden headlamps. The design's most unfortunate aspect was another version of that Classic-era throwback, the "bustle" trunk, which stuck out a country mile and disrupted the roof's natural downward line. Chrysler couldn't have copied this feature from Cadillac, which had used a similar treatment on its

The '81 Plymouth Horizon five-door sported a new grille.

Plymouth's 1981 Reliant Special Edition five-door wagon

1981 Plymouth TC3 hatchback coupe with Turismo package

1981 Plymouth Reliant Special Edition wagon: $7102.

1981 Plymouth TC3 Turismo hatchback coupe

1981 Plymouth Reliant Custom coupe with vinyl roof

1981 Plymouth Reliant Custom four-door sedan: $6325.

Plymouth's 1981 Reliant Custom coupe. Base price: $6192.

second-generation front-drive Seville sedan only the year before, but some people thought Imperial's tail actually looked better.

All things considered, 1981 was Chrysler Corporation's most hopeful year in a long time. Strong Reliant sales enabled Plymouth to reestablish its production supremacy over Dodge, building close to 400,000 units against 340,000 for its sister division. The K-car was a winner—a good thing, as derivatives were set to appear the next year—and the L-bodies were holding their own.

But offsetting these strong entries were too many backmarker models: the R-body sedans, the Cordoba/Mirada, and now the Imperial. Chrysler could only hope for an upturn in the market—or an easing of interest rates, which amounted to the same thing—to give it the time it had to have to get its corporate house in order. Chrysler had been pulled back from the brink, but its troubles were far from over.

1982

Highland Park continued its quest for stability and profits with a reorganized 1982 lineup, led by the promised luxury versions of the successful K-cars. This year's emphasis continued to be on smaller, front-drive replacements for old models. The languishing R-body sedans were quietly put to rest along with the rear-drive M-body coupes and wagons. The remaining M-body four-doors now assumed "full-size" status, while the company's nominal entries in the mid-size field for '82 were the new CV-series Chrysler LeBaron and Dodge 400.

Despite the different platform designation, the new LeBaron/400 was essentially a plusher, restyled K-car, sharing structure, major dimensions, drivetrains, even instrument panels with the less expensive Aries/Reliant. However, the new cars were slightly longer overall and far more deluxe. The LeBaron sported an Imperial-like

vertical grille, the 400 a Mirada-style horizontal-bar grille done in body color. Body styles for LeBaron were initially confined to the opera-windowed K-coupe/sedan and a four-door sedan with blanked-off rear door windows, while the 400 came only in two-door form. Later in the year, a LeBaron Town & Country wagon with plastic-wood side trim appeared, together with a four-door 400 (Dodge promised a 400 station wagon, too, but it never materialized). The K-car suspension was retuned for LeBaron/400, interior appointments were several cuts above Aries/Reliant furnishings, and there was extra sound-deadening for greater refinement. In all, the CVs represented a nice step up from the Ks. The front-drive LeBaron provided a big boost to Chrysler volume, sales going from 43,000 of the old rear-drive type to over 100,000 of the new. Dodge completed some 34,000 of its 400s for the model year.

What had been LeBaron was now the New Yorker (the Newport name was consigned to the history file). It continued the corporate M-body platform, which was more lavishly equipped in the manner of the now-departed

1982 Chrysler Cordoba coupe. Base list price: $9197.

LS was a Chrysler Cordoba variation for '82.

The "gunsight" grille of the '82 Chrysler Cordoba LS recalled that of the famed letter-series 300s.

R-body New Yorker. Styling changes were confined to a starchier grille, blind-quarter padded vinyl roof treatment, and broader taillamps. Further down on the price and prestige scale, the M-body Dodge Diplomat four-door continued with little change from '81, and it was now joined by a look-alike Plymouth Gran Fury. Both these were fielded primarily because tooling had long been amortized and the company could accordingly make money on them, primarily in the fleet market.

Partly in response to the bumbled K-car launch, Chrysler began adding to its compacts' standard equipment without raising prices a proportional amount, thus making Aries/Reliant a more attractive value in the marketplace. Changes for '82 included a counterbalanced hood (eliminating the manual hood prop), a nicer-looking silver-and-black paint treatment to improve the 2.2 engine's underhood appearance, tighter quality control, revised carburetor "computer" and idle speed control, and a cooling fan redesigned for less noise and power drag. Options were expanded to include power front windows, a new line of electronically tuned radios, center con-

The K-based '82 Chrysler LeBaron Town & Country wagon

sole (with manual shift only), four-spoke sport steering wheel, and 14-inch cast-aluminum road wheels.

The subcompact L-body cars also got some sprucing up for '82. The Dodge 024 and Plymouth TC3 coupes were now marketed separately from the Omni/Horizon sedans. New no-frills Miser versions of each body style offered

After disappointing 1981 sales, the Imperial got an increase in base price for '82, to $20,988.

The 1982 Imperial with the $1078 "Frank Sinatra Edition" package option (also shown above).

Chrysler revived convertibles with this mid-1982 LeBaron.

1982 Chrysler LeBaron four-door sedan: $8237 basic.

1982 Chrysler LeBaron coupe. Base list price: $8143.

The $10,781 Chrysler New Yorker sedan for 1982

The front-drive LeBaron was one of Chrysler's new CV '82s.

1982 Chrysler New Yorker sedan. Note roof treatment.

simplified trim, few options (no air conditioning or power steering in particular), and the familiar VW-based 1.7-liter engine as standard. Mid-range offerings were now fitted with the Chrysler "Trans-4," and sedans carried the name Custom. All five-doors acquired new grille inserts bearing the Chrysler "Pentastar" emblem. Also new was a "European-inspired" top-line Omni/Horizon dubbed E-type, identified by blackout greenhouse trim, standard cloth-and-vinyl bucket seats, Rallye instrument cluster, a mini-console for the shift lever, and a shorter (numerically higher) final drive ratio for better off-the-line go. All coupes except for Misers acquired thicker C-pillar appliques. There were sporty variants here too, essentially continuations of previous option packages. Plymouth stayed with Turismo for its enthusiast's TC3, while Dodge brought back the Charger tag for its corresponding 024. Charger/Turismo equipment and mechanical specs roughly paralleled those of the Omni/Horizon

E-type, but the Charger 2.2 stood out from the herd with its black lower body paint, simulated air exhaust vents in the front fenders, and a non-functional reverse hood scoop boldly emblazoned with the model name. The Turismo was far more subtle. A welcome, though hardly original, new feature for all L-bodies was reclining front seatbacks, available at extra cost.

An unexpected twist on the L-body turned up at mid-model year in the form of Chrysler's first-ever car/pickup. It was initially marketed by Dodge under the Rampage label, in line with the truck division's "Ram Tough" theme. Basically, this was a hybrid combining the front sheetmetal, power package, and forward passenger compartment of the TC3/024 coupe with an integrated double-wall pickup box on an extended 104.2-inch wheelbase. The rear portion of the cab roof was unique to this vehicle (developed under the T-110 project code), with forward-sloping pillars that were smoothly faired into the

1982 Dodge Aries Special Edition sedan: $7736.

The CV-series Dodge 400 convertible, a mid-1982 entry

The '82 Dodge Aries Special Edition coupe listed at $7535.

1982 Dodge 400 LS coupe. It cost $8308 in base form.

1982 Dodge Aries Special Edition wagon. Price: $8101.

Dodge added a 400 four-door sedan at mid-model year '82.

upper box sides. Unlike most pickups, construction was unitized, not separate body-on-frame. The only change made to the coupe undercarriage for the Rampage was to substitute a simple beam rear axle on semi-elliptic leaf springs in place of the normal trailing-arm suspension.

The result was a pleasing blend of sportiness, car-like driving ease, and pickup practicality. Dodge said the Rampage "Drives Like a Car, Works Like a Truck," and indeed it did. Customers could choose from a well-equipped standard model and a racy Sport, the latter decked out just like a Charger 2.2 But though the Rampage looked like a winner, sales proved disappointing. The main problem was that small, light-duty import trucks were now satisfying whatever demand had existed for car/pickups like Ford's Ranchero and the Chevrolet El Camino. And, as Chrysler itself later admitted, most buyers thought of the Rampage as more car than truck and thus not well suited to their needs.

The personal-luxury Chrysler Cordoba/Dodge Mirada were left alone, playing out a tired hand due to their bulk, thirst, and stodgy handling characteristics. Interior trim was about the only thing that changed. The Cordoba LS was still around, if little called for by customers. Evoking strong memories of the letter-series Chrysler 300, it looked particularly handsome with the optional "cabriolet" roof covering, though that did nothing for the driver's view from inside.

Few changes were ordained for Imperial this year and for a very good reason: the car wasn't selling. The Sinatra connection was reinforced with a new "FS" edition featuring special paint and emblems, plus a set of 8-track or cassette tapes containing "Old Blue Eyes'" greatest hits, mounted in a purpose-designed center console. If nothing else, this must have been a nostalgia trip for former bobby-soxers of the late Forties. Curiously, Imperial's base price was jacked up to near $21,000—still thou-

1982 Dodge Diplomat Medallion sedan: $8799.

Dodge's handsome 1982 Mirada CMX with "cabriolet" roof

1982 Dodge Diplomat continued to find fleet buyer favor.

The 1982 Dodge Mirada CMX: a "looker" from any angle.

sands less than a comparably equipped Cadillac Eldorado or Lincoln Mark VI—but it hardly helped sales, and dealers quickly resorted to heavy discounts and other forms of "distress merchandising." Production for the model year sank to 2329 units.

Considering his great emphasis on the "new" Chrysler Corporation, it might seem curious that Lee Iacocca would want to revive any ideas from the firm's past. But he did bring back two, and they garnered a lot of publicity that benefitted sales. The more interesting one—certainly the more nostalgic—was the company's first full convertible in a dozen years. Appearing at mid-model

1982 Dodge Charger 2.2 hatchback coupe: $7115.

1982 Dodge 024 Custom hatchback coupe. Base price: $6421.

Dodge's 1982 Omni Custom hatchback sedan. Price: $5927.

1982 Dodge 024 Miser sold at a low $5799 base price.

Plymouth Gran Fury adopted the M-body platform for '82.

Plymouth's Horizon Custom hatchback sedan for '82

1982 Plymouth Gran Fury Salon sedan: $7750.

1982 Plymouth Horizon Custom retailed at $5927.

year in both Chrysler LeBaron and Dodge 400 guise, it was a stylish line-leader and a fair commercial success, though less than happy on the road. Both convertibles were actually conversions carried out on CV two-door coupes by Cars & Concepts, a specialty coachbuilder located in Brighton, Michigan. It was a competent job,

with acceptable body rigidity for a ragtop. However, the weight of the necessary structural reinforcements hampered performance (for this reason, the torquier 2.6-liter engine was standard in the convertibles) as well as braking power. Also, the convertible top had a very small rear window and very wide rear quarters, which

1982 Plymouth TC3 Turismo. Like Charger 2.2, it cost $7115.

The 1982 Miser version of Plymouth's TC3 hatchback coupe

1982 Plymouth TC3 Turismo hatchback coupe

1982 Plymouth Reliant Custom coupe. Base price: $6898.

Plymouth's '82 Reliant Custom sedan listed at $7053.

1982 Plymouth Reliant Custom four-door sedan

The '82 Plymouth Reliant wagon in Special Edition trim

made top-up visibility something of a nightmare. Nevertheless, a lot of people were drawn into Dodge and Chrysler-Plymouth showrooms by the allure of open-air motoring. And for good measure, Chrysler released a glamorous LeBaron Town & Country convertible, complete with imitation wood side panels that rekindled the spirit of the original late-Forties T&Cs.

Another revival from Chrysler's past was a brace of stretched-wheelbase front-drive limousines, which proved that there was seemingly no end to the possible permutations the firm could wring out of the K-car. Again, these were coupe conversions, good-looking, well-built, and luxuriously finished. The chief difference between them was wheelbase and interior furnishings. The Chrysler Executive Sedan rode a 124.3-inch wheelbase, while the Limousine stretched that to 131.3 inches. Powered by the 2.6-liter engine and weighing about 3000 pounds, they were Chrysler's first attempt at the "carriage trade" since the demise of the Stageway Imperial limos back in 1970. The Executive Sedan offered sumptuous seating for

five, while the Limo could hold up to seven with its auxiliary jump seats and even had an electrically operated division window between chauffeur's and passenger compartments.

For a company barely off the ropes, Chrysler was beginning to look like a survivor again. Its new K-car derivatives displayed the kind of clever, cost-minded approach to new-product development characteristic of Iacocca and his hand-picked team, precisely the approach Chrysler had to follow to assure its long-term survival. Unquestionably, 1982 was a year of pleasant surprises. And there were more to come for 1983.

1983

By the start of model year 1983, it appeared as if Chrysler Corporation was nearly out of the financial woods. The company had managed to cut its losses to $475 million for 1981, thanks largely to the K-car's timely success and chairman Lee Iacocca's drastic belt-tightening measures. The following year the firm actually recorded a net profit of $170 million, though it was achieved with great difficulty. The national economy bottomed out in 1982, and car sales were well down on even 1981's dismal pace throughout the industry. But Iacocca was determined that Chrysler should survive as an automaker, so he decided to exercise the one major life-saving option left open to him: sell the lucrative Chrysler Defense tank-making operation. He found a buyer in General Dynamics. It was a painful, "last resort" step, but necessary in order to keep the faith with company creditors—and the government.

Organizationally speaking, Chrysler Corporation was now the leanest it had ever been. Iacocca, and Riccardo before him, had disposed of money-wasting subsidiaries and dead-end projects. What remained was a car company down to fighting weight: confident, assertive and, maybe, just a bit smug at all it had achieved in the face of seemingly insurmountable odds. If Chrysler once was, as Iacocca said, a symbol of all the U.S. auto industry's problems, it had now become just as much a model for the rest of the industry to follow toward the future. And a lot of people in Highland Park took justifiable pride in that.

On the strength of the K-cars, Chrysler had been able to boost its market share back above the 10-percent level for the first time in about four years, and it held onto this slice of the pie through 1982 despite the economy's continued sluggishness. By autumn of that year, signs of a turnaround had begun to appear: interest rates had levelled off and were now trending downward slightly, and swollen gasoline stockpiles were beginning to depress prices at the pumps. Chrysler reached a watershed about a year later, at the end of 1983, when Iacocca proudly announced the highest annual profit in the company's entire history: a breathtaking $925 million. Chrysler had come a long way since the dark days of mid-1980. And through it all, the firm had never once "drawn down" on the loan guarantees for which it had fought so hard.

The Chrysler Cordoba was in its final year for 1983.

1983 Chrysler Cordoba. Base retail price was $9580.

To emphasize that salvation was complete, Iacocca had decided that Chrysler would pay back its major creditors by mid-1983—seven years ahead of schedule. The boss announced the payback on July 13, five years to the day since he'd been fired by Henry Ford II. Iacocca called that an "eerie coincidence," but we're not so sure he didn't purposely time it this way out of a sense of irony. In any case, Iacocca was widely quoted as saying that his wife used to remind him, "Don't get mad, get even." He had certainly done that, and when reporters kidded him

about taking off after Ford for the number-two position in the industry, he simply grinned like the Cheshire cat.

In making the loan payback announcement, Iacocca cleverly paraphrased an ad slogan for a well-known investment house made popular by actor/director John Houseman, who occasionally appeared in Plymouth TV commercials, too. Said the chairman: "We at Chrysler borrow money the old-fashioned way. We pay it back." Then he added: "Maybe the Surgeon General should be standing by in case anybody faints." Actually, the

The 1983 edition of the LeBaron-based Chrysler Town & Country convertible, introduced for mid-1982.

E-body E Class sedan was a new Chrysler offering for '83.

1983 Chrysler E Class sedan. Its base price was $9341.

The Chrysler LeBaron standard convertible for '83

1983 Chrysler Executive Sedan (foreground) and limo

1983 Chrysler LeBaron Town & Country wagon: $9731.

E-body front-drive Chrysler New Yorker bowed for mid-'83.

Chrysler's 1983 LeBaron coupe sold for $8514 basic.

Heavy rear quarters marked the '83 Chrysler New Yorker.

bankers were so surprised at the move that they didn't quite know how to take it. In New York City a week later, Iacocca presented them with a check for $813,487,500. For added emphasis, the check was blown up to gigantic proportions as a backdrop for the presentation, thus making this literally the biggest check Chrysler's bankers or chairman Lee had ever seen.

Speaking of commercials, Chrysler's corporate ad agency had been featuring the boss himself to promote the cars and the radically changed way of doing business at "The New Chrysler Corporation." Iacocca thought this was an unwarranted ego trip, but he let himself be talked into it. He quickly wished he hadn't, despite his undoubtedly effective on-camera delivery: "The ads wrecked my privacy," he wrote in his autobiography. "I walk a block, and there are five double-takes, six people stopping me, and seven drivers yelling out my name. It was fun for

about a week. After that, it's a pain in the ass." He said he couldn't even have dinner in a restaurant without some guy coming over to talk about his '65 Mustang or Dodge Dart "that's still running—or not running!"

Doing the commercials and appearing in print ads led to a rumor about Chrysler's CEO running for President of the United States. "I got patriotic and said, 'Let's make America mean something again,' and people identified with it," Iacocca said. "Many people now think I'm an actor. But that's ridiculous. Everybody knows that being an actor doesn't qualify you to be President..."

Whatever it was—or is—Iacocca had, by this time, become not only one of the most respected business leaders in the country but one of the few whose name was widely recognized by the general public. Chrysler's charismatic chairman insists he did nothing that any other heads-up executive wouldn't have done. But there's no denying that by the sheer force of his personality—and ideas—he had saved Chrysler's pride and heritage and, with that, its very soul. Whatever else Lee Iacocca chooses to do in life—and his career is certainly far from over at this writing—he will likely be best remembered as a kind of wizard, a corporate "Mr. Fix-It" in the dynamic mold of Walter P. Chrysler himself. He will surely be remembered with deep affection by anyone who loves cars.

Iacocca's own love of cars was clearly reflected in an even stronger corporate lineup for 1983. The year's main new-model introduction was the E-body, essentially a stretched derivative of the versatile K-car platform, riding a three-inch longer wheelbase and offered in a single four-door sedan body style with considerably more passenger space. It arrived as the Chrysler E Class and Dodge 600, divisional siblings bearing the company's now well-established four-square body lines but distinguished from the K/CV models by a "six-light" greenhouse. Make identity was served mainly at the front. E Class wore an Imperial/LeBaron-like vertical-bar grille, while the 600 had an Aries/400-style louvered opening done in body color. The 600 was available in standard and sportier ES guise, the latter frankly imitative of certain well-known German sports sedans, at least in looks, but it fit in well with Dodge's ad campaign as builder of "America's Driving Machines." Joining this trio at mid-season was an upmarket New Yorker derivative, certainly the smallest car ever to bear the name. It was set apart from the others by a wide-quarter formal roof, with the rear third heavily padded to cover the small C-pillar windows, adorned with opera lamps and a brushed-finish wrapover roof band. Small front fender louvers and a more upright E Class grille with a wider chrome header were finishing touches.

One of the nice things about a front-drive platform like the K-car is that it's much easier and less costly to spin off model variations than with a rear-drive configuration. With all the powertrain components up front, there's no driveshaft, transmission tunnel, or rear differential to worry about, which simplifies structural engineering and enables greater component sharing among variations, thus helping to hold down costs. Chrysler obviously recognized these advantages, for the E-body duplicated the K/CV in engine offerings and suspension design. However, the new models did introduce a couple of new features that showed up in their smaller siblings. For example, the Chrysler "Trans-4" 2.2-liter engine generated 10 extra horsepower in all applications this year, thanks to redesigned manifolds, recalibrated fuel/spark controls, higher compression (now 9.0:1), and a modified catalytic converter. The result was a rated 94 bhp at 5200 rpm, which beat the Mitsubishi 2.6 by a scant 1 bhp, though the larger unit still had a useful edge in torque (132 versus 117 lbs/ft) that made it the preferred choice in the somewhat heavier E-cars. TorqueFlite automatic was standard for E Class/New Yorker and the base 600, but the 600ES could be ordered with Chrysler's newly designed five-speed overdrive manual transmission. This gearbox —one of Iacocca's promises to Congress back in 1980, remember—was also an option for the Aries/Reliant K

Rear-drive reminder: 1983 Chrysler New Yorker Fifth Avenue

1983 Chrysler New Yorker Fifth Avenue. Base price: $12,487.

The 1983 Imperial. Base price fell to $18,688 this year.

1983 was the last year for the "bustleback" Imperial coupe.

and CV LeBaron/400 as well as the L-body subcompacts.

Chrysler continued to differentiate its various K-based cars with a wider selection of trim and equipment than it had been able to field previously. A notable—and controversial—example was the Electronic Voice Alert system available in E-body and LeBaron/400 models. It appeared as part of a new gauge cluster set within the familiar K-car dash, with a large, rectangular

1983

speedometer and a "Message Center" warning light system that signalled when a door was open or fuel was running low on a Honda-style outline diagram of the car. The purpose of the Electronic Voice Alert (EVA) was to supplement these visual warnings with audible ones, "spoken" through the radio speaker by a little box able to imitate a human voice. It was a good idea, monitoring 11 functions including engine conditions such as coolant temperature and oil pressure, but the execution was clumsy. For example, the system was programmed to give an "all clear" signal ("All monitored systems are functioning") whenever you started the engine *and* all doors were closed *and* all passengers buckled in. But failure to observe the latter two would result in reminders that "A Door Is Ajar" or to "Please Fasten Your Seatbelts"—after which the little "man" in the black box would politely say, "Thank you." It doesn't take much imagination to realize how talkative the EVA could be in some circumstances. Garage attendants must have hated it. So did many owners, some of whom undoubtedly cut the system's "vocal cords" for the sake of sanity.

We mention all this because Chrysler would revise the Electronic Voice Alert the very next year, making it far more useful and much less intrusive. And that's significant, because it reflects not only the company's heightened concern over customer complaints but also its ability to correct design flaws with a speed it had never shown before. It was a benefit of the company's trimmer size, and it contributed greatly to Chrysler's strong comeback in the market.

Judged critically, the E-cars were more trendy than revolutionary, prettified rather than glorified, compared to the Ks, and they were anything but the driver's cars some versions were claimed to be. Nevertheless, they were another instance of Chrysler having the right product at the right time—another marked departure from company tradition. And in the much more competitive market of 1983, timing was everything. Together, Chrysler and Dodge retailed more than 80,000 E-cars for the model year.

Besides the changes already mentioned, the K/CV came in for a number of other minor refinements this year—nothing earth-shattering, just the kind of detail attention that Detroit had finally noticed that customers noticed and appreciated. Among these subtleties were standard halogen headlamps, a maintenance-free no-fill battery, gas caps secured on plastic tethers so they wouldn't get left behind at service stations, and an extra pair of dash vents (previously reserved for cars fitted with optional air conditioning). Aries/Reliant model offerings and price structure were shifted some, and LeBaron/400 was reduced from two trim levels to one "premium" class.

A similar realignment took place in the L-body clan. The Omni/Horizon five-doors both lost their strippo Miser and high-line E-type variants, leaving a better-equipped base model and a step-up Custom. The standard Omni/Horizon was now a really attractive buy (Chrysler had been steadily upgrading equipment here, too), priced at $5841 and boasting handsome cloth upholstery, full carpeting, dual horns, quartz clock, trip odometer, and an understated exterior. The 024/TC3 coupes changed

names, becoming the Dodge Charger and Plymouth Turismo, respectively, and offered a similar two-step line of base and sportier "2.2" models. The familiar 1.7-liter VW-based standard engine was scheduled to be replaced by a 1.6-liter unit supplied by Peugeot, but this was delayed until 1984. It didn't matter much, because most Omni/Horizon and Charger/Turismo sales were with the

Dodge's 400 four-door sold at $8490 for 1983.

1983 Dodge 600 ES sedan was European-inspired.

The '83 Dodge 600 ES retailed for $9372 in base form.

Dodge also offered this $8841 standard 600 for 1983.

Chrysler 2.2, standard in the sportier coupes and just $134 additional on other models. The Charger/Turismo 2.2 was quick, able to hit 50 mph from rest in about 7 seconds, but a special low-restriction exhaust system made the cars somewhat noisy, and their firmer-than-stock suspension yielded a jerky ride on bombed-out city streets. If not refined, they also represented excellent value, priced at around $7300 and typically optioned up to around $9000. Chrysler happily counted receipts from close to 200,000 L-body car sales for the model year.

The L-based T-110 car/pickup returned basically intact, but the Dodge Rampage now had a Plymouth cousin that revived the Scamp name from the Seventies. In an attempt to broaden the little truck's appeal, a hot-shot

1983 Dodge 400 coupe. Base list price was $8014.

Dodge's hot Shelby Charger debuted for "1982½."

The Dodge Aries Special Edition four-door sedan for '83.

The Shelby Charger boasted 110 bhp and aggressive good looks.

1983 Dodge Aries Special Edition wagon. Base price: $8186.

The Plymouth Gran Fury Salon four-door sedan for '83

The base Dodge Omni was a very attractive buy for '83.

'83 Gran Fury's base sticker price was $8248.

Plymouth Turismo 2.2, new for 1983, packed the "Trans-4" engine and five-speed gearbox as standard.

The Plymouth Turismo hatchback coupe listed at $6379 for '83.

Plymouth's 1983 Horizon Custom hatchback sedan: $6071.

Rampage 2.2 and Scamp GT were fielded, roughly equivalent to the Charger/Turismo 2.2 in equipment and specifications. It was a delightful package, but it didn't provide the hoped-for sales spark.

Chrysler was well on its way to the all-front-drive lineup that John Riccardo had once envisioned, but there were still a few rear-drive cars around to maintain the tradition of grand size and weight. Continuing to languish near the bottom of the sales charts, the personal-luxury Chrysler Cordoba and Dodge Mirada were in their final year. As is typical of outgoing, slow-selling models, they were virtually unchanged, holdovers from Chrysler Corporation's recent, stormy past that had no place in its now-promising future.

That was also true for the high-bucks Imperial, which returned as a virtual 1982 carryover, though rumor was that it wouldn't come back at all. The Frank Sinatra edition was dropped and base price was slashed to $18,688, about what it had been in '81. After dourly seeing 1427 examples out the door, management pulled the plug. Ironically, the car had failed to match the last of the original Imperial line in sales, and the '75 was considered a failure.

The M-body sedans stayed with their evergreen

112.7-inch-wheelbase platform, and saw no alterations of note. Not that any were really needed, as these cars were now selling steadily again, if not in really high volume. With the advent of the front-drive New Yorker, the rear-drive model became New Yorker Fifth Avenue, just to keep things clear.

Enthusiasts had a more immediate reason to appreciate Lee Iacocca. This year, Chrysler's chairman coaxed Carroll Shelby back into the business of dreaming up special performance cars based on production hardware. A living legend himself, Shelby was an old friend of Iacocca's from their days together at Ford in the Sixties, where he created the hot Mustang GT-350/500 and the otherworldly Cobra sports cars. Now, Iacocca set up Ol' Shel with an expensive development facility at Santa Fe Springs, near Los Angeles, fully equipped for research, design, and testing. The first result of their collaboration appeared at mid-model year as the Dodge Shelby Charger.

Not merely a cosmetic job on the front-drive L-coupe, the Shelby Charger was an enthusiast's machine through and through, a Charger completely reengineered end to end. Its only link with the Shelby Mustangs was Carroll's favored broad blue over-the-top and rocker panel racing

The 1983 Plymouth Reliant Special Edition four-door sedan

1983 Plymouth Reliant SE Wagon. Base price: $8186.

Sales success: 1983 Plymouth Reliant Special Edition coupe

stripes, done in blue or silver to contrast with the blue or silver body paint. Styling changes included an aggressive front spoiler, ground-hugging rocker panel extensions, a one-piece rear quarter window to replace the clumsy two-piece stock item, a rear lip spoiler, and wide 15-inch "Swiss cheese" aluminum wheels shod with fat 50-series Goodyear Eagle GT radials. Inside were color-keyed bucket seats with "CS" logo, revised accelerator/brake pedal spacing for easier heel-and-toe shifting, plus center console and standard five-speed gearbox. The real magic was under the hood, where Chrysler's workhorse 2.2 was considerably warmed up via higher 9.6:1 compression, wilder cam, optimized electronic controls, and a mellow, free-flow exhaust system. The result was 13 more horsepower (107 versus 94) and 10 extra lbs/ft torque (127 versus 117) compared to the normal 2.2. A numerically higher final drive combined with these tweaks to yield an average 0-60 mph time of around 8.5 seconds, amazing for a four-cylinder car of this size and not far behind much more powerful V-8 ponycars like the Mustang GT and Camaro Z-28. Heavy-duty shocks and taller springs produced slot-car reflexes and flat cornering response.

Though all these improvements were fairly modest, they added up to what *Road & Track* magazine termed

"sensual and emotional experiences…It's quick, tractable, and reasonably sure-footed in spite of some torque steer. It looks outrageous, which adds to the fun if you're willing to let your hair down and think young. It's relatively affordable [$8290 base, about $10,000 in typical form]." Shelby's first Chrysler effort might not have matched "the best the Europeans and Japanese can produce," as the company claimed, but it was a heartening first step. Five years before, anyone who would have predicted Chrysler would be building anything like this would have been sent to the funny farm.

1984

In just four short years, Chrysler Corporation had managed to pull off a miracle that had seemed impossible in 1980: it not only survived, but began to prosper again. This achievement would have been remarkable even in the best of economic times. But it was nothing short of astonishing for a period of unprecedented inflation, record interest rates, the strongest-ever competition from foreign manufacturers, and the U.S. industry's worst sales performance since World War II.

As we've seen, chairman Lee Iacocca and the young Turks he assembled around him had moved quickly to silence those in Washington and elsewhere who questioned whether Chrysler even deserved to survive, let alone could. With the hard-won federal loan guarantees as "collateral," they won key wage concessions from workers, negotiated more favorable contracts with suppliers, and streamlined company operations top to bottom to slash overhead. Yet they also managed to find money for modernizing the firm's aging physical facilities, in the time-honored tradition of Walter P. Chrysler and K. T. Keller. And they invested heavily in the advanced technology necessary to design and produce a new generation of Chrysler cars better attuned to the radically changed market of the Eighties–cars that would be more economical, better built, and better value.

Beginning with the 1981 K-cars, Chrysler had issued a stream of new products at the astounding rate of one about every six months. All sold well, bolstered by markedly improving workmanship and more competitive pricing. As news of its healthier sales spread, Chrysler began to look like a survivor and public confidence in the company returned. This only spurred sales further, and black ink began washing away the red on corporate ledgers. A modest profit for 1982 made it clear that Chrysler Corporation was in the midst of a dramatic, full-blown recovery that had all the earmarks of permanency. Now, the automaker so recently branded a failure was suddenly the most startling comeback story in the history of American business.

The U.S. auto industry began to reverse its three-year sales slide in 1984, with help from a world oil glut and declining gasoline prices, an easing of interest rates, and a continuation of the 1981 Voluntary Restraint Agreement (VRA) limiting Japanese car imports. Chrysler,

1984 Chrysler E Class sedan. Base sticker price: $9565.

1984 Chrysler E Class sedan with two-tone paint

which had been swimming against the sales tide, participated in the upturn and proudly announced record annual earnings for the year. At last, the nightmare seemed to be over.

Chrysler Corporation entered the 1984 model year with a vastly improved financial outlook and a group of cars completely different from what it had been producing only a few years before. By this time, the company was long able to boast the industry's highest corporate average fuel economy, with more fuel-efficient models than GM as a percentage of total production and a big lead over Ford Motor Company in adopting front-wheel drive. Chrysler also claimed the industry lead in robotics and computer-aided design and manufacturing (CAD/

The sportiest Chrysler in many years, the 1984 Laser XE boasted front drive and turbocharged power.

1984 Chrysler Laser XE Turbo. Base price: $11,418.

Base 1984 Chrysler Laser Turbo retailed at $9582.

The 1984 Chrysler LeBaron convertible: $11,595.

1984 Chrysler LeBaron convertible: better top-up visibility.

CAM) technology. And it was the first of the Big Three to establish a California design center, Chrysler Pacifica, to keep tabs on consumer trends in that bellweather market. As Iacocca would declare, all this was "not bad for a company that had one foot in the grave."

If Chrysler now seemed like an outfit that could be expected to achieve the unexpected, its two major new products for 1984 were proof positive. Of course, neither was exactly a surprise. The firm had revealed their existence in the uncertain days of late 1980, and accurate design information had been widely reported months before their showroom debuts. Nevertheless, both would be greeted with rave reviews and would have a major impact in their respective markets. Moreover, each could claim several "firsts" that would contribute as much to the growing Chrysler "legend" as Lee Iacocca and the K-cars. As promised, a brace of high-performance sports coupes arrived at the start of the model year. Called Chrysler Laser and Dodge Daytona, they were the first such U.S. cars to combine front-wheel drive and turbocharged power. Even more revolutionary was the industry's first compact "van," marketed as the Dodge Caravan and Plymouth Voyager, a front-drive "people mover" so different yet versatile that most observers didn't know whether to classify it as a car or truck.

Enthusiast eyes were naturally riveted on the fleet and beautiful Laser/Daytona. Developed as project G-24, they were yet another variation on the successful K-car theme, though you'd never know it by looking at them. Chrysler called them "sports cars," which they were not in the literal sense. Rather, they were civilized, well-furnished *gran turismos*, hatchback coupes offering 2+2 seating on a 97.1-inch wheelbase (3.2 inches shorter than the K/CV chassis). Styling was almost flawless: smooth and dynamic, with Porsche 928 overtones in the greenhouse and a little GM influence around the tail. The only design disappointment was a general lack of styling individuality between the two versions, highlighted by their shared nose and its bare, angular, undistinguished appearance. Differences among the five models initially offered were confined to body add-ons, no doubt reflecting a very limited styling budget during the G-24's gestation in the touch-and-go early Eighties.

The Laser/Daytona marked the first time that Chrysler had built anything like a ponycar since the demise of the Plymouth Barracuda and Dodge Challenger a decade

earlier. And indeed, the G-24 was conceived primarily as a reply to latterday ponies like the third-generation Chevrolet Camaro/Pontiac Firebird, not to mention a number of out-and-out sports and GT models from overseas. Accordingly, Chrysler put a lot of effort into reengineering the K-car platform for life in the fast lane—which explains why company officials objected so strenu-

Chrysler's unique Executive Sedan for 1984

1984 Chrysler Limousine

The $9956 Chrysler LeBaron Town & Country wagon for '84

The woody-look Chrysler LeBaron Town & Country convertible returned for '84 with numerous improvements. Price: $16,495.

1984 Chrysler LeBaron Town & Country convertible

The Chrysler LeBaron coupe for 1984. Base price: $8783.

ously to even the slightest suggestion that the Gs were simply more athletic Ks.

The changes began with the engine. Base Laser/ Daytona power was supplied by a new fuel-injected version of the reliable 2.2-liter Trans-4, making these the first injected production models from Highland Park since 1958. Unlike that earlier system, though, this newly developed throttle-body or "single-point" injection was Chrysler's own, and the firm's considerable expertise in electronics was applied to control ignition, injection timing, and exhaust emission functions. Rated output was 99 bhp at 5600 rpm and 121 lbs/ft torque peaking at 3200 rpm, a gain of 5 bhp and 4 lbs/ft over the carbureted 2.2 on the same 9.0:1 compression.

But the real excitement was the new turbocharged Trans-4, standard for the upper-level Laser XE and Dodge Daytona Turbo and Turbo Z. Painstakingly engineered, it featured a Garrett AiResearch turbocharger spinning out up to 7.5-psi boost, plus a more sophisticated port or "multi-point" fuel injection system, with individual injectors (made by Bosch) for each cylinder, again with Chrysler electronic control. A notable innovation was a water-cooled turbine end-shaft bearing, which promoted longer turbocharger life by reducing the tendency for oil to "coke" on the bearing. For this reason, it eliminated the inconvenience of letting the turbocharger coast down by idling the engine for a time before

shutting off. The normally aspirated 2.2's compression ratio was lowered, as is customary with turbocharging, to 8.0:1 via dished pistons. Though premium fuel was recommended, a detonation sensor linked to the engine's electronics (another customary feature of modern turbo powerplants) allowed the use of unleaded regular at a slight sacrifice in performance. Internals were beefed up to withstand the greater stresses turbocharging imposes: more durable intake and exhaust valve seals, better-sealing piston rings, and "select-fit" main bearings. Completing the modifications were a wilder camshaft, larger-capacity oil pump, and a low-restriction, 2.5-inch-diameter exhaust system. The result of all this was 142 bhp at 5600 rpm—better than the magic "1 bhp per cu. in."—and 160 lbs/ft peak torque at 3600 rpm.

Per now-standard Chrysler practice, both engines were transversely mounted under the sloping Laser/Daytona nose, and were linked to Chrysler's own close-ratio five-speed manual gearbox. TorqueFlite automatic was optional. For all its 1984 applications, the five-speed's linkage was revised for easier, more precise shifting, though there was still more work to do in this area.

The G-24's considerably modified K-car suspension had higher spring rates, harder bushings, and gas-filled shock absorbers to impart the desired handling characteristics. A new "dual path" upper mount for the front MacPherson struts helped better isolate road shock from the passenger compartment, a change also found on this year's K-, CV- and E-body models. Standard power-assisted rack-and-pinion steering also came from the company parts shelves, but a quicker 14:1 ratio was specified along with a higher-output steering pump for better road feel in the sports coupes. Brakes were 10-inch-diameter front floating-caliper discs and 8.9-inch-diameter self-adjusting rear drums, with the usual vacuum booster and front/rear proportioning valve, plus diagonally split twin circuits. One important driveline change was made for the turbo-engine Laser/Daytona: equal- instead of unequal-length halfshafts, which reduced torque-steer reaction ("wheel fight") in hard acceleration.

Acceleration was something the blown G-24s had in abundance. Magazine road tests roundly confirmed Chrysler's claimed 0-60 mph time of 8.0-8.5 seconds with manual shift, which put the Laser XE/Daytona Turbo hard on the heels of domestic V-8 rivals and imports like the Nissan 300ZX Turbo and Porsche 944. Top speed was in excess of 115 mph. Less weight than a hotshot Mustang or Camaro/Firebird contributed greatly to the turbo models' great go, and also enabled them to return unexpectedly good fuel economy, an EPA-rated 22 mpg city and 38 mpg highway with manual gearbox. The normally aspirated car seemed tamed by comparison, but could sprint to 60 mph from rest in a reasonable 10 seconds while returning up to 25/42 mpg, again with manual. It was also much more refined than the turbo, which suffered from a marked exhaust boom that may have fit the performance image but that an owner would soon find aggravating on a long trip.

Long-distance touring should be the forte of any GT, and in most respects the Laser/Daytona was worthy of those initials. Turbo models came with a Performance Handling Package that included extra-firm spring and shock rates, larger stabilizer bars front and rear, and fat 15-inch road wheels shod with Goodyear 60-series radial tires. Predictably, it yielded a harsher, thumpier ride than the standard chassis, but the payoff was sensational handling, with flat cornering response and gobs of grip. Passengers were treated to a snug cabin typical of 2+2s, with comfortable, adequately roomy accommodations in front on supportive, wide bucket seats. Another pair of buckets was found in back, but room was so tight there that the backrests were better left folded down to increase luggage space for a long trip. The driver faced a modified K-car dash with a well-placed and complete set of analog gauges. Exclusive to the Laser XE was a much less legible electronic cluster, plus a gimmicky travel computer of the sort first seen on the front-drive Chrysler New Yorker. The XE and both Daytona Turbos were equipped with a special "enthusiast's" driver's seat, with inflatable lumbar and thigh support bolsters reminiscent of something out of the Space Shuttle. All models had a center console housing the shift lever and switches for optional accessories like power windows and seat and electric rear window defroster.

Admittedly, the Laser/Daytona wasn't perfect. The turbo versions suffered from torque steer under power and that disconcerting exhaust boom, the manual gearbox linkage wasn't the best, fuel economy was well under EPA estimates (by 20 percent or so), and some ergonomic

1984 Chrysler Fifth Avenue. It sold for $13,990 basic.

Chrysler's front-drive '84 New Yorker listed at $12,179.

The 1984 Chrysler New Yorker sedan

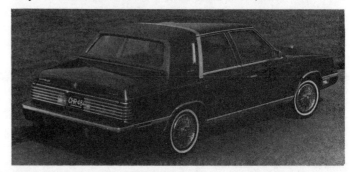
A revolution begins: the 1984 Dodge Caravan LE

The 1984 Dodge Caravan in 5-seat SE trim: $8915.

Dodge's 1984 Daytona Turbo Z cost $11,504 in base form.

1984 Dodge Daytona Turbo coupe. Base price: $10,227.

Dodge Charger 2.2 bore a fresh face for 1984.

The high-performance Dodge Shelby Charger for 1984

Racy 1984 Dodge Daytona Turbo Z featured deep front air dam and rocker panel extensions, plus two-toning.

details and the XE's "video arcade" instrumentation could have been better handled. Even so, the Laser/ Daytona was amazingly "right" for a first-year design. It looked right, felt good and moved fast. And the Daytona Turbo Z, with its eye-catching two-tone paint, deep front air dam, "ground effects" rocker panel extensions, and unique rear spoiler, was a tremendous image car. Chrysler had come up with another winner.

Though this book is primarily about cars, we can hardly leave out the other big event at Chrysler for 1984, the mid-year announcement of the Dodge Caravan/Plymouth Voyager. Here was not only a trend-setting new concept but vivid new evidence of the Iacocca regime's "think fast, think smart" mentality—a perfect symbol for Chrysler's resurgence.

It couldn't have been better timed. A lot of buyers were now looking for a thriftier, less expensive, and more maneuverable alternative to traditional big U.S. vans, including cost-conscious fleet operators and small businesses as well as a number of diehard "vanatics" who were simply tired of their old behemoths. Then too, a growing number of families were seeking a practical alternative to the conventional full-size station wagon, a species doomed to eventual extinction by government fuel economy mandates despite a sales reprieve resulting from the world oil glut. The Caravan/Voyager had natural appeal to all these groups. More importantly, it made Chrysler the first U.S. producer to go head-to-head with the innovative Japanese in what some observers forecast as the biggest growth market of the Eighties. After years of simply following its domestic competition, Chrysler was again leading it.

Though the Caravan/Voyager defied easy classification, Chrysler wasn't at all muddled. According to company officials, this was neither car nor truck but a "people mover." Even so, the T-115 internal code signified that the design project had originated in Dodge Truck and not the passenger-car section, and Chrysler itself touted this as the first "garageable van," the smallest vehicle of its type ever built in the U.S. Not surprisingly, the T-115 was tested and built like any Dodge truck, though it drove more like a car than anything that division had produced except for the T-110 Dodge Rampage/Plymouth Scamp pickup.

Considering its historic symbolism, it's ironic that the T-115 was really a product of the "old" Chrysler Corporation. The design effort had been initiated way back in 1973, but product planners delayed introduction, having concluded that the market wasn't ready for a minivan. By 1980, when the market *was* ready, Chrysler was struggling for survival and there was simply not enough money for getting the T-115 into production. Iacocca, who knows a winner when he sees one, gave it the production go-ahead that same year, but the whopping investment required for new tooling precluded imminent introduction, however much at that time Chrysler could have used what undoubtedly would have been the minivan's high sales. As it turned out, the firm spent $660 million on the project, most of it going to overhaul the Windsor, Ontario plant with new automated production equipment. And if anything, the potential market grew even stronger during the long delay. In fact, initial sales targets proved conservative, and once the minivans hit dealer showrooms, Windsor couldn't keep up with the demand. For Iacocca, the T-115 must have seemed like a repeat of the Mustang's phenomenal first-year success.

The T-115 arrived on a 112-inch wheelbase but was no longer than the familiar K-car station wagon. Compared to the B150, the smallest full-size Dodge van, the T-115 was about three inches shorter overall (175.9) but stood a significant 15 inches lower and was nearly 10 inches slimmer. Like a van, it had a sliding center door on the right, two front doors, and a one-piece lift-up tailgate. Compared to the K-wagon, however, it was a towering 11 inches taller and only about 1.5 inches wider. In essence, then, this was a compact station wagon with "phone booth" styling. Careful attention to body aerodynamics

1984 Dodge Diplomat Salon four-door sedan: $8832.

Dodge Diplomat was predictably little changed for '84.

For mid-1984, the $10,165 Dodge Diplomat SE sedan

resulted in an unusually low drag coefficient for this sort of vehicle, 0.43, and use of what amounted to the K-car chassis allowed step-in height to be kept quite low, only fractionally greater than the passenger car's.

Shrewdly, Chrysler decided to offer the T-115 in both consumer and commercial versions. The Dodge Caravan and Plymouth Voyager were the passenger models,

1984 Dodge Aries four-door sedan. Base price: $6949.

The Dodge Aries Special Edition wagon for '84: $8195.

Dodge released this hot CV-series 600 ES Turbo convertible for mid-1984. Base list price was $12,895.

"1984½" Dodge 600 Turbo convertible

The 1984 Dodge 600 sedan in standard form

Dodge's 1984 600 ES sedan was available with turbo power.

Dodge 400 coupe became a 600 for 1984.

offered in base, Special Edition (SE) and Luxury Edition (LE) trim levels with a choice of five- or optional seven-passenger seating. These effectively replaced the smaller window vans that both divisions had been selling in the Seventies. The commercial model was offered only under the Dodge nameplate and borrowed the Mini Ram label from a short-wheelbase version of the old truck-based rear-drive van. Mini Ram customers got only two front seats and no side windows aft of the doors, but Dodge made a pitch to the recreational van market with a ready-to-customize offering complete with full-length headliner and carpeting on floor and sidewalls.

T-115 powertrains and most suspension pieces were familiar corporate components, though engines were tuned a bit differently for this application. Base power was the two-barrel 2.2-liter Trans-4, rated here at 101 bhp at 5600 rpm and 121 lbs/ft torque at 3600 rpm, mounted transversely to save space, as in the K-cars. The standard transaxle was the five-speed manual overdrive, with TorqueFlite automatic optional. Available at extra cost and with automatic only was a new Chrysler-modified version of the Mitsubishi 2.6-liter "Silent Shaft" four, with 99 bhp at 4800 rpm and 143 lbs/ft torque peaking at 2000 rpm. Front suspension employed Chrysler's "Iso-Strut" MacPherson-type layout with coil springs, and power-assisted rack-and-pinion steering was included. At the rear was a newly designed lightweight beam axle suspended on multi-leaf springs instead of coils to suit the heavy loads some owners would likely carry.

The T-115 interior evidenced an unusual number of thoughtful touches. On passenger models the second and third seats could be easily removed via quick-release clamps. The seven-seat version came with a second set of locating slots in the floor, so that its wider three-passenger third seat could be moved up in place of the two-person second seat for more cargo room. Toward the same end, the third-seat backrest could be folded down and then pushed forward, and the spare was out of the way on the vehicle's underside in a special carrier you wound up and down from a special fitting at the rear of the cargo floor. The floor itself was only 14.6 inches above ground, which eased loading of heavy items. Low-effort needle bearings allowed the side door to be opened or closed practically with one finger. All side windows were mounted nearly flush with the body and were forward-hinged to keep wind noise low when open. A clever option was a remote control for the rearmost side windows, operated by handwheels mounted on the ceiling between the two front seats. Both driver and passenger sat on individual buckets with reclining backrests, and all riders enjoyed generous head and leg room as well as panoramic outward visibility.

In its driving position and general road manners, the T-115 was far more car than truck. Aside from leisurely acceleration with any drivetrain and a fair amount of engine noise, it was very impressive for ride, maneuverability, and general driving ease. In fact, CONSUMER GUIDE® magazine's editors judged it a highly practical proposition for people living in dense city centers. About the only criticisms that could be levelled at the minivan's dynamic behavior were a slight loss of rear-end adhesion over humpbacks taken quickly and marked body roll (what else from such a tall box?). But were it not for the higher-than-normal driving stance, you wouldn't know you were driving anything other than a car. It says a lot for the T-115's basic design excellence that two of our editors were persuaded to buy one, a Caravan and a Voyager.

Buying was easy, too, because Chrysler's new minivan was attractively priced. The LE, for example, listed at about $1000 less than the forward-control Toyota Van and some $2500 below the Vanagon, the latest in Volkswagen long-running rear-engine "bus" line. Even with automatic, the T-115 would outperform either of these with manual transmission, and was quieter and handled better to boot. Though it wasn't quite as economical, it was the only one with the traction benefits of front drive. With all this, it's no wonder the T-115 was a sellout, and the arrival of rear-drive domestic competitors for 1985, the Chevy Astro and Ford's Aerostar, did nothing to lessen its appeal. The Caravan/Voyager could even be

Also from mid-1984, Dodge's Shelby-tuned Omni GLH

"1984½" Dodge Omni GLH packed 110-bhp Shelby 2.2.

Still going, if not strongly, the 1984 Plymouth Gran Fury

1984 Plymouth Turismo 2.2 hatchback coupe

Plymouth charged $7288 for its '84 Turismo 2.2.

1984 Plymouth Horizon hatchback sedan: $5830 basic.

1984 Plymouth Reliant coupe. Base price was $6847.

1984 Plymouth Reliant Special Edition four-door sedan

The $7736 Plymouth Reliant Custom wagon for 1984

Plymouth's T-115 was called Voyager. Here, the top-line LE.

Open for pleasure: the 1984 Plymouth Voyager LE van

destined, as *Road & Track* magazine put it, to "become classics in their own time—the sales legend that once belonged to the Mustang." Lee Iacocca would like that. We know he was pleased in getting the jump on GM and Ford in the minivan sweepstakes.

Chrysler didn't neglect the rest of its lineup for '84, continuing to revise model offerings and to institute appropriate product changes to keep them competitive. With the demise of Imperial and the Cordoba/Mirada, the trio of M-body sedans were the only rear-drive cars left in the fleet. None saw significant change. However, the veteran Slant Six was retired as their base engine in favor of the 318 V-8, reflecting the nation's much-improved gas price/supply situation. The popular K-cars received revised grilles, a larger fuel tank, and standard all-season radial tires, as well as a restyled and more comprehensive instrument cluster with coolant temperature gauge, voltmeter, and trip odometer. The Dodge 400 four-door sedan

was dropped, and the remaining coupe and convertible were tagged 600. The Laser/Daytona turbo engine became an option for the CV-series Chrysler LeBaron/Dodge 600 and E-body Chrysler New Yorker and Dodge 600ES four-door. All these models were given restyled taillamps. Convertibles came in for a wider back seat, and their visibility was improved by fitting power-operated rear side windows and a redesigned top with narrower aft quarters. As noted (see 1983), the Electronic Voice Alert option for G-24, E-body and CV cars was changed to issue more pertinent warnings and fewer "thank you's," and its voice could now be shut off via a switch in the glovebox. The injected 2.2 was slated to replace the carbureted unit as the standard E/CV powerplant, but production hangups prevented it from appearing until late in the year.

The L-body Charger/Turismo coupes returned with their first major facelift since starting life as the 024/TC3 back in 1979. Up front was a reshaped nose with a simple bar grille flanked by horizontally arrayed headlamps, and the rearmost side windows were eliminated in favor of the Shelby Charger's solid C-pillars. The new nose did not show up on the rapid Shelby Charger itself, but was applied to the Dodge Rampage/Plymouth Scamp pickups. The Shelby-tuned 110-bhp 2.2 was now an option for all L-body models, which also picked up a more contemporary standard instrument cluster *a la* K-car. The Charger/Rampage 2.2 was toned down by deleting its fake hood scoop and gaudy side striping, while the Omni/Horizon soldiered on with new grille inserts.

1985

Shortly after Chrysler Corporation won Congressional approval for its federal loan guarantees, it took out a series of ads that simply said: "Thanks, America. Now, It's Up to Us." In the ensuing four years, Chrysler had certainly done more than enough to justify the faith of those who had urged their representatives to support the company in its darkest hour. On the occasion of its 60th anniversary in 1984, the firm paused to thank the country again, this time for buying its cars. Read one ad: "We wouldn't have lived to see 60 without you."

To be sure, Chrysler's amazing comeback since 1980 was helped immeasurably by the loan guarantees, not to mention the corporate fat-trimming of 1979-81, a world oil surplus, and the sudden market upturn often ascribed to the "Reagan Recovery." Yet none of this would have made much difference without the right products. And of all the innovations and pleasant surprises we'd seen since Lee Iacocca's arrival in Highland Park, it is the K-car that stands out most brilliantly as the key factor in the company's salvation.

Remarkably, the Dodge Aries and Plymouth Reliant continued to sell strongly through 1984 despite few changes since introduction. It was thus singularly appropriate that they received their first major design alterations for 1985, another public "thank you" from Chrysler. Immediately evident was smoother, more curvaceous sheetmetal front and rear, which brought a small claimed reduction in aerodynamic drag. Coupes and sedans sported slightly higher rear decks, and all models boasted restyled taillamps and a slightly longer nose with a mildly reclined grille and curved parking/side marker lamps at the corners. This more streamlined look was probably a reaction to the more rounded shapes coming from the competition, notably Ford. And that was too bad in a way, because Chrysler had been leading Ford and even GM so often in recent years that its supporters must have hated to see it following.

Then too, the curvy Ford products weren't as aerodynamic as they appeared. One GM designer commented to us that they had "perceived aerodynamics—they look slippery but in relative terms are not." Still, low-drag styling had become *de rigeur* by the second half of the Eighties, and the new-look K-cars were a clear sign that

1985 Chrysler LeBaron GTS "Premium" hatchback sedan

The '85 Chrysler LeBaron GTS in base "Highline" form

"Highline" '85 LeBaron GTS retailed at $9099.

1985 Chrysler LeBaron sedan. Base price: $9309.

Chrysler's 1985 LeBaron Town & Country wagon: $10,363.

The '85 Chrysler Limousine could be yours for $26,318.

1985 Chrysler LeBaron Mark Cross convertible

1985 Chrysler LeBaron coupe. It sold for $9460.

The exciting Chrysler Laser XE hatchback coupe for '85

1985 Chrysler Laser XE Turbo. Base price: $11,683.

the company had decided it was time for a change. If Chrysler's future production designs turn out to be anything like the advance projects we've seen in progress at Chrysler Pacifica, the firm may very soon be hailed once more as the industry's styling pacesetter.

Inside, the 1985 K-cars were spruced up with a new padded top that made the instrument panel took tidier and richer, accented by the handsome gauge cluster introduced with the '84s and greater use of black instead of bright trim. At long last, the old climate control panel with protruding chrome buttons was abandoned for an easier-to-use and much more modern flat-face design, adopted for all K-based cars this year, including the slick Laser/Daytona. Door trim panels were also revised and now carried convenient map pockets. A new standard item for manual-shift cars was a Volkswagen-style indicator light to tell the driver when to select the next highest gear for reduced engine rpm and thus better mileage. It

was advertised as the "Fuel Pacer," thus reviving a name from the early Seventies.

Following the series nomenclature introduced with the T-115 vans for '84, the Aries/Reliant lineup was expanded for '85 to encompass base, Special Edition, and new top-shelf Luxury Edition models. The list of no-charge extras was longer than ever, and there were interesting new options such as electronically tuned radios with AM stereo capability and a heavy-duty suspension with gas-filled shocks. Perhaps the best standard feature was the corporate five-year/50,000-mile warranty, another idea from Chrysler's past that Iacocca had brought back beginning with the 1981 season. It helped spark sales just like it had in 1963, and it continued to make the K-car the best buy among domestic compacts.

With the exciting Laser/Daytona solidly established in the sporty coupe market, Chrysler decided to go after another group of enthusiast buyers with a high-perform-

1985 Chrysler Fifth Avenue sedan: $14,205 basic.

1985 Chrysler New Yorker with optional turbocharged engine

'85 New Yorker listed at $12,743 in base form.

ance sports sedan. The result was essentially a four-door G-24, sharing suspension and running gear with the coupes but wrapped up in a spacious, smoothly styled five-passenger body with luxurious furnishings and hatchback practicality. Developed as the H-body project, it bowed at mid-model year as a pair of near-identical twins, one for each division. The C-P version was sold only with the Chrysler badge as the LeBaron GTS, an unfortunately confusing choice. The duplicate Dodge bore a perfect name, however: Lancer, recalling the make's flashy hardtops of the Fifties.

Scheduled to total 100,000 units for the model year, H-body production began in late 1984 at the firm's new, highly automated facility in Sterling Heights, Michigan, near Detroit. There was a peculiar irony in that, because this plant had been acquired from Volkswagen of America, whose fortunes had declined greatly since it had purchased Chrysler's unfinished factory in Westmoreland County, Pennsylvania, for local production of the Rabbit.

In size and general concept, the H-body was Chrysler's reply to mid-size domestics in the image of certain European sports sedans, competitors like the Chevrolet Celebrity Eurosport, Pontiac 6000STE, Buick Century T-Type, and Ford's LTD LX. To some extent, the H-body also had to tackle genuine Euro-sedans like the Audi 4000, BMW 318i, Saab 900, and Volkswagen Quantum. Stylistically, however, it was closer to the Mazda 626 Touring Sedan from Japan than any of these. Major design features were a sloped nose, flush-mount windshield, semi-flush side windows, doors cut into the roof slightly, and a short rear "deck" to help camouflage the hatchback configuration. As usual, only differences in grilles, nameplates, and taillamps set the two versions apart. The GTS bore a chromier, vertical-bar grille, while the Lancer displayed a simple black grille with prominent cross bars, a new Dodge Division theme for '85 that also appeared on the Aries and harked back to the great letter-series Chrysler 300s.

Though built on the same 103.3-inch wheelbase used for the E-body Chrysler New Yorker/Dodge 600 four-door, the H-body claimed slightly more interior volume despite being six inches shorter overall. Obviously, Chrysler had learned something about space utilization since the K-car was laid down. As on the Laser/Daytona, the suspension comprised MacPherson struts in front (with "dual-path" upper mounts for road shock isolation), a "torsion" beam axle located by trailing arms at the rear, coil springs all round, and an anti-roll bar at each end. A new wrinkle shared with the '85 Laser/Daytona was Chrysler's first use of gas-pressurized shock absorbers, which were standard H-body equipment. Fast-ratio (14:1) power steering was standard, along with power front-disc/rear-drum brakes. Two "Sport Handling Suspension" options with beefed-up springs and shocks and wider Goodyear Eagle GT tires were listed for improved roadability. Standard rubber was P185/70R-14 all-season Goodyear Vector or Michelin XA4 radials. Buyers could choose from a base and premium version of each model, the latter called ES if Lancer. The upper-level package included the basic Sport Handling Suspension, a "full gauge" electronic instrument cluster (one of the more legible ones around), plusher seat and door trim, rear seat headrests, and a 60/40 split (instead of one-piece) fold-down rear seatback.

There was no need for any major substitutions in the engine compartment, so the H-body's base power came from the normally aspirated version of Chrysler's revvy 2.2-liter "Trans-4" with electronic throttle-body fuel injection. Rated output was unchanged from 1984. Optional was the turbocharged 2.2 with port injection and a new electronic wastegate control that varied maximum boost from 7.2 to 9.0 psi depending on engine operating conditions (including the type of fuel being used). The new variable-boost system netted 4-6 extra horsepower (up to 146-148 bhp at 5200 rpm) and somewhat more torque (163 lbs/ft at 3600 rpm) compared to the previous turbo engine, a change that also applied to LeBaron/600, front-drive New Yorker, and Laser/Daytona models so equipped. Another H-body feature that showed up on these cars was a revised dual-rail selector mechanism for Chrysler's own close-ratio five-speed overdrive manual gearbox, which enhanced both shift feel and precision while reducing effort.

CONSUMER GUIDE® magazine's editors were duly impressed by the GTS/Lancer when we sampled them at Chrysler's Chelsea Proving Grounds in early June 1984. The stylish body provided generous four-passenger seat space (the rear proved surprisingly roomy and comfortable for adults), a spacious cargo bay, and the same exemplary underhood access characteristic of all Chrysler products with the intelligently laid out 2.2-liter four. The take-charge driving position made you feel instantly "at home," bolstered by a thoughtfully arranged dash, properly spaced accelerator and brake pedal, and a supportive bucket seat with reclining backrest. A full set of eminently readable analog engine instruments plus a tachometer made up the standard gauge cluster, which we preferred over the useful but still gimmicky electronic setup. Out on the demanding test track, the ride proved supple even with the handling suspension, though one particularly difficult "corkscrew" section revealed that the back end can go light at times. Aside from that minor complaint, the handling was superb: accurate, sharp, predictable, and sporting.

As for performance, the turbo engine put the GTS/Lancer in some fast company, indeed. We saw a little over 9.0 seconds from rest to 60 mph with manual, a bit more than 11 seconds with automatic—and that was with three aboard! The normally aspirated engine produced predictably slower times, but not that much slower, and it was

The 1985 Dodge Caravan in mid-level SE trim

miles ahead for refinement. Impressive performer though it is, the turbo 2.2 is still far too boomy and unpleasant, particularly at higher rpm and on deceleration, despite ample sound-deadening. We hope Chrysler's exhaust system engineers will attend to this, because it spoils what would otherwise be a world-beater.

Yet it's easy to second-guess engineers, and our personal criticisms should not obscure the fact that the GTS/Lancer emerged as a remarkably "finished" design, thoroughly executed and highly satisfying in most every way, just like the Laser/Daytona and the T-115 minivans. It offered more proof—if any be needed—of Chrysler Corporation's new assertiveness in every market sector, backed by engineering talent unsurpassed in Detroit.

1985 Dodge Aries LE four-door sedan. Price: $7792.

1985 Dodge Aries LE coupe. Base price: $7659.

Dodge's Aries LE wagon for '85 sold for $8378 basic.

The restyled 1985 Dodge Aries coupe in luxury LE trim

Handsome hauler: 1985 Dodge Caravan LE 7-seat van

Dodge's 1985 Caravan LE. Base price: $10,005.

And, of course, the firm never lost that talent—or the determination to apply it—even during the worst of its financial problems. Priced at around $9000 basic—competitive with domestic rivals and thousands less than most similar imports—the GTS/Lancer also represented excellent value for money, which buyers had been quick to recognize in all products of The New Chrysler Corporation and a not inconsiderable factor in the firm's amazing recovery.

With the updated K-car and the new H-body as this year's major attractions, the rest of the successful corporate lineup saw only detail changes for 1985. The hot Laser/Daytona received wider 205-section, 60-aspect tires as standard equipment, plus the fortified turbo engine

option, revised manual shift linkage, and reworked heat/vent controls. Inside, the standard remote releases for fuel flap and hatch door were relocated from inside the center console glovebox to a more convenient position outboard of the driver's seat. Outside, a wraparound rear spoiler *a la* Daytona Turbo Z was adopted for all versions.

The E-body models were left mostly alone, except that the four-door Dodge 600ES was cancelled to make room for the new Lancer and the Chrysler E Class was transferred to the Plymouth line to become the Caravelle. Continued from mid-1984 was the racy-looking turbo-powered Dodge 600ES convertible, a fast yet affordable way to enjoy "wind-in-the-face" driving. Those more traditionally inclined could get the same basic package in

1985 Dodge Charger 2.2 hatchback coupe: $7515.

Dodge Shelby Charger acquired standard turbo 2.2 for '85.

1985 Dodge Charger 2.2, now with 110 bhp standard.

1985 Dodge Shelby Turbo Charger. It sold at just $8995.

Turbo Z continued as the top Dodge Daytona for 1985. Note the ground-hugging stance, "Swiss cheese" wheels.

1985 Dodge Daytona Turbo Z. Base retail price: $11,620.

The mid-line Dodge Daytona Turbo coupe for 1985

nostalgic Chrysler LeBaron Town & Country form.

The blown 2.2 showed up in an even more torrid Dodge Shelby Charger for '85, an adroit amalgam of V-8 go and four-cylinder economy. Gas-charged front and rear shocks and larger rear brakes were ordained to cope with the turbo engine's extra power, and a new silver/black color scheme was offered in addition to the usual silver/blue. Those looking for a genuine Q-ship could get all the Shelby goodies—including the turbo—in the more practical five-door Omni shell as the GLH. Dodge said the initials stood for "Goes Like Hell," and the GLH certainly could. Another mid-1984 introduction, it packed the normally aspirated 110-bhp Shelby 2.2, but it really

flew with the optional pressurized engine. Either way, it looked great with its fat aluminum wheels, black grille and greenhouse trim, and front foglamps, all standard. The rest of the L-body line was substantially unchanged, except that the 110-bhp engine was now standard for the Charger/Turismo 2.2 to separate them further from their less sporting siblings. The cute but slow-selling Rampage/Scamp pickup was dropped.

The rear-drive M-body Chrysler became simply Fifth Avenue this year. Along with the carryover Dodge Diplomat and Plymouth Gran Fury, it remained the only reminder of the cars Chrysler Corporation used to build. An unexpected development was an improved 318 V-8,

Dodge's Diplomat SE sedan sold for $10,491 for '85.

The 1985 Dodge Diplomat SE sedan

1985 Dodge 600 coupe. It was tagged at $9060 base.

Dodge's new-for-1985 Lancer ES Turbo hatchback sedan

The E-body Dodge 600 SE sedan for 1985: $8953.

1985 Dodge Lancer ES Turbo: $11,169 in base form.

still the standard powerplant in these cars but now with roller-type camshaft followers for less internal friction, plus several other modifications that bumped rated output from 130 to 140 bhp, a gain of 10 bhp. Dodge dealers had been clamoring for a more luxurious Diplomat to counter the Fifth Avenue, and they got one in mid-1984 as the Diplomat SE. This model returned for '85, identified by a special cross-bar grille and a full complement of standard luxury features, though it was less ornate outside than the Chrysler.

Rounding out Chrysler's well-balanced '85 fleet was the T-115 Dodge Caravan/Plymouth Voyager minivans. They were still selling like cold beer on a hot August day, and

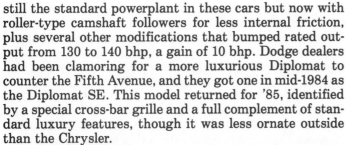

1985 Dodge 600ES Turbo convertible: a $13,995 sportster.

the trend-setting basic design was so good to begin with that only minor refinements were called for. Among these were a more conveniently sited remote fuel filler flap release, the "Fuel Pacer" upshift indicator for manual-transmission models, and a revised latch for the flip-out window in the sliding side door (first-year T-115s had to be recalled when it was discovered that the glass could shatter when the window was open and the door was closed hard). New to the options list were rear seats that could be made up into a bed, a front floor console with locking storage bin, an overhead console with reading lamps and compartments for sunglasses and garage door opener, and power door mirrors.

And that brings the Chrysler story up to date. But what of the future? Unquestionably, the outlook for the company is now rosier than it has been in years. And as long as there are people around like chairman Lee Iacocca and president Harold K. Sperlich, it seems safe to say that Chrysler's long-term survival is assured.

Iacocca has stated that only multinational conglomerates can make it in today's vastly changed automotive world. To this end, Chrysler continues to seek long-term relationships with other producers (as indeed it was required to do by the Loan Guarantee Board established by Congress). This means strong companies like Mitsubishi, not weak ones like the old Rootes Group. Chrysler already has a link to Peugeot-Citroën, which supplies the 1.6-liter four that's now base L-body equipment (Peugeot manufactures a French version of the Omni/Horizon under the Talbot badge, a joint design it inherited when it

The standard 1985 Dodge Lancer with turbo engine option

Without turbo, the '85 Dodge Lancer sold for $8788 basic.

1985 Dodge Omni hatchback sedan: a $5999 bargain.

Dodge's Omni GLH offered plenty of go for $7620.

1985 Dodge Omni GLH carried sill extensions, front air dam.

took over Chrysler's European subsidiaries). At one time, it appeared that Chrysler and Peugeot would collaborate on an Omnirizon replacement, the so-called P-car originally slated to be built only in the U.S., but it now looks as though Chrysler will go it alone on this project. It's a tough assignment, because the P-car will compete in the roughest sector of the market, the sub-2.0-liter class, where it has been increasingly difficult for Detroit to match the Japanese on production costs, and thus price.

An exciting new development is Chrysler's recent acquisition of a five-percent interest in Maserati, the famed Italian builder of high-performance, limited-production sports cars. Because of its small share, Chrysler's influence at Maserati is only minor, but the linkup does bode well for a new mid-engine GT that Chrysler is known to be preparing for mid-1986 or 1987. Known as project J-21, it reunites Iacocca with Alessandro de Tomaso, who recently took over Maserati and was responsible for the slinky mid-engine De Tomaso Pantera sold in 1971-74 by Lincoln-Mercury dealers. Whenever it appears, the J-21 will be strictly an "image" car, a low-volume showcase for Chrysler's best in high-technology design and performance. It will be somewhat shorter and lower than the Laser/Daytona, with styling that represents a further extension of the company's more rounded look, albeit not as radical as Audi or Ford design. Power will likely be supplied by a standard turbocharged 2.2 or possibly a blown 2.5-liter derivative of the Trans-4 known to be under development. Another possibility is a V-6, originally planned for a mid-size/rear-drive pickup, to be supplied by Mitsubishi. Price is anybody's guess at this writing, but a target figure of well under $25,000 is known to be part of the plan. And there's the prospect of a J-21 convertible, which would make Chrysler the only manufacturer in the world other than Ferrari to offer an amidships ragtop.

There are several equally interesting developments coming up. We can confirm the imminent arrival of Mitsubishi's new V-6 to replace that firm's aging 2.6-liter "Silent Shaft" four as the step-up power option in all of Chrysler's transverse-engine front-drive models. The new engine was designed for this application from the outset. It should arrive for 1986 with a displacement of around 3.0 liters and performance about midway between that of the turbocharged and normally aspirated 2.2s.

Being readied for mid-1987 is Chrysler's reply to sporty import coupes like the Toyota Celica and Nissan 200SX. Officially designated the J-body (perhaps to confuse outsiders about the forthcoming mid-engine sports car), it has been all but locked up at this writing. We've seen photos of the approved production styling, and it's a knockout: clean and smooth, with a GTS/Lancer-type front end mated to an SX-like structure aft of the cowl. The J-body should be close to the Laser/Daytona in size, but will have the more traditional notchback configuration and the requisite long-hood/short-deck proportions. Look for it under both Chrysler and Dodge nameplates.

Also in the works is a front-drive four-door replacement for the rear-drive M-body sedans being developed as project C-41 for a likely 1988 release. Expect a general appearance much like that of GM's front-drive 1985 C-body models (Buick Electra/Cadillac DeVille/Oldsmobile Ninety-Eight) but with a more pronounced wedge profile. Though it's unclear whether C-41 will be the basis for a new-generation Dodge Diplomat/Plymouth Gran Fury, we can tell you that the car will definitely be sold as a Chrysler New Yorker, and there may be a super-luxury edition reserved for a second revival of the Imperial marque. A two-door body style is unlikely.

Finally, truck designers are hard at work on the T-111, a downsized successor to the current full-size Dodge vans. Styling is known to be along T-115 lines but on a slightly larger scale. You can also look for a new generation of smaller big pickups from Chrysler, though it's not known whether this will be based on the T-115 or T-111 platform.

Chrysler's E Class transferred to the Plymouth line for 1985 to become the Caravelle. Price was $8879.

Plymouth's 1985 Gran Fury Salon sedan: $9469.

Frugal fun: the $5999 Plymouth Horizon five-door for '85.

Like Aries, the '85 Plymouth Reliant was nicely restyled. Shown: the top-line LE four-door sedan.

The base 1985 Plymouth Reliant coupe: $6924.

Plymouth's Turismo 2.2 for 1985: $7515.

1985 Plymouth Reliant LE wagon. Base price: $8378.

The 1985 Plymouth Turismo Duster

While all these projects build on the K-car design and Chrysler's production experience with it, company engineers and product planners are sensitive about their newer offerings being labelled K-car derivatives. At a 1983 press party, manufacturing vice-president Stephan Sharf was asked how Highland Park could produce such a diversity of models so quickly, as it had in 1981-84. Answering in a feigned German accent, he said: "Because we are smart. All of our new cars are based on the K platform." Later, he rhetorically asked a group of Detroit auto writers, "Does it matter to the public what a platform is? Do you ride in an underbody? Do you sit in an

A first-year sellout, Plymouth's Voyager returned for '85 with few changes. The LE model is shown.

New for '84, the Dodge/Plymouth Conquest was a rebadged Mitsubishi Starion from Japan. Here, the '85 version.

Plymouth's Reliant LE four-door sedan for '85: $7792.

1985 Dodge/Plymouth Colt sedan, another Mitsubishi import

underbody, or do you worry about the style of an underbody? Yes, the wheels are in the same places, the 'hard points' are all the same, but everything else is different, right? Let's assume the K underbody is the most beautifully developed underbody. Would you destroy it? Would you throw out your wife because she's just the same old wife? Your kids used to be five-two, and now they become five-eight, so now you throw them out because they are stretched kids?'' Then he concluded by denying any K-car origins in the T-wagons!

Mr. Sharf was right, of course: it doesn't matter how a car is derived as long as it fits the proper market niche

Woodgrain bodyside appliqués were standard on the Plymouth Voyager LE. The '85 was hard to tell from an '84.

and sells well—a place where it doesn't compete with its linemates but beats the tar out of the opposition. And this has been the Iacocca regime's most tangible accomplishment for Chrysler. For the first time since the "Forward Look" era of Virgil Exner and Tex Colbert, the company has a definite lead over its Big Three rivals in several areas—fuel economy, front-drive and four-cylinder engineering, computer-aided design and manufacturing—all of which are far more important than styling was even in the old days.

For five years now we've been enjoying the bright, well-conceived, new-generation cars from a company on which few would have bet a quarter back in 1980. Altogether, they've given The New Chrysler Corporation every right to claim that title. It really is a far different outfit today, producing a far better breed of cars than it has for a long, long time. And thanks to the new order and the right new products, it will certainly be around to celebrate its 75th anniversary in 1999. We can't think of a happier note on which to end this book.

A prototype "wagon of tomorrow" at Chrysler Pacifica

From Highland Park, a 2+2 for the late Eighties

Mid-engine sports car mockup from Chrysler Pacifica, 1983

Another aerodynamic concept from Chrysler Styling

Future forecast? Upcoming J-21 mid-engine sports car could resemble this Chrysler Pacifica design study.

Chrysler Show Cars

From parade phaetons to turbine-powered
experimentals to wild one-offs, Chrysler Corporation
has produced an amazing variety of "dream machines"
spanning more than 40 years. Here's a review of the
most significant and interesting ones from the
Forties to the Eighties.

Styled by Ralph Roberts of LeBaron and built by that firm in 1940, this is one of six Newport parade phaetons completed. All rode the 128.5-inch-wheelbase 1940 C-26 Chrysler chassis. Only four are known to survive today.

The innovative Thunderbolt was a companion to the 1940-41 Newport and shares honors with it as Chrysler Corporation's earliest show car. Billed as "the pushbutton car," it was styled mainly by Alex Tremulis of the Briggs Manufacturing Company and was also built on the 1940 C-26 chassis. Features included hidden headlamps and a fully retractable hard top.

Virgil Exner's earliest Chrysler-based show specials, all built by Ghia. Top: The K-310 toured with the "New Worlds in Engineering" show in 1951-52. Center: The derivative C-200 appeared in 1952-53.

Above left: A Ghia-designed Crown Imperial limo, later given to the Vatican. Above right: The Plymouth XX-500 sedan of 1950.

365

Left: 10 Ghia/Exner specials at Chrysler's Chelsea Proving Grounds circa 1954. Opposite page, clockwise from center left: Chrysler D'Elegance (1953), the modified version of the original Dodge Firearrow (1953), Dodge Firearrow convertible (1954 and inspiration for the Dual-Ghia), DeSoto Adventurer I (1953). This page, counterclockwise from below: Two views of the DeSoto Adventurer II (1954), a Derham-bodied Custom Imperial "sedanca de ville" (1954), the non-Ghia Plymouth Belmont (1954 and actually built on a Dodge chassis), and the modified Chrysler Special, built by Ghia for Export Division president C.B. Thomas (1953).

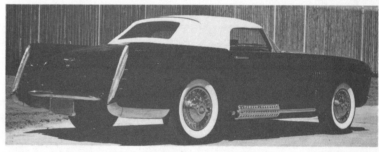

Opposite page: A collection of mid-Fifties studies from Chrysler's Advance Styling Studio. Clockwise from top: Plymouth Explorer (1954), Flight Sweep II (1955), two views of the two-seat Falcon (1955), and two views of Flight Sweep I (1955). The Flight Sweep twins helped promote Chrysler's "Forward Look" styling on the auto show circuit in 1955-56. This page (clockwise from left): George Huebner with his 1962 turbine experimentals based on a production Dodge Dart hardtop sedan and a Plymouth Fury hardtop coupe. The 1961 Dodge Flitewing featured "flipper" upper door sections and Exner's favored "mouth" grille and blade-type front bumper. Vignale of Italy crafted this unusual body for a 1955 Imperial chassis at the request of May Daugherty Carr of Corpus Christi, Texas. 1958's Imperial D'Elegance was rather garish. Unusually styled 1961 TurboFlite was the firm's turbine-engine showcase that year.

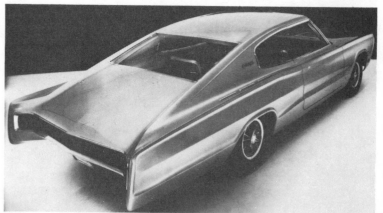

Opposite page: A quartet of Chrysler "dream cars" from the Sixties. From top: Virgil Exner's Valiant-based XNR roadster (1961), Elwood Engel's dramatic "production" turbine car (1963) of which 50 were built by Ghia, the Dodge Charger II (1965, a preview of the production 1966 Charger), and Plymouth's wild XP-VIP (1965). This page: As with other automakers, Chrysler's show cars were increasingly based on normal production hardware as the Sixties wore on. Clockwise from top left: Dodge Charger III (1968), Chrysler 300X (based on the production '66 convertible), the more radical Chrysler Cordoba de Oro (1970), and the Daytona/Superbird-like Dodge Super Charger (also 1970).

Despite its recent troubles, Chrysler has continued to produce showstoppers. Top: The Challenger-based Dodge "Yellow Jacket" (1970). Center left: Plymouth Turismo Spyder (1980).

Center right: Mercedes SL-style short-wheelbase Chrysler LeBaron turbo convertible (1983). Above: "Stealth" 2+2 turbo hatchback concept (1982).

Chrysler Corporation Trucks

From the first Dodge Brothers commercial vehicles in the Teens to the high-tech T-115 of the Eighties, trucks have played a key role in Chrysler Corporation history. Here is a brief, pictorial review of some of the more interesting types, models, and bodies offered under both the Plymouth and Dodge nameplates during the firm's first 60 years.

The Dodge Brothers company began selling chassis for commercial applications beginning in 1917. Here, a side-screen utility car from 1918. Priced at about $885, it was very popular among rural, urban, and military users.

Top: Dodge's hometown police department used this paddy wagon based on the 1930-31 DD-series passenger-car chassis. Center left: A 1931 Dodge DB-1 tanker. Center right: More streamlined frontal styling marked Dodge's 1934 K-series heavy-duty trucks. Here, a welcome sight on a hot day in Detroit. Above left: Dodge kept 1934 cab and front styling the same for 1935. Shown is a KC-series half-ton pickup. Above right: Plymouth began selling light-duty car-based trucks in the mid-Thirties. Shown is a 1936 panel delivery, priced at $605. Right: 1936 Dodge LC half-ton pickup.

Clockwise, from top left: A 1938 Dodge DeLuxe Suburban panel truck, $1020. 1938 Dodge RE-series with box body. Airflow styling was applied to Dodge trucks beginning in late 1934. This brace of beer trucks on the RX-71 chassis (body by Barkow of Milwaukee) dates from 1938. From 1940, a special soft drink carrier on the Dodge TH-series chassis. A 1940 Dodge cabover gets set to roll with a quartet of Plymouth cars. Glistening in black, this Dodge stake-body is one of the first of the new 1939 T-series built. Another look at the unique Dodge Airflow truck, here in basic cab-chassis form.

Clockwise from top left: 1940 Plymouth PT-series with special body. Dodge's famous Power Wagon 4×4 scout/command car from WWII. Dodge's B-series pickup design (1953 shown) dated from 1951. The 1951 Dodge B-series stake-body was offered in a variety of sizes and payloads. By 1960, Dodge pickups had progressed to this jazzy two-tone D-100 half-ton. A 205-bhp V-8 powered the 1957 Dodge K-series D-200 pickup. A short-chassis example of the Dodge Route Van offered in the early Fifties.

Top left: 1961 Dodge D-100 Utiline pickup. Top right: 1963 styling prototype for the Dodge A-100 compact truck. Center left: The production Dodge A-100 panel van of 1964. Center right: The Dodge A-100 served as the basis for the medium-duty L-series cabovers introduced in 1966. Above left: 1967 Dodge W-200 Power Wagon with Utiline Express box. Above: The big 1971 Dodge LNT-1000 heavy-duty tilt-cab tractor. Left: From 1968, the Dodge D-100 Sweptline pickup.

Top: Dodge offered its handy, extended Club Cab pickup beginning with 1973. The top-line Adventurer version is shown. Center left: Plymouth's 4WD Trail Duster sports/utility was new for '74. Center right: The Dodge double was called Ramcharger, here in fully open dress. Above: Dodge's 1975 "Big Horn 900" heavy-duty tractor.

Top left: 1977 Dodge D-700 cab-chassis. Top right: 1977 Dodge D-100 Warlock. Center left: 1977 Dodge B-series Street Van. Center right: 1977 Dodge D-300 wrecker. Above left: 1978 Dodge D-150 "Macho" Power Wagon. Above: 1979 Dodge Royal Sportsman. Left: 1980 Dodge D-50 Sport pickup.

Top: The 1982 Dodge Ramcharger Royal SE offered off-road opulence. Center left: Based on the front-drive L-body cars, the Dodge Rampage/Plymouth Scamp was a short-lived attempt at a car/pickup. Shown is the '83 Rampage 2.2 Center right: 1985 Dodge Power Ram 50, 4WD fun from Mitsubishi. Above: 1985 Dodge Mini Ram van (T-115).

Index